Page 245 to Page 253

Catholicism

Paganism

Sociology &
social life

aesthetic

aesthetic

Paganism
mahomedanism
Catholicism

A STUDY OF SOCIAL ELEMENTS

SOCIAL ELEMENTS

INSTITUTIONS, CHARACTER

PROGRESS

BY

CHARLES RICHMOND HENDERSON

NEW YORK

CHARLES SCRIBNER'S SONS

1898

Norwood Press
J. S. Cushing & Co. — Berwick & Smith
Norwood Mass. U.S.A.

PREFACE

This volume is prepared for readers and for students, and each person will treat it as he prefers. To students it is recommended that writing, map-drawing, and discussion accompany the reading according to the order suggested in the Appendix. If the reader can find a company of congenial spirits to talk over the subjects with him, the impression will be more distinct and clear. The matters to be discussed and explained are facts of our every-day life, not remote and unfamiliar. Emerson says, "Aristotle, or Bacon, or Kant propounds some maxim which is the keynote of philosophy henceforward. But I am more interested to know that, when at last they have hurled out their grand word, it is only some familiar experience of every man in the street. If it be not, it will never be heard of again."

In so brief a treatment more questions are raised than answered. The author has earnestly sought to stir and direct personal investigation and reflection rather than to furnish ready-made and dogmatic opinions. He has desired to be constructive and hope-inspiring rather than discouraging and destructive. The Marquis of Mirabeau said finely: "The method of suppression and of destruction is absolutely opposed to the art of government; it is the heroic mode of suicide. An ignorant surgeon knows how to cut off a limb; Esculapius would treat and heal it. Four treatments of the former kind, and there would remain nothing but the trunk" (*L'ami des hommes*). Controversy is avoided as barren. Guyau tells of two savages who fought for a pair of ear-rings. The victor carried away the jewels in triumph, but could not wear them, for the conquered competitor had succeeded in biting off both his ears! Reasons for personal conclusions are offered for consideration, and then the matter is submitted to the candid reader.

The philosophical belief which runs through all the chapters is not pessimism, and it is not optimism, but rather what George Eliot called meliorism. Well did our great Lieber say: "We must find our way through all these mazes. . . . There are not a few who, seeing the perversion of principles follow the besetting fallacy of men, and seek salvation from one evil in its opposite, as if the means of escaping death by fire were freezing to death. The opposite is hardly ever the cure of an evil. A glutton would not take the right step of amendment by the resolution of starving himself to death. . . . No good is done, when the ship of state is in danger, by cutting away the very ribs of the ship" (*Civil Liberty*, p. 19).

Quotations from the "literature of power" are freely used, and with a definite purpose. Poets, such as Goethe and Herder, have had a presentiment (*Ahnung*) of laws and principles which men of science afterwards develop, formulate, and verify. The references serve to give credit to our spiritual benefactors; to give readers a taste of the finer springs of wisdom, which shall make them thirst for deeper draughts from the same wholesome fountains; and to give the weight of authority where the judgment of experts have intrinsic value.

C. R. HENDERSON.

THE UNIVERSITY OF CHICAGO,
1898.

TABLE OF CONTENTS

PAGE

PREFACE V

PART I

BASIS OF SOCIETY IN NATURE

CHAPTER I

INTRODUCTION I

CHAPTER II

NATURE IN RELATION TO SOCIAL LIFE 13

PART II

THE SOCIAL PERSON

CHAPTER III

THE SOCIAL MEMBER: THE PERSON 41

PART III

SOCIAL INSTITUTIONS

CHAPTER IV

THE FAMILY 62

CHAPTER V

AUXILIARY INSTITUTIONS 78

CHAPTER VI

PAGE

SOCIAL ARTS OF CREATION, COMMUNICATION, AND OF THE ÆSTHETIC LIFE 94

CHAPTER VII

OUTLINE OF OUR INDUSTRIAL ORGANIZATION . . . 113

CHAPTER VIII

TENDENCY TOWARD ECONOMIC BETTERMENT . . . 141

CHAPTER IX

THE SOCIAL MOVEMENT FOR ECONOMIC BETTERMENT . 167

CHAPTER X

SOCIAL MISERY, PAUPERISM, AND CRIME 207

CHAPTER XI

THE SCHOOL AND ITS SOCIAL SERVICE 228

CHAPTER XII

SOCIALIZED IDEALISM. RELIGION AND THE CHURCH . . 259

CHAPTER XIII

THE NATURAL AND SPIRITUAL BONDS OF A PEOPLE . . 276

CHAPTER XIV

THE STATE AND THE GOVERNMENT 292

PART IV

SOCIAL PSYCHOLOGY, ORDER, AND PROGRESS

CHAPTER XV

PAGE

SOME PROBLEMS OF SOCIAL PSYCHOLOGY 318

CHAPTER XVI

HARMONY WITH THE PRESENT ORDER 342

CHAPTER XVII

SOCIAL PROGRESS 370

APPENDIX

DIRECTIONS FOR LOCAL STUDIES, MAPS, AND TOPICS FOR
DISCUSSION 395

PART I

BASIS OF SOCIETY IN NATURE

———◆◇◆———

CHAPTER I

Introduction

I. Outline of Contents and Statement of Purpose. — The particular object of this book will be to direct attention to the phenomena of human associations; to teach the methods of classifying facts of this order; to give training in the search for efficient causes; to show how to interpret social tendencies and movements; to interpret social duties which arise out of conditions and relations; to guide in the attainment and criticism of social ideals of welfare; to stimulate and direct interest in methods of betterment approved by experience; to indicate the foundations of social order; to disclose the principles of social progress, — forces, laws, and methods; and especially to show the connection of order and progress with the institutions and methods of education.

Sociology is a science of survey, synthetic, teaching us to comprehend what special sciences dissect, analyze, and treat apart. It will be the aim of the writer to indicate at the suitable points the relation of each special "study" or science to other studies and to the united interest of mankind. Social interest will be taken as an important principle for the co-ordination of studies. It is hoped that this method will impart a sense of unity, movement, progress, and utility to all branches of school work.

II. The Field of Study : the System of Human Associations. — Every one knows something of the state in which he lives, —

its boundaries on the north, south, east, and west, its surface, rivers, climate, soil, and natural productions, its people and their occupations.   There is the home, the business, the circle of friends, the church, the pleasure resorts, and all else that is of human interest.   One knows the county seat, with its streets of residences and shops, its offices and trades, its political schemes and public assemblies.   One can tell something of the capital city of the state, with its public buildings, its higher courts, and its urban airs.   From stories of old settlers, speeches on anniversary occasions, and from special histories or historical articles, the memory has preserved some fragments of the past,— the struggles of the early pioneers, the digging of canals, the introduction of railroads, the growth of various manufactures.   Every reader has something, at least a bud, of the flower of public spirit, something of the reformer's fire and zeal, something of the sacred flame of an ambition to leave the world better than he found it.

III. Means of learning the Facts. — Very good and familiar instruments of learning will be accessible to most readers: a school geography, with its maps and descriptions, a railroad guide, an article on the state in some encyclopedia, a history of the commonwealth, and newspapers published at the county town and at the capital.   Thus equipped we may start on a "little journey in the world."   All journeys and all voyages must start from home.   Voyages usually take persons into unknown regions.   This journey, "personally conducted," will start with familiar facts.   It may lead us to see that our own state is connected in various ways with the wide, wide world, and that we must even care something for "abroad."

IV. The Physical Basis of Society. — A rapid and superficial sketch will bring before our minds the main features of the facts with which we have to deal.   Afterwards we can take them up in more detail and ask for their connections and meaning.

School studies have already made the imagination familiar with the shape of the earth on which we live.   It may best be conceived as a ball turning and rolling through space, with a thin crust of soil and wide stretches of ocean covering its surface.   The inhabitants of this earth are as grass-hoppers, and at some distance the planet itself would look smaller than a grasshopper.

> " Each floats ever and on
> As the round green earth is floating
> Out thro' the sea of space,
> Bearing our mortal kind
> Parasites soon to be gone."

In some states, whose territory is small but furnished with "the great watch towers of mountains, purple-vestured, grave and silent," the student may climb to a height which will give him a view of that political area named a state. But any of us may, winged with imagination, and assisted by poetic bicycle or prosaic train, take a bird's-eye view of even a level and monotonous plain. Its silver streams glide beneath the shadowed banks and past rich pastures and fertile corn-fields. The dark forests tell of tree-trunks, ferns, flowers, and wealth of bird life. The stone quarry and the coal mine give promise of building material and fuel. Perhaps ores are dug, or oil is pumped, or natural gas forces its way to the surface. Without this firm resting-place, this soil, this sun-visited climate, these vane-moving winds, this water supply, these species of animal and plant creatures for food and clothing and other uses, man could not exist. Nature is not man, and natural forces are not society, and herds of cattle are not associations, but man could not build a society in the upper air, nor out of mere thoughts. The bare imagination of a feast will not still his hunger, and a logical argument will not render him that service which garden vegetables are able to supply. Men are a part of all this natural world. They have put themselves into the miasmatic swamps which have been cleared; they have mixed their ideas with the furrows which have modified the very climate and driven fever and ague into the outer darkness of ignorant communities, and with the railroads which creep serpent-like over the divides. Nature, therefore, must be brought within range of our thought on society.

V. The Social Person. — The community is composed of individual persons. It will be well for us to know something of the bricks which are to be built into our edifice. We cannot hope to construct a bridge of straws, or a warehouse of unburnt clay. These human beings on one side are animals, with the physical structure, organs, and appetites of the higher animals. In another aspect they are minds, beings who think, who aspire, who have emotions, who reason, who resolve, who have a capacity and an inclination for society.

VI. Classification of Institutions. — These animal-spirits, creatures of two worlds so strangely and wonderfully joined, have built what we call a community. Looking on this society steadily, and with the help of previous reflections and analyses, certain great classes of facts begin to come out, — institutions, customs, groups of persons.

The first of these with which memory begins is the family. The first we knew of ourselves we were already taking part in a social institution, sometimes as petted favorites, sometimes as disgraced rebels.

Our next personal reminiscence is usually that of a school-house, another social institution, where we were actors and sufferers. The teacher represented to us the officer of justice, the regulator of conduct, the guide of life. In the absence of parents she assumed some of the duties and powers of the father or mother. Under such tuition we learned the instruments of speech and thought more perfectly, and in the conflicts and plays of the recess we became acquainted with the desires, the wants, the elemental forces of society.

But if we were fortunate enough to have a country residence, we learned at home and in intervals of school life that there is such a mode of social activity as industry. This knowledge came first in the form of childish games, which often imitated the occupations of our elders. Social impulses of imitation and affection, of command and authority, led us to share more and more the occupations of kitchen, garden, field, shop, market. Thus the economic institutions of society were made familiar to us as personal experiences.

Within the home the theme of religion was discussed. Perhaps there was the rite of family worship, the child's prayer at night by the mother's knee, or the devotions led by one of the parents. Sometimes the Sunday School was an early introduction into this mysterious world where human beings spoke to an Invisible Person. We learned thus, step by step, the social meaning of the church.

All this time there was coming, more or less often, into the range of thought and interest, the government. At the table something is said of a shocking murder, of the search for the murderer, of his arrest, of his detention in jail, of his trial, and the unfolding of a terrible story of greed, lust, or revenge; of the night when the jury was shut up, debating the sentence; of the solemn verdict; and, finally, the awful doom hidden in the obscure shadows of a private execution. Or in some less sensational yet impressive way the functions of the state have been isolated in our thoughts from those of parents, teachers, pastors, and editors. The stirring scenes of a political campaign, the torchlight processions, the noisy crowds and bursting powder, so dear to the boy, the eloquent speeches, so wonderful to youth, have stirred the civic feeling and made each citizen become conscious of his powers, interests, and duties in relation to government.

Thus one by one, yet all together, out of the dark clouds of infantile ignorance each social member becomes aware that he has entered a world of institutions,— home, school, industry, church, state.

VII. The Internal Forces which create these Institutions. — The human mind asks very early after causes, although youths are too easily satisfied with almost any sort of authoritative answer they may chance to get from their elders. Some such questions as the following are natural enough when quite young persons have their attention called to the differences between the visible institutions of society mentioned above: Why do people go to the court-house? Why do they build schoolhouses? Why do they build railroads, establish newspapers, organize lodges, hold synods and conferences? These questions lead straight into the study of the thoughts, wants, desires of men. Every institution which is taken up compels us to look into the motives of human beings. Society soon comes to be regarded as a spiritual organization, and not merely a certain arrangement of forms of matter. Of course it is as constantly observed that the combined efforts of men are conditioned by the physical world about us, and that we must employ natural forces to realize our wishes and aspirations. The study of this interworking of mind and nature, of thought and things, is always with us in our consideration of social institutions.

VIII. Progress. — There is change, movement. That which moves attracts our attention. The people are always asking about a man, if he is growing richer; of a town, whether it is growing larger; of a newspaper, if it is increasing its circulation. American people, especially, are always studying statistics of increase in the production of grain, cattle, iron, and all industries.

IX. The Lessons of History. — The inquiry into present causes and changes sometimes induces us to to hear stories of the past. Studying the map of Boston, we wonder why the streets are so crooked, until we learn that these streets were laid out according to the early roads and paths of the colonists. At a wedding we are asked by the children why a gold ring is used in the ceremony, and a true answer would compel us to go back to very ancient customs. In a thousand ways we come to see that the present cannot explain itself, that the tree we see has hidden roots planted out of sight and deep in the past.

In the attempt to explain an institution by discovering what made it, we come upon forces which are not yet exhausted, and which are carrying us forward. It is natural for a reasoning being to be somewhat curious about what is going to happen to this world. Will it burn up to-morrow? Will it last long enough to get in the corn crop? Will parents be cruel enough to whip their children to death next week? Will wheat be worth two dollars a bushel next year? Will the governments of Europe combine to crush the United States? Will the criminal element be strong enough to burn our cities and make a new government out of the ruins? Will trade unions injure trade, or will they simply forward the interests of wage workers? These are specimens of questions which may be asked, showing the interests of men in the future. There are many times when we care comparatively little for the past; for it is gone, like the water which has already flowed past the mill and can grind no grist. The actual present is a mere point, and is instantly gone. Our hopes, ambitions, fears, desires, all have a forward look.

X. Social Problems of Duty. — Just as natural is it for us to ask in respect to each social institution and its transformation, what can we do about it? What ought we to do? How can we best prepare to meet the changes which are sure to come, and how can we diminish the pain, the loss, the evil, that must destroy us unless we take precautions and put forth united and timely effort?

The philosopher may not feel called on to go beyond the explanation of social life. It is perfectly proper for him to make a business of revealing all the causes, near and remote, which explain what we see. But the person who has studied the direction and strength of forces is best adapted to foretell what is likely to happen, and what means give most promise of promoting the common interest. The philosopher is also a citizen.

It is wise, however, to keep these investigations somewhat separate and distinct in thought and treatment. We must not adopt a theory and then select facts to prove it. It should be our aim first of all to understand the reality with which we are dealing; at the same time to seek its cause in past and present connections; and then to look forward to the direction of forces, so far as they are within our power, to the end of advancing human welfare.

XI. Method and Order of Study of Society. — The task of all sciences includes answers to these questions: (1) What is the fact — what has occurred? (2) In the particular facts is there anything general — regularly repeated? (3) What are the causes of this general element in the various facts? The social sciences, being concerned with persons as well as with things, must take account of the preferences, of the feelings, pleasures, and pains of men, and must answer, in addition to the above questions, three others: (4) What is the value of the facts observed to the persons concerned? (5) What ought to be — what is best and right? (6) What measures are to be taken in order to secure what is desirable for men? In the study of natural objects our interest is purely theoretical, and we desire simply to know. But when we come to political, economic, æsthetic, religious, — all human affairs, — we must proceed to deal with practical methods, ways, and means.

It will readily be seen that it is not the office of such a book as this to teach the contents of all the sciences. These must be learned of those who profess them, the masters in the fields of chemistry, physics, geography, biology, psychology. It is our present duty to exhibit the social whole in which these special studies form parts, and we shall borrow from each in order to relate all. The new element we add is comprehension, relation. That is an element which is implied in each, but cannot be displayed by each. In a watch factory the various parts of the instrument are first made by many workmen, and yet there is no timekeeper until they are all — springs, wheels, jewels, pivots, posts — "assembled"; and it is the business of a certain workman to bring all the separate parts into one effective whole. The artist who assembles the different parts may not be able to make any one of them as well as the person who devotes his life to that piece; and yet all parts are useless unless they are connected in one system and made complete by joining. It is the business of sociology to "assemble" the elements of social life, to present life as one, and not a heap of disconnected parts, each a sphinx so long as it is apart from the others.

Miss L. J. Sanderson (in the *Journal of Psycho-Asthenics*, September, 1897) tells of an experiment with feeble-minded children, who were trying to draw pictures of a duck. "A constant race is kept up between the cage and the blackboard; back and forth they go till the thing is done. Each excels in some one point. One duck revels in fine webbed feet; another has a most graceful bend in its neck; one has a shapely body; but all are caricatures, and it is necessary to write below the attempt, 'This is a duck.' They recognize their failure. . . . The next day the duck comes again. The different points are carefully noted and another attempt is made, this time with much better results." After many trials the pictures are at least so like the bird that it is not necessary to label them.

The world of our observation is one world, which the Greeks called a Cosmos, because they believed that it was an orderly fact, made by reason and that could be understood by reason. This world presents two sides, for it is composed of things and of persons, of humanity and of all beside that man can know.

General truths and laws can be communicated and learned only by coming into direct contact with things and persons, by feeling the tension of experience, and by setting up images of the appearances of the world. All that a book can do is to bring forward the images of thought to those who are daily living in contact with objects and men, and thus help to interpret that life which we all enjoy together. Spirits reveal themselves through visible, tangible, and audible realities. Institutions are the embodiments of social aims, and therefore with these we begin.

There are many ways of approaching our subjects, each good for its purpose and audience. It is sometimes best to begin with the careful study of a child in the home. Others have come to our study by placing the discoveries relating to race history in order, beginning with the lowest and earliest races and coming up to our own times. Spencer and Letourneau may be cited as notable examples. For mature students it is profitable to consider the theories of the masters of social philosophy, since they aid the mind with a large framework of conceptions by which the world is seen to be a whole.

The right method is to proceed from the present to the past, because the present is better understood, and then knowledge can be tested by reality. "The true scientific method is to explain the past by the present" (Bagehot, *Physics and Politics*, p. 60). The present we know or have at hand to reëxamine; the past is more difficult to realize and test. It is by interpreting the little events and objects under our eyes that we acquire the power of reasoning about the fragments of information relating to great movements of history. Newton's mind rose from the apple's fall to consider laws of the heavenly bodies and their motions in infinite space. Of the superior souls of early New England their eulogist says: —

> "With that deep insight which detects
> All great things in the small;
> And knows how each man's life affects
> The spiritual life of all."

Tennyson declares that if we could understand absolutely all about the flower which grows in the crannied wall, roots and all, we "should know what God and man is."

Archimedes was given the mean task of finding out for the king Hiero if the goldsmith had cheated him by mixing alloy with the gold of a crown. The philosopher went to bathe, and when he noticed that his body displaced a part of the water, a great principle flashed across his mind and filled his soul with the triumph of discovery. From so small an event and so inconsiderable an occasion, the great mathematician reasoned his way to the universal principle that a body immersed in a liquid sustains an upward pressure equal to the weight of the liquid displaced.

Bagehot (*Physics and Politics*, p. 167) tells the story of the origin of two important histories of Greece, those of Mitford and of Grote : —

"Some seventy years ago an English country gentleman named Mitford, who, like so many of his age, had been terrified into aristocratic opinions by the first French Revolution, suddenly found that the history of the Peloponnesian War was the reflex of his own time. He took up his Thucydides, and there he saw, as in a mirror, the progress and the struggles of his age. It required some freshness of mind to see this; at least, it had been hidden for many centuries. All the modern histories of Greece before Mitford had but the vaguest idea of it, and not being a man of supreme originality, he would doubtless have had very little idea of it either, except that the analogy of what he saw helped him by a telling object-lesson to the understanding of what he read. . . . And that is not all. Mr. Grote, the great scholar whom we have had lately to mourn, also recognized the identity between the struggles of our modern world, and taking violently the contrary side to that of Mitford, being as great a democrat as Mitford was an aristocrat, wrote a reply, far above Mitford's history in power and learning, but being in the main characteristic almost identical, being above all things a book of vigorous political passion, written for persons who care for politics, and not, as almost all histories of antiquity are and must be, the book of a man who cares for scholarship more than for anything else, written mainly if not exclusively, for scholars. . . . It is just because of the analogy between the controversies of that time and those of our times that some one has said, ' Classical history is a part of modern history ; it is mediæval history only which is ancient.' "

To study of the present should be added historical study. What help will it afford us in the attempt to understand the present and to guide its forces? The answer lies in the word "reciprocity." Men and ideas assist each other. If we can set clearly before us the simple forms of ancient social problems, we may discover universal motives acting without the complications of modern conditions. If we watch the mighty current of social movement which gathered head thousands of years ago and has swept into its awful stream many fancies, theories, and ambitions, we shall be less hasty and impulsive in pressing some sudden inspiration and private scheme until all sides have been considered. We shall be preserved from the illusion of taking a side eddy for the direction of universal movement. Perhaps we shall be more hopeful when we discover the might of what makes for general welfare and the weakness of efforts based on selfishness. At any rate, we shall come to the consideration of modern problems with more ample materials for a judgment, with an expanded mental horizon, with fewer mean and provincial prejudices, with more worthy conceptions of mankind.

We should take advantage of the intense and natural interest in social problems, in order to lead on to laws, principles, generalizations. The human race has entered the royal palace of chemistry by the kitchen door. People studied the science of atoms to discover what was going into their stomachs. The mediæval philosophers approached political economy to procure rational weapons against usurers. "The student is first attracted to concrete, definite problems rather than to general theories. In race development theories grow out of the solving of problems" (Professor G. E. Vincent).[1]

Many who read this book are teachers, — in school, home, church. They are seeking to fit youth to places in the world. They must then know the world. Professor Edward R. Shaw has said "that the child's position in the world is not appreciated; that he is suddenly forced into the midst of manifestations of varied phenomena, events in time, all at once, without any key that will enable him to see their relations to each other, or his relation to them. The failure to remember that children reason only from the things they know is the cause

---

[1] *The Social Mind and Education*, p. 142. Cf. Böhm-Bawerk, *Capital and Interest*, pp. 4, 5, 13, 14.

of much friction in education, and often results in building an insurmountable wall between parent and child, between teacher and child." Unless the youth knows something of the order and institutions, customs and laws, of the great world, he is soon "lost" in the motley throng. He cannot find his way. He becomes confused, discouraged, bewildered, and roams around in circles, without progress, a prey to chance influences.

Our age is restless and uneasy. Multitudes are looking forward with anxiety or hope, with fear or joy, with anger or yearning. All will confess to a division, a conflict, a want of understanding. Those who have much property to lose often manifest great hostility against any one who suggests any disturbance or change of present conditions. This is very natural. There are multitudes of others who regard the present condition or system as utterly and fundamentally unjust, cruel, and worthy of execration. Perhaps it is because they feel the pinch of want and disappointment; perhaps because they look out upon the suffering of their neighbors with pity and regret; perhaps because they do not realize the real value of the present order and the promise it holds of gradual betterment.

Now, for all these persons the right act is an honest effort to understand thoroughly what society actually is. The present order is all we have. We must work with it or with nothing. Until the new comes into being we can neither eat nor breathe without the present social system.

The order we know must have in itself the germs of the coming order, since life cannot arise out of nothing; and it may pay well to look carefully and closely to discover the opening buds of hope. Perhaps we may see that one of the best things about the present system is that it has articles in its constitution permitting amendments. If we are to act together, we must first think together. Coöperation in the majestic civic task waits upon agreement about ends and means. The common ground for radicals and conservatives, so far as they are sane, honest, and just, is a study of life as it is under our own eyes.

CHAPTER II

Nature in Relation to Social Life

"This brute matter is part of somewhat not brute. It is that the sand floor is held by spheral gravity, and bent to be a part of the round globe, under the optical sky, — part of the astonishing astronomy, and existing, at last, to moral ends and from moral causes." — EMERSON.

> "'So careful of the type?' but no,
> From scarped cliff and quarried stone
> She cries, 'a thousand types are gone;
> I care for nothing; all shall go.
>
> "'Thou makest thine appeal to me,
> I bring to life, I bring to death;
> The spirit does but mean the breath:
> I know no more.'"
>
> —TENNYSON, *In Memoriam.*

I. The World of the Astronomer. — It is well for us, before we become absorbed in the affairs of these swarming inhabitants of earth, to spend a moment with star-gazers and celestial map-makers, in order to see the true and widest relations of things. The advance of astronomic science enables us to regard this terrestrial ball from the outside, and imagination helps us realize that our society is simply a company of passengers on a very swift vehicle, which moves along an invisible track through the infinite spaces. By the aid of an artificial globe and the evening lamp we may assist our fancy and witness the rapid changes of day and night, the alternations of winter and summer, which so essentially determine the arrangements of associations of men on earth. From this large, general conception we may come down to the divisions and local interests of nations, cities, and families. The astro-

nomical point of view helps us to think of the population
of our globe as having at least one great possession in common, and suggests that we on earth really belong to a universe,
and that there may be similar beings in other worlds who
share our nature and who may come to be partners of a society much more extended than anything known of imperial
grandeur in earthly history.   Sociology does not presume to
take such flights of imagination; it finds more than enough
at present to do in trying to understand and comprehend the
doings and nature of the residents of this rind of rock and
soil crust on which we dwell.

II.   The Physical Elements and their Influence on Mankind.
— That one fountain of force which streams up through all
things takes three general forms, — chemical, vital, and social.
Not an ounce of this force is ever lost or destroyed.   It
changes its direction and its appearance but does not cease
to exist.   Heat may become electricity, or light, or animal
energy, or the nervous power which furnishes the basis for
thought and emotion and will, but it is not annihilated.   The
plant takes up energy into its tisses; these tissues of leaf and
grain becomes the source of the warmth and vitality of animals, the flesh of animals becomes the food of men, and re-
appears as the power of armies and governments, but nothing
is lost.

It is true that new elements enter when we pass by insensible
gradations from soils to plants, and from plants to animals,
and again from animals to human society.   These new factors
are the distinguishing marks of three worlds, physical, vital,
and social.   But there is no break from base to summit.   The
breath of the singer is like the zephyr, and the thoughts of the
architect or teacher depend on a certain consumption of fuel
in brain and stomach.

The geographer regards earth not as an on-looker, but as a
resident.   Human society, as we know it, is not a cloud of
bodiless ghosts, flitting from star to star, nor a congress of
ideas, nor a collection of fancies imitating each other.   Mankind is composed of complex beings who must have solid
ground for their feet.   They must at least have standing room.
They must have places to lie down to rest and sleep.   Their

necessities are not met, their existence is not assured, without space and soil for houses, gardens, farms, pastures, palaces, warehouses, and temples. What is going on among the people of other worlds might be interesting, but it does not belong to our subject. We are earth-dwellers at present, though we feel ourselves to be potentially cosmopolites, citizens of the universe at large.

Most of the surface of this planet is not habitable: the frozen regions at the poles and the vast portions covered by the restless ocean. It is true that the high seas are the industrial fields of sailors and fishermen, the sources of food supplies, and the paths of commerce; but waves are not the restful home of domestic and industrial life. No cities rise on the wild waste of waters, nor are habitations there constructed and boundaries of empires defined.

The land is the solid foundation of communities. Its soil is the product of corrosion of the rocks under the influence of frost and flood, of chemical action with the help of vegetable elaboration. When the geographer has laid out for us upon his globe the outlines of continents, the range of mountains, the valleys of rivers, the deserts and fertile plains, then comes the chemist to tell us of the elements which compose the soil, the waters, the air; and the physicist declares to us the forces of light, heat, electricity, and all the modes of motion and the instruments of force. At a certain point the chemist discovers, or artificially combines, the atoms of matter in such complex forms that the mass seems almost alive. But thus far men of science have not been able to produce living beings out of inorganic matter. Up to this date the man of science confesses he cannot explain the passage from non-living to living matter.

It is a very slight transition from some of the complex chemical bodies to the simple jelly-like creatures, plant or animal, which are disclosed to us under the microscope. Nature is able, in her mysterious laboratory, in the bodies of already living things, to transmute atoms into living creatures which produce their kind in unending procession.

And thus our sciences and, in less degree, our common knowledge, bring us to the field of biology, the world of living beings, plants, and animals.   This vast region is partitioned out among botanists and zoölogists in order that the study may be successfully prosecuted within our short lives and with our limited powers.

The Elements of the Physical Environment. — Without attempting to do the work of the geologist and instructor in physiography we may profitably illustrate the social interest in the physical world, and may notice the influence on human conduct of the atmosphere, the waters, and the solid land. In the enveloping atmosphere about the earth we are brought into contact with air, light, heat, electricity, winds, storms, and moisture.   The word "climate" suggests the more permanent conditions of the atmosphere as contrasted with the shifting and momentary changes.

The waters of the earth in rivers, lakes, and ocean determine many elements in social arrangements and ways of existence.

The solid land, with its mountain ranges, its valleys and plains, its natural highways, must decide or at least influence the direction of social action.

All these factors have a direct power over our lives at every moment and in every place.   They also affect us and our institutions through their influence on animals and plants, the food and servants of men.

The distribution of plants and animals, the effect of conditions of atmosphere, water, and land, of geologic change, enters into our thoughts and plans.

We pass from this dry catalogue of the elements of the external world to consider a few illustrations of the various ways in which they mould, affect, and determine human life.

The Influence of these Physical Elements on Man : on Physical Vigor, Health, and Aptitude. — A moderate observation will reveal the influence of temperature, barometric pressure, dark days, damp weather and climate in general upon the body.   This we can feel from hour to hour, from day to day, and from season to season.   We are different persons in summer and in winter. Gray skies may dampen ardor, and close, warm weather unfit us for the best service.   It is by this constant and varied experience that we learn to appreciate the effects of temperature, moisture, and other conditions on an entire people subjected to these agencies generation after generation.

In our temperate zone we have a great variety of weather, and we notice the effect of changes on our vitality. The same person who in January moved with brisk step and easy stride over miles of pavement comes into the torrid climate of July and becomes a different man; his motions are slower, he seeks the shady side of the street; he protects himself from the sun in the middle of the day as if he were a resident of India. If a northern man goes to a soft and warm climate, as in some parts of Mexico and South America, he learns that the habits of the natives are suitable to their physical surroundings, and if he determines to work with the same energy which was natural to him at home, he soon falls a victim to fever or exhaustion.

The very hardships met by the founders of New England, their contests with hunger, cold, and stubborn, thin soil, helped to develop in those who survived the ordeal a physical and spiritual vigor, which is still a store of available energy for the conquest of an entire continent. One of the greatest men of this fine race has noted this fact and its limitations: "Climate has much to do with this melioration. The highest civility has never loved the hot zones. Wherever snow falls, there is usually civil freedom. Where the banana grows, the animal system is indolent and pampered at the cost of higher qualities: the man is sensual and cruel. But this scale is not invariable. High degrees of moral sentiment control the unfavorable influences of climate; and some of our grandest examples of men and of races come from the equatorial regions, — as the genius of Egypt, of India, and of Arabia" (Emerson).

Charles Kingsley believed in the social value of natural science, and no doubt would confess that weather is a factor in our lives. But it is very evident that he thought the doctrine that climate determines character and institutions may be overworked. He wrote in *Yeast:* "But what is a description without a sketch of the weather? In these Pantheist days especially, when a hero or heroine's moral state must

c

entirely depend on the barometer, and authors talk as if Christians were cabbages, and a man's soul as well as his lungs might be saved by sea breezes and sunshine; or his character developed by wearing guano in his shoes, and training himself against a south wall . . . we must have a weather description. . . ." He tells us how Lancelot made a soul-almanac in this style: "Monday, 21st. — Wind S. W., bright sun, mercury at 30½ inches. Felt my heart expanded towards the universe. Organs of veneration and benevolence pleasingly excited; and gave a shilling to a tramp."

Illustrations may be given of the effects of the physical facts of soil, mines, vegetation, temperature, and other physical conditions on occupations. The reports of the state geologist are rich in materials for such a study. They reveal the material resources of the community and point out the best direction for the investment of capital and the learning of trades. Every commonwealth should have in its employ a corps of scientific students constantly busy with the investigation of the nature and value of different soils, the kind of vegetation which will flourish best in the given conditions of frost and heat, of rain and chemical constituents of the land. The mineralogist and geologist seek all possible information about coal deposits, hoards of natural gas, petroleum, building stone, ores, mineral waters of healing efficacy; and this knowledge, published in books and popularized through daily papers and magazines directs the energies of the people into the most profitable channels. Other men of science study the plant life of the territory, and publish information about grasses and grains, fruit trees and berries, and the conditions of the best investment of money and labor.

Men planted the first cities, centres of enlightenment, along rivers and near the coasts of seas. Each continent and each part of the continents may have peculiar local advantages in the production of the good things of life. There is a field for oranges, bananas, olives, and lemons in the warm south country. It is natural that the inhabitants of those regions should turn their attention to the growth of such fruits. The people of the rocky districts of Lake Superior, with the lake navigation at hand, spend their energies on the development of copper and iron mines. The ores are carried for smelting to New York, and Ohio, and Illinois, nearer to the great coal beds which furnish fuel for reducing them to ingots and transmuting the raw material into the rails of steel, into machinery, agricultural implements, beams for warehouses, and all the articles wanted by civilized man.

As in the village each artisan cultivates his own trade and exchanges his products for those of others, so the various parts of the world build up commerce with others because each land can contribute most of a certain kind of goods to the needs of the world. Out of these material differences of soil, climate, and mineral wealth arise the social bonds which knit nation to nation.

The arrangement of land and water, of plains and mountains, has great influence on governments and the formation of national institutions. In the early history of our country the original colonies were held compactly together, in great part, by the natural barrier of the Alleghany range of mountains and the dark mass of forest. It is possible that the fate of the war for national independence depended on this fact, that natural causes pressed the feeble people together into a relatively small space and gave them a sense of unity and power which sustained them in the struggle.

Who can overlook the tremendous significance of the shape of our continent and its position between the great oceans? Vast space has made it possible to build up a great nation, full of large ideas, conscious of possessing indefinite material resources. The existence of plenty of free land, to be had simply for the taking and clearing, suggested to the hireling and serf, as soon as he touched these shores, to set up for himself. If the employer did not like to give him good wages, he could go to the forest, clear a patch of ground, and soon possess a homestead in his own right. The traits of independence thus planted have become national characteristics and made permanent despotisms impossible.

The comparative monotony of our country, its wide and level plains occupying the great interior, with no serious separating ranges of mountains after the first pioneer days were over, and roads were constructed, have determined the similarity of habits and customs which travellers and observers, like Mr. Bryce, have called to our attention.

Our material resources are a theme of perennial interest to our orators and eulogists. On the Fourth of July they are brought to our complacent attention almost as if we had some merit in their creation. Of course we are not the creators of this material, and credit can be earned only by a wiser use than we have hitherto known how to make of it all; and yet, it is worth while to fill our imagination with these pictures of the physical greatness of our land, and its countless riches, for thus the idea of our national call to duty becomes more impressive.

A wide area of fertile soil, with different climatic conditions means that we can have varied industries, many types of character, large conceptions of nationality, splendid schemes of governmental achievement. The unity of the continent impresses upon the motley population a sense of our national oneness, and gives a material symbol for patriotic sentiment. The vigorous climate inspires energetic action, while there are places suitable for weak lungs, and other localities free from malaria for those who cannot acclimatize themselves in the rich valleys where the wheat ripens in prolific soil and the corn tassels fly the flags of prosperity and also warn of possible fevers.

The policy of national peace and mediation seems our destiny set by geographical position. We are too far away from that great camp of soldiers called Europe to be enticed into their fratricidal strifes and bickerings. It is dignified for us to pursue the constructive arts of civilization undisturbed by the warlike diplomacy and intrigue of continental courts. Situated between two mighty oceans, midway between the most advanced nations of Europe and the slow peoples of Asia, just now awakening to the stir of modern life, we have a position most favorable to a mediating policy dependent more on wisdom in council than on force of arms and ships. No foreign nation could gain anything by attacking us, and an enemy would be sure to lose a great deal. Nature seems to have indicated our national duty in most distinct language. Our commercial competition will be severe enough to tax and spur our inventive genius without seeking the burdens of sense-less and destructive war.   So geography seems to teach.

Man is a Geological Force. — The works of man, especially those constructed by associated enterprise, and made possible by the marshalling of many persons under one control, have made a deep and abiding mark upon the face of the physical world.   There is space for only a few illustrations.

Men have cut down and burned immense tracts of forests and, in consequence, the climate has been changed over vast areas.   The average rainfall has diminished, and formerly fertile tracts have become desert.   The waters, no longer re-strained by the roots, leaves, and trunks of the trees, have rushed down into the valleys in floods and carried destruction before them.   Vast systems of drainage have carried off the water from the surface, and the drained, parched land has raised the temperature of the district.   Agriculture has trans-formed bogs and swamps into fertile fields and pasture lands. If man has sometimes stripped the hills and laid them bare, he has in other instances turned desolation into bloom and verdure by planting trees and flowers.   The Hollanders, brave people, few in numbers but with mighty hearts, have built a wall against the sea, and held its threatening tides at bay for centuries.   The Mississippi River has been enclosed within banks, its currents tamed by jetties, its floods controlled by vast walls, and the method seems already devised to check its floods at their source, and to divert them into the desert for purpose of irrigation.   The immense irrigating canals of the southwest have driven back the borders of the "Great Ameri-can Desert."

By excavating the Suez canal two oceans have been made practically one, and the long, costly journey around the con-tinent of Africa has been shortened by many weeks.   Man is counted among the geological forces, along with volcanoes, glaciers, ocean tides, and summer storms.   His cities cover large portions of the land, and the structures of man's craft, dug out of the mountain sides, suggest their lofty elevation. From the top of Milan cathedral one may look over the plain to see the white scar of the hills whence the marble walls have come.   These changes may not be so large in bulk, but they are so full of evidence of human intellect, and bear so directly on human happiness, that we must regard them as full of significance.

III.   The Physical Side of Human Life, as a Part of Nature. — Man is much more than an animal; but before we can do justice to his social life we must for a time consider him as if he were a direct descendant and a relation of the humble living creatures which occupy the earth with him.   We may first study some of the physical elements of human life apart from the modifying influence of his superior intellectual qualities, which distinguish him from this lower world.   At a later stage of our inquiries, we shall see how the merely animal factors are modified by forces of a more exalted kind, and the conclusions we now reach must, for that reason, be considered as only a part of the whole truth.

First of all we may give attention to the *"Law of Diminishing Returns."*   The human intellect and will are powerful elements, but they find limits in nature.   By improving our methods of ploughing, fertilizing, seeding, draining, we may increase the average production of the soil in a very great measure.   Larger vegetables, finer fruits, more perfect oxen, sheep with heavier wool and with more meat on their bones, are the achievements of improved methods in agriculture and related industries.   Science and practical arts based on advancing science show encouraging results, and no one will pretend to prophesy the end.   There will be no end of improvement as long as man lives on the earth, and he will be pushed to make improvements by the very law which we are now studying.

Take a garden under your own observation for illustration of this law of diminishing returns.   Last year it was not drained, and the water drowned the tender plants at one corner, and half the crop was lost.   This year a drain prevents that loss.   Last year the seed was defective, and this year a gain is made by examining the seeds under a microscope and by testing them in a warm room in the winter to see if the germs are alive.   Here is another source of profit.   Last year one part of the soil was worn out and yielded little; this year fertilizing material has been applied and plant food furnished in abundance, and here is another cause of gain.   Last year the weeds were permitted to suck up much of the strength of the soil; this year more careful tilling has kept these parasites out and given the vegetables full sway. This year the product is more than doubled, and you have enough for two families. Can you double the product next year? Probably you can increase it somewhat, with this experience, but never can you double it again. With increase of labor and expenditure on seed and fertilizers the product will increase up to a certain point, but even the increase may not pay for the greater expenditure. The returns have diminished in relation to the work and capital expended on the soil. A limit is reached at last. And what is true of this little garden is true of the whole country. We have not approached the limit of possible product as yet, and will not for a long time. But many a farmer has already come to this point and knows it. In older countries millions of persons suffer because they cannot, even by putting forth their best effort and wisdom, compel their soils to yield any more food for man. We can get increased paying returns up to a certain point for our outlay on land; then comes the point where the increased returns do not pay for the outlay.

The Doctrine of Malthus. — If we are really to make any progress in understanding society, we must be aware of another tendency in nature, this time in the animal nature of mankind. Nature without is niggardly; human nature is prolific. The animal appetites tend to cover the earth with a population larger than the soil, even under the highest cultivation, can feed and otherwise provide with necessaries. It is true that man has not always yielded to this animal disposition, but has held it in rein by foresight of consequences, as merely animal natures could not do.

But in some parts of the earth, as in India, we see this tendency producing its most terrible consequences. Millions of human beings starve to death because they multiply beyond the productive power of the soil, even when carefully and diligently cultivated. It may be objected that the cause of famine is unjust distribution of the product. But the best intelligence, philanthropy, and statesmanship have thus far failed to discover a better way. When we come to study our industrial system and economic reforms, we shall consider some of the attempts to mitigate these causes of suffering and to remove the elements of human injustice.

We do not require to travel beyond our own acquaintance to discover some families whose numbers are too large for the earning capacity of the parents. Even when we make allowance for inequitable distribution of wealth, all competent persons must admit that the average product would not supply the wants of as many human beings as would exist if animal appetite were not curbed by some action of the intelligence. Morality demands that these facts should be known and understood. Social progress depends on such knowledge and on suitable action. The high rate of mortality among young children in the poor quarters of cities helps to keep down the excess of population, and the effects of this excess are seen in the idiotic and other defectives who burden our charities and fill our asylums and poor-houses and prisons.

Of course population cannot actually pass the limits of subsistence. There will always be some kind of an adjustment of these two factors, because the supply of food is the actual condition of the existence of human beings. But this adjustment is now secured at awful cost of sickness, starvation, suffering, and death. And that is in fact the method by which the balance is maintained, as every physician and every charity worker knows. If all the children lived who are born, there would not be enough to provide nourishment for them, and so nature carries them off by starvation, diseases, and by all the cruel processes of competition of the under-fed and enfeebled with the strong and competent. The unlimited gratification of animal appetite, without regard to social welfare, is the direct cause of much of the misery which gives us distress, and such want of self-control and recklessness is therefore brutal and cruel.[1]

The Law of Variation. — We may at this point direct attention to the fact of variation in the natural process of inheritance. The causes of the unlikeness of children as

---

[1] The view in the text is the author's conviction. Mr. Henry George, in *Progress and Poverty*, and S. Nitti, *La Population*, may be consulted for a different doctrine.

compared with their parents and with all other persons are numerous, and many of them are not yet clearly known. Each parent is unlike all other persons, and the offspring take something from both father and mother. Many external causes, as food, heat, climate, and millions of forces act upon the formation of human beings as they come into life. The result is all that now concerns us: variety of physical and mental characteristics. Each human being makes a new start. This unlikeness of individuals must be kept in mind as we proceed, for we shall have to make further use of it in our studies.

Inheritance of Likeness. — But this tendency to variation is crossed by another natural effect of inheritance, — likeness to parents and to the race. The two physical tendencies work together, side by side, and represent apparent opposites. Variation makes possible both progress and degeneration, while direct likeness tends to preserve the type as it is on the average. One tendency gives us all that is new, the other stereotypes what is useful until something better is struck out.

This conservation of species and genus by inheritance of qualities may be observed in plants and in animals. It is the result of physical causes deep as the beginnings of life, even deep as the chemical laws of the material world. It gives us a sense of the reliability and stability of nature, helps us to count on what has been accomplished. But it is not absolute. It is not exclusive. The actual situation of the race is determined by a combination of two tendencies, one toward fixed outlines and forms and modes of conduct.

The Law of Conflict. — At this point we must consider another law of animal life which will pursue us to the end, — the law of conflict. In business we are familiar with this law under the name of "competition." Whenever ten persons apply for one position, it is manifest that some one must be disappointed. But the conflict of interests began long before man existed on earth, and it is observed wherever there are organized and living creatures.

The garden will give abundant illustrations to any careful observer. In the spring the soil and air are full of seeds of all kinds. When the warm sun and rain have caused these various seeds to germinate and break through the crust, it becomes manifest that some of the plants must perish. Usually we kill out the weeds, "thin" the beets, select the best plants, destroy the beetles and worms, starve or kill the birds which injure the vegetables, and so permit the best vegetables to enjoy the soil and grow to perfection. But sometimes a garden or field is neglected, and then we have nature at war in truly primitive style. The field of the sluggard is the battle-field of individual plants and of kinds of plants for the possession of the space.

On a summer day one may discover the conflict going forward in the animal world. Seated in the quiet woods by a brook or pond the tragic history of millions of years passes before the eye. Down there in the warm waters the larger fishes are darting after the small fry and devouring them, and this furnishes the original of the proverb of modern business: "The big fishes eat up the little fishes." But the little fishes are not innocent, for they also are out hunting for insects. Frequently the surface is broken by a swift leap of a minnow eagerly springing after its prey. Its life depends on consuming other life. The waters are teeming with cannibals. Up there on a tree branch sits a kingfisher, waiting for his opportunity, and soon he swoops down to the shallows, where a fish is struggling up stream exposed to the clutch of his hereditary enemy. The bird of prey takes meat home for her brood. The hawk's shadow bodes ill to the dove or hen, and chickens seem born with an instinct of dread which has been inherited from generations of fowls who had reason to be afraid of that peculiar shadow.

Examples might be multiplied. Conflict is the universal state of plant and animal existence. Men may strive to be vegetarians, but the microscope shows how vain the attempt must be to carry out the principle in all strictness. In the market-place stand a thousand men waiting for employment. Every one of them wishes to serve that he may win food for himself and his wife and children. If he fails, as fail he may, there will be more hunger and cold.

Advertise for a clerk in a great newspaper, and at eight o'clock the office of rendezvous will be crowded with applicants. Life means competition. That is not all it means,

as we shall see. Other sides of existence deserve our attention. But we cannot escape from this fact. Tears and protests, passionate outcries against the injustice of it, laws
forbidding it, Utopian schemes to bring it all to a sudden
end, are in vain. The universe is made on this principle.
To deny it is simply to deceive ourselves; nature will have
all the less pity.

This struggle exists because the provisions of nature are
limited and the demands of individuals are persistent. If
there were no pressure from the presence of competitors, there
would still be a necessity for toil in order to wring from soil
and sea the means of life.

Natural Selection. — Let us now consider the issue of this
conflict. It is usually said the consequence of the struggle for
existence is the "survival of the fittest"; but the phrase needs
explanation. If we connect with this phrase the idea that
the "fittest" are always the most beautiful, the most gentle,
the most refined, the most agreeable, according to our best
ideals of what is desirable in character, we are apt to find
many exceptions. We may be grievously disappointed.

What is true may be summed up in this statement, although
any brief statement must be incomplete: the struggle for existence issues in preserving those individuals, families, races,
and those modes of thinking, acting, and doing, which on
the whole are best adapted to the conditions of existence in
a given age and land.

In a general way the primitive conditions of human life
demanded physical strength, compact family life, or close
organization of groups, and power to resist attacks with force
and cunning. In some situations it was more important to be
sly than strong and aggressive. Whatever the type of man
that was needed, those would live and have successors who
had these qualities.

The process was rude and attended with immeasurable
suffering, although the earlier men were not as sensitive to
pain as their more delicate descendants. Perhaps the pain
of the process may have been exaggerated, for certainly there
are still among us rough people who enjoy nothing better than
to take and give bloody blows. It is the form of amusement

most agreeable to savages in all countries, and the savage and tiger element is not entirely bred out of our blood even in this smiling century.

We are not trying to defend this method on ethical grounds. We are just now simply trying to state one aspect of the past and of the present. But it may be noted at once that this severe discipline has helped to produce fine fruits, the man of the twentieth century. On the average this man has nothing to complain of in the conduct of his ancestors, for he is very well satisfied with himself, their child.

"The homing instinct of the fur seal, concluding its long swim of three thousand miles by a return to a little island hidden in the arctic fogs, to the very spot from which it was driven by the ice six months before, excites our astonishment. But this power is not an illustration of animal intelligence. The homing instinct with the fur seal is a simple necessity of life. Without it the individual would be lost to the species. Only those which have the instinct to perfection can return; only those who return can leave descendants. As to the others, the rough sea tells no tales. We know that not all of the fur seals who set forth return. To those who do return the homing instinct has proved adequate. And this it must always be, so long as the race exists, for general inadequacy would mean extinction of the species " (President D. S. Jordan).

Even a brief statement of natural selection would be incomplete without noticing another product of the process, the birth of love, of sympathy. Leaving out of account the parables of attachment in the flower world, we may discover deep down in the animal world the early beginnings of affection. Very simple animal structures show a drawing together in response to touch and sight and motion. Much higher up, among the birds and mammals, the collections of stories by naturalists will illustrate characteristics almost human. Mother birds will risk their own lives to save their young. Ants will toil unceasingly for the nest. Fierce tigers seem to be as tender to their own young as gentle domestic creatures.

And these affections are part of the product of the struggle for existence. Animals which did not develop such impulses would neglect their offspring, and the species would die out.

Nature has long been offering premiums for sympathy as well as for cunning and for strength. All the qualities which we have come to value originated in variation in the upward direction, and were preserved by the struggle for existence helped by the tendency of offspring to be like parents.

Thus far we have considered man just as we might any other animal. Further study will show how this blind and unconscious process has come to a stage where it produces and is modified by higher forces. But so long as man is composed of body as well as mind, these forces will still be part of his social experience and cannot be left out of account.

IV. Races. — One of the facts of the life of mankind is the distinction of races. As this distinction had a physical origin, and retains physical elements, this is the right place to consider it. The social problem of race is very serious for us in this country. There is the southern problem of the Negro race, the California problem of the Mongolian, the Hawaiian question of the native people, the Cuban difficulty of mixed races, the national problem of the assimilation of immigrants from European races.

Perhaps the following general definition of the *Century Dictionary* will be sufficient for our purpose: "A great division of mankind having in common certain distinguishing physical peculiarities, and thus a comprehensive class appearing to be derived from a distinct primitive source: as, the Caucasian race, the Mongolian race, the Negro race."

The origin and causes of race differences are only dimly made out. Monuments of Egypt and remains of early men preserved for our study prove that the differences now known are very ancient. It seems highly probable that they were caused by the long operation of the physical world upon the human body, and by modes of living which were adopted in order to meet the needs of various conditions of life.

The eminent ethnologist, Quatrefages, bases his divisions of the human races on three sets of characteristics, — physical, intellectual, and spiritual (moral and religious). (*a*) The physical differences are partly external, as the color of the skin, the form of the face, the height and proportions of the body; (*b*) anatomical, varieties of size and form of cranium, skeleton, jaws, the structure of brain and nerves; (c) physiological, the modes of growth, the changes of adolescence, the diseases to which the persons are liable, and other peculiarities of the bodily life. The marks of the grade and mode of intellectual life are evidenced by the kind of language used, the utensils, weapons, implements, and other works of art, and the methods of support, as hunting, fishing, pastoral occupations, agriculture, and trade. Moral and religious conduct is another sign of the characters of a race.

Our immediate social interest in the question does not depend on the primary origin of races, but rather on the effect of race mingling in our own country. The questions which thoughtful citizens are asking are such as these: What must be the influence of a large volume of alien elements upon our institutions of culture and religion and government? What must happen if a multitude of laborers come among us with low standards of life, willing to eat coarse food, wear cheap clothing, and accept very low pay? And, finally, what must be the result in respect to the quality of the stock of people which will at last inhabit this continent?

Such questions compel us to inquire whether the lower races can be improved, or whether they must gradually be suppressed or die out by natural processes and the diseases of civilization. Or may it be possible to find localities better adapted to some races than to others, so that the population may be varied and yet each people enjoy the home best adapted to its physical peculiarities?

V. General Considerations as to the Influence of Nature on Society. — Nature sets a limit upon social action. The climate restricts the number of crops man can raise in a year. The motions of the earth among the heavenly bodies set up certain barriers of seasons, certain rhythmic effects in his body beyond man's power to change. The products of mines and soils determine our industries. There is a necessary connection between the climate or soil and the occupations which are followed in various parts of the earth. The warm temperature of the tropics creates a type of character and makes impossible the habits natural to the north temperate zone. The attempt to study races, governments, industries, and churches without reference to the forces of nature is irrational. There is, and must ever be, an interchange between man and his physical environment. There is even a certain mystic sympathy between the physical features of the earth and the life of its inhabitants. "This globe is not, as we are informed, a perfect sphere, but slightly flattened at the poles; and in like manner this world is by no means a perfect world, though it be not quite so easy, as in the other case, to say where or why it is not" (J. R. Lowell).

The eminent economist, President Francis A. Walker, has counted the parsimony of nature among the causes of poverty.

" Easily chief among the causes of poverty is the hard condition of the human lot as by nature established. The prime reason why bread must be so dear, and flesh and blood so cheap, is that the ratio of exchange between the two has been fixed in the constitution of the earth, much to the disadvantage of the latter. When it is written that God cursed the ground and bade it be unfruitful, bringing forth briers and thorns, that man should only eat his bread with dripping brow, the Scripture does not exceed the truth of the unceasing and ever-painful struggle for existence. Taking it by and large, it is a hard and cruel world, in which little is to be got except by toil and anguish; and of that little not all can be kept by any degree of care and pains. There are, indeed, regions where the earth spontaneously brings forth fruit enough for a small population, and where a moderate effort will largely increase that product, while the climate is so benign that life is easily protected from exposure. But these are not the regions where man ever has, or seemingly ever can, become a noble being; and even here, in the midst of tropical plenty, the serpent stings, the tiger prowls at night around the village, the earthquake and the tornado work their frightful mischief, cholera and malaria kill their millions, while every few years gaunt famine stalks over the land, leaving it cumbered with corpses.

". . . The socialist is simply dishonest when he charges human misery upon society. Society has done vastly more to relieve misery than to create it."

We gain nothing by intoxicating ourselves with golden dreams about an earth as we might picture it, — rich, fertile, responding to easy touches. We do not live in such a world. Let us face the facts. Some genial and optimistic minds are promising us to make bread directly out of stones by chemical processes, thus delivering us from the uncertainties and toils of agriculture and gardening. But their prophecy of chemical pellets of nutritious manufactured substances, even if it were appetizing, is a mere fancy as yet, and no sensible man will build a social theory on a guess, no matter how pleasant it may be.

The Epicurean gods are represented by the poet Tennyson as looking down from serene heights careless of man's fate:

" For they lie beside their water, and the bolts are hurled
  Far below them in the valleys, and the clouds are lightly curl'd
  Round their golden houses, girdled with the gleaming world.
  When they smile in secret, looking over wasted lands,
  Blight and famine, plague and earthquake, roaring deeps and fiery sands,
  Clanging fights, and flaming towns, and sinking ships, and praying hands.
  But they smile, they find a music centred in a doleful song
  Steaming up, a lamentation and an ancient tale of wrong,
  Like a tale of little meaning tho' the words are strong;
  Chanted from an ill-used race of men that clear the soil."

This stern discipline of nature has been described with terrible and realistic force by J. S. Mill: " For how stands the fact? That next to the greatness of these cosmic forces, the quality which most forcibly strikes every one who does not avert his eyes from it, is their perfect and absolute recklessness. They go straight to their end, without regarding what or whom they crush on the road. . . .

" In sober truth, nearly all the things which men are hanged or imprisoned for doing to one another, are nature's every-day performances. Killing, the most criminal act recognized by human laws, nature does once to every being that lives, and in a large proportion of cases, after protracted tortures such as only the greatest monsters whom we read of ever purposely inflicted on their living fellow-creatures. . . . Nature impales men, breaks them as if on the wheel, casts them to be devoured by wild beasts, burns them to death, crushes them with stones like the first Christian martyr, starves them with hunger, freezes them with cold, poisons them by the quick or slow venom of her exhalations, and has hundreds of other hideous deaths in reserve, such as the ingenious cruelty of a Nabis or a Domitian never surpassed. All this Nature does with the most supercilious disregard both of mercy and of justice, emptying her shafts upon the best and noblest indifferently with the meanest and worst; upon those who are engaged in the highest and worthiest enterprises, and often as the direct consequences of the noblest acts, and it might almost be imagined as a punishment for them.''

Over against these extreme representations of the hatefulness of nature we may set the words of Shelley, who imports into the external world something of his own spirit.

> " Earth, ocean, air, beloved brotherhood !
>   If our great Mother has imbued my soul
>   With aught of natural piety to feel
>   Your love, and recompense the boon with mine;
>   If dewy morn, and odorous noon, and even,
>   With sunset and its gorgeous ministers,
>   And solemn midnight's tingling silentness;
>   If Autumn's sighs in the sere wood,
>   And Winter robing with pure snow and crowns,
>   Of stony ice the gray grass and bare boughs —
>   If Spring's voluptuous pantings when she breathes
>   Her first sweet kisses — have been dear to me;
>   If no bright bird, insect, or gentle beast,
>   I consciously have injured, but still loved
>   And cherished these my kindred; then forgive
>   This boast, beloved brethren, and withdraw
>   No portion of your wonted favor now."

The terrible and tragic pictures drawn by Mr. Mill are not a representation of the whole truth. They personify nature, whereas nature is impersonal. Many of the evils described are within the power of man to remove or greatly mitigate by his science, his art, his intelligence and education. All the institutions we are to study are parts of man's successful striving to bring the merely physical world under control. We have no reason to "blame" nature, for it is not a responsible being. Our business is to domesticate forces and matter by improving ourselves and our institutions. So far as our miseries are due to our own ignorance, injustice, oppression, social iniquity, we must not excuse ourselves by laying all to the account of nature, but resolutely turn against organized human error or selfishness. Dr. James Martineau, in *A Study of Religion*, has shown that Mr. Mill's indictment of the cruelty of nature is at some points an exaggeration.

It is not in place here to answer the question which inevitably arises, What is the meaning of this war of nature

D

against man? If we mean to inquire why the Divine Being has introduced these disorders, miseries, and hardships into the world, we may properly hand the investigation over to theology and metaphysics; it is not possible for strict science to give an answer, and perhaps the theologians may have some difficulty with a problem so knotty that Job and Plato struggled with it, as Kant and Schopenhauer have done. Robinson Crusoe's man Friday asked, "Why did not God kill the devil?" and Crusoe floundered in that deep sea. But if we ask what *use* men can make of hardship, scarcity, and struggle, we are on more solid ground. Perhaps in dealing with present reality and duty we may be on our way to speculative satisfaction. If struggle brings out the higher faculties of men, compels them to be alert, inventive, and industrious; if the hardships of existence educate us in sympathy and finer social organization, in the progressive victory by coöperation,— then we can understand at least a little way the meaning and use of pain and trial. It is in society, not in nature, that morality emerges.

Nature as our Ally. — Over against the tragic and one-sided statement just given, we may draw a brighter picture. Nature not only limits the possibilities of human action, but also assists and provides. Out of the material world of unorganized and organized matter come the materials and forces which sustain us. The energy which is stored up by the sun rays in plants is energy of higher potency in animals; and man eats both, not merely to supply heat and strength, but to make thought possible.

Nature is more than a kitchen, it is a library and a gallery. Its scenes furnish the memory with objects of beauty and sublimity. The study of the laws of the outward world fill the mind with suggestions of the unity and harmony of all existence.

Nature once entrusted with the works of human art keeps them manifest in visible forms from age to age, as monuments, pictures, fountains, aqueducts. It is true that disintegrating forces are at work,— frost and earthquake, wind and acid,— but man can calculate the probabilities and balance one tendency against another and compel the matter of earth to keep his message and his story through thousands of years.

Professor O. T. Mason gives illustrations of four different ways in which nature ministers to man's life:

"And first we cannot help seeing that the environment is the provider of all raw materials. . . . An Eskimo collection is white; the same ideas are expressed by the Haidas south of them in jet black. The art of the British Columbian is red, of Oregon and Californian yellow, of the Pueblos écru, of Mexico gray. All this is plain enough when you know the color of walrus ivory, of slate, and mountain-goat horn, of cedar, of grasses, and spruce roots, of fire clay when baked, and of volcanic building stones. People express themselves in the material at hand. The Egyptian was furnished with limestone and sienite, so he hammered away at that. His ideas could mount no higher than the material. On the other hand, the Greek was provided by environment with the whitest, finest, and thickest quarries of marble on earth. It was expected of him that he should give the highest expression of the æsthetic faculty in sculpture and architecture, though his pottery was somewhat inferior. When the whole world is brought into one environment by the art of transportation, then other lands have hope to imbibe some of the genius engendered and fostered by the quarries of Pentelicus.

"Nature or environment appears to us, secondly, in the light of a *purveyor of force.* At first our race had only the force of its own frail but versatile bodies to depend upon, yet men will never cease to marvel at this mechanism as an economic device for storing and utilizing power. Whether we regard a machine in the light of saving fuel, of speed, of ability to change rectilinear motion readily into that of any curve or succession of curves, the body of men will ever remain for inventors to wonder at and imitate. Long ago backs and hands and feet were wearied with ever-increasing burdens, and so the dog, the reindeer, the horse, the ass, the cow, the camel, the llama, the elephant, and even the sheep, were handed over in innumerable packs and herds to give additional power to industry. These creatures not only fed and clothed men, they made men's legs longer, their backs stronger, their hands more skilful. Then came the wind to blow upon the mat, the sail, the mill, and the water, moving in its natural currents and then in artificial channels, to turn the wheels of industrialism. How bountiful has nature been in the supply of force! Who ever dreamed of exhausting it? How many ships upon the sea would it take to use up all the winds that blow, and how many turbine wheels would it require to take up and transform into useful arts the force of all waterfalls ? . . .

"In the third place, the environment manifests itself as the teacher of industries. . . . There were cave-dwellers before there were men; spiders, mud wasps, beavers, and birds spun and worked in clay and cut down trees and made soft beds for their young long ago. Plants reared vessels, and mollusks produced dishes that even now are the patterns of the most skilful potters. There were hammers, gimlets, pins, needles, saws, baskets, and sandpaper at hand when the human artisan first became an apprentice.

"Lastly, the environment itself is capable of unlimited education and improvement in relation to the commonest wants of life and our ways of satisfying them. . . . An industrious and wise farmer settles upon a piece of land. Soon you behold remunerative crops replacing the forest and the waste. The man is enriched; he then enriches the land, and by a kind of mutual admiration they two grow fat together. When a progressive race has settled down in a part of the earth not too icy, not too torrid, not discouragingly luxuriant, not absolutely a desert, the same has been true. The wild and coöperatively relentless wolves have become faithful dogs. The capability was slumbering there. The feeble grasses are transformed simply by giving the best a chance into prolific grains."

It is in the art and profession of agriculture that man comes face to face with nature in all its varying moods of glory, beauty, and terror. The farmer is dealing at first hand with the physical environment, and shares with miners the honor and toil of extracting from the earth the raw materials of all social arts and commodities. Nature studies should be of highest interest to these primary producers. "The plough-man who is also a naturalist runs his furrow through the most interesting museum in the world" (Lowell).

The dependence of society upon nature is, perhaps, relatively less than it was in ancient ages. It is easy to understand that savage people who live from hand to mouth, without stores of food, without roads and means of communication and transportation, cut off from distant communities by dark, dense forests and high mountains, isolated by feuds and hatred, must often utterly perish in case of a local drought and famine.

"In the days of Turgot, the French minister of finance under Louis XVI, there were at times in certain departments of France such abundant harvests that wheat was almost unmarketable, while in other and not far distant sections of the country there was such a lack of food that the inhabitants perished of hunger, and yet, through the absence of facilities for transportation and communication of intelligence, the influence of bad laws, and the moral inertia of the people, there was no equalization of condition. This experience of France in the last quarter of the eighteenth century has repeated itself at the present day in China. General Wilson, in his *Study of China* (1887), states that over ten million of people died from starvation about ten years ago in the provinces of Shansi and Shensi alone, while abundance and plenty were prevailing in other parts of the country. Every effort was made to send food into the stricken regions, but owing to the entire absence of river and canal navigation as well as of railroads, few of the suffering multitude could be reached." — D. A. WELLS.

In the pioneer days of our great West, as the aged settlers still repeat, our forefathers suffered from the absence of salt, condiments, and medicines, because these articles could not be secured without a journey to New York, which cost many weary weeks and intense hardships. The inventions of our age enable us to become independent of the direct gifts of nature, to rely upon stores of goods, and to substitute one article for another in times of scarcity. Irrigation makes a plain independent of rains. Electric lighting turns night into day. New modes of curing and preserving fruits and meats give more varied diet at all seasons, and railroads serve the same end by carrying the vegetables of south to north and of west to east.

Knowledge and art bring freedom from the limitations of nature, and make of speechless things and forces the drudges of mankind. This is the meaning of the story of Prospero and his magic, in the pages of Shakespeare. The spirit Ariel and the magic wand represent modern science. Winds and waves are servants of the prince who reads the secrets of Nature and learns how to command her at his will. Caliban, the savage, the brute, is the unwilling instrument of the intellect of the man who knows.

Man's civilization is conditioned by nature, but climate and soil are by no means the only factors, not the most important. Think of the conquest of dunes and oceans by Danes and Hollanders. "The Mississippi has always been the same lordly stream as to-day, but so long as only red men inhabited its banks, it was not a commercial highway" (H. von Treitschke).

We find the modern Greeks in very much the same outward conditions as those which affected the ancient Greeks; but how different the people! In the same climate, in view of the same mountains, tilling the same soil, eating the same food, in Africa, in the islands of the Pacific, and in India, we know that many races and kinds of men reside, century after century, side by side.

This mastery and freedom of man are only relative. There is a limit even to genius and to science. Society must ever rest, in the last analysis, on mother earth. The land, the mines, the forests, the sea, must ever bound his pretensions and supply his means. The physical world will ever have the last word. Decrees forbidding comets to approach the earth are dead letters. Engineering plans based on the hope of water flowing up hill must come to grief.

VI. Relation of Nature Studies to the Study of Society. — Systematic knowledge of soils, minerals, stones, as presented in mineralogy, geology, and chemistry, helps us to understand the means of human welfare, the boundaries and limits of organized effort to provide for man's wants. Systematic study of plants enables man to discover food supplies, materials for garments and shelter, dyes, medicines, and hints of æsthetic forms, and thus botany finds its place and rank among the "humanities." Systematic study of animals, in anatomy, physiology, zoölogy, enables men to discover the best means of securing animal food, skins and wool, silk for clothing and ornament, and to guard health against countless foes. Physics reveals the laws of motion, of heat, light, electricity, and actinism, and assists the mind to grasp the order and unity of the world. It is in seeking the human uses of the various kinds of knowledge, in relation to social ends, that we discover their value, their beauty, their connection with each other, and their place in the school. To use a current phrase, our nature studies are correlated in the one inclusive study of society, its nature and its needs. As the spokes of a wheel are "correlated" by their insertion in the hub and the felloes composing the rim, so each nature study finds its rank and position by its relation to the demands of the community, that is, the common life of our kind.

And these human needs are not merely animal wants, as of nutrition, comfort, and protection, but also the intellectual desires for orderly knowledge and the æsthetic demands for beauty.

Natural Forces are not Social Forces. — Important as are the services of the physical world about us, and indispensable to every act and movement of society, yet the external environment is not human, is not a social force. It is only as man thinks nature, as his mind responds to its power and manifestations, that nature enters into the very current of social causes. "The geographical environment may limit or hinder social life, but it cannot be a force or moment in that life" (Baldwin). It may be more correct to say that nature does more than limit and hinder, it offers actual and positive aid to man and bears his burdens for him. But genuine social forces are mental and not physical.

Wind and wave, stream and tide, soil and climate, plant and animal, are not social forces, but human thoughts about these realities are among the social forces. Knowledge and superstition, science and belief, accurate information and gross prejudice in relation to the external world, are to be counted among the social causes.

The Sources of our Interest in Nature. — Our interest is utilitarian in the narrow sense. A gentleman of economic habits declared that he preferred to take care of his own furnace, because he did not feel comfortable to have an ignorant man building fires under his parlor and bed. All men, working as individuals or in companies, must know what forces are at work under them and around them.

Our interest is intellectual, and knowledge is itself useful, since it gratifies the hunger for truth. Granted that nature study may not give us more bread or softer beds or more pleasant houses, still one craving of our minds would be met by the science of things.

There is æsthetic enjoyment in the contemplation of nature. Beauty is "in the delicate forest flower, with scented breath and look so like a smile." The clouds of evening spread the sky with the glories of a panorama impossible to be produced by any save the Divine painter. When once the external world has been interpreted to us by poets and artists, the most common objects are invested with a charm which entrances us and enriches life.

The study of nature has an interest because it comes to be a common pursuit of members of society and binds them in the bonds of higher ends. It subdues selfishness and enlarges sympathy for all that breathes.

While we no longer pretend, as did earlier students, to determine the exact thought of Providence for every insect and shape of stone and arrangement of nerve-cells, yet nature, in its majestic movements, its orderly progress, its suggestions of infinite power and thought, never ceases to be a revelation to the human spirit.

Alexander von Humboldt closes one section of his great book, *Cosmos*, with this passage:

"From the remotest nebulæ and from the revolving double stars, we have descended to the minutest organisms of animal creation, whether manifested in the depths of ocean or on the surface of our globe, and to the delicate vegetable germs which clothe the naked declivity of the ice-crowned mountain summit, and here we have been able to arrange these phenomena according to partially known laws; but other laws of a more mysterious nature rule the higher spheres of the organic world, in which is comprised the human species in all its varied conformation, its creative intellectual power, and the languages to which it has given existence. A physical delineation of nature terminates at the point where the sphere of intellect begins, and a new world of mind is opened to our view."

PART II

THE SOCIAL PERSON

———◦◦◦———

CHAPTER III

The Social Member: the Person

"There is no prosperity, trade, art, city, or great material wealth of any kind, but, if you trace it home, you will find it rooted in a thought of some individual man." — EMERSON.

"What is thy art? to be good. And how is this accomplished well except by general principles, some about the nature of the universe, and others about the proper constititution of man?

"Every man is worth just so much as the things are worth about which he busies himself."

"Whatever any one does or says, I must be good, just as if gold, or emerald, or purple were always saying this, Whatever any one does or says, I must be emerald and keep my color." — MARCUS AURELIUS ANTONINUS, *Meditations.*

> "Turn, Fortune, turn thy wheel with smile or frown;
> With that wild wheel we go not up or down;
> Our hoard is little, but our hearts are great.
> Smile and we smile, the lords of many lands;
> Frown and we smile, the lords of our own hands;
> For man is man and master of his fate."
> — TENNYSON.

SOCIETY is composed of persons, of human beings. We shall not stop to discuss the question whether there are animal societies, whether flocks, herds, beehives, ant-hills, and companies of cunning crows may properly be called societies. We admit that there are many points of agreement, but there are also vital differences, which will appear more clearly as we develop the conception of human society and the peculiar marks of human community life.   At present notice is served that we are studying mankind.

Since we are to study human institutions, we certainly may well begin with an inspection of the being who makes society. We may take at random any one out of the millions of persons who live in civilized lands, and by study of his mode of being we are at once in contact with the facts of society.   The nature of man helps us to explain the community.   What is the meaning and purpose of schools and states, of factories and banks?   The answer to these questions must be secured by asking particular men what they mean and what they desire. The study of humanity in general is possible only by taking the particular specimens and reasoning from these.   By carefully following the order of development of persons, we have some hint of the development of mankind in the past.   We speak of the "childhood of the world," and the phrase has meaning when we compare some of the traits of children with those of savage peoples.

Whether we wish to deal with a mob to understand it, or with a city ward to elevate its life, we must take with us some clear notion of the way in which outward conditions affect thought and sentiment, and the process by which beliefs and feelings are communicated from person to person.

The world in which we live is composed of things and of persons, of physical objects and of spiritual beings.   Each man carries in himself the elements of both worlds, and is himself an illustration of the unity of this world in its two aspects.   Man is both body and soul, and these are so intimately bound up in him that it is impossible to separate them, and each profoundly affects the other.   A man can know natural objects, as trees and flesh, because he knows his own body.   He can enter into the thought of other intelligent persons because he has thoughts of his own.

I. The Physical Man. — Social studies and common observation make us more or less familiar with the structure and activity of the body.   It is at this point that our scheme of study might insert a treatise on anatomy and physiology.   We must take it for granted that those subjects have already been considered; that the reader is familiar with the cells, the tissues of bone muscles and nerve, the organs of mastication digestion respiration circulation and nervous energy. It is to the works on physiology that we must go for our knowledge of the uses or functions of the different parts of the body.

In the physical history of each person there are indications of the social origin and dependence of men. There are the familiar facts of differences of sex which condition the family, and have such profound influence on social customs, laws, and sentiments. Marriage itself would not exist, would have no meaning, without the powerful incentives which arise out of the physical nature of human beings. The merely instinctive passions are brought under rational control, are hidden by modesty, are transfigured by poetry and religion, are brought into subservience to the highest interests of the race.

> " Flesh and bone and nerve that make
> The poorest, coarsest human hand;
> Are objects worthy to be scanned
> A whole life long for their sole sake." — BROWNING.

All social study must begin with a clear understanding of the structure and functions of the body. Many of the social problems are directly problems of health. This is a fundamental social interest. Health is a condition of all higher activities. Disease reduces vitality and strength, diminishes the amount of force available for social work, disturbs the order and peace of social relations, endangers the very existence of the community. The laws of health become laws of duty binding on the conscience, and at last find themselves enacted into decrees of legislatures and ordinances of councils and boards of health.

The bodily structure and functions determine those appetites which play so important a part in human history — hunger and love. It seems to be the object of nature to construct men so that the race shall be maintained and continued through the active demands of these two impulses. Industry, from the simple gathering of shell-fish and nuts by savages to the complicated machinery of modern city factories, has its origin and support in the demand for food and clothing and shelter.

All other wants wait on these and are attached to them. Out of the sexual instinct grow families, throngs of children, inhabitants of towns, armies, school population, nations. The regulation of these powerful animal instincts is the slow achievement of civilization, of morals, government, custom, public opinion, and religion. Their abuses constitute the perils of order and progress. Their right direction secures the ends of existence. "So far as he is a social animal, that is, an animal liable in various ways to make his neighbor uncomfortable, it is certainly prudent to remember always that, though his natural impulses may be restrained, or guided, or even improved, yet that they are always there and ready to take the bit in their teeth at the first chance which offers" (J. R. Lowell).

The suitable regulation of the appetites must be determined primarily by physiology. The ethics of the temperance question turn on the discoveries of physiological science as to the effects of alcohol in various forms and quantities upon the health. The legislator and the advocate of total abstinence would have no powers of persuasion without the verdict of the medical profession. Common observation needs to be supplemented by the nicer discriminations of experimentalists before we can decide whether a regulation should be applied to all persons or only in certain cases. The argument for legislation in favor of periodical rest is largely based on accumulated knowledge of the effects of unremitting exertion on the muscular and nervous tissues.

There are physiological ideals for social legislation. When physicians declare that six hundred cubic feet of air are necessary for each person, and that allowance must be made for the consumption of oxygen by gas jets or lamps, there is a basis for a rule of building and occupancy of tenements. When physicians agree that one day in seven must be taken for recuperation of bodily energy, we have at once a principle for the direction of action by trade unions, clubs, legislators, and public opinion. Bodily integrity conditions knowledge, for the first materials of knowledge come to us first through the senses, as of sight, hearing, taste, touch, smell. No picture of Raphael would mean anything to the blind. Rossini's music would remain dead to the deaf. The perfumes of flowers would give no pleasure to those deprived of the sense of smell. The emotions which accompany the processes of knowledge would be forbidden enjoyments to those deprived of the physical organization through which alone these forms of knowledge enter the spirit.

The stages of physical development and decay furnish serious social problems. Infancy, adolescence, maturity, and old age bring with them difficulties and crises which concern the community and demand rules of reason, laws, modes of discipline, special sacrifice, and appropriate sentiments.

The prolongation of the helplessness of human infants is at least one important cause of the rise and refinement of parental feelings and sentiments. It is the feebleness and dependence of the babe which makes the family. When affections have grown more responsive and tender, and men begin to care for the sick and the aged, just because their suffering and need awaken sympathy and pity, the very defects of existence become the occasion of new virtues and nobler qualities.

Here, also, we must notice the inheritance of spiritual qualities and dispositions through physical inheritance. So intimate and real is the organic connection between mind and body that mental characteristics go down with bodily traits and conditions.

In order to understand the race question, we must begin with a careful consideration of the differences in the cranium, skeleton, brain, muscular system, and other inherited marks which distinguish one people from others. We must discover the intellectual, emotional, and moral qualities which have come down from remote ancestors and have fixed the limits within which change is possible.

In the study of economic conditions in various countries, problems of poverty and riches, of great and small incomes, of adaptation to creative and merely routine labors, we cannot leave out of account inherited powers and capacities. Even crime and pauperism are not to be understood apart from the inheritance of bodily peculiarities.

From ancient times poets and statesmen have loved to compare society to the complex and unified system of organs which constitute the body. The ancient Roman orator who sought to quell the mob by showing them that the stomach must work for the hands while the hands fight and toil for the entire body, and who drew the inference that there must be laborers as well as soldiers and rulers in the state, employed this analogy as an argument. Paul, in his first letter to the Corinthians, used the same picture: "For as the body is one, and hath many members, and all the members of the body, being many, are one body," and applied the parable in persuading to harmony and humility. Each separate cell has a life of its own, but it cannot remain alive apart from its place in the body, and it is only in union with millions of other cells that it can share in the exalted mode of being peculiar to mankind.

II. The Mind of Man. — We know that as the nervous system grows the mental powers increase, and that when brain and spinal cord are impaired by disease or old age that the mental powers are disturbed or fail. Without touch, sight, and hearing, by which the body feels its way in the material world, the soul never wakes from its infant slumber.

Psychology takes up the consideration of the growth of the mental acts and states, analyzes them, studies the conditions under which they arise, change, and disappear.

The Soul's Life. — For what we are about to consider there is no need of external witnesses, proofs, and authority. The mind of each student is highest authority and original document. Discussion can do no more than waken the mind to observe itself at work. We are studying modes of associated human activity, institutions, and their causes. All these causes lie in the souls of men, and each soul is of kin to all others. Let one master the contents of his own mind and he is prepared to read off the secret sources of all the institutions of mankind, from the laws of Solon down to the regulations of a base-ball club or evening party.

The Mental Contributions of the Senses. — That hidden " I " which is born with each begins with scant faculties and skill, but has capacity to attain to mastery of the world of matter and of spirit. At first blinking and uncertain of the meaning of lights and colors and forms, the child comes gradually, and by many blundering experiments, into fair possession of the power of seeing. Into the spirit there flows by this gate all fair forms and sights, colors, shapes, hues, shades, — materials afterward for guiding conduct, for combining into paintings and machinery, into poems and orations and laws.

Hearing contributes other elements to the inward wealth of the spirit life. Consider the waking of the babe at the soft sound of the mother's voice, and think of the dreamy waiting for the merry laughter of brothers and sisters. Its own cries, merely instinctive at first, discover to the ignorant immigrant into this world that the cry will bring nourishment and comfort and gentle caress and warmth. The discovery of the power of its own voice is a step outward into the social world. Fortunate is that infant whose ears are long spared the jarring noises of strife, the din of harsh and disagreeable sounds, the exclamations of impatience and ill temper. Fortunate that man whose ears have drunk in melodies of concord from the dawn of existence in the home. "The ear is the way to the heart. Envelope an infant in an atmosphere of sweet sounds, tender and happy, and you work for his immediate happiness, and do much for his future disposition and morality" (Perez).

Thus, also, we might enter in detail into the various contributions to our knowledge made by the senses of touch, taste, smell, temperature, organic sensations, and muscular feelings. Each of these forms of sensations has its own peculiar gift to bring to life, each combines in various ways with all the others to furnish the mind with the elements of memory, and all together lay a foundation for all the higher processes of learning and doing and enjoying.

Pathetic is the case of those who not only suffer from the mutilation or destruction of the special nerves of hearing and sight, but whose interior brain is so defective or diseased that even the wisest and most patient tuition can go but a little way to establish communication with the outer world of things and living beings. Here in the feeble-minded, — imbecile and idiot, — we discover how narrow the range of spiritual activity when the physical medium of thought is not supplied at birth. Some are themselves insensible to pain, and therefore can inflict wounds upon themselves or upon their companions without shrinking and remorse, and even with a sort of animal satisfaction. In such ways we may realize the debt our souls owe to the senses for their early and continual supply of reliable reports from the outer world.

Step by step the fabric of knowledge is woven by ever more complex methods and with richer materials, the shuttle flying back and forth at each moment to weave together into one soul all that is learned from every source, and to construct new patterns. Memory collects these images and holds them, by the help of the nervous structure in which, as in leaves of books, the characters of impressions are stored.

Not in some irregular and disorderly way, but according to laws quite clearly stated by psychologists, these images and records of experience are laid down in the memory, ready to spring forth at call of occasion or of choice. Objects which resemble come up again together when they are wanted or needed, as sunrise and lamplight suggest each other. Objects which have come into the mind in company are apt to come out in recollections at the same call, as when we hear the airs of a music-box bought in Germany we are at once transported in imagination to the distant city where the tones were first heard. Strong contrasts are also apt to be associated; and it is easier to remember two men very much unlike in height and appearance than to recall two soldiers made to appear almost alike by uniforms and lost in a mass of soldiers, all dressed in the same way.

Imagination recalls the impressions thus stored away, sometimes much as they entered the mind, but often in new combinations, especially when the "creative" genius of the artist surprises us with a composition of figures and landscape which borrows elements from many places but is itself a new object of contemplation, not just like any picture that nature ever showed.

It is not possible here to do more than mention the processes of thinking by which conceptions are formed and minds come to connect objects and remembered events in judgments and long processes of reasoning.

Out of all this process of mind-growth each one comes at last to realize that he lives in a universe where he can distinguish himself from the external world and have glimpses of that Higher Being who lives in all and must be thought of as the Perfect One.

Accompanying this history of learning is the development of the emotions. When objects are brought before our minds, they excite in us feelings corresponding to their nature and our relations to them.

We may next set down some of those feelings which arise in connection with the mind's search for truth. Wonder is a common experience in the presence of appearances which we cannot yet account for. Take, for an example, the long roll of thunder, repeated many times after the flashes of lightning. It awakens eager desire to understand the source and cause of it. This wonder acts as an incentive to inquire and make experiments until it is found that the clouds themselves reflect from their surfaces the movements of air caused by the explosion whose flash first attracted attention. There is also an emotion of satisfaction and pleased gratification when the cause is found and the fact is explained. The pursuit of truth and the discovery of truth are but the sources of emotions of pleasure, while uncertainty and defeat are causes of painful feelings.

The emotions accompanying the perception of beauty are of a different kind. To refresh the memory in regard to this emotion one may recall a visit to some famous picture, or the hearing of a great work of musical art, or the enjoyment of a charming landscape.

Our experiences in society call out emotions of a different order, as love, hate, anger, jealousy, sympathy. These feelings are aroused by our contact with our fellows, or by thoughts of them.

Professor Tracy adopts the classification of Professor Prever in regard to the movements with which a child begins to develop will. First, there are the impulsive movements of children which proceed from within and are not excited by any action or happening external to the person. The infant moves his limbs, turns his eyes, yawns and stretches, curls up into a ball, or reaches out his hands without any apparent cause. There is no distinct act of the will in this kind of

E

movement, although the child discovers himself and feels his body through just such action. He remembers these involuntary movements and the comfort they give him, and he repeats them afterwards with evidence of intention.

There come next the movements which arise in consequence of some external influence, but are not the result of purpose, as in blinking, or removal of a finger from a briar or hot lamp.

Then come the instincts, by virtue of which animals and young children seek food and protection and companionship, but without any deliberate plan or reflection.

And highest of all is the real act of choice in view of many considerations and ideas. It is here that man becomes consciously himself, a being of reflection, thought, and will.

The permanent results of choices are for the individual certain permanent dispositions and ways of acting, called habits. The complete result is a character which becomes one of the facts of life with which we must take account.

We have thus hastily sketched the elements of the mental life, and now ask ourselves what this means for social doctrine.

Thought determines action. "The end of action must be a function of the content which arouses the action. The dog acts with reference to perceptions, they are the best he can do. The man acts with reference to concepts, with distant aims before him in space and time; he can do it because he is able to feel the value of the distant and the general. The nature of the knowledge is that which determines the sort of action, and the action must terminate upon this knowledge, not on some other knowledge, be it better or be it worse knowledge " (Baldwin).

Our interest in the world advances from particular objects to larger ranges of objects, and extends to persons and ideas which did not at first command the least notice. It may be said that sympathies and desires attach themselves to our thoughts, and that they are the expression of our endeavor to attain the objects of life.

If we wish to know why men have acted in a certain fashion, we must discover their modes of thinking, the contents of their intelligence. If we have a practical purpose to move them in a direction thought better by us, we must find some way of gaining possession of their attention for the forms of knowledge which will naturally kindle their interest.

The Similarity of Mental Operations and its Meaning. — For our purpose it is very significant that an analysis of sensations, emotions, mental processes of learning, are good for India, China, Africa, and Nevada. A standard work on psychology, translated into any language, would be intelligible to any competent person who had sufficient maturity to reflect on his own inner life. Even in men who are too undisciplined to understand books every one of the essential elements of thought, feeling, and volition is present. Think how far this carries us! It means that humanity can communicate; that there is a bridge over the chasm which divides races; that souls are akin.

All spirits arise out of one Spirit, and are related to each other, as children of one father are alike by virtue of common spiritual origin. There is one reason, and in that reason all persons are united.

The differences among individuals are also of great interest, as well as their likenesses. Age makes one set of differences. The spiritual nature of each human being passes through many stages of development, — infancy, adolescence, maturity, old age.

> " All the world's a stage,
> And all the men and women merely players :
> They have their exits and their entrances;
> And one man in his time plays many parts,
> His acts being seven ages. At first the infant,
> Mewling and puking in the nurse's arms.
> And then the whining school-boy, with his satchel,
> And shining morning face, creeping like snail
> Unwillingly to school. And then the lover,
> Sighing like furnace, with a woful ballad
> Made to his mistress' eyebrow. Then a soldier,
> Full of strange oaths, and bearded like the pard,
> Jealous in honor, sudden and quick in quarrel,
> Seeking the bubble reputation
> Even in the cannon's mouth. And then the justice,
> In fair round belly with good capon lined,
> With eyes severe, and beard of formal cut,
> Full of wise saws and modern instances,
> And so he plays his part. The sixth age shifts

Into the lean and slippered pantaloon,
With spectacle on nose, well saved, a world too wide
For his shrunk shank; and his big manly voice,
Turning again toward childish treble, pipes
And whistles in his sound. Last scene of all,
That ends this strange eventful history,
In second childishness, and mere oblivion, —
Sans teeth, sans eyes, sans taste, sans everything."
— *As You Like It*, II, vii.

Mental differences are also due, in marked degree, to sex. Illustrations may be supplied by mothers and teachers from common observation. Social theory and practice must take account of differences of temperament, talent, and taste. Other differences are due to race. Stages of civilization mark their elevation in the character of the members of a community. Other distinctions are due to the moulding influence of callings and professions, as those which mark actors, lawyers, artists, clergymen, judges, managers of industry, salesmen.

Collect from the newspapers of a month the biographies or brief chapters of conduct of individuals there recorded. The death of a statesman calls for an account of his education and public career. The arrest of a burglar recalls the story of neglected childhood, wayward youth, undisciplined manhood, and final ruin. The corner of a wheat market causes the ubiquitous reporters to investigate the past of the venturesome dealer in grain and sound his praises while he stands for a brief period in the blaze of notoriety. The union of trunk lines in a far-extended railroad system reveals in detail the most minute acts of the captain of industry.

The experience of daily life brings us into contact with characters of many kinds and colors. The teacher of the village school must discriminate between the dull, the bright, the industrious and the lazy, the conscientious and the unscrupulous, the grateful and the rude. The merchant learns to read the characters of customers, and the bank president must know how to recognize the man who can be entrusted with borrowed money. All our lives we are compelled to guide our action by these discriminating studies of persons. Our success and failure are largely determined by our acuteness and fairness in judging the inner capacity and disposition by face, gesture, voice, acts, conduct.

Biography and descriptive history furnish many examples of distinctive characters, and they should be studied by the person who would understand the amazing variety of factors which have entered into the formation of the community life of our age. If some historians have given too much emphasis to the value of particular heroes and leaders, and too little to the general forces which move the multitudes, others have given too little attention to the impression made on mankind by the gifted men who break paths for their followers and show the method to those who are groping in the dark.

It takes all kinds of people to make a world. To our imperfect understanding some people are hard to explain on any reasonable view of a moral universe. Certainly one would think the world could have staggered along without Nero, the bloody emperor, and without the madmen who deluged Paris with blood in the days of the Revolution. No philosopher has ever given a completely satisfactory excuse for mosquitoes, gnats, cobras, typhoid and tuberculous bacilli, and still less for murderers and perjurers and seducers. Perhaps, however, larger wisdom will make even these things clear, and meantime we must make room for them as facts in our system of society. Even if we dislike certain kinds of persons, we must make our plans with reference to them.

The painters and sculptors assist us to enrich our conceptions of the vast variety of forms taken by the human spirit. Portraits, busts, and statues set before us the outward aspects of men and women who have graced or cursed the world.

In fiction and dramatic literature we discover multitudes of types and characters. George Eliot gives us Felix Holt, the Radical. In another story there. rises before our minds the grand figure of Adam Bede, the honest carpenter, who sings at his work: —

> " Let all thy converse be sincere,
> Thy conscience as the noonday clear,
> For God's all-seeing eye surveys
> Thy secret thoughts, thy works, thy ways."

And again the shrewd Mrs. Poyser, or the weak beauty, or the sweet, primitive Methodist woman preacher is the centre of imagination.

Shakespeare crowds upon his stage in bewildering variety all sorts of men and women,— kings, rogues, jesters, severe judges, grave-diggers, braggarts, drunkards, innocent children, fiendish and heartless assassins, knavish traitors, noble women, — all unlike, yet all akin.

The novels of Charles Dickens form a gallery of characters of surpassing interest. How dull the world would be if all were cut after the same pattern! How impossible it would be to live in a world where the worst could reign in a majority. Take the pictures at random, for only a library could present them all. There is Little Nell, "a small and delicate child of angelic purity of character and sweetness of disposition, who lives alone with her grandfather, an old man possessed by a mania for gambling, his object being to make her rich and happy." There is Mr. Pickwick, founder of a club whose members give themselves unlimited liberty to pursue scientific research, upon the understanding that each shall pay his own expenses. We see in Mr. Pecksniff the incarnation of hypocrisy. He is a surveyor and architect, who never surveys, and whose only plans seem to be to squeeze gain out of deluded victims of his dishonesty. He is a very moral man,— his own word being proof of it. His genius lay in ensnaring parents and guardians and pocketing premiums. The dark under-world of city life reveals itself in Nancy, a thief in Fagin's service, and mistress to Sikes, to whom, brutal as he is, she is always faithful and devoted.

Genius is a special development of humanity of the highest social interest. When a happy combination of hereditary gifts, physical endowments, outward circumstances of education, and favorable habits have conferred on the world a Milton, Newton, Descartes, Darwin, Washington, Lincoln, the cause of civilization is advanced more than by an army of mere imitators.

These differences between human beings are not of kind, but of degree and proportions. All belong to one kind,— mankind. There is only one species, though there are many varieties. Wordsworth has helped us to see that there is a common element worthy of our veneration. "He who feels contempt for any living thing, hath faculties that he hath never used."

These *differences are the ground and cause of unity*. Special aptitude and special ability give pleasure to their possessor in their exercise; he cultivates his gift, and it brings him success, rewards, praise, honors. He specializes still more, and with finer results. He is imitated by others, who become his disciples, and thus a profession or trade is built up, a class in the community. This calling is found to be indispensable to the members of society. In like manner other trades and professions arise. The products must be exchanged; the trading and banking classes emerge; all persons are bound together by bonds of interest and necessity and can no longer live in isolation. Hence cities and even international commerce.

Unity is not sameness, uniformity. It is just the opposite. It is founded on differences. But these differences are of persons of the same kind, persons who use a common language, live by similar food, and are tolerant and capable of compromise and concession for the sake of peace. The peculiarities are accidental; the likeness is essential, fundamental.

If the peculiarities are excessive, then arises unfitness for social coöperation, and we have the criminal, the insane, the pauper, the defective. Disease, misfortune, or vice may remove one so far from useful ways that he is out of his orbit, and the attractive forces of society no longer hold him to his task. Then there remains only severe and special discipline or seclusion, and even exclusion.

III. The Process of Development. — The individual grows into possession of self with the help of the environment. In modern "Child Study" we have opened to us a method of investigation which promises to throw much light on the nature of social life, on community bonds, and on the progress of the race in knowledge and character. Many proofs have come from physiology and from child study that the order of development of each modern child follows, in a very general way, the order in which human races have ascended from primitive savagery to civilization. This suggestion leads us to pursue two directions of investigation: first, we are prompted to watch the development of the child to discover hints as to the probable past of our race; and, further, we are led to study the development of the race in order to understand the order in which the mental traits of children must advance from animal simplicity to adult fulness of life.

IV. Heredity as a Factor in Traits and Powers. — The mental powers must be studied in the light of their origin and development.

Here three elements require attention,— heredity, education, and the personal assimilation and recomposition of what is inherited and learned from others. All these elements are mingled, like the waters of three fountains, and who can tell exactly how much is due to each? In a child's face we see something of father and mother, something of the race to which he belongs, and something which gives him his own character, and which makes him fit to carry an individual name.

It is not enough to satisfy our scientific curiosity and reason to trace influences to our infancy and to our immediate ancestors and neighbors. We are compelled to ask how our ancestors and our neighbors came by those qualities which they have had the goodness or badness to hand over to us with or without our personal permission. How far should we go back? Whither will the quest lead? There is no end of inquiry until we have exhausted the materials of knowledge. At present we may postpone this large and general inquiry and take the point up again when we come to consider the general causes of social order and progress.

V. The Individual Mind is the Only Centre of Social Forces. — There is no "social" mental experience outside of individual persons. There is no social brain or consciousness apart from the separate brains and inner lives of the millions of individuals who compose the race. Take away the particular persons, one by one, and no society would be left.

It was said of an eminent Frenchman, that he had but to consult his own heart and he knew instantly the thoughts, ambitions, and hopes of the French people. It is by studying the man within that we learn what is going on in the souls of our neighbors. Each person is a man and knows mankind.

We may therefore study the social element in each of the forms of mental action which psychology analyzes. These forms may be conveniently summed up in the words, "knowing," "feeling," "willing." But we must never forget that these modes of consciousness all belong equally and essentially to oneself. At a given moment the same person is thinking, is enjoying a pleasant state of consciousness, and is making a resolve to take measures to prolong the agreeable condition. But one or the other of these modes of mental life may be selected for particular consideration and attention, and one or the other may be uppermost.

The Social Element in Knowledge. — We cannot here go beyond illustration of the main factors in thinking. We may begin with a perception. Let the object chosen for attention be the port of a lake town, with ships sailing in and out, with smokestacks of steamers visible in all directions on the water. Along the wharf on a warm summer day may be gathered a thousand persons, all gazing out upon the scene, watching the movement of the vessels. It is true the lake does not look exactly alike to any two persons, but the picture impressed on all minds is the same. If there are artists in the company, they might sketch substantially the same outline of objects, so that each drawing might be recognized as a representation of the same port. By comparison of impressions the people can have a common object of conversation. Thus while each retina will take a distinct photograph, all can find themselves in agreement in the assertion that they see the same lake, sky, breakwaters, steam and sail vessels.

There is a common content in the imagination of objects, as we can readily prove by describing a scene and asking a hundred persons to make a picture of it.

In the various processes of thinking, forming concepts, judgments, reasoning, and classifying facts into a system, we discover in each mind a social factor. Watch the process of mental interchange in a conversation or in a public assembly. The reader interprets the author to a company of persons who have never heard or read the poems or the orations. Something goes over from him to the audience from the author's soul. The look of interest reacts upon the mind of the reader and assists him to give more truth and power to his presentation. Thus there is a constant passing of all kinds of mental contents from one mind to another in daily intercourse.

"There is no individual man for ethics, for psychology, for logic, or for sociology, except by abstraction,— that is, if by individual man we mean a being not influenced by social forces,— nor are there any feelings, thoughts, or volitions in any man which are independent of such forces. On the other hand, there is no social or collective sentiment which exists except in the medium of individual consciousness" (Professor J. H. Tufts).[1]

The Sociable Nature of the Individual. — The individual is debtor and creditor, imitator and creator. Each human being at every moment of his life is trading with his fellows, consciously and unconsciously. He copies from others and sets the pace for others. He follows and then leads. The growth of each person is forwarded by the process of taking in impressions from others, by imitation succeeded by new compositions of ideas. The child of a king, suckled by a wolf, and never permitted to see a human being, would probably know no other language than a howl. It is possible that with superior hereditary equipment he might imitate birds, and invent some sounds that would surprise his foster-parents. But it would remain true that without intercourse with his kind the range of thought and language would be little above that of brutes.

VI. At this point we may call attention to the many-sided relations of the individual. If we take up each social institution and relation in order, we may discover that the same citizen may be connected in some way with each. By following this clue we shall be preserved from the serious error of imagining that social institutions are merely isolated groups of distinct persons, and that these groups are separated from each other by high barriers.

The citizen belongs to a family and occupies there a place

1 "There are no thoughts which think themselves, no language which has existed except in the speech of the individual, no belief and no science which has shone like a universal sun above the heads of individuals, no constitution which has existed elsewhere than in consciousness, the will, the feeling of duty or fear, of the particular citizen." — SIGWART, *quoted by Professor Tufts.*

as son, brother, husband, or father. He attends the annual
meeting of the family stock,— the Browns or Smiths, the descendants of some Norman chief or pioneer of the *Mayflower*.
He gives receptions to his neighbors, although the companies
are composed of persons of many different families, churches,
and parties, just because they are neighbors and friends. He
may be a banker and belong to a bankers' club in the city,
and yet as director or stockholder be associated with twenty
corporations, unions, and mutual benefit organizations. One
may belong to the "upper four hundred," and have his name
in the Blue Book to mark his social rank. He may also have
his circle of congenial friends and meet regularly with them
for amusement and recreation. If you touch his philosophy,
you may find he holds with Kantians or Hegelians, or is a
disciple of Spencer. He has a name in politics,— Republican, Democrat, or Mugwump. When he goes to his church,
he finds that a democratic Hegelian is at his right, a single-
tax admirer of Wordsworth is on his left, and a high-church
reader of Walter Scott is behind him. By race he is connected
with Irish and German peoples; his mother tongue is English,
and he has acquired French and Italian. Thus a single citizen
may be so variously related that the threads of society are
woven into his inmost soul, and he himself serves to weave a
thousand others into the tapestry of the community life.

*VII. The Value of the Individual to Society as Means, and
his Social and Personal Worth as End in Himself.* — The individual is the end of social organization and yet finds his true
and larger self, his culture, and his satisfaction only in society.
The institutions of society which we are to study are not
created for their own sakes, nor for some vague abstraction
called the state, but for persons who can enjoy them and get
good from them. Some writers have declared that if there
were only one man on earth, there would be no science of
sociology. Very true. It would also be true that if there
were only one man on the earth, there would not be any other
science, nor art, nor interest. But the supposition is pure
chimera. There never was such a creature, such a monster, as
the isolated man. Even Robinson Crusoe was not a solitary,
for he carried with him the tools and weapons of civilization,

and bore in his own brain and memory the gathered results of social coöperation of the ages whose riches he inherited. His own nervous system and his intellect were social products of European life. Society could not exist without people, and people are by nature sociable. It is a waste of effort and words to attempt to think them apart and wonder what would become of our study if every person tried to live in an airtight bottle. Of course the forest would disappear with the trees, but each tree is itself child of the forest. The cells and tissues of the body make the body possible, but what would a hermit cell or separated eye become without the body?

The Worth of the Individual. — We can get no large sum by adding millions of zeros together. A mountain of corals has not in it one thought beyond coral instincts. What gives dignity and worth to mankind is the nature of its members. Here we pass beyond what is called "science," to a truth which rests on beliefs. The beliefs which give worth to the individual man are those which relate him in our thoughts with God, the eternal life, with immortality as the limitless sphere of his development, and with duty as his endless task. Take these beliefs away and the individual shrivels and becomes akin to what is beneath him more than to what is above him, and invites him upward. I am quite aware that a belief like this cannot be "proved" in the same sense that we can demonstrate a law of chemistry or a fact in biology. But the ground of ultimate certainty of these sciences is not in themselves, but in some form of belief in our own intelligence, in the uniformity of law, in the veracity of our senses and of our logical faculties.

Indeed, it would seem that even those who deny the religious view of life and the world, when they devote themselves to the pursuit and discovery of what yet lies beyond knowledge, are acting on the same theory on which the devout man prays and hopes and aspires. The chemist declares by his acts, whatever his professed creed may be, that this world is built on truth, that it will not put our intellect to confusion, that it will show itself veracious and reliable. As bees work to an end without comprehending the end, and as migratory birds fly toward a land which they have never seen, impelled by a trustworthy instinct, so men of science reveal a devotion, a spirit of sacrifice which is touched with religious quality. Only too often this martyrdom is not appreciated by men who call themselves religious, and it is not fully understood even by many who endure it.

Man is

> " crown'd with attributes of woe
>   Like glories, move his course, and show
> That life is not an idle ore,
>
> " But iron dug from central gloom,
>   And heated hot with burning fears,
>   And dipt in baths of hissing tears,
> And batter'd with the shocks of doom
>
> " To shape and use.   Arise and fly
>   The reeling Faun, the sensual feast;
>   Move upward, working out the beast,
> And let the ape and tiger die." — TENNYSON.

Man's sense of worth comes largely from his hope and faith. Our social estimate of man, apart from the outward recommendations of wealth and position and intellectual achievement, must rest on some forward-looking belief in respect to his place in eternity.   The obscure and poor and weak are likely to be despised and trampled as mere things unless there is diffused in society some ideal of them yet to be realized under more favorable conditions.   Knowledge, science, cannot affirm our vast estimates of man's worth, but the hope itself is an earthly fact.   Tennyson was not singing to a deaf nation when he voiced this belief: —

> " I trust I have not wasted breath;
>   I think we are not wholly brain,
>   Magnetic mockeries; not in vain;
> Like Paul with beasts, I fought with death;
>
> " Not only cunning casts in clay:
>   Let Science prove we are, and then,
>   What matters Science unto men,
> At least to me?   I would not stay."

PART III

SOCIAL INSTITUTIONS

———◦◆◦———

CHAPTER IV

THE FAMILY

The Social World in Miniature

> "God give you in requital all the amends
> Your heart can wish, a husband, family,
> And good agreement.   Naught beneath the sky
> More sweet, more worthy is, than firm consent
> Of man and wife in household government."
> —CHAPMAN'S *Homer*.

IF any social institutions could stand alone, it would be the family.   There are found all the elements for the satisfaction of individual wants and provision for the continuance of the human species.   There are the most tender and sacred affections, the most beautiful hopes, the most intense interests. Think of the home upon a Western prairie, far from cities and distant even from neighbors.   Out on the wind-swept plain, where the fierce and frosty blizzard howls wolfishly at the door, the cheerful fire of the living-room, the bright companionship of loved ones bid defiance to nature and assure the essentials of human joy.   There is aged grandmother in the warmest corner, representative of the venerable Past, her head full of history.   At the table are masterful father and gentle, tactful mother, planning campaigns for the spring, busy with thought for those who look trustfully to them for the means of life. The parents are the grand Present in heroic mould. The boisterous Future is romping on the floor, in the persons of lusty children. The infants are buds of opening flowers, the heralds of a new order.

I. The House. — The dwelling is the visible structure which reveals in its very form and appearance its adjustment to family needs. It is not a member of the family but it is humanized matter, and becomes the symbol of all hallowed memories. It has grown out of man's wit and serves his ends. Man on the frontier wants protection from wild beasts and savage men, and the house becomes a fortress, a castle. In the calm days of peace the walls are still a defence against excessive cold and heat. The furniture provides for rest in sleep, for the distribution of food, for congenial intercourse in friendly conversation. The clock keeps time with sun and stars and with the movements of mankind. The roof does more than shed rain, for form and ornament of gable and cornice gratify æsthetic feeling. The walls are covered with pictured paper or delicate tints, while framed engravings, photographs, and colored prints minister in humblest homes to the sense of beauty.

The house has had a history. The lowest races of men live in the open air, like monkeys, where the climate is warm and friendly. Hollow trees, natural caves, or caverns dug with rude implements out of the hillside, serve for shelter and rest. Huts of bark and conical tents of skin may still be seen among the more backward Indians. In Northern Michigan the scattered groups of aborigines still prefer to dwell in such primitive lodges rather than in close and stifling houses. Those tribes which have advanced to the weaving art may use some cloth material for their temporary covering. As settlements are effected, unburnt clay and stone may be piled up to form walls, the roof being branches of trees, grass, or clay. The history of architecture enables us to follow the details of style and fashion in all lands and ages. We thus see that the house has a history. It will change in the future.

One of the most marked differences between town and country, between past and present, lies in the arrangement of dwellings. In great cities it is seldom possible to own a separate house. Land is costly and taxes are high. Tier above tier, the city families live in lofty and crowded hives or in fashionable hotels. House building follows the order of consolidation and coöperation. Isolation is more and more difficult. Privacy is disturbed. Very often there is no suitable provision for children, and it is to be feared that boarding-house and hotel life is responsible for a dangerous decrease in the number of children born and reared.

II. Housekeeping was the Primitive Industry. — The word "economics" means simply the art of the house.[1] All social industries are specialized housekeeping, carried out on the grand scale. The earliest industry was the finding, gathering, and preparation of food. There is an art which does not threaten to become obsolete. Nutrition conditions spiritual life and all else.

What will the future bring? It is no longer common in town houses to preserve meat, vegetables, and fruit. Large factories can pickles and fruits. Bakeries furnish bread and cakes, more or less digestible and wholesome, for the table. We are slowly getting away from kitchens. Public establishments are drawing to themselves functions once performed by the members of the household.

The making and mending of clothing has always been a household industry. Clothing for protection and for ornament was long a part of women's work. Among lower races it has ever been so. The ladies of ancient classic lands were often represented in works of art with spindle and distaff. The ideal Hebrew woman, described by the Book of Proverbs, looked carefully after the garments of her charge. In our own country gradual changes have been going forward. Wool and flax, the materials for clothing, are no longer, as with our ancestors, prepared for use in the course of domestic life, but their manufacture has become almost entirely a public industry. These illustrations reveal a social tendency.

III. The Personal Organization of the Home. — By courtship and marriage, two friends, a man and a woman, found a new household. But there is no complete family until at least two children are born. Marriage and family are not synonymous.

[1] Aristotle, *Politics*, I, 19, Jowett's translation.

The man becomes a father, the woman becomes a mother, and then they are conscious of new powers, new faculties, deeper forces, and larger motives. Other persons, as grandparents, dependent relatives, domestic help, boarders, may come into very close relations with the household, but they are not essential members of the family.

IV. The Care of Children is one of the Functions of the Family. — Future citizens are nourished, protected, nursed in sickness, taught the first lessons in friendly coöperation, fitted for social life, within the home. The spiritual culture of the household is one of its highest uses. The first elements of knowledge of objects in nature, of plants and animals, of earth and sky, of social relations, of music and poetry, of religion and patriotism, are communicated by parents and companions even before the kindergarten age. Mothers and fathers, if they have suitable education and are intellectually alive, can assist their children to store the memory with a multitude of pictured impressions of stones, soils, clouds, rain, plants, elements of food, animals, and types of human beings. Here is laid the foundation for later systematic studies of chemistry, physics, botany, astronomy, zoölogy, biology. Parents can encourage children to make collections of leaves, pressed flowers and roots, sections of woods, fossils, insects, — and they are wisest who teach them to do this without inflicting pain on any sentient creature. Simple experiments with light, heat, and electricity are within the reach of moderate means and knowledge.

It is from imitation of parents and playmates that children learn the wonderful art which binds man to man, race to race, and present with past and future, — the art of language. Beginning with inarticulate cries of pain, hunger, and loneliness, the infant advances in its first years to acquire the product of race struggles of centuries. With the assistance of the social experience of the home the baby leaps over æons while it is learning by imitation. It hears the language of the house, — the "mother tongue." If the language is German, French, or English, it is copied, word for word, accent for accent, gesture for gesture. If the language offered as example is rude, coarse, with scanty vocabulary pieced out with signs and

F

slang, with defiling expressions and debasing images, that is the foul matter which goes into the young mind. This fact is of supreme importance in education. When a child comes to school, his habits of speech have already been formed. If they are wrong, it is hard to break them down, sweep them out, and build up new habits. Sometimes the articulation is so indistinct that the boy is not able to make himself understood, and sometimes he has a voice so elegant and refined as to make the simplest expressions give pleasure.

The range of knowledge of nature, man, history, and literature will be determined largely by the topics of the table and of familiar conversation. The sentiments and beliefs, the religious ideas, the moral ideals, the history of heroes for imitation, are all furnished in great measure by parents. Etiquette, forms of courtesy, modes of dress, care of the person, and consideration for the rights and feelings of neighbors are home products. The home is the real primary school, the original temple, the first government. Within its narrow walls may be a company of young actors whose hourly play, whose fanciful pursuits and activities, take them through the range of individual types and social occupations. Watch this wayward and varied journey of the grave child: inventor, composer, draughtsman, painter, orator, preacher, nurse, soldier, horseman, bandit, musician,— undifferentiated and raw material for anything. The child tries all experiments, tests his powers on each particular trade and calling in turn, and out of this world of possibilities finds at last his own place and part.

It is very evident that this social situation defines the duties of parents and shows the nature of the education which fathers and mothers should have for the due performance of their sacred office. The highest degree given by universities does not represent superfluous knowledge. All sciences and all arts would be worthily employed in mother work.

V. The Domestic Republic. — The first experience of social regulation comes with the discipline and government of the family. At first the infant is restrained from acts which would injure or destroy it, by physical force, if necessary. Later a command may be understood, or a loving request, having back

of the word authority and power. When we look over the
course of domestic discipline for many years, we can discover
tolerably distinct evidence of household legislation, administration, and sanction,— the apparatus of a government. It is
not often that the rules are printed and posted on door or
bulletin-board. The orders in council are issued on occasion.
Parents are not aware that they are day by day framing a legal
code of wide extent. But it is true and significant. It was
thus the earliest laws of mankind were made, as accident
decided, as difficulties arose. The fragmentary edicts of the
family emperor and empress are collected in the memories of
parents and children. The decision of yesterday is made the
precedent for an appeal to-day to settle a dispute about a doll
or a wagon. Ownership or use of playthings, articles of clothing, or a garden space may be fixed by a rule which holds
from infancy to manhood.

This collection of unwritten laws covers rights of person
and rights over things, the relations of parents to children
and of brother to sister. If it were all written out, the code
would fill a book. It regulates the time and quantity and
quality of eating, the hours of sleep, dressing, bathing, and
all physical habits. The jealous sense of property manifests
itself even in infancy, and leads to mimic war when cherished
articles are wrongfully taken away. It covers the case of games
and insures "fair play." It brings attack and defence under
the modifying influence of public rule, with appeal to the
crowned heads in case of misunderstanding. Before the
supreme court at mother's sewing-table the controversy is
argued out with lawyer's logic, and a favorable decision is
often invoked with tears and sobs for dramatic effect. In
table and parlor etiquette, the mode of eating and sitting, of
salutation and reception, of asking and answering, is completely regulated by the code current. Thus also studies and
religious practices are made to conform to a law. The judges
and administrators of household codes are the parents. The
advocates are the children themselves. They have no use for
hired attorneys. The procedure is summary, and decisions
of appeals are usually announced at the time of the plea.

And as for sanctions, they are all the hopes and fears, the

affections and attachments, the habits of thought and feeling, the customary ways of the home.   Penalties and rewards are both employed.   In fortunate instances, where skill and tact are possessed in high degree, resort to physical pain is reduced to a minimum.

VI. Social Regulation of the Family. — When we look at the isolated home, we can regard it as making its own rules and doing its own will.   But when we take a wider view, we discover that each family is one of many families living in connection on the same territory.   The people of a neighborhood or of a "flat" are not likely to permit a family to do as it pleases, if it does not please to regard the common belief and interest.   If a father neglects to support his children or to educate them, others suffer, and the community is burdened. If a man divorces his wife and leaves her without means, perhaps with broken health and helpless babes, he injures society. Therefore in all ages communities have been compelled to make laws relating to marriage, divorce, support of children, and all the interior habits of the household.

If we ask after the origin of these household codes, we discover that, while they are in the home, they did not first arise there.   Looking a little further, we are struck with the fact that in the same country or community or class of society there is a very great similarity in the laws which parents make and enforce.   What does this mean?   Chiefly this, that the family itself is a part of surrounding society, that its laws and customs are social products.   The young mother, a mere girl, begins to rule her child from the start much as her mother had ruled her.   If she seeks to be too original, and the neighbors hear of it, they are apt to send hornets of censorious remarks to trouble her.   These rules are traditions, or even instincts, with parents.   They are not thought out to suit the circumstances, in the main, but simply express the social way of regarding life.   They are handed down by social inheritance, diffused by imitation, enforced by public opinion.

VII. The Family holds a Distinct and Unique Place among Social Institutions. — It is not to be classed directly with state, church, school, and industrial organizations.   Some kind of a pairing arose before the times of authentic history, and may be found among other living beings,—plants and animals. In origin the family differs from other social institutions, because it has its rise in simple, direct, and primitive attraction of men and women for each other, and in the vague parental instincts which yearn for the presence of children, and which protect and nourish them when they come into life. It is true that the family gathers to itself other sentiments and attractive bonds. As human beings widen the range of their interests and become engaged in the pursuit of science or art; as they improve in taste and culture; as they come to paint pictures and carve in wood and marble; as they learn to like books and noble conversation; as they enlarge religious thoughts and make the world's wide activities their own concern,—all these subjects will be brought home and will add to the daily occupations which make the hearth the centre of all the soul's pleasures. But the essential and initial impulses are very lowly and simple.

Thus the family is not a product of society in the beginning, but it produces general society. The race comes into being through the domestic institution. Other institutions, as they arise, react upon this primitive association, but they could not produce it.

The organizations arise out of very complex wants. The industrial system has grown up in order to supply the material means for satisfying all human wants. The state has grown out of needs of defence, ambition for power and territory, the desire for an organ for securing order, education, and the convenience of civilized life. The family came before all these, and supplied the foundation on which they could be built.

The family differs essentially from all other associations in the fact that its members have their place defined by their physical and spiritual nature. Thus the wife and mother cannot change places with the father; the children are what they are because they are dependent and undeveloped. But in the industrial system one person may occupy at various times several positions and offices, as laborer, foreman, messenger, master, owner. And in the church a man may be transferred from office to office according to changing circumstances or his growth in adaptations.

It follows from all this that the form of the family is more fixed and unchanging than is true of other institutions. From the earliest time the essential form of the family has been that of the union of two parents with the children. It is true that this union has varied in duration from a short period of days to lifelong companionship. It is true that polygamy, in various modes, has been common in many lands and ages. It is true that divorce has often made changes of husbands and wives frequent in varying degrees. But through all these changes the essential form of the family has been preserved, and the form of permanent union of one man with one woman, together with their children, has come to be protected by the innate instincts of the higher races.

There is no other institution, and never can be one, which can so nearly satisfy all the essential desires and affections of men as the domestic group.

Another important distinction is to be noted: there are few states, churches, and schools where there are multitudes of families. It is essential to the family that it should be small. We shall never have a domestic "trust."

VIII. Relation of the Family to Social Order and Progress. — The family is conservative of all social possessions. Property is acquired and held by families from the strongest and most enduring of motives. The title to a large part of the world's wealth descends from parents to children, because the universal instinct of civilized parents, itself the product of ages of domestic affections, from savage to modern, is to care for offspring. This instinct is not always entirely reasonable or wisely manifested. It sometimes sacrifices substance to shadow and prompts the transmission of property to incompetent, indolent, wasteful, and dissolute children. The right of bequest is not to be thought of as absolute, since wealth is a social product and a social interest, and must be guarded from abuse and dissipation. But after all, wealth has been accumulated and added to the sum of common resources because of those parental affections and interests which appear in the transmission of property.

Also in and through the family is there a conservation and preservation of spiritual goods, their symbols and their material embodiments. Thoughts, forms of knowledge, books, proverbs of the wise, maxims of concentrated race experience, are treasured in family life. Home libraries, coins, furniture, pictures, manuscripts, letters, diaries, account-books, are among the means by which social goods of the spiritual order are kept from the tooth of time.

IX. *The Family is the Primary Agency of Society for securing New Beginnings, Variations from the Old, Chances of Improvement in Persons and Ideas.* — This introduction of new elements, giving starting-points for progress, happens first of all from the consequences of pairing. Parents come together from unlike stocks. Their children are not exactly like either of them. There is a family likeness, it is true, but there is also a difference. The better form is likely to be favored when it comes into existence. The more vigorous, more beautiful, more intellectual, are endowed for the struggle of life with superior equipment. Differences in body and mind come from causes which are now carefully studied by biologists. It is in the crossing of persons from various families that these new varieties appear.

It is within the family that ideas are debated, new plans are struck out, discussed, and tried. Every infant is a discoverer, finding a new world. The new tooth, the new shoes, the new pain, the new pleasure, are disclosures which pique curiosity and lure the traveller onward. Here is set up a habit of investigation, which endures through life.

X. *Perils of the Family and Modes of Amelioration.* — First of all, as to marriage and its consequences. Observing persons have noted the too great frequency of premature marriages, "child marriages," as they are aptly called. Medical authority of the highest order gives warning that physical injury must follow the marriage of adolescent persons; nervous diseases arise; the offspring start in life with inferior physical powers and stunted members and defective tissues; the discipline of self-control is too early suspended; the poor family is burdened with children before it can provide suitable food and care for them; society is taxed for an increase of the pauper brood; discouragement and neglect, bred of desperation, lead to separation and divorce, after bitter dissension;

and social unrest and rebellious dispositions are the certain accompaniments of the decline of well-being.

On the other hand, observers and statisticians note the fact that others neglect marriage or defer it to an age at which family relations are not easily established with the best individual and social results.

Among the "proletariat," the reckless poor, there are too many children; while thousands of those who are best able to support children have none. In France the population is almost stationary. In the United States the average size of the family is declining. Probably many causes contribute to this tendency: the increasing love of luxury, unwillingness to fall below the customary rate of expense, the desire to see their children enjoy even greater advantages, perhaps even a loss of care for what becomes of future society if the present is made to yield all the enjoyments possible to extract from it. At any rate, the fact deserves study, and gives occasion for serious reflection. No general and ethical law, binding on each particular case, can be announced.

One of the most dangerous elements is the unhistoric and anti-social theory of the family which is frequently urged and has gained wide popularity: the theory that marriage is a merely private affair, and should not continue under the regulative influence of social censure or legislative enactments. At present, society governs marriage relations on the theory that it is, once formed, a public interest. No one can be constrained to enter marriage, and free choice is of the essence of the institution. But when the man and woman have once become wedded, the social interest is very great. At that instant society must protect the property rights of each, as it need not do before. The care of children devolves upon the state in case of neglect to provide or in case of separation and divorce. Only when society consents to act as artificial nurse for all children in minority can it consent to relieve married persons of responsibility to each other after marriage. It is true that there are cases where it would be gross wrong to continue in this relation, for man or woman, and for such extreme cases law must provide. Society cannot escape from the necessity of regulation, even at risk of error. But the extreme facility of desertion and divorce seems to excite a volatile and frivolous temper, to exaggerate the incitements to wandering desire, and to present the thought of abandonment as something not falling under the just censure of the community. A loose and easy moral theory intensifies these savage dispositions and justifies them by a sort of moral philosophy.

Defective housing is the source of many evils. Every citizen, by the study of good houses, should erect in his mind at least a minimum standard of decency, health, and spiritual welfare, by which to judge and condemn unfit habitations. This criterion must first of all include the demands of hygiene, as laid down in books on public health. The cities of this country frequently publish handbooks for their building inspectors, which give minute and complete details in respect to the cellar, walls, drains, plumbing, closets, windows, ventilation, cubic space in relation to occupants, surface of lot that may be covered, space reserved for light and ventilation, wall paper, distance between buildings, and all the necessary conditions of health.

But to these essential requirements, these merely animal demands, should be added a minimum of æsthetic provision, since morals and taste are closely connected. Compared with such a moderate standard, many houses fall far short. In the country the laws of health are frequently violated, but there is at least plenty of fresh air and oceans of sunshine. There the problem of disposing of decaying, poisonous waste is comparatively simple, because the earth soon transforms the most offensive matter into plant food if the waste is buried near the surface. But in the cities the situation is different. There one finds families crowded into one or two rooms, where modesty and health require four or five rooms. Ignorance and greed, along with the helplessness of abject poverty, are to blame for the windowless dark dens where multitudes of human beings are condemned to dwell, quarters less favorable to comfort than the cells of penitentiaries.

Maladjustments of the Family to Economic Life. — We should trace the domestic results of inadequate wages of the natural breadwinner of the household. If the earnings of the father fall short of supplying the means of physical existence,

with a margin for human culture and enjoyment, then one of
two effects must follow: either the family is physically and
spiritually starved, or the mother and children must assist in
labor to make the living. It is not generally understood
among fairly well fed people that starvation diseases are very
common among the very poor. The most evident effects of
insufficient food and clothing and fuel are seen in the case of
young children, with whom the rate of mortality in such conditions is very high. Most pitiful illustrations of starvation
may be seen at hospitals in the children whose crooked legs
and distorted spines, pale color, and aged features, reveal the
story of defective nourishment in infancy. If the father works
in a shop where the atmosphere is foul, the hours long, the
toil exhausting, we have an added cause of physical and moral
degeneration. It is true that sensual vices and drunkenness
add to these ruinous tendencies, and we cannot too strongly
paint the sin. No colors are lurid enough to depict the horrors of these immoralities and their dread brood of weak and
degenerate offspring. But those who are comfortable must try
to understand that vice is itself an effect, and that among the
causes of vice are unwholesome external conditions, low pay,
uncertain employment, and unkind treatment. It is the particular duty of the prosperous and well-fed to consider the
relations between the "labor movement" and the temperance
movement.

But now add the fact that many wives and mothers are compelled by poverty to leave homes and children to earn, or help
earn, a living in factories and mills. All admit that the evil
is great. Why is factory work of wives and mothers such an
evil? Because it takes the woman from a work which requires
all her strength. The proper care of a household is labor
enough for a poor woman, and if she must be away from the
home during many hours each day, it is impossible for her
to maintain a clean, tidy, healthy house, and provide food,
clothing, and comfort for husband and children. But if it is
an evil to have mothers leave young children to earn a living
in a factory, it is even worse to turn the scant room of the
cottage or tenement into a workshop. The worst abuses of
modern industry are found in these "sweated" domestic

shops. The conclusion is that poor mothers have no place in the factory, and that garment-making and like low-paid industries are not suitable for mothers. Shall not society permit poor mothers to earn a living? The question is not easily and quickly answered. A poor woman has done her full industrial task when she has performed mother work. Normally, wages of men should be high enough to maintain families. In abnormal cases philanthropy should find a way of relief.

The factory employment of girls and unmarried women is not so serious a social problem. It was perfectly natural that young women, having no longer the household industries which occupied their grandmothers, as carding, spinning, and weaving, should follow those occupations to the establishments which are provided with modern machinery. And yet, there are some dark features even here. Statistics do not seem to show that immorality has been deepened by this custom, although it may be said generally that crime does increase with women in countries where they are most exposed to the friction and collision of public affairs. But as machine industry advances in the newer states it will be found necessary to guard women from the perils of night work and the improper conditions of crowded shops.

In this connection we must refer to the evils of child labor in factories. Growing children must be kept out of factories until they are well matured, for many reasons: that the tissues and organs of the body may have a full development; that they may not be poisoned by chemical odors and their vitality sapped before the energies of resistance have come to their climax; that they may have a chance at the play time of life and not be changed prematurely into old men and women, decrepit before life has fairly begun; that their intellectual progress at school may not be cut off before they have mental equipment for the intellectual struggles of modern competitive existence.

It will thus be seen that those engaged in the "labor movement," trade unions, mutual benefit societies, factory inspectors, and reformers of legislation, are really contending for the very cradles and altars of national life.

Housekeeping is yet to be made a beautiful art; now it is too often regarded as drudgery and slavery. When we despise a necessary task, we slur and spoil it. No work can be done finely unless it is thought to be dignified. Housekeeping has no place as yet in a liberal education; it is the only occupation to which a democratic society dares to give the name "service." About it linger the contempt and shame of slavery. It has no place in the schoolhouses, save here and there as a hated and hunted "fad." And with what consequences? Dyspepsia, stomachs full of ferments and undigested and indigestible food, with a myriad of diseases, bad tempers, family quarrels, resort to drink for stimulant and to the saloon for companionship.

There also is the aggravating problem of domestic help. Many a household is made unhappy and anxious because there is unrest, uncertainty, and restless change in this department. Many feel themselves driven to boarding houses and hotels because of this terrible affliction. It is a vulgar topic of conversation in two hostile camps of the nation.

XI. Associated Efforts to better Home Life are Engaging Increasing Attention in all Christian Lands. — Perhaps one of the most important associations for the betterment of domestic life is the National League for the Protection of the Family.[1] This society acts for the people of the country on behalf of every means of elevating the state of domestic welfare. It investigates the facts relating to the perils of the home and sets the results of investigation before the world. Its educational influence is very great. It conducts a constant study of laws and administration and it arms reformers and philanthropists with the weapons of truth and reasons. It corresponds with congressmen and members of legislative committees and commissions, and secures improved laws. It collects the suggestions of judges and lawyers of high character and learning, and publishes the results. It was the means of securing from the general government one of the most important statistical investigations on the subject of divorce which was ever given to the world. It deserves the support of every patriot and of every church. There ought to

---

[1] Secretary, Rev. S. W. Dike, LL.D., Auburndale, Massachusetts.

be funds sent for its work from every town in the land, although the sum required from each community is not large.

Of the coöperation of the schools with the home, in the educational activities of the family, we may speak later, in the chapter which deals with the school. In the proper place, the aid of the church and Sunday-school will be invoked in the promotion of the higher life in the household. Child-saving work is now being directed primarily to securing new homes for the homeless, instead of placing orphans in huge institutions where mother care is impossible. But it is also discovered that many homes are unsuitable for the proper rearing of the young, and now we are seeking to build up the life of such families for the sake of the future generation. Defective children, as the feeble-minded, who never can support themselves and care for themselves in competitive life, should all be cared for in special asylums, where a safe custody will preserve them from injury and save them from becoming the parents of hapless and miserable offspring, so that the stream of heredity shall not perpetuate the suffering and pain beyond the present lifetime.

Every one of the reforms and improvements to be discussed in this book, if rationally and successfully conducted, will contribute to the happiness and social efficiency of the home.

CHAPTER V

Auxiliary Institutions

WE have here to deal with a number of public institutions which are necessary to the working of all other institutions, and are presupposed by them. They have gradually grown up, as all institutions grow, by minute improvements and inventions, and through experiments tried for acceptance or rejection, and they have been made more or less general by unconscious imitation, by general perception of their utility, and have been sanctioned and made authoritative by custom or law. No individual or private association thinks of inventing or creating one of them. It is sometimes necessary for the individual to procure for himself what he usually relies on society to provide. But these exceptional cases simply bring out the general fact with more emphasis. By observing, analyzing, and explaining the auxiliary institutions, we shall advance in our understanding of social thinking. For every common work or structure is the embodiment of a common idea or feeling.

I. The System of Protection. — All the factors which enter into the complex of society are constantly threatened by forces of dissolution, — the bodies of men, their property, and their character. Life is one long and unceasing struggle to push back the day of death. Much of the energy at our command is consumed in this battle, and much of our wit is evoked by it.

The dangers are above and below, in nature and in our fellow-men. From external nature come the pitiless frost, the deadly miasma, the fever germs, the floods and lightnings, the hungry flame, the poisonous plant, the flesh-eating wild beast, the venomous reptile. Our foes are of our own kind:

78

criminals who live by fraud or robbery; rebels who revolt against social order; aggressive foreigners who seek to enlarge their territory. So, also, there are insidious enemies of morality and purity, unsound teachings, vicious and sensual books, pictures, plays, and companies, and all the constant and restless agencies which seduce and debase the mind. All that man possesses he must win and defend.

Social Organization for Protection. — Each institution has some means of defending itself from its enemies. Each family has clothing, house walls and roof, locks and bars, the medicine chest, and the holy Book.

Quaint George Herbert wrote : —

" Lord, with what care hast Thou begirt us round!
Parents first season us; then schoolmasters
Deliver us to laws; they send us bound
To rules of reason, holy messengers

" Pulpits and Sundays; sorrow dogging sin;
Afflictions sorted; anguish of all sizes;
Fine nets and stratagems to catch us in;
Bibles laid open, millions of surprises;

" Blessings beforehand; ties of gratefulness;
The sound of glory ringing in our ears;
Without, our shame; within, our consciences;
Angels and grace; eternal hopes and fears; —
Yet all these fences, and their whole array,
One cunning bosom-sin blows quite away."

The social system of protection cannot be entirely classified under the functions of the government. The family, the neighborhood, the school, the church, the factory, provide parts of the system. It is social, an arrangement made by the entire community through all its organs, and not by the state alone. In increasing degree the organ of the general will, the government, undertakes this task of protection.

The Mississippi valley would not be secure from the floods of the monster river if it were left to private or local enterprises. There must be a long series of dikes, and the expense of these is so great, and the interest of the nation is so clearly involved, that national resources are taxed to provide the defence. Army and navy are organized against foreign foes. In cities men do not carry pistols and swords to defend themselves, but a special body of policemen are paid for that task. But in new frontier towns and mining camps every man, like the primitive savage, must be ready to defend his body and his property. This irregular method soon gives place among civilized men to a regular and efficient method of resisting encroachments upon rights.

It is coming to be felt that a *rural police* is desirable, such as the older European countries have long enjoyed. Frequent and disgraceful instances of lynch law have given some localities a bad name among Christian peoples. Until adequate protection is afforded by a complete system of mounted police and detectives all over the country, these violent outbursts will occur. They will disappear when it comes to be felt that effective agents of justice are alert and ready to arrest all who prey upon property or who attack persons.

Boards of health, in cities and states, are part of the machinery to ward off the dangers of disease. The entire medical profession may be regarded as a corps of experts supported by society for the purpose of defence against physical enemies. That is their "function" or use. They accomplish their duty partly by prescribing medicine and diet, or by performing surgical operations for individuals, and for this they are paid. But in addition to this, and gratuitously, they diffuse in the community knowledge of hygiene, of methods of preventing the spread of infectious diseases, and they act on commissions and boards whose purpose it is to remove the causes of disease.

II. The Public System of Comfort and Convenience. — Closely related to the auxiliary systems for the protection of health and spiritual good are those which provide a supply of the necessities of existence and which dispose of the waste incident to large communities.

Among the essential conditions of life we must count, in the first place, food, water, and light. In cities a special form of organization is required for the supply of these elements. Even in village life it is necessary to make arrangements for the distribution of food and other materials of daily use, especially of coffee, spices, and all foreign products. In large towns the system by which meats, milk, vegetables, and other foods are supplied as required is highly developed and intensely interesting to study. While the machinery is by no means perfect, and is often needlessly wasteful and slow, still, at its worst, we find marvellous provision made for multitudes of families. In response to a demand there springs up the means of supply. Goods are stored of the kind needed, they are exposed for sale in each neighborhood, and they are delivered at the door of each inhabitant. These food materials are collected from the ends of the earth; and one may almost fancy that he sees ships, trains, wagons, and pack-horses moving with their various burdens toward the home of the humblest citizen, in obedience to his wish.

In the country one has usually only to dig or bore a well in order to secure wholesome water. The soil is friendly, — the source of food and drink. In the city these conditions are reversed: the soil is saturated with poison; it is sterile and deadly. Water must be conducted at great expense from long distances. "Free as water" is a phrase full of irony, because each family must pay a regular water tax. But this water tax is a cheap payment for the service rendered. For if each inhabitant were compelled to carry water ten, or even fifty, miles for himself, or buy it by the bottle in drug stores, poor people would suffer desperately, and the means of cleanliness would be denied them.

One would think that no social arrangement need to be made for light, a commodity which delivers and distributes its riches gratis. This is true in the country, far from the lofty walls and narrow trenches between mountains of houses; but in large towns, where the buildings are lofty and densely packed together, it is necessary to make social regulations to secure the access of light from the sun. Experience has shown that public lighting is essential to order and comfort. It is not practicable for each person to carry his own lantern; at least it is not economical. Far more desirable is it for the city to light its inhabitants by some general plan which provides lamps of oil, gas, or electricity in all places. Crime hides its head and vice fears the piercing and revealing rays.

G

Thorough lighting of streets, alleys, and courts is a measure of protection and police, as well as of comfort.

The disposal of waste is a serious problem in all towns. On farms it is not difficult, with a little care and intelligence, to convey the rainfall along channels to the tile drain or to the open ravine. It is not difficult to dispose of all offensive and decaying matter by burying it just under the surface of the earth, where minute organisms and chemical agents soon transform it, solid or liquid, into plant food. In the farming region it is necessary to avoid the contamination of wells which comes from permitting this waste to sink deep into the ground in cesspools, which poison the soil in every direction for many rods.

But in towns, to bury waste matter would be to invite the plague and call down the horrors of epidemic. It must be carried to a distance, mixed with earth, or purified by fire or water. One of the most difficult problems of modern science and municipal art is to find a safe and economical method of taking the refuse of cities and transforming it into fertilizers or something else that is useful, as well as to prevent it from becoming the cause of pestilence and destruction. In the earlier cities, before the birth of modern science, ignorance of sanitation caused the death of multitudes of the population in many countries. Even in our own country and age, where the principles of science have been neglected through ignorance, whole cities have been driven to despair by death-dealing fevers which would have no terrors for a clean town. The system must provide for the removal of rainfall, of liquid waste, and of solid garbage which cannot be reduced to fluidity. Our towns are busy on this problem, with the help of the best advice. One of our great cities — Chicago — has already spent nearly thirty millions of dollars in the construction of a drainage canal, in order that its supply of water from Lake Michigan may not be poisoned, and that the sewage may be diverted into less dangerous courses. Each city is obliged, in consequence of its local surroundings, to study and work out its own system. City life must always be more artificial than rural life. This socialized provision for common wants is one of the distinguishing features of town life.

It is not necessary to describe and discuss in detail the various social organizations by which these systems of comfort and convenience and health are controlled. The water supply, for example, may be furnished by a private person or corporation, or by the town government. The same alternatives are open in case of lighting and food supply. But it is very rare for a city to do anything more than regulate the food system, and equally rare to find the authorities leaving the sewage to the care of individuals.

III. Social System of Adaptation to Space. — All that a community does must occur within determined limits of space. We may think of society as at rest, simply occupying a certain area; or we may think of movements from place to place, of persons and of things. In other words, we may study the arrangements made by societies for location, and those made for transportation and communication.

Location and Edifices. — Our survey of the facts of nature has shown us that human society could not exist without room, and that its members live by means of the materials which the physical world supplies. The external world furnishes the conditions of social arrangements and partly determines them. Let us now see how societies make their adjustments to the earth as they advance in coöperation.

From a tower or hill one may sometimes overlook a town, or even a wide plain on which are several villages. Each family has its home, usually with a lot or garden or adjoining field. The manufacturing establishments must occupy ground to the exclusion of other uses. Every institution must have its edifice, covering a portion of the limited earth.

There is also necessity for some kind of social arrangement and understanding about the use of this space. Two bodies cannot occupy the same space at the same time. Occasionally we are made to feel the necessity for social understanding, when a title is disputed, or when two farmers quarrel about the location of the line fence, or when a landlord causes a delinquent tenant to be thrust out upon the sidewalk with all his household furniture. The penniless wanderer, out of employment, driven from hotels, rejected at farmhouses, chilled by winter's wind, realizes that, while the world is wide, it has

no room for him. The first task for the head of a household
is to secure a place for his family. The schoolhouse and the
church must have a lot. All persons and institutions must
arrange for a definite place and home.

*Reasons governing the Selection of Sites for Houses and
Towns.* — In former ages, when war was general and neighbors
were enemies, sites for residence were selected with reference
to security against invaders. Thus the banks of the Rhine
are made interesting by the remains or ruins of castles built
long ages ago, by men who lived by plunder or sought to protect themselves from robbers. Lofty eminences, tops of steep
cliffs, deep cañons and defiles, have often been the places on
the whole most suitable for residence. But with the establishment of settled government these considerations yielded to
others. Healthy ground has been selected, and low, damp,
malarious levels have been deserted. Even where there was
scant knowledge of sanitary science, experience taught its
costly lessons to colonists in new regions, and drove them
from even fertile spots where the fever swept away their children and weakened their numbers. Along with considerations
of health and security, especially after the rise of trades and
commerce, the settlers in new regions thought of waterways,
of nearness to productive soils, quarries, and ores. Sites
which are beautiful commended themselves to those who had
taste and were not compelled to forego such considerations
by fear of poverty. The study of the reasons for the selection
of sites for residences or cities is an admirable exercise in
social psychology, for here we discover in the acts of men
their methods of reasoning and choice, and the way of har-
monizing their separate choices as individuals.

Houses in settled communities must have some kind of
order, especially if there is a degree of crowding. They must
be arranged in streets or along highways. This arrangement
of houses of all kinds seems to give even a defined shape to
society. There are few towns in this country, or in any
country, which have been built upon a far-seeing plan.
Philadelphia, in its central parts, was laid out in very regular
squares, and the effect is monotonous and wearisome, while
in its newer portions modern feeling has departed from the

Quaker simplicity of a former age and introduced great and pleasing variety. The capital city of the nation, Washington, was laid out upon a magnificent ground plan, and its splendid streets and avenues are the pride of the nation. Among the towns occupied by wage-earners, perhaps none can excel Pullman. Although the site is level, yet the arrangement of grounds, lakelets, trees, houses, public buildings, and shops is so artistic and harmonious that the general effect is delightful, especially in the summer. We are not thinking of the terms of ownership, nor commending the rate of rents or the accommodations, but refer simply to the external method of occupying the space with buildings. This admirable result was attained by having the control of the town in one mind, so that the landscape gardener and the architects could carry out one consistent and beautiful system. After a town or city has grown up haphazard, it is difficult to make any essential changes.

If the people of a community are willing to employ a competent artist to arrange the new additions and to lay out improvements in the old portions, they can enjoy beautiful designs. But if the disposition of houses and grounds, streets and open spaces, is left to individuals, the town is sure to be ugly. What Mr. Pullman accomplished as a single master of a large tract, villages and cities can accomplish by giving authority to boards of improvement and to landscape gardeners.

Tendency to Expansion. — The constant growth of population which is characteristic of most peoples implies an extension in space. If we compare maps of the United States at intervals since the colonial days, we shall be impressed by this fact. The crowded nations of the Old World have sent their superfluous population to find homes on the wide continent of America. This led at first to struggles for territory. Spanish, French, English, went to war with each other and against the Indians, and the primary motive of those bloody conflicts was desire for territory. Out of those terrible struggles came at last a peaceful solution, and the boundary lines of possession have been fixed and made secure by the building of a nation strong enough to protect its citizens in quiet use and ownership of the soil.

But the struggle is not over. It has simply assumed new forms. Multitudes of men are toiling, building, competing, for the possession of titles to farms, city lots, gardens, sites for factories and shops. With increasing density of population the difficulty of securing ground is greater, and the young press on to the West. Now that cheap and desirable land becomes more rare, we hear of schemes for irrigation of arid plains, in order that more space may be provided for our excessive population in congested towns.

Out of this struggle for land comes the necessity for legal regulation of titles to mines, farms, forests, and pastures. Hence such social problems as the Single Tax, Inheritance Tax, Homestead Laws, Exemption from Assessment, and many similar questions. The possession of a large territory has many important effects on the nation at large, on its spirit and plans.

"The spaces into which we must fit our political ideas and plans are measured by the general space in which we live. . . . A great territory invites to bold expansion; a small one engenders a faint-hearted huddling of the population. The range of the inward, as of the outward, vision is capable of being increased in every individual, and while he gages the extent of his geographical space by his freedom of movement and his right to enjoy it, he shapes accordingly his ideas and his habits, and so as a whole does a people." [1]

This is true of our country, as foreign witnesses testify. Large farms, vast systems of railroads, governmental systems covering the continent, industrial enterprises reaching out from ocean to ocean and to foreign lands, tolerance of all sects and schools of thought without legal persecution or interference, missionary societies with world-wide aims, are among the illustrations of the sublime conceptions fostered by the ownership and control of wide national domains. While large areas alone cannot produce great ideas, and while small territories have produced men of splendid intellect, yet the enlarging influence of territory on thought and sentiment cannot be denied.

Movement in Space. — Arrangement must be made not only for orderly location of houses, lots, farms, and factories, but

[1] F. Ratzel, *Am. Jour. Soc.*, Jan. 1898. "Political Areas."

also for systematic transportation of goods, persons, and the material expressions of thought.

Transportation. — The first element in a social system of carrying and travel is the way. The path of transport may be a road, street, watercourse, or railroad track. The second element to be considered is the vehicle, as the shoulders of a porter, the back of an animal, the wagon or cart, the coach or the train. The third element is the power that moves, as wind, current, muscles, steam, electricity. The progress of invention is marked by the advance in modes and means of travel and carriage. More and more the forces of nature are substituted for the muscular energy of man.

Communication. — The social system of communication is really only another mode of transportation, since it merely provides for the movement of the physical embodiments of ideas. The telegraph line runs along the railroad. The mail trains serve the postal system. The telephone wire "carries" our spoken message.

The development of this social system of communication is full of interest. Savages conveyed thoughts chiefly by words and signs in presence of each other. · Hence, among primitive peoples the group which can be in spiritual touch must be small. Signals of fire from peak to peak were invented to call rude tribes to the rendezvous of war. Flags are used at sea where colors and shapes must take the place of vocal utterance. The earlier postal system depended upon footmen and riders. The introduction of the railroad made swifter communication possible, at an ever-cheaper rate, between cities and widely separated nations. The electric telegraph and cable joined in spiritual union peoples who had been isolated from each other. The telephone still further facilitated commercial and sociable intercourse.

Improvements in transportation and communication have great significance for civilization. Imitation becomes more rapid. Inventions, fashions, ideas, plans, styles, technical processes travel from the point of invention and discovery with great rapidity. In former times, in a city state, where the number of citizens was small, the entire population might be reached by a single orator speaking from the public platform.

This kind of influence of one person over many is impossible where the members of a community cannot be instantly reached by the voice. But the telegraph has almost brought the members of all nations into one vast assembly, where the same words sway all minds at the same instant. The printed page takes the place of the speaker's voice and gesture.

Thus the citizens of modern countries dress and think very much alike at a given time. But when a change of any kind arises, it is very quickly made universal.

The pictures of costumes, carriages, and furniture are seen in shop windows in Vienna, Budapesth, Paris, London, and Oshkosh at nearly the same time. A riot in the Austria-Hungary Parliament is discussed an hour later in New Orleans. Berlin and Chicago exchange ideas about municipal lighting in the same month. The discovery of a new asteroid or satellite in the Lick Observatory is flashed to all the astronomical towers of the world before the next dawn.

A medical missionary in China tells us that she buys her butter from France, her bed from New York, her bicycle from Michigan, her medicines from Germany, her vegetables and most articles of clothing from her Chinese neighbors. Let the reader make a list of articles daily used for necessity or comfort, and trace them to their origin, and thus count up our obligations to the system of transportation which invests the world.

Thus merely mechanical devices and organizations have a profound influence on the contents of the social mind and therefore on coöperation in conduct. "When the Indian trail gets widened, graded, and bridged to a good road, there is a benefactor, there is a missionary, a pacificator, a wealth-bringer, a maker of markets, a vent for industry" (Emerson). The sea has been a great civilizing agent. The very sight of it provokes a desire to travel and see the world.

Improvements in our Postal System. — Persons in high position have suggested various points wherein our already excellent postal service may be made to minister more completely to the wants of civilized communities. It is suggested that the free delivery system which is already so convenient in cities, and which is extended to rural communities of Europe, should gradually be extended to farms, mining camps, and all settlements; that the money order and registration system should be extended and made cheaper; that small parcels might be carried, and that circles of small offices might be consolidated under better managements, so as to provide for better supervision. "No other country conveys a letter 6849 miles within its own territory for a single rate of postage, as we do, from Key West, Florida, to Circle City, Alaska. In no other country does the transportation of inland mails require twenty-one million miles of travel during the year, over railroads, lake and river steamboats, and stage lines."[1]

While our system is already doing a great service for civilization, at cost of an annual deficit, further improvements may justly be expected, although their introduction must be along the lines of careful experiment with new devices.

The telephone system is just beginning to produce its most interesting results. In cities, after the patents have expired and municipal control or legislative action has compelled reasonable rates for use, we may expect even more important modifications of social customs. In rural neighborhoods we may look for desirable improvements in social customs. The lonesome farmhouse can be easily and cheaply connected with the village store, the house of the physician, and with neighbors. In Kansas it is said that the wire fences have been employed to perform a double task: to protect the crops and to convey messages between the homes. The extension of some such device would rob rural life of many of its terrors, and would increase the warmth and depth of social feeling, the source of our highest pleasures and motives.

IV. Social System for Time-keeping. — In a well-regulated household, about a certain moment in the morning, one hears a bell, feels the stroke of light upon the eyeballs, hears the swelling sounds of activity, looks at his watch, and begins another day. There is the breakfast hour, the factory whistle, the school bells, the church chime, the shriek of a regular train, all reminding us that every event of our existence is measured and dated in time. The regulation according to

[1] Mr. Perry S. Heath.

time periods constitutes a social system which governs all our conduct in all institutions.

In the chapter on Nature as the basis of human life, we saw that the physical world fixes certain boundaries for our doings. All natural forces are changed by the touch of the human hand, but they are necessary for our existence, and we cannot understand ourselves without referring to them. The rhythmic alternations of day and night have acted upon vegetal, animal, and human beings from the first appearance of life on the planet. There is a sleeping and a waking for all organized creatures. As the earth revolves on its axis in twenty-four hours, the sun now shines and now is hidden. As the earth moves around the sun in its orbit, the seasons come and go with regularity. Man is compelled to notice these changes in order to adapt himself to cold and heat, to sowing and reaping, to providing food for winter and plans of work for summer. The changes of the moon mark distinctly a natural division by months, and the passing of seasons and months give us the year. Thus we have in the external world the foundation for our time system. Man did not invent this system, but discovered it. We set our watches by the sun and the other stars.

> "'Tis easy saying they serve vast purposes.
> What's a star?
> A world, or a world's sun: doesn't it serve
> As taper also, timepiece, weather glass,
> And almanac? Are stars not set for signs
> When we should shear our sheep, sow corn, prune trees?"
> — BROWNING.

That the heavenly bodies have other business need not be denied, even while we find them incidentally convenient to ourselves.

It seems probable that the earliest calendars were made by religious leaders, who taught the worship of natural objects and who had an interest in the regulation of offerings, festivals, and rituals. But these more careful calculations of times and seasons were simple and natural outgrowths from the early efforts of man to make his actions agree with the motions of his fellows.

With advancing civilization accuracy becomes important. While life is simple, wants are few, and groups of coöperating workers are very small, time is not very significant. An hour, less or more, is of no consequence. But when a thousand people are waiting for a train or a ship even one minute is of value. A thousand people waiting one hour means the loss of one hundred days of precious working time.

The improvements in science and art make it possible to measure time more exactly, by parts of a second, instead of by hours. When a good system has been adopted in one country, it is copied by others because of its obvious convenience, and so a calendar becomes more general and authoritative.

The measurement of long periods or eras is reckoned from some great national or religious event. The most widely used era is that which is dated from the beginning of the Christian history, *Anno Domini*, the Year of the Lord. People of various nations, races, and religions have different eras for their dates. Owing to the wide diffusion of Christianity and the colonizing, missionary, and commercial enterprises of European peoples, the Christian era is best known and seems to be most likely to be universally adopted.

But time order is necessary not only to knowing but also to doing, and especially to associated doing. In the family regularity, precision, and punctuality are necessary for health, for convenience, and efficiency. The hours for meals must be determined and kept or the food is cold and indigestible. Irregular sleep is disturbed and fails to refresh. In industry time is increasingly essential. Think of two thousand workmen waiting a half hour for the engineer to get up steam and start the wheels! Imagine a locomotive driving along a track without reference to the schedule of trains!

Experience in school life reveals the vital importance of observing the moment of opening and closing. Disorder, waste, loss, confusion, careless habits, grow up with irregularity about beginning and ending. Those who come late to church lose the first music of the organ, often the finest opportunity of life to hear noble compositions. Late comers disturb the others.

The government must keep time. Its courts must sit when expected. Its legislatures must have hours of hearing petitions and considering bills. Statutes must take effect at a given day and hour. The social system of time-keeping is not an affair of one institution, but regulates or serves all.

There is an entire code of morality bound up in the social methods of regulating action by time. The reason for the duties of promptness, punctuality, and regularity lies deep in nature and in human relations. They are not the sport of individual choice. Our duties grow out of our relations, and our business is to conform, not to transgress.

V. Social System of Standards. — Weights and measures, the regulation of quantity and quality, must be common and general, not local and personal. Daily experience in buying and selling, trading, cooking, dressmaking, tailoring, building, making contracts, prescribing medicine and compounding drugs, demonstrates the necessity of having a uniform and universal system of weights, measures, and tests of fineness and strength. With a uniform system of weights the prescription of a Cincinnati physician, filled by an apothecary in Rome, Italy, broke up a malarial fever. An order for a wedding ring, so many carats fine, means the same in Venice and Chicago, to all who understand the terms. "No. 1, White" wheat, graded in Chicago elevators, means the same quality in Liverpool. So long as exchange of goods is confined to a small territory, it is sufficient to have a merely local standard. But when the inhabitants of different parts of a large country are trading with each other, it is very convenient to have one system of weights and measures, of quality and grade, for them all. And now that commerce between all countries has assumed world-wide proportions we see the gradual growth of the "metric system" common to all civilized peoples.

Very much of social coöperation rests on contracts and agreements, oral or written. The language of these agreements is meaningless unless the terms relating to quantity and quality carry the same impression to all parties. The system of time-keeping, transport, and communication serve all other institutions of society. They are not merely instruments of business, but of family, school, church, government.

They are managed, usually, as forms of business.   Street-car lines, canals, railroads are often in the hands of firms, corporations, syndicates, who manage them for personal profit.   But as these systems serve all society and all its interests, they are sometimes owned, and they are always regulated, by society. Gradually toll roads are bought up and owned by the counties. Rivers, seas, lakes, are left free for all who choose to travel upon them or use them for transport.   Bridges over streams may be owned either by private parties or by the local governments; but in any case they must be made free from the caprice and arbitrariness of private owners by means of public regulations.   Whether the means of transport and communication should be owned by corporations or by the government is to be determined by economic and political considerations, which we shall notice at a later point.

CHAPTER VI

Social Arts of Creation, Communication, and of the Æsthetic Life

CLOSELY allied to the Auxiliary Institutions just described and explained are other social institutions which are implied in all the modes of association and coöperation yet to be studied. These are the arts, language, and the modes of publicity.

I. The Useful Arts. — The arts are the means and methods by which society secures its satisfactions. Science deals with knowing, but art implies both knowledge and power to do or make. Each of these subjects has its own literature, text-books, schools of instruction, all of them in our age highly specialized, so that it requires a lifetime to master any single branch. Our purpose here is to exhibit the arts in their systematic connection, and to explain their relations to each other and to society. Indeed, it is only as we see them serving the entire community that we understand their function and meaning.

Requirements. — Every art makes use of certain tools, utensils, or other material means of carrying into effect the thoughts and designs of the mind. Thus the hunter uses bow and arrows, spear, or gun; the fisherman must have hook or net; the cook has vessels for baking and boiling; the painter, colors and brushes; the musician, organ or piano; the orator, his vocal organs.

But implements, tools, and machines are dead things without knowledge and skill. The great organ lies silent in the dim religious light until its master unlocks the keyboard and touches the keys. The chisel and plane create no articles

94

of use and luxury unless wielded by the trained mechanic. Society must, therefore, provide in some way for the instruction of its members in their several callings. There are some forms of knowledge which are required by persons who are to follow all callings, elementary instruction. But at a later period in life it is necessary to specialize, since it is impossible for a person to make goods or perform service for the community in more than one calling or one general direction of kindred activities.

This technical skill may be communicated in two ways,— by apprenticeship with older workmen or by special schools where the trade is taught. Even where technical schools exist, it is still necessary for the young workman to have experience in actual industries in order to acquire quickness and to adapt himself to the rough conditions of every-day life. As society becomes more complex, as the use of costly machinery extends, and it becomes impossible to take time to instruct awkward apprentices, society must gradually increase the range and variety of its technical and professional schools. This has already been done for physicians, lawyers, musicians, painters, and many of the textile trades. Here and there pioneer schools of manual training and special arts indicate the direction of progress.

One of the most important and complicated of arts is that of agriculture, with the auxiliary art of rearing domestic animals. In a former day it was possible to wrest a coarse living out of rich virgin soil by very rude methods, by almost brute force. That day is rapidly passing. Severe competition with the grain fields of India and Siberia and Argentina is pressing heavily upon our farmers. They must learn more economical methods, get more out of an acre at less cost, use better machinery, employ the organization of the large industry, or suffer countless miseries. The struggle for existence, in the form of international competition, will not permit us to rest. We must learn the best ways or pay heavy fines for ignorance and awkwardness. Hence the necessity for agricultural colleges and experiment stations, of institutes and classes, dairy schools and gardening instruction.

America has vast resources, but science and art are necessary

to enable us to use them.   Competition is costly and hard;
often it seems cruel, but it does prevent laziness, lethargy,
and mental stagnation.

Classification of the Useful Arts. — It is somewhat difficult
to classify the arts, on account of their very great complexity
and multitude.   A visit to a great exposition or a manufacturing city is bewildering, because the variety of callings and
products seems to defy the mind's power to arrange the objects
in any order.   But our minds are so constituted that we cannot rest while the facts lie before us in confusion.   Let us,
then, attempt to arrange the various arts upon the single principle of their relations to the organizations which minister to
social welfare.   The enumeration will here extend beyond
what are usually called "useful arts."   (1) The arts of the
direction and organization of what we have called "Auxiliary
Institutions"; the public arrangements for adapting ourselves
to the relations of time, location, housing, movement, transport, communication, protection.   (2) The arts of domestic
life.   Within the home there are the rearing, care, and education of children, the parental art.   Physicians, nurses, cooks,
teachers, ministers, and members of all trades and professions
assist in these tasks.   Originally we may think of the arts having sprung from the family, and now in their independent
development they still pay tribute to the mother institution.
(3) Next there come into view the arts of economic organization; the callings of men who produce and exchange and
prepare for consumption.   (4) Then follow the industrial arts
in their various stages.   In a great factory there are two sets
of men, those who carry on the business from the office and
those inside the works, who understand the processes of making the goods.   Some of the industries make articles directly
for human use, as foods, clothing, houses, and the like.   But
there are other important industries which make the tools and
machinery for these primary industries, as machine shops,
engine works, manufactories of agricultural implements.
(5) We may next distinguish several classes of art having
more directly to do with the spiritual interests of human life,
as those devoted to pure science,— the labors of chemists,
biologists, mathematicians.   (6) There are others who pro-

duce works for contemplation and direct enjoyment, as poets, musicians, novelists, painters, sculptors, architects, all kinds of artists. (7) The teaching profession, in all its branches, is an art, based on knowledge, but requiring special methods and skill. (8) The art of social influence is practised, in some degree, by most of the members of society; but there are some professions in which this function occupies a specially marked position, as in that of preachers, editors, teachers, parents. (9) Finally, there is the art of social regulation and control, in which all citizens share, but whose details are in the hands of lawyers, judges, administrative officers, and other persons of special training and experience. As the problems of government become more complicated and difficult, it will be still more necessary to educate a special body of experts for the work of legislation, and especially of administration.

The Study of the Useful Arts in Common Schools. — It is evidently impossible to teach all pupils all the arts which supply the wants of men to such an extent that they can take them up and make a living by them. Any one trade is enough for a life. But it is possible in the course of school years to give to all citizens sufficient knowledge of the various contributions of the principal arts to fit them for forming intelligent social judgments.

But what is the value of this kind of knowledge? In the first place, a general survey of the arts, their processes and products, would enable the young citizen to select his particular calling. Where the range of information about industries is narrow, the person is confined to a narrow range of choices. He merely knows what he sees in his own little neighborhood. It is not fair and just to shut up a youth to such a range of vision. In after years he may have a right to blame his early teachers, if he misses the best opportunity of employing his powers because he did not know what was going on outside of his immediate field of vision. Such knowledge has a high economic value. We are all purchasers or sellers of goods. Shopping is not a mean art, if it be done with intelligence. The buying of groceries and other commodities in the Saturday market day asks for all the education which schools can supply. The socializing influence of this knowl-

H

edge is not beneath notice. It is incredible that a community should be brought up in familiarity with the customs and arts of other peoples, without some larger and juster estimate of the service of each to all. Morality means social sympathy, and this comes from knowledge. The intellectual value of the study is very great. It awakens interest on all sides by presenting in endless variety new objects and modes of action. By reducing the facts to order the mind itself acquires organizing capacity. It learns to sift evidence, to trust reliable sources, and to respect testimony. The grasp of the imagination is made more sure and comprehensive. As the citizen comes to years of political responsibility as a voter, and is called upon to help determine questions of tariff and assessment, of home and foreign trade, of competition and treaties of commerce, his mind is stored with an orderly fund of information about the facts which should direct his judgment.

The method of securing this knowledge should be taught in normal schools. There is room here for only brief illustration. The first step in the process is to have and use a garden, the miniature of the agricultural world. There flax and hemp may be planted, and in due time their fibres may be studied in the fingers of inquisitive children. With some degree of ingenuity and industry a teacher may even erect a simple loom and illustrate the process of weaving. Cocoons of moths are easily gathered in the bushes, and may be made to illustrate the culture of silk. All teaching should begin with action, and there is boundless room for action in teaching the nature of the arts which minister to mankind. Kindergarten methods are well adapted to the beginning of the process. Drawing and all kinds of sloyd and manual training find their place under such a controlling idea.

Many teachers have gathered valuable museums for their schoolrooms, by which they can illustrate the products of many places, at home and abroad. One teacher of a modest school began a system of correspondence and exchange with persons in distant countries, and after patient and shrewd trial found herself in possession of an apparatus of considerable value. Maps, pictures, and charts are helpful means of presenting the facts which are typical.

The best point at which to begin in our ordinary school system is with geography and history. And here it seems very clear our central point should be the human interest. The world should be studied, not merely as a system of natural forces, but as the home of mankind. "Geography is not merely a description of the earth as an inert mass, or even as a mass undergoing geologic changes and transformations, but a home for man, and interesting to us chiefly as it affects man. The question therefore arises, whether the earth itself is the chief object of study, or whether man and his surroundings become the leading idea" (A. E. Winship).

From the direct handling and observation of the materials and tools of industry the pupil will easily be led to the study of the stages of the process, the methods of raising domestic animals, the shearing of sheep, the dyeing of wool, the preparation of the fibres, the shipment. A single illustration must suffice. Dr. Winship gives a story of the various breeds of sheep and their specific merits; of the kinds of wool, the machinery for making cloth and carpets, and the history of inventions; the competition of various markets, the tariff legislation demanded by the producers, the statistics of manufacture in the centres of the business, and the sources of wool supply in the world. In the same way he deals with silk, cotton, flax; and the method might be extended to ores, foods, and every kind of manufacture.

The Useful Arts must not be overestimated. — "These are arts to be thankful for, — each one as it is a new direction of human power. We cannot choose but respect them. Our civilization is made up of a million contributions of this kind. . . . These feats that we extol do not signify so much as we say. These boasted arts are of very recent origin. They are of local convenience, but do not really add to our stature. The greatest men of the world have managed not to want them. Newton was a great man, without telegraph, or gas, or steam coach, or rubber shoes, or lucifer matches, or ether for his pain; so was Shakespeare, and Alfred, and Scipio, and Socrates" (Emerson).

II. Language. — Among the social systems which have grown up gradually in response to human needs, and out of the infinite interchange of thoughts and experiences, is the institution of language.

Under the head of language we include all means of communication — oral speech, writing, gesture, signs, pictures — which can give a reliable sign of ideas to two or more persons.

What is the Social Function of Language ? — It is a means of communication, the interchange of mental life in the community. Whether we wish to learn and get or teach and give, we must use some kind of language. There could be no society without this medium. Even a serious defect in hearing shuts one off from his fellows, leaves him in the silence of a cell while he may be walking the public streets. In the concert hall or the political meeting deafness builds a wall about the soul. Where blindness and deafness go together, the mind is still more isolated, as in the instances of Laura Bridgman and Helen Keller, only that in these prophetic and hopeful cases loving science and art made openings in the barrier and brought those souls into touch with their kind.

This social intercourse is the only possibility of developing the mind in powers of knowing, feeling, and reasoning. Only by communication are the dormant powers awakened and developed. The infant knows nothing at its birth, and must learn all by sharing the common fund of experience. Unless there is some gift of language, the infant cannot grow into free use of its inherent powers.

Language, in its more advanced forms, is a means of registering and preserving knowledge. Each discovery is costly and painful. The results of experiment need to be kept for posterity or held in trust for coming ages. Language embalms and treasures the results of thinking and trials with the forces of nature, the processes of art, and the combinations of human activities. Thus the very pigmies of our age stand on the shoulders of the ancient giants, and sometimes imagine themselves very tall. One who has climbed a mountain and put it under his feet has a wider range of view than when he was on the plain, yet personally he is no greater in stature than when he looks up to the heights. Perhaps we have no larger average brains than the men of Greece and Rome, but then we have all the knowledge they left the world. We begin where they left off, at the end of long and earnest toil. Our schoolboys of ten years recite facts which Socrates, and even Newton, could not have discovered. Our scholars at twenty have the equipment of forty centuries, down upon which they look.

Knowledge is not merely preserved, but transmitted through language. Thoughts travel across the æons of time and across the oceans and continents in space, to reach the most distant children of the race. This is its magic power. The half-brute monster, Caliban, in Shakespeare's play *The Tempest*, marvels that his master, Prospero, has such wondrous power stored up in books. Language thus distinguishes the full man from the mere animal, although animals have a less developed form of speech.

With communication of thoughts, knowledges, come awakened emotions and quickened wills. A fine example is seen in the Renaissance, the re-birth of European art, science, and social energy. It was primarily due to the re-discovery of the books and art works left to the later world by the Greeks, Romans, and Hebrews. All men, all institutions, are served by language. We cannot trade, travel, study, visit, save by means of this medium.

Language has a Social Origin. — It is futile to attempt the task of imagining what might have been if human beings had lived apart as individuals. We know that they have always lived in groups. They have seen the same visible objects, heard the same sounds of winds and waves and wild beasts. They have needed the help of each other in the struggle for existence. Hence they have learned the need of expression of thoughts and purposes and wishes. Reason has grown up along with words and by their means. Thinking and speech are merely two aspects of the same experience. Man talks because he thinks and feels, and he thinks more clearly because he talks and writes. "Why cannot the ape speak? because he has nothing to say." That is the story of the rise of reason and language together (Blumenbach, quoted by von Treitschke, *Politik*). As Mr. Tarde says, "The soul, philologically, makes itself a body."

The individual adds little to a language in the course of his life. He inherits it as a legacy of supreme value from his ancestors. Slowly through the ages words are added as emergencies arise, as new objects become known or interesting, as human relations become more complex. Every school girl finds a great dictionary full of words, the inventions of centuries gone by. A vocabulary is a treasury of ideas. Words are full of philosophies and histories, provoking to thought. Slang and profanity betray strange neglect of inherited resources. Until one has exhausted the more than one hundred thousand words of an ordinary dictionary it seems superfluous to inject corrupted phrases into conversation. We can understand why thieves should desire to have a dialect of their own, but it seems quite unnecessary among good citizens. Very rarely a bit of picturesque verbal invention does actually enrich the language, and it then becomes common property.

Modern comparative philology is opening a vast field of amazing interest in revealing the nature and growth of all languages. This science has made much progress during the century in classifying tongues according to their elements and forms, as animals and plants are classified in descriptive botany and zoölogy. Not content with the mere arrangement of the materials, the students of language are tracing, by means of words, the evolution of the race in different parts of the world. Every word is a monument, petrified history; it embalms in itself the contents of thinking and volition of races dead or still on earth.

The acquisition of language by each person is a social process and depends on two factors, heredity and education. Each person inherits physical organs for speech and a disposition to communicate. Long before imitation has begun the baby utters a great variety of sounds in the cradle, even when alone. But no great advance can be made without hearing and imitating others in acts of speech.

III. Social System of Publicity. — The Greeks have left to us the image of the messenger of the gods, blown forward by the unseen winds, himself endowed with winged feet and cap, swiftly moving on some errand of information or command. Language is our social messenger, our Mercury, and the system of publicity is the machinery of power and the wing of speed.

Classification of Means. — First of all there is conversation, the publicity of the personal presence, the limited audiences of parlor, gossip, saloon, street, dinner party, and social reception. The assemblies for political, commercial, religious, and educational discussion are agencies for extending publicity of ideas. Next come the official documents printed, posted, and circulated by schools, associations, churches, governments, for the information of the public or of persons directly interested. Illustrations will readily occur to any one : the statutes of councils and legislatures, bulletins posted in factories or shops for the direction of employees, reports of synods and conferences, of relief societies and village boards.

The system of transportation and communication, already discussed, is tributary to this system of publicity. The railroad, the telegraph, the postal service, the express companies forward packets of knowledge, germs of ideas, impulses of feeling.

The Newspaper. — The daily and weekly newspaper is the most conspicuous organ of modern society for receiving and transmitting thought. It is not under the direct management of the state, but is a system built up by private enterprise to serve the public.

The function of the newspaper may be considered from two points of view, that of the owners and that of the community. With the private motives of the publishers we have little here to do. The proprietors are much like other men, and they carry on their particular form of business like other human creatures in the same society. Philanthropy, public welfare, ambition, ten per cent., amusement, desire to leave something to their children, revenge, religion, — these are quite like the forces which inspire rolling mills, missionary societies, tobacco factories, national education associations, and all the rest. "We are of one flesh, after all."

But if we turn from the impossible task of judging private and personal motives to the clearer field of social uses, we are not so liable to error. Society needs and wants to know every morning, when it rises and goes, half-clad and eager, to the doorstep, what men were doing and saying yesterday. Newspaper men are the experts who study what it is society wishes to know, who find it out and print it, serving it hot for break-fast. The newspaper is the social machinery for interpreting what happens to be uppermost in the public mind at a given moment. It sells information and takes a small commission on each item. It is a labor-saving machine, which spares us the necessity of loafing about the town square and the city hall trying to find out what only trained men can dis-cover.

The materials of a newspaper are classified, roughly speak-ing, into news items, general and local, interpretations of these items by experts, and advertisements of goods and services. The news items are reports of the recent words and deeds of men in all parts of the world, so far as they are interesting to the readers of a particular locality. The first item one can see through a blanket sheet of forty-eight pages, is his own name. It may be in an obscure corner, half-way down a tedious column of the egotism of other people. It is a dull page that lacks this lustrous bit of news. Next to the "Ego" is the expanded self of our neighborhood. We do not care to pay for the society sayings and doings of some town a thou-sand miles away. Such items grow cold in the next county and freeze to ice at a state line. Yet we do wish to know some things, as citizens, of our own commonwealth, such as the acts of the legislature, the decisions of the highest court, the pageant of a governor's ball (if he permits it), or the agricultural show. As citizens of the United States, we all have some interest in the discussions and acts of Congress and the declarations of the President and his cabinet. Thus, as the area widens the item must be very large and striking which can attract our attention. This instinct is not altogether in-sane and wicked. It is necessary. Our purpose in reading news is to make better personal adjustments of our own envi-ronment. If we have goods to sell or service to render, it must be to persons close at hand. The opinion of great people in a distant country does not much affect us, while the con-tempt or hatred of our meanest townsmen stings us to death. The newspaper gives us a picture of the state of things about us, and enables us in the morning to plan our day so as to sell our grain at the highest price, to correct a falsehood which may be circulating, to suit our time of making a trip to agree with the motions of a customer or a rival.

The interpretations of news are made by experts whose business it is to receive with meekness the numberless suggestions about the method of conducting their business and — to do as they please or must. As an item comes flying into a telegraph office it is like the broken wing of a bird, or even a single feather, a fragment without meaning. The editor must name the kind of bird to which the fragment belongs. He must give a history of the affair up to the moment when the message rushes upon the community.

The advertising columns are hired out to people at fixed or contracted prices for them, to tell on their own responsibility, what they think of themselves and their wares. Presumably a man knows more about himself and the goods he offers than any one else. Society desires to enjoy his special opportunities of information. Hence the advertisements. The newspaper serves the public, and takes a commission, money or other consideration, from pumpkins to fortunes or foreign consulships.

Thus in its several departments, with a bountiful *menu*, the daily journal lays before us knowledge about the world we live in. This is its social function. To state the function is to give the explanation, and at the same time to form a standard by which the institution must be judged. According to its social efficiency in giving the community the truth, the truth worth telling, and nothing but the truth, should we pass social verdicts upon the daily journal. It is here mentioned as one of the chief agencies of publicity. As such it is indispensable in modern life.

The Periodical Magazine as a Means of Public Communication. — The immense sale of the magazines in this country is a phenomenon of vast moment. The periodical can be more deliberate than the daily, and can be made more trustworthy, even if it is a little slower. It can be printed on finer paper and offer really artistic pictures as illustrations. The artist has a poor chance to show his skill on the thin, coarse paper used in the daily journal. It is not surprising, therefore, that the attractive cheap magazines should have a large circulation.

It is disheartening, however, to note the quality of many of them. Of course it is desirable that each class and calling should have periodicals adapted to its own professional or educational needs, and that amusement should be supplied from this source. But it is pitiful that so many of the articles should be written by persons who have no adequate preparation for their work, and that so large a body of misinformation should be kept in circulation. But we do not require a public censor. Under the rule of liberty and competition among institutions we have reason to hope that the best periodicals will at last gain confidence, and that a generation educated in the public schools will detect and punish those who seek to mislead them. At present there is abundant need for careful criticism and exposure of ignorance and fallacy. There are so many such papers of the highest order that the inferior ones have no reason for existence.

The Book as a Means of Publicity. — The function of the book is very different from that of the newspaper or of the magazine. The book has for its function the publication of the ripe results of thinking and investigation, or of completed artistic production. In speeches and lectures, in occasional fragments of essays and articles, one may test his partial thoughts by submitting them to criticism. If there is anything vital in the study it may be worth while to give it a more permanent form. Where a connected presentation of a large subject is required, the daily and the magazine both fail. A more adequate form is demanded by those who seriously undertake the mastery of a difficult subject. The organ for publicity in such a case is the book.

The Publishing House is the social agency for manufacturing and marketing intellectual and artistic wares. The great publishing firms have been among the most important agencies for the diffusion of culture. It is true they have made mistakes and have left genius in obscurity. It is true that many of the most thorough scientific works cannot be published for general circulation by private enterprise. It is also true that many an ambitious author, heart-sore when his manuscript was rejected, has hastily concluded that all publishers are a bigoted and narrow-minded and mercenary body of men. But even

authors sometimes make mistakes in their judgments of themselves, and probably it would be found that the better publishers
have, on the whole, acted as "fool-killers" for the people, and
protected them from a deluge of ill-considered words. They
have a direct and economic interest in discovering, as quickly
as possible, a work that has any sort of value or interest, and
they bring to this task special gifts and training, and those
who are successful are selected by a process of extirpation of
the incompetent who have tried and failed. The declaration
of the social function of the publishing house reveals its cause
and the criterion of judgment.

The Public Library is an institution of publicity of increasing importance and growing power. Its function is to select,
purchase, store, and keep in convenient form the various
journals, periodicals, and books which are required by the
community, and to keep them in circulation. A public library
is a coöperative medium for the town. Each citizen can by
this means enjoy access to hundreds of books and magazines
in a collection too large for the mansion of the most wealthy
citizen. The public free library is to be more and more the
centre of the intellectual life of our nation, in city and country. Its power as a medium of communicating knowledge
and diffusing the ripest thought on all subjects is beyond calculation or prevision.

All these organs of publicity gather the impressions and
thoughts of men from millions of private sources, hold them
up in the blazing light and promote the process of testing, of
judging, and of diffusing ideas.

IV. The Fine Arts and their Social Ministry. — "What is
called civilization is not only an unveiling of the laws of politics, agriculture, mechanics, hydrostatics, and magnetism, but
it is also a perpetual production or discovery of all that is
pleasing to the sentiments. . . . It is impossible for the
human mind to unfold strength without unfolding toward
beauty. . . . When wisdom founds a republic, then taste
comes to adorn the republic" (David Swing).

The Institutions of the Fine Arts exhibit an element so attractive and important that they deserve a special study. Let
memory recall the various manifestations of decorative taste,

of æsthetic creation, of artistic fancy which appear in all the works of man. The dwelling and its surroundings, where the residents have risen above the merest animal life, show a touch of beauty which deserves, even in partial failure, our sympathy and cheer. It is happily not unusual to see a hut of logs, where the pinch of poverty is severely felt, covered and adorned with climbing vines. In summer kind nature assists the gracious hand of the weary mother, and the rude shelter bursts into blossom. The front yard of very plain habitations may display a delightful array of flowers, hedge, and velvet lawn. In the packed tenements of crowded cities, the dreary hideousness is frequently relieved by a white curtain edged with cheap lace, a row of flowers on the window ledge, and a picture on the wall. As the very snows of arctic regions produce their own objects of beauty, so the wintry life of penury will persist in showing that the artistic instinct is never quite frozen out. In the mansions of wealth and taste, where refinement is endowed with purchasing power, we discover the prophecy of what all homes will have in the good time coming.

Art finds its way into industry and manufacture. Perhaps it is a step-child in those arid and smoky regions where roaring machinery, black chimneys, blasted heaths, and disorderly array of broken materials have invoked the impatient curses of Ruskin. Machinery can never get beyond the lower forms of imitation, and must "follow copy." It is more the minister of animal comfort and mediocre neatness than of angelic beauty. Yet we see the locomotive driver, himself in grimy garments, decorating his engine with flags, and polishing the brass and nickel plate until it shines again. Useful tools, made for dusty places, will often show the marks of artistic finish and decorative design. An impulse which can survive in such a famine of opportunity must have deep roots in human nature.

In the free and open highway, along the streets and boulevards, and in the parks, there are nobler opportunities for art. The bright sky is a canopy, and floating clouds of changing gray and gold and crimson glorify its wondrous depths. The broad spaces of land lie ready for the touch of grace. The landscape gardener plans rows of trees, masses of bushes, beautiful crags and ravines, and compels even forbidding elements to satisfy the love of beauty.

Public buildings display the taste of communities. Photographs have made familiar the magic and fleeting glories of the White City, whose memories are transforming our towns. Public libraries offer their walls for mural paintings, statuary, carving in wood and stone, and display of grace where all can enjoy.

The church has always been a patron of art. Devotion always called for fitting expression. Worshippers think that the best work must honor the alone Perfect. Nothing inferior seems suitable or morally correct. The edifice is made as noble, vast, and finely proportioned as the means of the congregation and the talent of the architect can make it. The windows are glorious with color and suggestive with historic pictures. The organ, from behind its decorated screen, becomes the majestic interpreter of musical masterworks. The people in their assembly bring to the help of their faith and aspiration sublime anthems and chorals. The enjoyment of the beautiful mingles with the incense of prayer.

When some great event is to be celebrated, — a declaration of independence, the birth of a hero, the completion of a railroad, the rebuilding of a burned city, — then the people become a procession, and the fête is an artistic triumph. Art is a social possession and a social product. It belongs to all social activities and institutions, pervasive and universal.

The Forms of Art are endlessly diversified and combined. Literature may be regarded as the central stock of all fine arts, the direct heir of the primal beauty. Perhaps early men imitated the notes of birds, the murmur of waters, the rustle of leaves, the plaintive cries of stricken animals. From early ages have come down to us rhythmic utterances which were composed and carried in memory until the art of writing came to embody them in lasting form. Indian Vedas and Homeric songs of battle, love, and worship have thus been preserved. They have lived because they were musical, and full of appeals to the common human heart. The ugly tends to perish; the dull and uninteresting decays; the merely technical, individual, and egoistic falls into the grave; but that which speaks to all is cared for by all, and this remains. Oral and written speech — poetry and prose, epic and lyric, history and fable, maxim and oration, myth and fiction — carry down to us the life of our ancestors. They set us singing and speaking. Homer and Hesiod and numerous nameless bards and prophets are our contemporaries.

From the beginning, some form of dance has accompanied rhythmic speech. Animals, savages, children, and civilized adults seek to express, in regulated motion, the feelings of the soul. Religion, love, warlike anger, fierce courage, find expression in march and circling dance.

Music is that art which, alone or married to immortal verse, is most nearly akin to worship. On its material side music obeys rigid mathematical laws, while on its emotional side it speaks out of the depths of the spirit, out of a mystic sense of what is public and general.

The drama is that ancient art which responds to the universal desire to enact life artificially. Men grow weary of the monotony of their little individual existence. They tire of the repetition, stale scenery, the level and barren life. Old joys lose flavor and interest. Personal callings bring up the same threadbare stories. But in the drama, read and acted, all human life comes into view. Kings move in pomp across the mimic stage; nobles of mediæval times rise from the dead to talk as courtiers and lovers; groups of distant peoples assemble to show their unfamiliar costumes and reveal their thoughts. Life in an hour becomes rich with a world's experience. The spectator is transported out of himself and lives a thousand lives in one. Hence the power for evil as well as for good in this fascinating art which paints with the intensity of life itself. In the opera, poetry, music, acting, dance, painting, sculpture, fencing — all arts — seem to be combined. It is the luxury of dramatic art.

In architecture man takes the forms of dwelling, and transforms the rude hut, the primeval cave, the circle of unhewn stones, into palaces, temples, and galleries. It is not enough to keep out frost and rain. Man is a creature of large discourse, and not easily satisfied. He must build something noble, large, spacious, lofty, beautiful, for his home, his justice, his music, his worship.

Drawing and painting are forms of speech, of communication from man to man. On the margins of his manuscripts, the handles of his tools and weapons, his very cooking-utensils, man has wished to manifest his thought of beauty. Savage and child, seeing an elk or bird, is eager to reproduce its image. Any material that nature offers will be used — ivory, walrus tusk, an edge of flint, a tooth. At first the story is rudely told, afterwards more gracefully and adequately. From the first sketch of the cave-dweller to the Madonnas of Raphael there was an unbroken succession of artists. Each genius taught his pupil how to excel himself.

The Aim of the Æsthetic Effort is to express Life. — It is not concerned with beauty and sublimity alone, but with all that is interesting. Ugly objects are made interesting by artists. "We believe that the æsthetic sentiment is identical with self-conscious life, with life that is conscious of its own subjective intensity and harmony; beauty, we have said, may be defined as a perception or an act that stimulates life simultaneously on its three sides, sensibility, intelligence, will, — and that produces pleasure by the immediate consciousness of this general stimulation" (Guyau).

Art is a Social Instrument. — It serves the social end of setting before many a common sense of enjoyment and inspiration, of truth, larger reality, common purpose. Art unites and harmonizes, attunes the discordant earth sounds to the dominant tones of widest human interests. It introduces new elements into life, as with fresh strains of the orchestra a course is served at a banquet.

The Fine Arts are in their very Nature Sociable. — The pleasures of fine art are essentially in a communicable order of pleasures. A house, as a dwelling, can be used by only one family, but if it is beautiful it becomes a possession for the multitudes. It contradicts the very idea of art to enclose a flower garden behind a high stone wall, or to keep great pictures shut up in private collections. Raphael did not paint for a few rich nabobs, but for mankind. It is the insolence and meanness of riches to buy up the works of genius and reserve them for the delectation of nobodies.

The pleasures of fine art are disinterested as well as communicable. "They are not such as nourish a man's body nor add to his riches; they are not such as can gratify him, when he receives them, by the sense of advantage or superiority over his fellow-creatures; they are not such as one human being can in any sense receive exclusively from the object which bestows them. . . . It is evidently characteristic of a beautiful building that its beauty cannot be monopolized, but can be seen and admired by the inhabitants of a whole city and by all visitors for all generations. The same thing is true of a picture or a statue. . . . Music is composed to be sung or played for the enjoyment of many at a time, and for such enjoyment a hundred years hence as much as to-day. Poetry is written to be read by all readers forever who care for the ideas and feelings of the poet, and can apprehend the meaning and melody of his language" (Article "Fine Arts," *Encyclopædia Britannica*, by Professor Colvin).

There is a Special Need of Art Culture in America. — Our people have long been engaged in a struggle to gain mastery over nature. Millions of immigrants have flocked to our shores as refugees from poverty. Puritan founders were busy with austere questions of conscience. We have been an agricultural people, and plough handles make strong rather than graceful hands. It is time for our century plant of material conquest to blossom into art. Our expositions of 1876 and 1893 have wakened the nation to a new yearning, a thirst which beauty alone can quench. Illustrated magazines are making the works of artists popular. Public schools diffuse a taste for finer literature, drawing, designing, modelling. Nature studies attract attention to forms and colors in the world about us. Ecclesiastical traditions bring from the mother country the pre-Puritan suggestions of illuminated anthem books, "storied windows richly dight," reverent rituals, and stately worship. Landscape gardening is transfiguring our vast expanse, our broad boulevards, our parks, our river shores, our wild reserves, our Niagara and Mackinac, our country lanes, village squares, and railway stations. Ugliness is losing sacredness and becoming intolerable.

CHAPTER VII

Outline of our Industrial Organization

"The division of labor, the multiplication of the arts of peace, which is nothing but a large allowance to each man to choose his work according to his faculty, — to live by his better hand, — fills the state with useful and happy laborers ; and they, creating demand by the very temptation of their productions, are rapidly and surely rewarded by good sale : and what a public and ten commandments their work thus becomes ! " — EMERSON.

"I do not know the history of that five-pound note, but well aware I am that it grew slowly out of pence and silver, and that Jamie denied his passions many things for this great hour. His sacrifices watered his young heart and kept it fresh and tender. Let us no longer cheat our consciences by talking of filthy lucre. Money may always be a beautiful thing. It is we who make it grimy." (Jamie was a true Scotch son who saved money for a gift to his poor widow mother.) — J. M. BARRIE, *A Window in Thrums.*

A RIDE across the state on a rapid train will present to the watchful observer in the course of a few hours many kinds of industrial activities. Most of the space is covered with farms, divided into meadows, pastures, ploughed lands, orchards, gardens, yards, and all these are devoted chiefly to the production of the materials for food and clothing. If the forests have not already been destroyed in our wasteful way, the trees may furnish boards and beams for houses and wood for fuel. Oil wells are bringing up materials for warmth and light. The sooty miners issue from the dark caverns whence they are blasting out coal for hearths, furnaces, and locomotives. At the smallest cross-roads village a blacksmith is shoeing the feet of horses, repairing wagons and agricultural implements, and exercising his universal genius on setting right all kinds of damaged utensils and machines. At the large towns there are glimpses of general stores, carpenter shop, mill, photograph gallery, cheese factory, and canning establishment. In small cities the industries are still more varied and special, and when we arrive for the first time at the capital city, it bewilders us with its variety and tempts us to spend more than we can afford. Each man has his trade or calling, and seems bent on making one article, or, at most, very few objects. The shoemaker makes more shoes than his family can wear in a lifetime; the farmer raises enough grain in a year to feed him and his children many years; the "store-keeper" buys a huge mass of cloth and groceries only to get rid of them as rapidly as possible. The laboring man toils at his narrow task though he may dislike it. The berry-picker dares not consume the fruit she gathers in the employer's field. What does it all mean? Can we discover any order, purpose, system, in this motley picture of the day's ride?

In order to map out the province of social welfare it is necessary for us to ask the economist for permission to cross his field, since it constitutes a very essential district in the territory we have undertaken to survey. The political economist will not object to this trespass on his preserves, for he is a good-natured person, by no means given to a "dismal science," as Carlyle ungraciously called economics. His is a science of entrancing interest and immense social value. The economist studies that he may deliver knowledge of his region to other students of the larger aspects of society, and he holds the power to check the vagaries of speculation by his severe and painstaking methods, to which the world owes so much of its deliverance from visionary and impracticable schemes. One of the perils of our time is the disease of economic hysterics. Genius, it is well said, is characterized by sanity, self-control, balance, and all-sided consideration. It is our duty to wait until we have taken into account all the materials for a judgment. Heat without light is a real danger. Patience is a duty of every person who proposes in any way to influence public opinion or lead in social action. A hasty glance at certain economic topics may at least serve to prevent the formation of a judgment of our problems of welfare without even knowing of the existence of economic elements. Their further and adequate discussion belongs to the particular field of study called political economy.

I. Wants. — The wants of men show through all their in-dustries. Economic study is a consideration of the social method of satisfying wants. Our study of the individual in our third chapter has already revealed to us the appetites and desires which are in all human beings and prompt them to effort. The woman bakes bread because she is hungry or knows that she and her family will soon become hungry. The farmer fattens swine and salts pork in autumn that there may be meat for the winter. The girl learns to play on the piano because she likes music, or because she will earn money by the art. Thus we make, buy, and sell in order to satisfy our wants.

The desire to consume, to use, to enjoy, is the prime spring of work and business, from the simple act of roasting potatoes to manipulating a railroad. Our wishes are indefinite, prac-tically boundless and endless. Pearls, meat, music, books, tobacco, — where is the end of the catalogue?

Industry and business rest on all other forms of activity and interest. Our animal nature demands food, drink, clothing, dwellings, comforts of many kinds. Our æsthetic craving calls for pictures, beautiful ornaments and decoration, lawns and flower beds, statues, music and musical instruments. Our intellectual cravings make us hungry for books, papers, libra-ries, schools, lectures; and all these cost money. Our religious beliefs and aspirations call for churches, ministers, sermons, missions, organs, singers; and these require wealth. Industry and business are created by all the human desires.

On the other hand, all life waits for material goods from industry and business. All the articles and services which satisfy our various intellectual, physical, and religious wants are supplied out of the busy system of industry and profes-sional toil. Economic life is the means of meeting these higher demands. Work itself shares the dignity and honor, or the shame and wrong, of the ends it serves.

The water of a mill-race is the direct material force which sets in motion the great and small wheels of a grist mill, but the miller's purpose to make money is the spiritual force inside all wheels, and the purpose to make money is the effect of many kinds of desire. Man's wishes blow on the sails of all

the ships of lake and ocean.   Man's ambitions fire his engines
and propel his trains.   Steam and lathes, pulleys and bands,
are but the dumb slaves of man's soul, its longings and resolves.

The civilized man is a person of many more wants than the
savage, and he has larger foresight.   The savage, especially in
a warm climate, is content with a few articles of diet, an apron
for clothing, a roof of bark, and fifty cents' worth of tools and
weapons.   Until a group of men desire the comforts and refinements of civilization they will work fitfully and rest a good
deal.   Until the lazy and irregular workman begins to want
three rooms to his house, instead of one chamber with its clay
floor, and until he sees the value of glass in the windows and
a door-bell, he will lie in the sun four days of the week and
trust Providence for the rest.   Civilization implies the multiplication of wants, the improvement in methods of making
things, and the elevation of grades of goods.

But wishes and desires are not the immediate cause of
wealth.   We may have a wishing-cap on the head, but we must
take a trowel in the hand.

II. Work. — These wants, in all their variety, cannot be
satisfied without work upon nature.   The physical world contains what is indispensable to our life.   There is the material
for food and shelter and clothing.   There are the possibilities
of paper, music, railroads, and all that nourishes the body, is
interesting to the intellect, and charming to the taste.   The
heat that warms us, the stores of energy by which we move
and strive and think, are in nature.

But the objects of desire will not come to man without work.
Even those savages who subsist on nuts and berries must pick
them and devour them.   If we enjoy a few of the bare necessities of life, we can sometimes secure them, in sparsely settled
regions, with very brief effort and by simple means; but in
older communities, where wants are multiplied and industry
is complicated, the simple old ways would leave us to perish.

It is true that certain classes in most communities do not
work and yet enjoy, as tramps, thieves, beggars, robbers, parasites, gamblers, the idle rich, and all the drones.   But even
for these nature supplies nothing without toil, the toil of other
people.   The predatory members of society exist because

others delve and strain.   The possession of wealth may mask the reality, but nothing can unmake the fact that an idler lives upon the stores gathered by workers.

It is our duty, however, to recognize the services of all classes of useful workers.   The manual laborer is apt to fancy that he is the only productive agent.   But the work of mothers in bearing and rearing and educating children; the work of teachers, ministers, physicians, lawyers, artists; the toil and anxiety of merchants, bankers, managers of great affairs, of statesmen and officials,— are in the category of productive industries.   The rich are by no means all useless, and they have the best opportunity to be serviceable to society; they have the largest resources and the most numerous ways of promoting the happiness of mankind.   Those whose sole business is to cut coupons and collect rents may be, through a noble use of their leisure, repaying their fellow-men a thousand times for all their material support costs.   There are many methods of working for the increase of the common sum of satisfactions.   But of the man who only cuts coupons and collects rents, what shall we say?   What should society do for *him ?*

Work usually means cost to the worker; it is ordinarily painful, and requires sacrifice.   This is most visibly manifest in the labors of those who lift and pull, bend and lift, sweat and struggle, in harvest field and factory, in the dark mines, lying on their sides and creeping along the low tunnels, often toward the deadly fire-damp and the falling roof.   But it is also known in hidden places, out of sight of the multitudes.

Even in our day, long after Thomas Hood sang in pity the classic of poverty, *The Song of the Shirt,* the friendly visitor and the faithful missionary may discover the maker of cheap clothing in the attic room of a great city : —

> " With fingers weary and worn,
>   With eyelids heavy and red,
> A woman sat, in unwomanly rags,
>   Plying her needle and thread, —
> Stitch ! stitch ! stitch !
>   In poverty, hunger, and dirt;
> And still with a voice of dolorous pitch
>   She sang the ' Song of the Shirt.'

> " Work — work — work !
>   Till the brain begins to swim !
>   Work — work — work —
>   Till the eyes are heavy and dim !
>   Seam, and gusset, and band,
>   Band, and gusset, and seam, —
>   Till over the buttons I fall asleep,
>   And sew them on in a dream ! "

III. Economy. — Since productive work costs sacrifice, it is natural that rational beings should get what they want at as low cost as possible. This is what we mean by "economy." It is true that many kinds of activity are pleasurable, and men will put forth great exertions in sports. Artistic work has a delight in itself, apart from the price it brings. It seems probable that this kind of pleasant useful labor will increase with improvements in machinery and social organization. But practically men are pushed by the most powerful motives to get the object of desire at the least cost and in the most economical method. It is rational to buy in the cheapest market, even when we intend to make a present. Since the amount of energy and materials at our command is limited and our wants are unlimited, we must act on this principle of economy or come to the end of supplies. The instinct is like that of a dog, which instinctively runs along the diagonal path across a pasture, just as if he knew the geometry of a triangle. None but the insane act habitually on the principle of doing an act twice where one effort is sufficient. Some one has said that men are just as lazy as they dare to be. If this saying is extravagant, we may still admit that it indicates a truth; men will gain their ends by the most rational method known to them or available, and they will count any other conduct irrational.

IV. Hence the Industries and the Arts. — We have already studied the various classes of useful arts, the tools, machines, skill, and technical training by which social wants are satisfied. The development and perfection of these arts are furthered by the economic impulses of society. Inventions are made under the spur of desire. The intellect works from the goading of the purpose to get goods by the shortest method.

Necessity is the mother of invention. The invention becomes general property.

These social inventions are the most valuable and permanent kinds of capital. Material things perish with the using. Gorgeous palaces, solemn temples, iron machinery, staunch ships of steel, stores of grain, are dissolved by worm and wear, by rust and fire. But the invention of an axe or hammer, a millstone or a water-wheel, lasts for ten thousand years, long after the savage genius who first made the discovery has been forgotten. Ideas and methods survive; it is things which decay and pass away.

V. Hence Social Organization for Production; Division of Labor. — In order to produce an article most rapidly and perfectly, one must be in the habit of making that one object. Illustrations of the division of labor should be sought by the reader in some shop, factory, or mill. No written page can make the principle clear to one who does not observe for himself. Fortunately, the nearest blacksmith shop may furnish the primary lesson. If a man works alone at forge and anvil, his productive ability is very much restricted. If he has a helper to hold the heavy and white-hot bar, or to strike alternate blows in welding at the critical moment, he can undertake kinds of tasks impossible without such coöperation. In making a wagon some men have greater skill in shaping the wooden parts, and others excel in iron. If one man attempts to make the entire vehicle, he succeeds, if at all, only imperfectly and slowly. A piano factory, a watch factory, or a planing mill would give still more complex instances of fine division of tasks. In a great shoe factory the trade really means many trades under one roof. There are those who cut out the leather, others who form the heels, or sew the uppers, or peg the soles, or finish the edges.

The Regulation of Industry is essential to its efficiency, and the methods of government have changed from age to age. In the earliest history of mankind the father seems to have ruled the household arts, although in a subordinate way the woman directed some parts of the labor, especially in the preparation of food and clothing. Under all systems of slavery, regulation is in the hand of the owner and lord, who controls the laborers according to the customs of the time. This control does not always rest entirely on fear and force, for the slave himself recognizes his subject condition and assents to it, especially if he has inherited his state and is of mild disposition and feels himself inferior. So natural was slavery in ancient times that poor men sought to place themselves under a master in order to secure support and protection.

Slavery belonged to an entirely different social state from our own. Slaves were captives of war or purchased from conquerors. There was a need of protection as well as of support, and the condition of the slave secured both. But at a later stage in European history it was gradually found that man would produce more for the landowner if he could be sure of his home and family and had a share of the product of his toil, according to his industry and skill.

Serfdom displaced slavery, because it was more profitable to landowners and gave them larger and surer returns. No doubt the diffusion of more humane sentiments and nobler conceptions of the worth of man aided this movement of liberation. Finally serfdom disappeared in Europe and a new mode of regulating labor gradually arose.

Slavery, after it had ceased in Europe, was established in America. The economic cause of this was the necessity felt by the Europeans for having under their control a body of laborers who could not run away and set up as farmers on their own property. We were long in discovering that this kind of control was wasteful to the land and did not train workmen fit to manage modern machinery at a profit. In the meantime the moral and religious sentiment was coming into revolt against slavery as a degradation of man by man. The Civil War killed slavery in the United States and left us with a vast multitude of persons who had no proper discipline for self-government.

The Factory System. — The most general method of control in our age has grown naturally out of the two preceding stages. It is still true that wage-workers are subject to the directions and command of the landowners, managers of manufactures, and other employers. This system may be called the Factory or Business Manager System. It is governed by the will of the Capitalist Employer, the "captain of industry." The manual workers, and others under control, are appointed their tasks and are supported during the process of production by the managers. Why do not the wage-workers go upon the land and be their own masters? Why do they submit to the orders of the business managers? There are many reasons, all of them found in the advantages of the system in the present state of public opinion and national character. In the first place, a great many men *have* chosen to become self-employing farmers, owning their own land and working under their own rules. Multitudes of our people, especially in earlier times, when free land was plenty or when farms could be purchased for a small sum and on credit, have thus provided for their families. And many others are doing the same thing now in various parts of the country.

But multitudes of others have found it less difficult, for various reasons, to work for employers on farms and in cities. In our times, the immigrants of older countries have flocked to our shores without enough money to carry them to the great West and South, and provide seed, horses, ploughs, and subsistence until they could raise a crop. These persons discover that they can at once find support in manufacturing establishments, without capital, and, frequently, without skill. It is no longer possible, as a general rule, to start business with a few dollars' worth of tools and materials. Clothing, shoes, machinery, the parts of houses, and most articles sold in the market, can be made more cheaply by steam power and in large quantities. These small shops are closed out; the workmen hire themselves to the manufacturers; the number of wage-workers increases and the relative number of employers diminishes. The man who sells his time and energy does, indeed, lose control of his person thus far; but, on the other hand, he is not vexed by having to seek customers, or collect bad debts, or make complicated plans for introducing inventions and better methods. He is responsible for his own task for so many pieces or hours, and then he is free. Many mechanics can thus secure a larger income than if they owned their own farms and tilled them. The comfort of living in a town, with its amusements, excitement, and other attractions, is another motive which holds the wage-workers under this kind of control. We may be sure that this method is fairly well adapted to our average condition, or it would not be so general, and would not continue.

Direction of the working groups is a necessary social function. It is as much a part of the process of production as labor at bench, or plough, or lathe, or counter. Any person can verify this assertion for himself by watching a gang of road-menders, or a group of car-makers, or a crew of sailors. The larger the establishment, the more important is this function. A man who tills a field for himself needs no supervision; but then, his product is small in proportion to his exertion. A thousand men working under skilful supervision can produce much more than a thousand times more than one person could produce working by himself. The supervision adds to the product, and is a real contribution to wealth.

Of course, if workmen are indolent, dishonest, careless, awkward, the cost of supervising them is greater than if they are intelligent, industrious, and honorable. And here is a point where manufacture and business can be made much less costly to society by advance in morality and education. But there will never come a time when it will not be necessary to have a directing head for each large body of producers. The materials must be ready, the plans must be at hand, the task of each person must be assigned so that others shall not be kept waiting. Every machine must run steadily all day, and the combination of materials and workers must be calculated exactly. The duty of the "boss" requires ability of a peculiar kind, and as the complexity of elements increases it is more and more difficult to find men competent to carry all the details in mind and to reach decisions swiftly and accurately. Those who are at the head of great railroads and steel works are frequently paid very high salaries because they are in demand and have a sort of monopoly of their kind of talent.

During the hours of work, the manual laborer or the salaried servant of the house is subject to the master of the establishment. He may, within very rigid limits, choose his master, but even this power is restricted and does not carry him out of the sweep of the system. When he engages to give his time he accepts a foreign will and is directed from without. If he objects to the demands made upon him in respect to the duration, intensity, or quality of his work, or the treatment of the overseers, or to the wages, he is liable to discharge. If he is known to be a constant objector, he finds it difficult to secure employment in any place.

Under these circumstances it is inevitable that friction should arise. Men accustomed to the atmosphere of political freedom, taught to consider all as equal before the law, are not likely to bow meekly to the yoke of arbitrary discipline. Power soon becomes arbitrary if it is not met by other power. There never was a body of men on earth who could be entrusted permanently with the control of others without responsibility. The habit of being obeyed instantly and unquestioningly, without murmur or criticism, without opportunity for revision or complaint, makes tyrants of the best supervisors. Experience has taught men in politics and in manufacture to organize checks on irresponsible government.

The Trade Union as a Governing Body. — The trade union is an organization of wage-workers to secure a share in the control and regulation of business. It is part of the general democratic movement of this age to give men a place in the management of their own persons and destinies. This is the central meaning of the movement and of the organization, and this should be better understood. These organizations are new in regions where manufacturing has been but recently introduced. They are often composed of persons who have had little experience in them, who are strangers to each other and to our institutions. It is not wonderful that they should make mistakes, that they should come into collision with the law which they have never been taught, and that their own sincere sense of injustice should sometimes move them to anti-social acts. All these abuses can be corrected. Experience, discussion, and law may remove many of the objectionable factors. But the essential aim and principle are sound. The trade union is a method of democratic self-government. It enables the wage-workers to gain a hearing and a representation in a regular way. It gives them power to enforce their wishes. It provides a parliament for debate, in which the extreme notions of radicals are tamed down by the sober counsels of conservative men.

Just as there is a government in the family, in the school, in the church, and in every club, lodge, and association of every kind, so there must be in the factory. With advancing intelligence and more general education, there will be more general fitness for sharing in such interior government, and there will also be a stronger demand for it. Men who have become accustomed to exercising their suffrage in choosing their political representatives will inevitably ask for a voice in governing the factory, that institution which most closely affects their health, morals, and happiness.

The right of wage-workers to a share in the government of the institution which determines the very essential conditions of their lives is disputed. It is frequently claimed that the proprietor himself is the only one who can be trusted with authority over the management of his factory. The capitalist employer may be conceded the right to control his machinery and plant, while he has no such right to govern the human beings whom he employs in a fashion which is against their will and judgment. There are two sets of instruments, the men and the things. The manager has no right to govern men arbitrarily and without taking counsel with them, as to the mode of using and consuming their physical and mental powers.

The extension of the great corporations, such as railroads, steamship lines, mining companies, irrigation associations, and other large enterprises, has modified the function of superintendence. The direction of large business in its details formerly belonged to the managers of finances, to be noticed later. But when a form of business becomes greater, and the real owners are scattered stockholders, and not one or two large capitalists, then the technical direction falls more and more into the hands of a new class of men, the various grades of salaried directors of manufacture or transportation who were educated in technical schools and have worked their way up from the bottom according to a merit system. This is a social change of far-reaching importance. Its effect may be to diminish the relative importance of the capitalist manager, and render his service less indispensable to society.

VI. Management of Business. — From the division of labor in production of goods arises the necessity of trade and exchange.

We may read of people who produced all they consumed, but they were not much raised above the conditions of savage life. Trade, beginning in barter, marks an important step in the progress of mankind. The farmers, in many regions, discover that it does not pay to make butter and cheese, because this can be done more economically in dairies and cheese factories. The dairy farmers bring milk to a central place and receive in return the butter and cheese they need, and in addition money which will enable them to purchase all they require.

The "middleman" or merchant, acting with agents of transportation, serves the community at this point. Oranges can be grown most cheaply in Florida and California. Cattle flourish on the plains of Texas. Sheep can be raised where there is suitable pasture and climate. The streams of rocky New England furnish water power, and the inventive people, heirs of mechanical traditions, furnish contrivances. Our very necessities compel us to be sociable. We might become isolated, shut up in narrow valleys of conceit and ignorance and prejudice, but for the system of trade.

Business. — It is not enough to manufacture goods for the market; they will never serve man until they are brought in good condition and on time to the market. Let us here consider, in outline, the social organization for this purpose. For an adequate discussion of each point, we must go to the ordinary works on political economy or "economics." Enough must be set down here to show the place of business in the grand scheme of society.

Exchange. — There is not only a division of labor among the workmen of a factory or mill, there is diversity of production in different regions of the earth. The shoemaker wishes to exchange nearly all the shoes he can make for other articles which he desires. The farmer has more wheat than his family can consume, and he wishes to send for books, wagons, tea, coffee, spices, tobacco, calico, woollen cloth, blankets, and other commodities.

Business began with barter. This is a stage of commerce which may yet be studied among school boys and the residents of Africa and other primitive folk. The boys trade so many marbles for a knife, so much string for so much candy, a definite quantity of slate pencil for an agreed quantity of leather. In the African forest, a few shining beads or a yard of bright-colored cloth will purchase elephant tusks of precious ivory. Barter is the earliest form of exchange.

In more settled agricultural and manufacturing communities, the number and variety of articles exchanged increase; and it becomes clear that there must be a common standard of exchange. Thus, a man who has more cows than he can use will purchase ten sheep for one cow. A horse may bring ten cows or a hundred sheep. A very attractive bracelet of gold may exchange for ten horses. Now, if cattle are the most common sort of wealth in that community, a custom may grow up of estimating horses, tents, and cloth in terms of cattle. Thus we come to the word "price."

Price is the common measure of the value of goods. But experience has shown that this price needs some well-known and convenient form of wealth as its representative. If a man wishes to sell a cow worth ten sheep, and his customer has only three sheep to sell, it is impossible to make a trade, because the cow is not valuable if she is cut up. Hence the use of money.

Without entering upon the controversial questions relating to money, we simply notice its social functions, — it is a standard of values and a medium of exchange. While in former times actual commodities were used for these purposes, — cattle, blocks of salt or tea, hides, iron, — advancing civilization adopted the precious metals and various symbols of these. As a matter of fact, the banking system is the chief medium of exchange, very little money being passed from hand to hand compared with the volume of wealth recorded in books and transferred by checks, notes, and various devices of the commercial world. The regulation of currency and exchange by government is one of its most necessary and delicate functions; the study of public finance is a duty of every citizen; and the administration requires the highest order of commercial ability in statesmen.

Capital and its Social Function. — As soon as industry and trade have grown to considerable proportions, there is need for large collections of tools and implements, of machines and buildings, of stores of food and fuel, of lumber and raw materials for manufacture. Capital is not very important in savage conditions and in frontier life. But when population is dense, and trade is widely extended, it becomes necessary to have immense resources ready and under competent control. These supplies of subsistence and machinery constitute "capital." They are the product of labor and thinking, and they are the result of saving, in the first instance, a part of the product from immediate consumption. The function of capital is to produce more wealth. The food supplies support the workers; the raw materials, as cotton and ores, are manufactured into goods demanded by the community, and thus the process of production is kept up in endless series from generation to generation. The capital may be owned and controlled by individuals, by the entire people in common, or by corporations. Frequently the capital employed in a railroad is largely owned by the employees, who have bought its stock. The owners of capital are not all wealthy persons; many of them are relatively poor. But whoever owns the capital it is absolutely essential to progress that masses of wealth should be brought together for production and exchange.

The Capitalist. — Any person who owns wealth used for production is so far a capitalist. The word is ordinarily used to designate a person who owns a very large amount of wealth. But a child who invests a dime in the savings bank, or the widow who buys stock in a bank or mine, becomes to this extent a capitalist; and the number of such investors constantly increases.

The Manager. — The most interesting figure of modern time is the "undertaker" or business manager. Perhaps it is safer to use the term "manager," because the word "undertaker" has a rather too sombre and funereal suggestiveness in our language. This business manager is the man whom Carlyle called the "captain of industry." We have just seen him directing the laborers in the factory, or delegating his duties to a superintendent from whom he requires reports.

There is another side to the duties of the manager. He is the man who provides capital for all kinds of enterprises. He is the man who walks the floor of nights when credit is hard to obtain, and immense sums of money must be raised to pay "the hands." He is the man who must wait for his pay, perhaps for years, and lose everything in the end by some error of judgment or by some unforeseen change in the public demand. He is the man who is cursed for his success and for his failures. He is more abused than any other person in the country. He is more bitterly hated. On him rests the burden of keeping his machinery busy, so that interest and taxes may not eat up its value, and his goods be forgotten in the markets. He must look for sales to the ends of the earth. He must watch the prices in Liverpool, London, and Pekin. When his ships with valuable cargoes are tossing on the waves, his head tosses on the pillow, though it be of down. Nearly all the men who try this occupation fail. Here and there one succeeds. But the son of a born leader often fails, and there are only two or three generations "from shirt sleeves to shirt sleeves."

If the difficulties of this perilous position are great, the rewards are also great. Of the merely economic rewards we shall speak under the head of "profits." But in passing we may point out the other social rewards which come to the successful man of enterprise during his brief enjoyment of control. He may live in a great mansion and keep a boarding-house for servants of all kinds. He can have dainty food, more than a regiment can eat. He can go to the opera and pay a hundred dollars for a box where all can see his shirt-front and diamond pin and splendidly dressed wife and daughters. He is the object of constant flattery and praise. He is called "Napoleon," more than a captain of industry — he is a general. Sometimes he succeeds in keeping his winnings till he dies, and then his estate is cut up, the lawyers and heirs and inheritance taxes dividing his earnings among them. He is conscious while he lives of performing for society a most important service. If he is a philanthropist he has the resources of society at his command, and can do all that money can perform, for it is his own. Professor Sherwood thus states the conditions which have given the undertaker his importance : —

"(1) Cheap and rapid transportation; (2) the existence of vast accumulations of loanable capital; (3) a high degree of civilization, shown in the effective anticipation of wants in the remote future; (4) the formation of great political empires bringing under community of law and administration the industries of vast territories; (5) the general development of the spirit of international trade and of democratic ideas; (6) the existence of a real world-market with its greater stability of prices and its extension of sources of demand and supply; (7) greater division of labor, increasing the technical difficulties of undertaking; (8) greater economy of production on a large scale."

Let us suppose that the present tendency should continue, that the function of superintendence of great industries and business should pass to salaried men, that the risk of capital should be taken by vast corporations having countless capital, as is already true in many railroads,— then the independent business manager would disappear, and the important position he now occupies would be vacant. This would have a certain effect on profits, — the reward of the manager. But that day may be far off. There are still magnificent chances for men who can discover new fields of enterprise, where powers of invention are required. Only when business is reduced to a degree of customary routine can it be directed by salaried superintendents.

The Banker and Banking. — The banker shares the responsibilities, the advantages, the honors, and the criticism of the manager. Many are asking, "What is the banker good for? How does he earn his wealth? Is he a blood-sucker or a blood-maker?" Let us see. Let it be remembered that when we sought the function of a trade union we left out of account the abuses and the immoralities. Every institution and group should be judged by its normal function and not by its crimes. The justice we asked for the trade union we now request for the banker. If the banker steals, there is the penitentiary, and the pardoning power should not rob the penitentiary of its due after the so-called respectable banker has been convicted of stealing a million of humble deposits. If he lies, he will lose confidence. If he cheats, we must trust the de-

K

tectives and eternal righteousness to look into his accounts. But if he transacts our business, he deserves at least candid consideration. What is his task in the great army of industry?

It is to gather the "many mickles that make a muckle." Ten sticks apart cannot make a fire; they must be heaped in one place. A million dollars in separate stockings and stove-pipes, suspicious of each other, will not supply a rolling-mill or railroad with capital to employ hundreds of men. Gather all these separate and idle dollars into one fund, pay the owners of each a little interest, keep it secure from rats and robbers, lend it to business managers of genius for industrial organiza-tion, and wealth is multiplied. That is one function of a banker. Visit a bank and see for yourself.

But the service of the banker does not end here. Society cannot afford to have the wrong managers get control of their hard-earned savings. An incompetent, ignorant, dishonest manager would soon squander the money which comes from stinting and sparing, from bleeding fingers and weary nerves. The banker must be a man who can read men and judge them, and measure their ability, find out their resources, and discover their modes of doing business. He must be a man who would not lend to his own brother if that brother were unfit for the trust. He must not show mercy to a bankrupt, even if he plead for credit with tears. He must be absolutely without compassion in business hours, although he may be merciful as an angel with his own money. He must be the embodi-ment of justice, that he may be good to his clients. They trust him with their hoards for a specific purpose. He has no right to make subscriptions to churches and missions and charities out of those funds. His sole duty is to find shrewd, upright, capable borrowers, who know how to make cents into dimes, and dollars into eagles, for the community. If a banker does this in business hours, he does his whole duty, and if he fails in this duty, he betrays his trust, no matter how generous and philanthropic he may be.

VII. Combinations of Capital. — Large combinations of capital are the natural growth of our conditions and stage of culture. It is desirable that all citizens should understand this tendency, for it is universal and necessary. The first step toward an understanding might be taken by a visit to a shoe factory, a watch factory, or any large establishment which employs many persons and assigns them different tasks.

Explanation. — The advantages of massing capital and labor are obvious to the careful observer. What can a farmer do with his wheat, if his best market is Liverpool? Can he carry it to the seaboard in his wagon and then row it in his own little skiff across the sea? The picture is absurd. And yet men complain at the aggregation of capital. They are astounded, confused, terrified by seeing the immense wealth under control of a few men. We have seen that control of capital does not always mean ownership of capital. Many of the greatest manufacturers and merchants do much business on borrowed money. It is the centralized management of capital which makes it productive.

If a farmer has coal, or natural gas, or petroleum in his farm, he cannot turn it into money and purchasing power. Simple ownership will not profit him. He must take his goods to market. This requires a pipe line or train of cars and a vast apparatus for preparing the crude product for use. Therefore he must join forces with his fellow-men; he must organize a joint-stock company, that is, he must make a combination or go without the advantages of his possessions. Perhaps he has not the business ability or knowledge to form a combination. Then he may find one already formed, to which he may sell or lease his land and its contents. He will naturally take the course which offers him the best terms.

It has been found that a large ship can carry the cargo of several small ships with less expense per ton for crew and coal. The cost for each bushel of grain carried is smaller with the great boats. Hence the large ships can offer lower rates for transportation, and the dealers give them the business. This explains the disappearance of the smaller ships.

It does not follow that the "large industry" will swallow up the small shops and industries altogether. People will buy where they can buy best and most cheaply. They will consider price, quality, and convenience, and they will build up the form of business which supplies their wants in the most satisfactory way. It is the consumers who determine the

method. If there is a little shop around the corner, it may
be able to make a living for its owner even if its prices are
somewhat higher than those of the "department store" simply
because the shop is in the right place.   Most clothing will be
made in large shops, but a really artistic tailor may still find
customers who prefer his style, though they must pay higher
prices for the finer fit.   The business of the dentist, the physician, and the lawyer are so personal that they cannot be very
greatly extended by the employment of wage-earners.   All the
finest art work, as painting, sculpture, wood carving, em-
broidery, may always be kept out of the wholesale form of
manufacture.   As taste improves there will be a larger demand
for this class of goods.   Perhaps the extension of electric
motive power, which is easily carried a long distance on wires,
may make it possible for little shops to compete with great
factories in certain lines.   It is not at all settled that the factory system is bound to be universal, although it will greatly
increase.

The Perils and Evils of Combinations of Capital. — Return-
ing to the principle that men cannot be trusted with irresponsible power in any relation of life, we may apply it in this case.
The control of wealth is a mighty power.   It enables rich men
or corporations to secure for their services an enormous reward,
to hold their goods for an exorbitant price, to make keen bargains with railroads, so that smaller dealers, having to pay
higher freights, cannot compete with them in selling; they
can buy votes in city councils and state and national legislatures; they can maintain lobbies to bribe and corrupt the
representatives of the people to betray and cheat their masters.
All this and much more great corporations can do, and have
done.   Their deeds, when fully written, — even when cleared
of all false charges and unproved suspicion, — will be a dark
blot on the history of this century.

Remedies. — If the dangers of combinations are so great,
and the acknowledged evils so vast, in what direction shall we
look for relief and escape?

Not to suppression.   The tendency to production by large
means and on a grand scale is fatal as the tides.   It was a
foolish woman who tried to sweep back the waves of the sea

with a broom. The movement toward the great industry has been coming for a thousand years, and it will never go backward. We must count upon and provide for its increase and continuance, just as we provide for winter. Winter is not wicked, and the great industry is not wicked. It is merely a natural fact which has terrible possibilities of evil, and is yet necessary to the very existence of the race, unless we kill a majority of the population and reduce the others to savagery. That way is blocked up.

Competition, our old acquaintance "the struggle for existence," lends us some help. It is not impossible for a hundred men to combine their capital and get possession of a market. But it is far more difficult to keep possession of the market than some imagine. If one manipulator buys up all the wheat in America, there are still Siberia and India to reckon with. But let us imagine that all these fields are insufficient; then we can eat corn and oats, meat and fruits, and dozens of other substitutes; and we do. When the price of the most desirable article advances, men turn to substitutes. If coal oil is higher than they like to pay, people will use some vegetable oil or return to animal fats. Monopoly has limits. It is too shrewd to raise prices too high, for fear of calling human inventiveness into the field. Thus we see that many forms of goods which are controlled by monopolies are sold at constantly reduced price; not out of philanthropy, but because high prices arouse invention and call substitutes into the field.

During the Civil War sorghum largely took the place of cane sugar, because that article was largely cut off. When coffee cost too much, rye was asked to take its place at the breakfast table, although it did not give entire satisfaction. Now that the sugar business has fallen into the hands of a trust, the beet sugar industry comes to the public relief.

Competition does not always run to the rescue of the popular interest. Is there any other way of escape? Let us turn to an illustration of a local gas monopoly in a city. There is only one company. It would not pay to start another company, tear up the streets for two sets of mains, and then find in the end that the owners combine under one management.

The supply of gas in a given area is of necessity a monopoly. Competition on any considerable scale is impossible. Substitutes are not easily found. Coal oil is unpleasant and dangerous in city rows. We do not desire to return to such inferior means of lighting. Since competition fails to offer assistance, we appeal to the regulative power of the legislature. This body, which represents all the people and not the monopolies alone, has the right to fix the rate at which gas shall sell, if it does not fix a rate so low as to be unjust to the owners and impair the capital. Sometimes city councils are given authority to make regulations on the subject. Sometimes contracts are made with companies which secure the rights of the inhabitants.

"But our legislators and aldermen deceive us and sell out our interests." Serves us right. We should elect honest and competent men.

Government as Business Manager. — Still another mode of escape is open to us, — the method of public ownership. This is no new and "socialistic" device. We are already familiar with the conduct of business by the national government in the case of the postal service. It is true that the postal department makes use of private enterprise, of railroads and steamship lines, but its own share in management is immense. While there have been gross abuses, and many things yet remain to correct, we have reason to continue the system and to extend it. If the government should carry parcels, the rate of express charges would diminish, and better methods would be devised.

In cities the public has become accustomed to buying water of its own government. This is a business which is largely routine and is not liable to sudden changes of method. There is, of course, a chance to steal in the water department, but experience seems decidedly in favor of extending this enterprise. In the care of waste and sewage the direct management by the city seems to be the most economical.

The government of a city is not compelled to manage its own property, any more than any other capitalist. If it chooses to let out any function to a corporation of private capitalists on good terms, that may sometimes be found the wisest course. The rights of the people are secured by means of a contract.

Government Commissions. — The Interstate Commerce Commission is an example of a legal method of controlling great corporations. For many years there were bitter complaints from certain merchants that railroad companies gave special rates of freight to their competitors. It was found that a powerful circle of directors would even ruin a town against which they had a grudge, by refusing to carry their freight or by demanding a rate which was not asked of competing towns. There was a great opportunity for directors to make themselves rich, even at the expense of the stockholders, by levying blackmail on customers and selling special privileges. These complaints were so general that the government was moved to interfere, in order to secure just and equitable treatment of men and of localities. It was not thought best to buy up the roads, nor to become responsible for their management, but to bring them under the supervision of agents of the people and compel them to give public account of all rates and to make the rates equal to all customers for similar services.

In a similar way the government has guarded the action of the national banks and promoted their honesty of management. When a business has grown so great as to pass the limits of a merely private enterprise, when it has gained the power to enrich or to ruin a whole community, then it may justly be required to publish its accounts, its rates, and all that concerns the public to know in order to protect stockholders and customers from imposition.

VIII. Forms of Income and Modes of Support. Rent and Interest. — A very brief and imperfect notice must be given to the rewards of capital, labor, and management. We have seen that capital is indispensable to modern society. But we cannot have accumulations of the means of production without a motive. Rent and interest are the premiums offered by society for the accumulation of the instruments of increasing wealth. If a man will watch the operation of motives in his own life, he will understand the meaning of rent and interest. It is not necessary to take the teaching on authority. Outside of the ordinary acts of friendly and neighborly accommodations in little things, men lend for a reward and save that they may secure the reward. If one lends the use of his farm, he wants it returned to him as good as he gave it into possession, and he wants something beside. The livery-stable keeper hires out a horse and carriage, and he keeps the horse and carriage for gain. It is his business. Those who do not wish to own or are not able to own, must pay for use to those who do have title and right. The full explanation of interest and rent does not belong here, but the social justification of both is found, and must be found, at last in the social usefulness of the system.

If a man owns a hundred horses and hires them out for riding, driving, or ploughing, he derives an income from ownership. If he sells these horses, and with the money buys a farm and rents it to one who has no land, he still enjoys an income from the same wealth. If he afterwards sells the farm and buys bonds or notes, he draws interest. So that, from the standpoint of society, rent, interest, and "hire" belong to the same class. They are all sources of income without direct and important effort. They are often called unjust, and many proposals have been made to declare them illegal, especially in the case of interest. But not without an absolute and radical revolution of modern ideas of business justice and expediency can such a crusade be successful. Usury laws generally raise the rate of interest, because they force the poor to borrow of the most unscrupulous lenders, who will take the risk and charge heavily for it.

Profits. — While this word is ordinarily used to cover all that is left to a business man after expenses and wages have been paid, it is convenient to separate the element of interest on capital from the other sources of the gains of a business manager. Indeed, a business manager may borrow all his capital and pay interest on it, and yet make gains. Let us suppose that a manufacturer is using a capital of $100,000 invested in a mill, in wages, and in raw materials, and that all this is advanced by others. He pays for the interest on this sum $5000, at 5 per cent. But after paying interest and all other expenses, he has property at the end of the year worth $115,000. There is a gain of $10,000 above the payment for interest. Whence does this come? From management. That means that he has had such skill in buying, in directing the men, in economizing materials and machinery, in securing a sale for the product, and such good "luck," that he is richer by $10,000. If the owners of the capital get their $5000, and are secured, they gain all that they can expect at current rates of interest on well-secured loans. Can it be denied that the manager should be paid for his service? The only question asked by competent critics is whether he gets too much for his service; for all confess that he should be well paid. If he makes no gain, he gets nothing for his labor and skill, although interest and wages have been paid, and those who furnished the materials have their pay. There is the risk of the manager, and he should have pay for that.

Wages. — Another form of income very familiar to all is wages, the reward of the operative, the laborer for hire. The wage-earner makes a contract with the employer for a specified sum to be paid as the work goes on, by hour or day, or week or year; or he may contract to be paid by the piece, according to the actual amount of work done. While the modes of agreement vary considerably, the principle is the same throughout.

The wage-earner also has his risks, and they are serious. If rain falls, he may be obliged to stop work and lose time. If he is sick, his income stops. If the market is glutted and the factory is closed, he loses his income. We hear of the "risks" of capital and managers, but sometimes the risks of labor are overlooked. Frequently the wage-earner suffers from the mistakes of business men, from the general causes of depression for which he has no responsibility. It is not true that laborers are to blame for being poor when these causes of non-employment are at work far beyond their power to control.

Charitable gifts are also forms of income of considerable significance. Many thousands of persons in every civilized land are supported, partly or entirely, by private gifts or public relief funds.

IX. The Income of the Government. — In the chapter on government we shall see the social service of the political system; and here we stop to notice the relation of government to industry and to wealth.

It is manifest that government cannot be carried on without income. Officers must be paid salaries, and expense is incurred at every point in the activity of armies, navies, courts, police, schools, signal-service, and of all the institutions through which the state ministers to social wants.

Income may be derived, in a subordinate way, from gifts, bequests, endowments, and sale of wild lands; but the main source of income, and the only one on which we can rely, is taxation.

X. The Limits of Economic Study. — The very useful and noble science of political economy, in order to pursue particular topics with great thoroughness, must confine itself within certain limits. This is to the credit of its students and teachers. It is merely an example of the advantages of division of labor in the intellectual sphere.

Political economy assumes the formation and organization of society as outlined in sociology. It assumes the existence of a government and of laws which will protect men in the free pursuits of objects regarded by them as desirable. It assumes that men will not defend their property by private warfare, but will refer disputes to regular tribunals. It assumes that education has advanced far enough to make communication between large numbers of men practicable. Moral and religious influences regulative of conduct, a high degree of tolerance of differences, are also supposed to be existing. All the explanations of economics are based on these social institutions and on the whole system of which they are parts. The function of economics is to describe and explain the affairs of business which have been mentioned and illustrated in this chapter

But it is highly desirable that all students should see just how this discipline is related to the entire structure and life of society at large. On this point, it may be best to let economists of highest authority speak for the sociologist. While there are some political economists who would not agree with the definitions and statements now to be given, it will not be disputed that the view here presented has high authority, and is in itself reasonable. If any one thinks that the province of economics is large enough to include sociology we shall not object; only it would seem best in that case to enlarge the name of economics and call it by some title equivalent to sociology.

" Economics must be constantly regarded as forming only one department of the larger science of Sociology, in vital connection with its other departments, and with the moral synthesis which is the crown of the whole intellectual system. . . . The economic phenomena of society cannot be isolated, except provisionally, from the rest, — in fact, all the primary social elements should be habitually regarded with respect to their mutual dependence and reciprocal actions. Especially must we keep in view the high moral issues to which the economic movement is subservient, and in the absence of which it could never in any great degree attract the interest or fix the attention either of eminent thinkers or of right-minded men. The individual point of view will have to be subordinated to the social; each agent will have to be regarded as an organ of the society to which he belongs and of the larger society of the race. The consideration of interests, as George Eliot has well said, must give place to that of functions. The old doctrine of right, which lay at the basis of the system of ' natural liberty,' has done its temporary work; a doctrine of duty will have to be substituted, fixing on positive grounds the nature of the social coöperation of each class and each member of the community, and the rules which must regulate its just and beneficial exercise. . . .

" It will be seen that our principal conclusion respecting economic action harmonizes with that relating to the theoretic study of economic phenomena. For, as we held that the latter could not be successfully pursued except as a duly subordinated branch of the wider science of Sociology, so in practical human affairs we believe that no partial synthesis is possible, but that an economic reorganization of society implies a universal renovation, intellectual and moral no less than material. The industrial reformation for which western Europe groans and travails, and the advent of which is indicated by so many symptoms (though it will come only as the fruit of faithful and sustained effort), will be no isolated fact, but will form part of an applied art of life, modifying our whole environment, affecting our whole culture, and regulating our whole conduct, — in a word, directing all our resources to the one great end of the conservation and development of Humanity." [1]

" Political Economy, or Economics, is the name of that body of knowledge which relates to wealth. Political Economy has to do with no other subject, whatsoever, than wealth. Especially should the student of economics take care not to allow any purely political, ethical, or social consideration to influence him in his investigations. All that he has, as an

[1] J. K. Ingram, *A History of Political Economy*, pp. 242–246.

economist, to do is to find out how wealth is produced, exchanged, distributed, and consumed. It will remain for the social philosopher, the moralist, or the statesman, to decide how far the pursuit of wealth, according to the laws discovered by the economist, should be subordinated to other, let us say, higher, considerations. The more strictly the several branches of inquiry are kept apart, the better it will be for each and for all. . . . The economist may also be a social philosopher, a moralist, or a statesman, just as the mathematician may also be a chemist or a mechanician; but not, on that account, should the several subjects be confounded. . . . Political Economy is the science, not of welfare, but of wealth. There may be many things which are better than wealth, which are not yet to be called wealth." [1]

[1] F. A. Walker, *Political Economy*, pp. 1, 6, 28. Cf. Boehm-Bawerk, *Capital and Interest*, p. 2; Professor J. L. Laughlin, ed. of Mill's *Principles of Political Economy*, III, pp. 200, and 523; Davenport, *Elementary Economics*, p. 24.

CHAPTER VIII

Tendency toward Economic Betterment

" Well, whiles I am a beggar, I will rail,
  And say, — there is no sin, but to be rich;
  And being rich, my virtue then shall be,
  To say — there is no vice but begging."

  The logic of this sad cynicism leads to the resolve : —
  " Gain, be my lord, for I will worship thee."
                                        — SHAKESPEARE, *King John.*

  "The property owner who employs his time in correcting the mistakes
and raising the methods of work in his district, does as much good as the
best of doctors. If one relieves the sufferings of a few men, the other helps
to cure the wounds of his country." — BALZAC, *The Country Doctor.*

Is this a dark world? It is often dark at night. Is it a
bright world? It is bright when the sun shines. No one
formula will cover all the facts, for life is a tangled maze. If
we would be true we must not be in haste to define and describe. As George Eliot said, the truth may be neither black
nor white, but some shade of gray, and it is truth we seek.
A short walk will take us past the abodes of misery and destitution and the mansions of luxury. Contrasts vex and depress
us. When the great Ferris wheel is turning, some of the passengers are going up and some are going down — a parable of
the great world.

      " Will Fortune never come with both hands full,
        But write her fair words still in the foulest letters?
        She either gives a stomach, and no food;
        Such are the poor, in health; or else a feast,
        And takes away the stomach; such are the rich
        That have abundance but enjoy it not."
                                        —*King Henry IV,* IV, iii.

Let us not attempt just now to answer the question whether mankind, as a whole, is advancing or going backward. It will be wiser to confine our attention to civilized lands, and particularly to the United States. If it can be shown that the path of betterment has been found here, then it may be followed by other peoples in their turn, for we trust that we are marching in the foremost files of time. We boast that we are carrying the flag of progress for the race. At least, we can test for ourselves the dolorous theories of despair, and facts of social life are here most accessible to us. In this discussion the assertions which are made, and on good faith as to their substantial correctness, may be verified by the reader out of official sources and from high authorities. Absolute infallibility is not claimed.[1]

I. The Definition of Social Progress viewed from the Economic Side. — Some one started the saying "The rich are growing richer, and the poor are growing poorer." Is that true, or is it just a fine-sounding phrase?

What do we mean by "industrial progress"? Until we define the word "progress" we cannot properly argue about it. Economic progress implies the increase of wealth in the countries we are now considering. It means that every year there is a larger production of the good things of life. It means that these goods can be more easily and promptly delivered at the place where they are wanted and at the right time. As to the division of these good things, it means that the majority of the population are receiving higher wages and salaries, greater money income; that commodities are cheaper as measured in money, and that the dollars received for service will buy more desirable things and of better quality than the dollars of our fathers could buy. Progress means the enlargement of the "comfortable" class of citizens.

Industrial advance ought to mean that the goods produced

---

[1] The author begs the reader not to judge this chapter by itself, but to suspend verdict until the Chapters IX and X are read. The bright side is first presented, and then the exceptions, objections, miseries, and difficulties are considered. The three chapters together constitute one presentation. Differing views are referred to ; and objections to authorities are pointed out. The intention is, without concealing the author's own conviction, to deal fairly by others.

are made in fewer hours of painful toil, so that more leisure is left for living after the livelihood is won by labor. And if the amount of dirty, unpleasant work is diminished, and the clean, pleasant labor is increased, all the more satisfactory is the situation.

But the social student will go further and inquire what effect these changes in industry and business are having on the well-being of the workers. For if wealth is increasing while man decays, it is a sorry outlook. Wealth is for man, and not man for wealth. The final test of our system will be its influence on the physical and spiritual nature of man, the Social Member. Industrial progress, therefore, must signify longer life of the workers, better health, more abounding vitality, surplus energy for recreation, amusement, and education. While the defects in character may not all be due to defects in factory and trade, yet we should be suspicious of our industrial order if it could be shown to increase the moral degradation of men. Hence the statistics of pauperism, crime, illiteracy, use of libraries, newspapers, musical and other artistic agencies must be considered.

All these factors and others must be included in our idea of economic progress, and not merely one or two of them. Wealth must be translated into well-being of the many, or it is not social wealth, national wealth, but only class wealth.

II. Evidence of Economic Progress in the Sense Defined. — We have to prove that the sum of wealth has increased since the present industrial system began its march, early in this century, that a greater number, absolutely and relatively, enjoy this increase, and that this multitude has made good use of this larger fund of resources.

We must at once notice that it is not proposed to show that this progress has cost nothing, that many have not suffered, that no wrong has been done, that all has been just as kind and fair as it might have been. No one but a crazy optimist would attempt to demonstrate such a wild proposition as that. Our venture is more modest, and it is confined to the evidence of the assertion that, through great conflict and trial, toil and pain, with much injustice and many blunders, the great majority of the population of civilized lands have made progress in the possession and enjoyment of the resources of the best existence; that we are on the right track, moving in the right direction. It is true we must still, as pilots of the ships, remain on watch, and be alert to avoid shoals and rocks.

The Annual Production of the Wealth has been vastly increased in the Present Century, and Great Improvements may be expected. — This fact is so seldom disputed that a few illustrations will be sufficient.

"Taking the true valuation of the real and personal estate of this country for each decade, beginning with 1850, we find that the total wealth was: —

> In 1850, $7,135,780,228, or $308 per head.
> In 1860, $16,159,616,068, or $514 per head.
> In 1870, $30,068,518,507, or $780 per head.
> In 1880, $43,642,000,000, or $870 per head.
> In 1890, $65,037,091,197, or $1036 per head.[1]

Wealth is three times what it was in the fifties." These figures are by no means exact, but they illustrate the upward movement.

Steam power has increased in the United States from three and one-half millions, in 1860, to seventeen millions horse-power, in 1895; Great Britain and Ireland from two and one-half to thirteen millions; Germany from seven-eighths to seven and two-thirds millions; and France from one and one-sixth to five millions horse-power.[2]

The increase of productive power has been most manifest in manufactures.

"The first complete census of manufactures was that of 1850, and the returns for 1890 show that they increased in value ninefold in forty years; in the same period the number of operatives multiplied only fivefold, one operative now producing nearly as much as two did in 1850."[3]

Manufactures in our country are moving westward and southward. In 1850, New England represented 28 per cent of manufactures, but in 1890 only one-sixth.

---

[1] C. D. Wright, *Atlantic Monthly*, September, 1897, p. 302.

[2] Mulhall, *Industries and Wealth of Nations*, p. 379; W. T. Harris, *Forum*, October, 1897.

[3] Mulhall, *Industries and Wealth of Nations*, p. 292.

The daily earnings per inhabitant increased as follows: —

		Cts.	Cts.
United Kingdom	. . . . . .	1860, 43.8 to	49.3 in 1894–95.
France	. . . .	1860, 32.0 to	42.0 in 1894–95.
Germany	. . . .	1866, 25.6 to	34.2 in 1894–95.
United States	. . . .	1860, 38.6 to	58.8 in 1894–95.
Russia	. . . .	1864, 10.9 to	12.6 in 1894–95.
Austria	. . . .	1869, 19.6 to	21.7 in 1894–95.
Spain	. . . .	1860, 18.5 to	20.6 in 1894–95.
Italy	. . . .	1860, 16.3 to	18.6 in 1894–95.[1]

Of the increase in agricultural production in the United States, the distinguished English authority says: "The growth of American agriculture in the half century has been unparalleled in any age or nation, the production of grain showing as follows: —

	Wheat. (Tons.)	Maize. (Tons.)	Oats, Etc. (Tons.)	Total. (Tons.)
1840	2,100,000	9,500,000	3,800,000	15,400,000
1895	11,700,000	53,800,000	23,900,000	89,400,000

"The grain crop of 1895 was equal to eight tons per hand employed in farming, the average in Europe being two tons: the superiority of the American agriculturist is due to improved machinery. Nevertheless, all parts of the Union have a deficit of grain, except the Western states; but for the surplus crops from those prairies it would be necessary to import eight million tons yearly for the food of men and animals."

"There has been such an improvement of agricultural machinery in late years, that the area of cultivation per farming hand rose from 32 acres in 1870 to 37 in 1880." The value in money of agricultural products rose from $866,000,-000 in 1840 to $3,903,000,000, in 1893.

Absolutely and *relatively* the *number of persons who enjoy the increase of income has steadily grown.*

That there are vastly more people in the civilized world than there were one hundred years ago is familiar to all. The population of Europe has doubled during the last one hundred years. In 1801, the number of inhabitants was estimated at 175 millions, and in 1891 at 357 millions. The

---

[1] W. T. Harris, *Forum*, October, 1897, p. 197.

population of the United States increased from 3,929,214 in 1790 to 62,622,250 in 1890.[1]

While this fact is generally known, its full significance is seldom realized. With the social arrangements, the tools, and machinery, the modes of transportation and business of the last century, modern lands could not support the present number of inhabitants. The very existence of so many people proves that our economic arrangements are improving. If deep misery were really, and on the whole, increasing, as some boding prophets of calamity profess, this fact of increasing population could not be explained, for misery kills. In the seventeenth century men said that the land of England was full, and could not support the much smaller population of that age. If methods of industry and business had not been made vastly better, famine, pestilence, and war would be necessary to keep down numbers even with the output of productive agencies.

The *number and ratio of bread-winners is increasing in our country.*

"In 1870 there were 12,505,923 persons engaged in supporting themselves and the remainder of the people; that is to say, 32.43 per cent of the total population were so engaged. In 1880 the number of bread-winners was 17,392,099, or 34.67 per cent of the total population. In 1890 this number had risen to 22,735,661, or 36.31 per cent of the total population. By 'bread-winners' is meant all who are engaged either as wage-earners, or salary-receivers, or proprietors of whatever grade or description, and all professional persons — in fact, every one who was in any way employed in any gainful pursuit. The figures show that the proportion of the total population thus employed is constantly increasing."[2]

This means, in part, that many occupations have been created by specialization of industry, by multiplication of wants, by the invention and display of articles of convenience, luxury, and beauty. It also means that more than four hundred modes of earning an honest living are now open to women instead of a dozen or more to which they were shut up early in the cen-

[1] Mayo-Smith, *Statistics and Sociology*, p. 368.
[2] C. D. Wright, *Atlantic Monthly*, September, 1897, p. 303.

tury. If it be true that women are doing work which men once did, it is just as true that they are busy with the creation of values which would not exist if men had all the work to do. It must be admitted that little children have been improperly employed by the machine industry; but the evils of that custom can be regulated by factory laws, as is done in older manufacturing countries.

The Average Rate of Wages and of Annual Income for Wage-earners is increasing in this Country. — One of the chief sources of information on this subject is the report of Senator Aldrich, of the Senate Committee on Finance, submitted in March, 1893.[1] The following conclusion has been drawn by Mr. C. D. Wright from the facts gathered in that report.

The report gives the course of wholesale prices and of wages from 1840 to 1891, inclusive, a period of 52 years. It deals with seventeen great branches of industry, and they are the principal ones in the country. By it we find that, taking 1860 as the standard at 100, rates of wages rose from 87.7 in 1840 to 160.7 in 1891; that is, an increase of 60.7 per cent from 1860 and of 73 per cent from 1840. Taking an average according to the importance of the industries, it is found that the gain from 1840 to 1891 was 86 per cent.

Census reports show aggregate earnings, and also the number of persons among whom the earnings are divided. In 1850 the average annual earnings of each employee engaged in manufacturing and mechanical pursuits, including men, women, and children, in round numbers, were $247; in 1860, $289; in 1870, $302; in 1880, $347; in 1890, $445.

"These statements for the United States can be supplemented by the figures for the state of Massachusetts. By the report of the Massachusetts Bureau of Statistics of Labor on the annual statistics of manufactures (1895), it is found that for 2427 establishments in 1885 and in 1895, wages were reported which, divided among their employees, amounted to $361.62 in 1885 and to $418.99 in 1895."[2]

[1] This report has been much criticised and charged with partisanship. Some of the criticisms seem just, and the darker facts are occasionally concealed. But this report, as to the main results, agrees with the other authorities used, — English, French, and American.

[2] C. D. Wright, article cited.

It is desirable to correct a wild notion, which seems to be popular, that if the wealth and product of industry were equally divided, on some communistic scheme, that every man might roll in luxury. Nature is not so liberal as that, and with all our improvements in machinery we cannot produce riches by magic. If we take into account all forms of income in this country,— agricultural, mining, transportation, manufacturing,— it comes to $11,751,728,858, or $1.5432 per person each day, or $10.80 per week. Any one who receives $11 a week has more than his share. If this calculation of Dr. Harris is correct, each wage-earner now receives very nearly all that it is possible on the average to divide among so many. Mr. Edward Atkinson has made similar calculations, with practically the same result.

The eminent Socialist, Mr. Sidney Webb, agrees with these hopeful writers in the main result, so far as England is concerned. "There can be no doubt that the incomes of the English wage-earners have, on the whole, risen ; prices of commodities have fallen; and the general prosperity of the country has greatly increased." [1]

If we turn from income to possessions which represent savings and accumulation, we have other cheering evidence that the distribution of wealth is approaching a better basis. Taking illustrations from Great Britain, whose experience is always instructive for us: "The ratio of persons (in the United Kingdom) above want rises steadily, in spite of the congestion of wealth. The following table shows the relative progress of population and of estates over £100 since 1840 : —

	1840	1877	1893
Population	100	126	146
Estates over £100	100	205	251

"Thus in 53 years population has risen 46 per cent, and in number of persons who left estates of more than £100 at their death, 151 per cent; in other words, the class of society which · may be considered above reach of want has grown since 1840 three times faster than the general population" (Mulhall, *Industries and Wealth of Nations*, p. 109).

[1] *Industrial Democracy*, II, 636; *Labor in the Longest Reign*, London, 1897; T. H. E. Escott, *Social Transformations of the Victorian Age*, 1897.

In the statistics of savings banks we find another sign of improving conditions. In the United Kingdom "the improved condition of the working classes is evident from the increased number of depositors in savings banks; it was less than 4 per cent of the population in 1850, and it has now arisen to 19 per cent."[1]

Mr. C. D. Wright is authority for saying of the United States that the total deposits at the present time in the savings banks of this country are about two billion dollars, one-half of which belongs to wage-earners.[2]

For the United States,

> In 1840 the amount due each depositor was $178.
> In 1850 the amount due each depositor was $172.
> In 1860 the amount due each depositor was $215.
> In 1870 the amount due each depositor was $337.
> In 1880 the amount due each depositor was $350.
> In 1890 the amount due each depositor was $358.
> In 1893 the amount due each depositor was $369.
> In 1896 the amount due each depositor was $376.

The Dollars of the Present will buy More Goods than the Dollars of Our Fathers. — Money has a greater purchasing power, because the articles of constant use can be bought more cheaply. It is true that some commodities cost more than they did formerly; but then they are better in quality, and the additional price is more than offset by the cheapening of manufactured and imported wares.

Here, again, we may sum up the evidence of statistics in the words of Mr. C. D. Wright: "If prices decrease or remain stationary, the increase in the rate of wages is a positive gain. Taking all articles on a wholesale basis, and as compared with the standard of 1860, the prices of 223 articles were 7.8 per cent lower in 1891 than in 1860, and taking 1840 as the standard, with 85 articles the difference was 3.7 per cent.

"Examining prices of articles on the basis of consumption, leaving rent out of consideration, the cost of living is shown to have been between 4 and 5 per cent less than in 1860; and taking all prices, rents, and everything into consideration, it

---

[1] Mulhall, *op. cit.*, p. 101.
[2] Reports of Massachusetts Bureau of Statistics of Labor, 1873-1874.

must be concluded that living was not much, if any, higher in 1891 than it was in 1840, while the rates of wages had increased as stated." [1]

Owing to the superior methods of production and the higher rate of income the articles of consumption and enjoyment are of better quality. The people, on the average, enjoy more of the good things of life than their fathers.

Who has not listened to some old pioneer reciting, with that pleasure which only the remembrance of conquered difficulties can give, the story of early privations? Land was free in those early days, and any one could have all he would take and till, for it had no commercial value. But life was hard, and the means of enjoyment were meagre. The cloth was coarse and made by hand. Those were the days when man possessed all he produced, and did not divide with a capitalist. But all he produced was a miserable sum of goods.

MacMaster, in his History of the United States, has given us many details of the modes of living in 1784 in the United States. "The tomato was not only uncultivated, but almost unknown. Apples and pears were to be had in abundance, but none of those exquisite varieties, the result of long and assiduous nursing, grafting, and transplanting, which are now to be had of every green-grocer. The raspberries and strawberries were such as grew wild on the hills, and the best of them could bear comparison neither in flavor nor in size with the poorest that are often to be seen at county fairs. Oranges and bananas were the luxury of the rich, and were, with all the tropical fruits, rarely seen; for few packets could then make the voyage from the West Indies under several weeks. Since that day our dinner-tables have been enriched by the cauliflower and the egg-plant. No great companies existed as yet for the distribution of ice. This article, since come to be regarded as much a necessity of life as meat and bread, and which, in ten thousand ways, administers to our comfort and promotes our health, was almost, if not quite, unused. The coolest water the tavern could afford came from the town pump. Every thunder-storm curdled the milk. The butter was kept in the dampest and coolest nook

[1] Article cited.

of the cellar, or hung in pails down the well." The newspapers were small, printed on inferior paper, and gave scant information. "Few came oftener than thrice in a week, or numbered more than four small pages. The amount of reading matter which the whole forty-three contained each week would not be sufficient to fill ten pages of ten daily issues of the *New York Herald*."

The Larger Income of Wage-workers has been earned in Days of Shorter Hours. — A few generations ago our ancestors in this country worked nearly all their waking time, and lived to work rather than worked to live. Severe toil, with poor tools, was the universal lot. Children were fortunate in frontier life if they could go to school a few weeks in the year, and they were expected to share the labor of the parents from the earliest possible moment. Abraham Lincoln was a type of his class and time, and he gained his education in the intervals of exhausting labor. "Between 1840 and 1891 the hours of labor have been reduced 1.4 hours in the daily average. In some industries the reduction of hours has been much greater, while in others it has been less" (C. D. Wright).

The Forms of Labor are Higher. — Much of the most dangerous and disagreeable labor has been taken up by machinery and various mechanical devices. The number of unskilled laborers is decreasing, and the number engaged in tasks requiring more intelligence is increasing. The inventions connected with plumbing and sewage have taken away some of the most disagreeable tasks in household life. Ditch digging, one of the most trying of occupations, has been greatly facilitated by machinery unknown in former times. The appliances for lifting and stowing away hay in lofts have come as a deliverance from hours of hot and dusty and stifling labor. In all modern manufacturing states the laws require the introduction of devices for removing dust and fumes from the workshops, much to the advantage of the health of the toilers. As the laws placing the liability for accidents and injuries upon the managers improve, the business itself will at last, as is already true in Germany, carry the insurance risk, and the consequence will be that employers will provide the best inventions to reduce the causes of injury of all kinds.

Many of the most disagreeable industries of the home are now made comparatively pleasant by the use of machinery in factories. Thus soap-making is no longer a general household industry, and the residence is certainly more comfortable for the change. Candles are made by machinery. Fruit is canned on a wholesale scale. The public laundry, with its rapid and effective methods, is gradually driving the ill-smelling and unhealthy wash-day terror out of the home. Even the washing of dishes promises to be handed over to some modern gnome of a machine.

If we divide the persons engaged in gainful employments into four classes, — proprietors, salaried men of fair income, skilled artisans, and unskilled laborers,— we find that the number of the first class rose from 10.7 per cent of the whole population in 1870 to 11.22 per cent in 1890; that members of the second class were 0.91 per cent of the whole population in 1870, and has risen to be 2.15 per cent in 1890; that members of the third class were 6.59 per cent in 1870 and 8.75 per cent in 1890. But during the same period the members of the lowest class fell in numbers from 14.76 per cent in 1870 to 13.44 per cent in 1890 (C. D. Wright).

Employment for Capable Workers seems to be relatively more Certain than at an Earlier Period. — It is true that severe vicissitudes have been experienced at the introduction of some new invention and in years of depression and financial uncertainty. It is also true that there is always a large number of persons "unemployed," although this vague term needs a good deal of definition. Many are forever out of employment because they choose to live on charity or theft; others because they have never been taught to do anything that is wanted done; so that a great part of the army of the "unemployed" could not be used in the best of times without some training. But if the foregoing argument is approximately sound, then the deduction is fair that work for the capable and willing is more certain than it formerly could be. "Rates cannot be increased if industrial conditions are degenerating, nor can they be increased or sustained in the presence of a very large body of unemployed really seeking employment. If, therefore, rates constantly increase,— and they have increased steadily in the economic history of this country,— the conclusion is inevitable that conditions themselves have improved" (C. D. Wright).

The Wage-workers have Improved in Health. — They live longer and they lose fewer days through illness. They have higher vitality, and presumably more physical capacity for enjoyment.

It seems that, owing to sanitary progress, the rate of mortality was so reduced from 1838–54 to 1871–80 that in the latter period the gain in years of life in England and Wales was 2,000,000 years of life. That means that a much larger number of the people lived to become producers of wealth, that there was less loss of time, that suffering was diminished and happiness increased. The expectation of life at birth increased for males 1.44 years and for females 2.77 years, between 1838 and 1881.[1]

The Wage-earners of Civilized Lands have, on the Whole, improved in Intelligence. — In 1885, in Massachusetts, only 6.12 per cent of the population could neither read nor write, and 88 per cent of these were foreign-born. In England the illiterates who could not sign their marriage registration were, in 1843, 32.7 per cent males and 49.0 per cent females; but in 1873, schools had so improved conditions that only 18.8 per cent of males and 25.4 per cent of females failed under this test.[2]

A woman who uses a sewing-machine employs more intelligence in her task than a woman who worked with a simple tool like a needle. A locomotive engineer exercises more intelligence than the coach driver whom he displaced. Machinery, by enabling men to do far more work in fewer hours, has redeemed time for reading, and the immense circulation of newspapers shows that readers have increased enormously. In some occupations less intelligence is demanded in the lower and more mechanical processes, but even in these lines there is "more room at the top" for persons of quick minds.

The *æsthetic result* of the factory system is not at all satis-

---

[1] R. Mayo-Smith, *Statistics and Sociology*, p. 178.
[2] *Ibid*, p. 194.

factory. "It vulgarizes the product, it stultifies the workman, it deteriorates public taste; the very buildings in which its operations are performed, the emanations they emit, give added gloom to life."[1]

While this picture contains only too much truth, it is not the whole truth. The buildings in which the earlier hand-work was carried on, in the "good old times" of household industry, were not altogether sweet and tidy, and could not be. Nor is an ugly building essential to the factory system, as many of the factories of New England and the Pullman shops prove.[2]

The Workers are, on the Whole, improving in Character. — The pictures of immorality and debased conduct in England early in this century among working people are now almost incredible. Drunkenness was almost universal and a matter of course. It was common among the upper classes and copied out of respect for their position by all below them. The laborer aspired to be "drunk as a lord." But the use of fiery liquors has diminished in Great Britain and in this country. The drinking of beer has come to be more general, but actual brutal excess is nothing like as general as it once was.

The regularity of discipline required by the factory system and machinery is conducive to temperance and self-control. An old compositor quoted by Mr. Webb said: "I always observed that those trades who had settled wages, such as masons, wrights, painters, etc., and who were obliged to attend regularly at stated hours, were not so much addicted to day drinking as printers, bookbinders, tailors, shoemakers, and those tradesmen who generally were on piece work, and not so much restricted in regard to their attendance at work except when it was particularly wanted."[3]

The Wealth owned by the Community has vastly Increased. — If we consider the services rendered to all occupations without charge, as by the postal department, the signal-service, the lighthouses, the life-saving corps, the agricultural experiment stations, and by scores of other agencies, it becomes

[1] R. W. Cooke Taylor, *The Modern Factory System.*

[2] Pidgeon, *Old World Questions and New World Answers.*

[3] Webb, *Industrial Democracy,* I, 326; Ludlow and Jones, *Progress of the Working Classes,* pp. 1–25.

apparent that each sailor and mechanic, each carpenter and ploughman, enjoys the use, occasionally or continuously, of the riches and the organizations of the nation and state.

In municipal property and service this form of common wealth is literally brought home to us all. Year by year the park systems and the facilities for reaching them are extended. The poorest youth has near at hand a high school which is, in many respects, far in advance of the college of our grand-fathers, where instruction is given gratuitously to the children of the nation. Large libraries are furnished, and free reading rooms, so that the poorest man can have at his command a stock of books and a supply of periodicals which would be beyond the power of the millionnaire to buy and keep. Gradu-ally the costly pictures and other works of art are gathered by cities into museums and galleries accessible on certain days without fees for admission.

Let us imagine this kind of property extended, as it cer-tainly will be in the near future, and it will be seen that most of the beautiful and delightful things of existence will be fur-nished by the community, in addition to wages, in return for the labor which supplies the means of support and pleasure. It is not customary to count up wages in this way, but the real income of a workingman who uses public wealth must include these elements, for they are true factors of the sum total of reward for industry. They are not the gifts of charity, but the product of the toils of the people, and the more civil-ized we become, the more these higher and common forms of wealth will be multiplied and appreciated.

If a man has a park near his home, he will have less need of a large private yard. If he can borrow books from a public library, he will require only a few choice classics at home, and classics are very cheap. If he can daily visit the great galleries where walls are glorious with color, he need not be envious of the rich man who pays $40,000 for a single French painting. If the city furnishes a free concert in the public parks and halls, as it well may do, he will have no occasion to envy those who pay large sums for boxes at the opera. And when the city itself, in all its parts, becomes a grand work of exquisite art, as parts of central Paris are, the workmen may truly rejoice in the wealth which each citizen owns and helps to purchase.

The true measure of general welfare is not equality of wealth, nor even of income, but of enjoyment. Since the means of enjoyment owned by the entire community is constantly increasing, the real well-being of the people is more liberally served. With universal suffrage the matter is in the hands of the people; they can acquire for all just what the majority demands, through taxation, so long as taxation does not cripple capital engaged in industry.

But *are the wage-earners happier* than their ancestors who lived in hovels and shared mean huts with animals and looms? Who can tell whether people are happier or not? All we can attempt to prove is that they have the means for larger satisfaction and culture; but happiness cannot be reduced to statistical form. The census-taker can easily discover the number of paupers in the population, the number of illiterates, of criminals, of families having insufficient room, but he never seeks to discover the number of people who call themselves happy. In fact, the report for ten o'clock in the morning might require amendment by noon, when the workers are hungry. As there are no statistics on this subject, we abandon it to those who like to amuse themselves with conundrums. The measurement of the immeasurable belongs to those physiological psychologists who, it is said, having measured the time taken for its reactions by the physical apparatus of nerves, declare that they can now exactly report the height of a joy, the depth of a grief, the length of an idea of immortality, and the number of ounces in a weighty consideration.

III. Causes of Economic Progress. Causes of Increased Production and Accumulation of Wealth. — Knowledge of nature is power. The splendid growth of the physical sciences in this century has added to the resources of mankind during all coming ages, as well as our own. All beginnings of command over nature come from new knowledge of the forces of the material world, of water, wind, gas, ores, steam, electricity, heat, magnetism, light, and the mechanical principles which underlie the arts. It is in the laboratory of the chemist, physicist, mineralogist, and in the observatory of the astronomer, that the first gains are made. Only after the lover of pure truth has done his work, can the practical man harvest the crop of his sowing. The general public sees the brilliant and immediately useful invention of the mechanic; but it often forgets the years of obscure toil given without hope of reward or immediate practical service by the man of science.

The inventor follows the scientist and discovers the utility of the labors of the laboratory. Sometimes one person may unite in himself the two kinds of ability, that of discovery of general laws and that of useful application. Usually, the two forms of genius are not found in one person.

But neither scientist nor inventor can make a device practically useful to society, on a large scale, without the intervention of the business manager; and it is largely to the more perfect organization of the factory, the railroad, the bank, and the wholesale trade that increasing wealth and comfort are due. This organization is a very high form of intellectual work. It costs effort, and can be achieved only by men of rare and peculiar talent or genius. These managers have not seldom become rich by using the inventions of mechanics, not always giving a just recompense.

The great systems of transport, made possible by science, art, and business sagacity, have been a mighty factor in the multiplication of the material comforts of our age. To sanitary science and medical art are due the improved conditions of city and country life, the suppression of once destructive plagues, and the heightened vitality of the people of all occupations.

Political power has been gained by the wage-earners during this century in England, France, and Germany, and the share of control enjoyed by them has been used to enlarge privileges and securities without number. Legislation more and more tends to protect their rights, to enable them to help themselves, and to foster their enterprises. Government is no longer a mere night watchman, to control and repress; it has become the organ through which the people can produce wares, secure advantages, open parks, museums, and libraries, and make accessible all the means of intellectual and spiritual culture.

None of these gains would be possible without general intelligence; and therefore the multiplication and improvement in institutions of education must be counted as factors in forwarding the interests of wage-earners.

The culture of the higher life reacts upon the lower. Where there is general refinement, noble feeling, a spirit of fraternity, a devotion to religious ideals, there we have reason to expect security of property, a just regard for the rights of labor and of possession, and a diminished friction in the processes of industry. While there may be less churchly feeling than formerly, there is more of the principle and of the fruit of religion than ever before.

Causes of the Increase of the Share secured by the Wage-earner. — There is more to divide; that is the central reason. In a poor country, without machinery and free from the tyranny of capitalists and managers, all are poor together. Their chief luxury is that they have no one above them to blame or envy, for all are in the dust. In a rich country, the capable workers gain something and the managers gain still more, if they are successful.

The successful managers are competitors of each other for the best workers. Their capital lies idle, their machines rust away, their own talents are useless, without "hands." In order to secure helpers wages are offered, and the price goes up to a point where men are willing to work. The most intelligent manager, with the most perfect machinery and organization, can pay the highest rates, and he takes the first choice of wage-earners. Competition is the guaranty to the wage-earners that they are getting the market rate for service.

But the families of wage-earners are consumers, and all business men are competing with each other to gain their custom. Competition acts to secure the highest income to the workers and the lowest cost of the commodities they consume.

But competition is not the only fact: the interest of all competing capitalist managers is to get work done at as low a rate as possible; to employ children, for example, if they can thus run machines at less expense. Competition does not always work to correct abuses. To meet such cases social organization on the side of the wage-earners is demanded. The action of trade unions will be considered at a later point, and the help of legislation will also be mentioned.

The effect of increased efficiency of production is to enlarge the amount of products available to the laborer as a consumer. What does he do with this surplus? Four possibilities are open to any group of laborers. " (1) They may increase their numbers, making the average size of their families larger. (2) They may shorten the hours of labor. (3) They may enlarge their consumption of the products of other laborers. (4) They may save money; that is, they may waive the enjoyment of a part of their income and put it at the disposal of other members of the community, for the sake of a future return which they anticipate from such present abstinence" (Hadley, *Economics*).

IV. Objections to the Factory System. — Before we pass from this point, it is desirable to notice some of the complaints often heard against the methods of industrial organization employed under the modern capitalistic management and termed the "factory system."

Some of these objections are not altogether devoid of reason. There are evils incidental to earthly life under any circumstances, and there are some evils which attend the development of the particular form of industry under consideration.

The Displacement of Wage-earners and Loss of Employment by "Labor-saving" Machinery. — The workman who has lost his place because a machine has been introduced which does the work of four or even of fifty men, thinks that machinery is certain to take the place of human hands. It is so natural to judge the world by our own little brief experience. The fact is admitted that at one point, and for a limited time, machines do drive out men. But in doing this they give goods at less cost to the community, and the inconvenience to the workman is temporary, though it may be severe, and for persons without savings may be tragical.

But look at the whole range of facts. Where most machinery is used there are the best wages and the most rapid increase of the number of persons employed. The railroad did indeed make stage coaches useless, but they opened up an industry which now employs 826,620 men, and pays in wages and salaries annually $468,824,531.[1] And more wagons are necessary than ever before to bring goods to the stations.

Physical, Intellectual, and Moral Injury to the Laborer in Consequence of the Use of Machinery. — This criticism takes many forms. Sometimes it is claimed that machine workers are physically injured, and facts are given to prove the assertion. The monotony of certain processes is very great. In some occupations the dust, fumes, and deleterious materials hurt the workmen. But over against these defects it may be claimed that under the former system such perils were even greater than they are now; that so far as they can be corrected, the way is open by trade union and legislative action; and that the increased leisure gives a chance for variety of exercise which was not possible with hand work. Much ill health now charged to the factory arises from bad sanitary conditions in the tenements, and corrective means must be directed to that point. Health has improved under the factory system and in consequence of its introduction.

Industries carried on in homes cannot be so easily inspected as those exposed to public notice in great establishments. The worst sanitary conditions are not found in the mills and factories, but among the poor people who do work in their own miserable and narrow homes.

It is asserted that the machine industry degrades the intellectual life of the workmen. In many trades the educative value of the process is much higher than that of old simple industry. This method of specialization is the price paid for our progress, and workingmen, on the whole, are far more intelligent than their ancestors in similar grades of industry, and have far wider opportunities for enjoying the educational agencies of the age.

It is sometimes said that the factory debases moral character. But the statistics in France seem to indicate that men in machine industries are less addicted to drunkenness than those in other occupations, and this is probably true in the United States. Prostitution is not so general under factory conditions as in some other situations.

It is charged against the factory system that it *increases the*

[1] *Chicago Daily News Almanac*, p. 247.

employment of women and children, and robs them of home advantages. It is admitted that work which takes mothers away from home is a serious social evil, but the extent of it has often been exaggerated. The fact that women and girls, without the responsibilities of housekeeping, are employed may not be entirely ideal, but if they must work to help make a living, it is better that they should have the best machinery and be surrounded by good sanitary conditions, such as household industry can never afford.

So far as little children are concerned, their employment in factories must be prevented by factory legislation and by compulsory education acts. The suitable place for a child is in school; his present duty is to play, grow, and learn. The employment of infants is no essential part of the factory system.

Our grandmothers were by no means idle, and most of them toiled hard and long. Many of them died from the hardships. The difference is in favor of the modern factory girl, who has a purse of her own. Some express the fear that this independent purse will make girls unwilling to marry, and so the family will die out. Statistics do not support the fear. The factory girl is not compelled to take up the first vagabond who offers. She can afford to wait till the eligible person puts in his appearance. Her very independence places a premium on sobriety and morality in men. Cupid takes care of the rest; for factory girls spend much of their earnings making themselves pretty, as is natural and proper; and statistics show they soon find husbands.

In backward countries a larger proportion of women and children give their entire lives to toil than in capitalistic lands. The census reports show for our own country an increasing proportion of men engaged in manufactures, a nearly stationary proportion of women, and an actually decreasing proportion of children.

"*But the rich are growing richer, and that of itself is enough to condemn the modern system of industry and business.*" — This is an objection hard to answer because it is based on a fact and is uttered very frequently in a state of mind which does not admit argument.

M

Take the state of mind first. If we assume without argument that inequality of riches is itself bad and dangerous, then the working of our social system is vicious, for not only are there great inequalities, but the inequality is growing greater all the time. When this fact is published, there are always plenty of people to jump to the conclusion that the nation is in a bad way and that nothing short of a revolution will save us from ruin. It seems to do no good to these excited persons to show them that they are themselves growing richer. The bitter drop is, that some other persons are accumulating wealth still more rapidly. It is difficult to reason with envy. Almost as difficult is it to persuade the generous philanthropist who has adopted a theory of "liberty, fraternity, and equality," when he fixes emphasis on equality and forgets liberty. One may as well try to conduct a concert in a thunderstorm as to convince the good man whose conscience is chained to a prejudice.

But, assuming that we are dealing with persons who simply wish to know the truth, let us look calmly at some of the facts. "The rich are growing richer; many more people than formerly are growing rich" (C. D. Wright). "Nearly 80 per cent of the total wealth is held by one and one-half per cent of the adult population. The middle class stands for 11 per cent of the population, and holds 18 per cent of the wealth." The largest fortunes are increasing most rapidly. Such are the statements of Mr. Mulhall, although he does not tell us clearly how he reaches his results.[1]

Admitting the charge that the rich are growing richer, and even more rapidly than the rest of society — what of it? Are we thereby made poorer? Are we deprived of any comfort or enjoyment? May it not be worth considering whether this arrangement may not be, on the whole, better for us? All can see, and socialists especially insist, that production is best promoted by the concentration of capital.

The capitalist, as capitalist, does not eat and does not burn

---

[1] Mr. Spahr, in *The Distribution of Wealth in the United States*, has given figures based on various public records, and "estimates," and which emphasize this tendency. See the criticism of Mr. Spahr's method of reaching his results, in the *Pol. Sci. Quarterly*, 1897, Vol. XII, p. 395, by Professor R. Mayo-Smith.

capital, but invests it, pays wages and salaries, employs men, produces goods, acts as the trustee and agent of society for the conduct of its affairs. If rich men get more income, they serve more people and on a larger scale.

Why have these vast accumulations of productive wealth fallen into the hands of their present possessors? Is it not at least largely due to the fact that they are the most suitable persons for the business? The very fact that they have succeeded where others failed proves that they are the right persons. Could there be a better test? If there is a better test and one more just, has it ever been revealed? We are not now discussing the cases of clear stealing. There are rich thieves as well as poor. But to assume, without proof, that dishonesty, rascality, oppression, injustice, and utter want of conscience are the supreme qualifications for business success is monstrous. The business of the world is made possible by credit. Billions of dollars pass from hand to hand every year without more evidence than entries in books and promises to pay. These enterprises are spread over the world, from Siberia and China to San Francisco and London. The credit system is the grandest proof the world ever produced of integrity and its commerical value. The man who violates his trust is a pariah. The petty confidences of ordinary life have nothing to compare with the gigantic structure of commercial credit, a word which carries on its face the triumph of honesty in the great world of capitalist managers.

"There are two origins of very large fortunes.[1] First, the founders may have been persons of great ability to make combinations,—such combinations as reduce the cost of collection and distribution of goods. Combinations that do this save, first, to the producer, who can get more for his goods, and, second, to the consumer, who is saved something in the expense of procuring his food, clothing, fuel, etc., from the producer. This class of wealthy men helps society by reducing the number of middlemen and by managing more efficiently collection and distribution. The laying of a pipe-line

---

[1] There are two points of view to this question. Mr. Lloyd's *Wealth against Commonwealth*, and Mr. H. George, *Progress and Poverty*, may be consulted for the other side. *Encyclopedia of Social Reform*, Article " Wages."

from the oil regions in the West to the great commercial markets and centres of distribution on the Atlantic coast, for instance, saves immediately in the distribution of oil, rendering it possible for the producers to lower the cost of oil in the cities of the East to one-third its former price; at the same time it enables the oil company itself to amass large fortunes on the balance of saving reserved for the stockholders. Another example is furnished by the trunk railroads connecting the Atlantic with the Mississippi valley. Vast combinations of capital consolidate roads into through lines; and, by building extra tracks, using steel rails, larger engines, and better cars, the cost of freight, which, thirty years ago, was from three to four cents a mile, is reduced to one cent a mile per ton. The amount of money added to the fortunes of the capitalists by these combinations is enormous; but the amount of money added to the value of the Western farms, oil wells, mines, and house property by saving in the cost of transportation, is much larger than the amount that capital obtains for the combinations. Besides this, the consumers resident on the Atlantic coast, engaged in manufactures, the consumers of the agricultural products of the West, pay but one-third as much for transportation on the bread materials, the coal, and other items brought by railway, and thus share in the aggregate of saving made by the financiers who created, by the aid of capital, the combinations which decrease the cost of connecting producer and consumer." [1]

Speculation. — A more serious criticism of business leaders is directed against their speculation. It is popularly thought that a few men on the boards of trade in grain centres can send the price up and down and change the price of the necessities of life at their will. How far this is possible need not be argued here. The modern modes of exchange, on the testimony of the greatest economists, tend rather to even prices throughout the year than to make them extreme. If wheat and corn are to be supplied in right quantities, and at the places most needed, it is essential that there should be social machinery for purchase and distribution, and this machinery is a service to the world. A comparatively few men take the

[1] W. T. Harris.

largest risks of the uncertain future, and frequently gain immense riches out of the ventures. More frequently those who attempt the enterprise fail; and those who are foolish and wicked enough to trade from outside, in utter ignorance of the conditions of the world-market, suffer, as they ought to suffer, severely, for meddling in a most intricate business which they have not learned. Probably speculation, on the whole, does not raise the average prices for the people, because these prices are set by world-wide causes beyond the control of the most powerful merchants; and the influence of speculation is rather to steady and lower prices, and to prevent local famines.

Connected with the necessary and legitimate speculation of cities is a vast amount of sheer gambling. It is difficult, perhaps impossible, to distinguish this from ordinary trading. It is difficult to frame laws which will suppress this form of gambling without injuring honest commerce. There is much betting on the speed of Atlantic "liners," but no one ever proposed, as a cure for gambling, to fine captains of twin-screw propellers for breaking the record. It were a wicked action to fire grape-shot into a holiday multitude in order to kill a thief who was making his escape from a policeman. Ingratitude is one of the basest of vices, but no lawyer would try to frame a penal law against it. We must trust something to the growth of enlightened conscience, to the codes of professional honor, and to the natural penalties of anti-social conduct. For the more obvious violations of justice criminal statutes can be devised. The tares cannot be pulled up until the harvest, for fear of uprooting good wheat with them. We remember what happened to the tares when the gathering-time did come.

If any one thinks that the present chapter is too bright and hopeful to be true, and that it does not contain the whole story, let him observe carefully the limits of each proposition, and then read the following chapters as part of the same discussion. There is another side, and it is gloomy enough. Perhaps we should not dare to look upon it if we were not sustained by first fortifying our hope with the consideration of the tendencies which make for happiness. To this sombre picture we shall turn attention. But first we must consider the Social Movement, the conscious and coöperative effort of society on behalf of the masses of independent and self-supporting population. For the progress whose principal facts we have just summarized is the effect of many causes, among which are the deliberate and coöperative action of human beings.

CHAPTER IX

The Social Movement for Economical Betterment

"Behold, the tears of such as were oppressed, and they had no comforter; and on the side of their oppressors there was power; but they had no comforter. . . .

"Two are better than one; because they have a good reward for their labor.

"For if they fall, the one will lift up his fellow; but woe to him that is alone when he falleth, for he hath not another to help him up.

"Again, if two lie together, then they have heat; but how can one be warm alone?

"And if one prevail against him, two shall withstand him; and a three-fold cord is not quickly broken." — (Ecc. iv. 1, 9–12.)

> "Have ye founded your thrones and your altars, then,
>   On the bodies and souls of living men?
>   And think ye that building shall endure
>   Which shelters the noble and crushes the poor?
>
> "Then Christ sought out an artisan,
>   A low-browed, stunted, haggard man,
>   And a motherless girl, whose fingers thin
>   Pushed frcm her faintly want and sin.
>
> "These set he in the midst of them,
>   And as they drew back their garment-hem
>   For fear of defilement, ' Lo, here,' said he,
>   'The images ye have made of me.' "
>   — J. R. LOWELL, *A Parable.*

I. Definition of the Social Movement; Its Meaning and Typical Forms. — We are to consider at this point the conscious positive and organized efforts to enable the operative members in the population to secure an increasing share in the increasing goods of our civilization.

What is the "meaning" of the movement as thus limited? The meaning of the social movement is its end, the goal toward which social thought and action are tending. This end is not seen with equal clearness by all who are engaged in it; and, in fact, a social movement is a voyage of discovery even to the most far-seeing men. Columbus could look further than his ignorant crew, but he could not see across the ocean. He himself must travel to discover the new world. "The baby in the cradle cries, for reasons that he does not understand, and would not admit if they were explained to him. The instinct of mother and nurse finds out what kind of pain produces the cry. The social movement is to a considerable extent a spontaneous cry of pain and a spasmodic clutching for pleasure; the sources of the pain and pleasure are not known by the majority who make the demonstration. They are not altogether beyond analysis and explanation" (A. W. Small).

The unconscious workings of the human spirit propel a nation forward along a path never before trodden. Deep below conscious and reflective thought there seethe and ferment the dim aspirations, the inarticulate hungers, the unspoken cravings, of the growing soul of man. Some day a leader arises among them who puts into clear and impressive speech just what they mean, and they recognize and applaud. Discussion and interchange of views make the purpose still more clear; the merely accidental elements are dropped; the selfish factor is sifted out; the large human interest is defined, based on solid argument and presented to the entire community as a thing ready for adoption and action. The leader of insight is often a man of the literary class, a poet or essayist, as Coleridge, Macaulay, George Eliot, Dickens, Mrs. Browning; or a statesman from among the people, as Lincoln; or a philanthropist of large culture and sympathy, as the Earl of Shaftesbury; or an economist, like some of the great teachers of the "historical" and "socialistic" type in Germany and other countries; or one whom some polite people sneeringly call "demagogues" and "agitators," men who keep close to the wage-earning population and understand them. The "settlements" promise to furnish us persons of education who acquire this insight by residence among the struggling multitudes, as Miss Jane Addams, Canon Barnett, and a goodly company of others.

Professor R. T. Ely, who has studied the literature of the Labor Movement very patiently, thus defines it: —

"The labor movement in its broadest terms is the effort of men to live the lives of men. It is a systematic, organized struggle of the masses to obtain primarily more leisure and larger economic resources; but that is not by any means all, because the end and purpose of all is a richer existence for the toilers, and that with respect to mind, soul, and body. Half conscious though it be, the labor movement is a force pushing toward the attainment of the purpose of humanity; in other words, the end of the growth of mankind, — namely, the full and harmonious development in each individual of all human faculties — the faculties of working, perceiving, knowing, loving; the development, in short, of whatever capabilities of good there may be in man."

This statement need not be changed in a single word to express the purpose of education and the school. Indeed, the school, the church, the state, are simply various forms of one great movement of society, in which the "Labor Movement" is one current. The larger tendency would be fruitless without this factor.

The Social Movement is more than the Labor Movement as Professor Ely defines it, because almost all classes in the country are interested in the means of securing diffusion of the means of well-being by various modes of coöperation. Mere individual enterprise, severed from association, is less and less promising. Managers of trusts have shown us the true way to security, the path of concentration and combination. Their example is instructive.

"The social movement is thus more than a class movement. It includes among its active promoters people of all social strata, except perhaps the enormously rich, or the idle rich, and even these do not always oppose the tendencies that I am describing. The social movement is popular in the most inclusive sense, *i.e.*, it is made up of all sorts of people. Property is universally conservative, but in our day great property holders who on the whole sympathize with the main tendencies of the social movement are by no means rare. The social movement is thus not the inertia of the many slightly disturbed by the few, it is the momentum of the many, hardly restrained by all the arts that the few can contrive."[1]

[1] Professor A. W. Small, *Am. Jour. Sociology*, November, 1897.

If one member suffers, all suffer. Therefore the oppression of one class is an injury to all others, and most of all to the oppressor. It is better to suffer wrong than to do wrong; and there is no element in the community to which universal justice is so vital as the small class of the rich. It is not only necessary that they should be just, but that other men should believe that they are just. The smallest class is the most helpless. If the majority should ever come to have the conviction that our social system rests on falsehood and unfairness, the first to suffer would be those who are conspicuous for their wealth.

In still another sense the movement of which we are thinking is a social movement: it is more than a particular problem of a special science, as demography, statistics, economics, or jurisprudence. Attempts to ameliorate the conditions of life for the multitude must borrow knowledge from all these studies, must seek advice and help from practical leaders in industry, politics, and education, and even in practical arts; but the social movement must organize the thought of all these departments; must proceed not in sections but as one army; must unify the various theoretical considerations; and must move onward with each particular measure in its right place with reference to every other measure of contemporary life. It is this very fact, more than any other, which has created a demand for some such a study as sociology,— a demand which is made first in the interest of practical guidance, and then in the interest which always follows, the scientific desire for unity and completeness. We may dislike the title of the study, and we may rightly think that the achievements of the discipline up to date are very doubtful and scanty, but the human mind will most certainly proceed, now that it is started, with this bold enterprise. Nor is this systematic knowledge of society needed by the statesman alone, but by all citizens of influence. The state by no means covers all the sphere of the life of a citizen.

II. The Scope of the Social Movement. — The differentiation of a wage-supported class, distinguished from the employing class, in modern industry, is the primary occasion for our present study. The social question becomes acute first of all among the multitudes of factory hands, who are brought closely together in large establishments, and have an opportunity of comparing views and debating common interests and grievances. These men are congregated in manufacturing towns and cities. It is in these centres of crowded populations that a class opinion is formed, which seems natural and just to those who are in the circle, and often seems strange and even immoral among those who are not in touch with the wage-earning body.

The agricultural laborers in all modern countries have scarcely touched this movement as organized bodies with clearly defined policies. Aggregation and congregation precede discussion. Men who never meet are not able to clear up their ideas and shape a definite line of action. Very little attention is given to the wage-workers of the farms, because they have few organs for the publication of their wrongs and hopes. The members of this class are widely separated. Many of them are young men who expect, at least in this country, to become owners of land and employers of others, and therefore have not that feeling of separate class interest which is natural in factory hands, who never hope to become managers of business.

As the number of capitalist managers becomes relatively smaller, a growing number of the salaried classes discover that they have many interests in common with others who are excluded from a direct share in controlling the industry of the land. Clerks, salesmen, government servants, school teachers, and multitudes of others find out slowly that they are related to members of the operative class. They have no share in "profits," but must live mainly by regular earnings and from the income of property which brings a low rate of interest. Thus we see the cause of the organization of members of each profession on principles quite similar to those of the trade unions.

The professional and salaried classes have this in common with the humblest wage-workers, that the instruments of production, machinery, factories, and business, being under the control of the manager class, all other classes are, in great measure, at their mercy. The men who possess and direct the great establishments of manufacture and the systems of transportation constitute a relatively limited part of society at large. Over against the capitalist directors stand all the other members of society, as consumers. For certain purposes there is unity of interest between the wage-earners and the great majority of other citizens.

In the cities the vivid contrast between riches and moderate means is forced daily upon the attention. Even if the wealthy do not purposely display the signs of their power, it comes out in a thousand ways. The beautiful carriages drawn by richly caparisoned horses along the boulevards, the charming costumes of the women, the gay parties at the operas, the luxury of the pew-holders in fashionable churches, the reports of splendid interiors of mansions made beautiful by the gifted sons of art, the precious collections of fine bindings and gems and porcelain, visible only to the children of privilege, are but a few of the evidences of a good beyond the reach of the populace. This populace has eyes that see, ears that hear, and an instinct which demands that the good of a few become the possession of all. Liberty, suffrage, and social respect have widened their boundaries in modern times. Each man thinks the best things are coming his way. The hope excites his desire and makes it seem more reasonable.

It is not increasing poverty and depressing pauperism and desperate misery which incite social unrest and discontent, so much as it is the taste of better means of living. The poor are not growing poorer but richer, as we have proved, and they find it so agreeable that they naturally wish for more nectar of the same kind. Who will blame them? If they sometimes seem to desire more wages simply to consume it upon coarse pleasure, they have only too many examples among those who have succeeded in winning the financial prizes. It is permitted us to hope that the uplifting forces of education and culture will awaken higher aspirations and desires in all classes.

III. The Forms of the Social Movement. — In order to have any distinct conception of this vast and impressive social tendency, we must briefly notice the various combinations which enter into it, those of the wage-earning and salaried classes; those initiated by employers and corporations on behalf of their employees; those formed by the friendly agreements of managers and men; those sustained by the community at large; and the Utopian schemes which so largely influence both theory and action in all modern lands; and practical legal reforms. It will not be possible to go much beyond conditions as they exist in the United States, nor to give full details of organization even within these limits. The general citizen does not require to know all about the technical arrangements and functions of these organizations unless he wishes to take direct part in them; but he does need to understand their principles of action, their motives, and their programme. Each of these subjects has its own literature.

IV. Organizations of Wage-earners as Members of the Productive Force of Society; the Trade Unions. — These societies have already been introduced to us as part of the governing and regulative arrangements of industry. But they constitute so important a factor in the social movement, in the wider sense, and they have such a powerful influence on municipal and other political institutions, on local improvements, on education, and on the division of the product of industry among citizens, that we must here give the essential elements of their structure and policies. It ought to be remembered that trade unionism labors under peculiar difficulties in the United States. The trade union is an institution characteristic of manufacturing populations, and our country has been accustomed to the modes of thought peculiar to a population overwhelmingly agricultural. Our traditions belong to a social state, in which it was easily possible for men to get homes of their own, and to become owners of valuable lands simply by cutting down the trees or by ploughing the prairies. Much of the land given to the state colleges sold for ten or fifteen cents per acre. Obviously that time has passed away from this country forever. When the immigrant seeks a place, he finds it full. "Poor Pussy wants a corner," but each corner is occupied. Those who came first wonder why the later immigrants should think different thoughts or seek their welfare by different means. Thus trade unionism is misunderstood, because it is an adjustment to new situations.

Those who have always lived among the employing or professional classes have a difficulty in understanding the trade union, because they are likely to take the tone of feeling peculiar to employers.   Class prejudice blinds us all, especially if we are not trying to understand by sympathy and by investigation at first hand.

A further cause of misunderstanding is that the unions have at times caused or tolerated many acts of lawlessness and crime or of gross injustice.   In our cities the members of these bodies have come together from many nations.   They do not speak the same language, or they learn to speak English imperfectly and with difficulty.   There are large colonies of persons of foreign birth who never learn our tongue, and who are separated by race barriers from each other.   Therefore the movement is not yet as fully under discipline as it has come to be in the trades of old England.   With such an unorganized and untrained mass to deal with, it is natural to expect occasional acts of violence, though they are fewer and rarer than many suppose.

The uncertain state of labor laws in this country promotes unrest and uncertainty of action.   In a new state, where manufactures are just becoming important, the legislatures and the courts have no experience in dealing with the industrial problems, and law itself has not yet accurately defined the duties and the responsibilities of employees and their combinations.

We must add to all these facts another which is not creditable to us: we assume that the wage-earners know the law even when the government has taken no pains to inform them. Here is a just ground for a grievance, and it is a cause of lawless conduct.   The workman sometimes never knows of the existence of a rule of the legislature until a policeman strikes him.   It is natural that an untaught foreign laborer should come to think of the government simply as a mighty force owned and controlled by the master of the shop.   Until our educative machinery can diffuse a general knowledge of our law and of the beneficent aids of government, and until justice shall be gratuitous, this provocative of antagonism will rankle.

The trade union has come to stay.   It is fixed in the affections of wage-earners in all Christian lands; it is established in customs; it has at last fought its way to legal recognition;

and it has even gained a place in the plans, if not the affections, of the great employers of the world. Opposition now is chiefly secret and indirect.

What our modern industrial community needs is a just and intelligent estimate of the social value and place of the trade union; of its worth and possibilities in relation to universal welfare, and not merely as viewed by workmen and by employers through their particular class interests and prejudices. A frank recognition of the union, a cordial sympathy with its fair demands, and a rigid determination to hold it responsible to the law of the common good are much to be desired. A summary statement of the objects and methods of trade unions will assist in gaining this balanced and sober estimate, although important considerations must be omitted.

Statistics of Trade Unions. — The relative importance of these associations can be partly judged from the numbers of their members. There were in the United Kingdom about 1,114,440 in 1894. These men were members of about three principal organizations. In the United States the figures are less reliable and the numbers seem to be more fluctuating. In good times, when hopes of success rise, the numbers are larger, while in hard times it is more difficult to keep up payment of fees, and membership declines. It must be remembered that it is almost impossible for farm laborers to unite, because they are so widely scattered and communication between them is so difficult. In other cases, the wage-workers are afraid to join unions because their employers would discharge them if it were discovered. There is always a multitude of unskilled laborers in cities who are too ignorant to form unions or who have no particular trade which gives them common bonds of interest. Thus it happens, that of all wage-workers in the country only a minority are likely to be organized in this way. But a minority organized and compact, with a plain theory and a practical programme of action, is more powerful and influential than a disorganized multitude. It is the difference between a regular army and a crowd of rioters. It was estimated, in 1896, that the American Federation of Labor embraced 80 national labor organizations, about 7000 local bodies, and an aggregate membership of over 650,000. The

1903- ＊ 2,000,000

1378 Local Union
Cinais
280 Weekly + monthly papers published

Knights of Labor still hold many organizations, and have reported about 75,000 members.

The General Objects of Trade Unions. — Workingmen do not differ in any essential particular from other citizens. They naturally and properly wish to secure the highest possible income with which to buy the comforts of life for themselves and their families. They have their appetites and their ambitions, their affections and tastes. They desire their share of the product of industry and know that they have a right to it. The wage-earners belong to all grades of refinement and intelligence; some of them resemble certain richer neighbors in having coarse and low ambitions as others are under the influence of lofty ideals. They share with the communities, of which they form part, in the gradual elevation of nature which comes with universal education, free libraries, and better church life.

Trade unions have for their primary specific object the assurance of a good rate of wages, the highest it is possible to obtain. Just as the money-lender seeks the highest possible rate of interest, on good security, and as the managers seek the highest rate of profit, and as the professional man wishes to obtain the highest fees or salary that his gifts can command; so wage-earners naturally strive to make the best possible bargain in selling their labor, the use of their bodies in the productive process. If they do not take care of themselves, no other class of society will take pains to care for their interests. They have found this to be true; and trade unions are the means adopted to make good bargains. Of course they know that if they ask too much it cannot be paid, because employers will not and cannot long pay wages which cause the impairment of capital and certain bankruptcy.

It is a universal principle with the unions to insist on a standard rate of wages below which they shall not fall. The employer may pay more than this minimum, if he thinks it to his interest to do so, in order to keep workers of superior skill. There is no general opposition to unequal payments for varying services, although the very nature of machine and factory work tends to uniformity of rate. If the men permit the rate to fall below this minimum, they are threatened with "the adulteration of labor." Law does not permit a dealer to mix cheap materials with flour, or coffee, or sugar, and thus lower the quality of the mass. Why should society permit a custom of payment which tends to degrade the physical and moral quality of working people?

Another vital concern of working people is the length of the labor day. Every minute costs energy and may cause pain. With effort life flows out and atoms of the body are burned up. The manager, having expensive machinery and materials, is naturally disposed to make them produce as many hours as the men are willing to work. His bias favors long hours up to the limit of efficiency. The working people believe that if they give long hours it will not only disable them earlier in life, but will tend to lower their wages.

Another interest of wage-workers is security of health and proper appliances to protect them from dangerous machinery in shops and on railroads. The worker not only agrees in the labor contract to labor so many hours, but he also submits his body to all the perils of swift and dangerous wheels and cogs and bands. Thousands of men are poisoned, maimed, or killed. Combination to secure the introduction of fans, guards, and other means of protection is demanded by the situation, and is supported by humane and enlightened public opinion. Experience shows that employers, even where there is a law making them liable for injuries, are disposed to insure themselves with some company rather than to introduce appliances which cost money, far more than insurance premiums. The unions in such cases are compelled to go to legislatures for help.

Another specific object of trade unions is to avoid the tragic losses attending the sudden introduction of new inventions. In recent years the unions have not been open to the charge of opposing the use of better machinery. Educated mechanics have discovered a better way, especially where trade unionism has had a long trial and training. The unions make contracts with the employers so as to gain for themselves, in shorter hours and in reasonable wages, their share of the new benefits. Every new process at first tends to enrich the employer alone and to give him extra profits; while at a later

N

stage the general community receives the advantage in cheaper commodities. Meantime, the skilled workmen find that they have lost a trade which cost them years to learn. Their only capital is sunk and lost. They are too old to learn a new calling, and are ousted by young persons who easily learn to work the machines. In these transitions thousands of skilled men suffer as martyrs to progress, as victims of a change which increases the wealth of society. Reason teaches that it is their right and duty to see that the change shall not be their ruin. Therefore social opinion should justify them in sober and orderly attempts to protect themselves by favorable contracts. And it would seem only justice if society should, in some way, make good their loss by paying them some kind of indemnity for their abandoned capital in skill.

One of the most severe trials of the workingman is the uncertainty and irregularity of employment. He may at any moment be thrust out of the opportunity of earning his living by causes absolutely beyond his control. The discharge falls like lightning out of the clear sky. Frequently this uncertainty is artificially increased, especially in the lower kinds of occupations, by the competition of a reserve army of men who are given just enough work to keep them hanging around "waiting for a job." This mass of unskilled and incapable labor is the curse of the lower grades of industry in cities. Trade unions take measures to diminish this competition.

The Methods of the Unions. — In order to secure better wages, sanitary surroundings of shops, reasonable hours of service, and other elements of welfare, the unions must have a consistent working plan of action. They must hold together and act in concert, since the entire value of combination is lost, and the individual is left in his weakness to make pitiful terms with society alone, unless the union remains intact.

Benefit Funds. — It has been discovered that if a society can collect funds in small amounts during time of steady employment, available for assistance of members when they are sick or out of a place, that these funds serve to hold the members together. So long as there is plenty of work, those who meet with illness or are disabled by accident can receive aid from the common treasury. And when one of the men refuses to work for a wage below that demanded by the union he can be supported during his protest in order that he may not be forced by starvation to accept any terms that are offered him and so become a competitor of his comrades and help to break down their rate. The stronger unions annually expend vast sums of money to support members who cannot find employment, so that they really furnish insurance against non-employment, one of the most grievous causes of suffering in the modern industrial world. For this reason, among others, the members of old unions seldom appear on the list of recipients of alms, and trade unionism has come to be one of the chief bulwarks against pauperism. When a strike becomes necessary, this same fund is used to support the members while they are out of work; and one union will help another, which seems to be making a just and reasonable fight for better terms. As mere insurance societies, to provide for times of sickness or accident, the unions are not so good as mutual benefit organizations; but the supreme interest of workingmen is in holding up the rate of income on which all else depends. The possession of common stores of wealth is one of the bonds of the association.

Collective Bargaining. — The very centre of unionism is seen in their mode of marketing labor and service. In warfare the army would invite defeat if it should send one soldier at a time against the solid front of the enemy. The individual workman has nothing to offer in the market but his strength and skill. If a thousand workmen seek a place as competitors, the manager can dictate his own terms, and sad experience has shown the wage-earners that if one master is merciful, he will be forced by his rivals to drive hard bargains. The alternative of this divided action is a union offer of labor through representatives chosen by the entire body. This has been called "collective bargaining," and it is a method dear to the great multitude of wage-workers all over the civilized world. It is tardily coming to be accepted by employers, and the refusal to treat with accredited representatives is universally regarded as a deep insult and an attack on the rights of laboring men. The delegate speaks for all. And a slight put upon him rankles for years in the hearts of the men, even though circumstances compel them to conceal their sense of wrong.

Legislation. — Wage-workers are citizens and have the common right of all citizens to ask for the protection of their rights at the hands of government. They can claim even more than this, since government functions are extended to render service to all members of the state, wherever the common welfare can be best promoted by such action. Employers may be required to keep their workshops in a sanitary condition; may be forbidden to employ young children before they are mature in body and have enjoyed the opportunity of elementary education; may forbid the employment of girls and women at hours and places where they are exposed to insult or peril. It is to the interest of the entire community that the home shall not be broken up; that women shall not be compelled to leave their young children in order to labor in public factories. In order to supply the country with healthy, strong, efficient, and intelligent workmen, it is proper to employ law and administrative measures to do anything that will save the workers from degradation and raise the standard of living.

Legislation is of three types: mere protection, enabling acts, and positive public service of benefit to all citizens. An example of protective acts is the law which requires manufacturers to fence dangerous machinery where employees are likely to be caught and injured; the requirement that railroads shall introduce new forms of couplers to save railroad men from being crushed; the law that boys shall not be permitted to manage engines and boilers, at the risk of injuring themselves and their companions.

Examples of enabling acts are those laws which provide that men may form associations for their common benefit, so long as they do not violate the laws.

Acts relating to the common good, in which all classes share, are sanitary measures, boards of health, free schools, and public libraries.

The state is compelled to provide officers to see that wholesome laws are enforced, as no law works automatically. Hence the appointment of factory inspectors, who have the legal authority to enter shops and stores and report for prosecution all managers and merchants who refuse to make the changes and provisions required by law.

V. An Estimate of Trade Unions. — Are trade unions helpful to the common welfare, or are they merely selfish bodies? The final test of any organization must be its effect on the general welfare. No community can tolerate an association which is in conflict with the general well-being, nor can permit any course of action which is injurious to the body of the people.

If it can be shown that trade unions, on the whole, are essential to the furtherance of life for the wage-earning class, that of itself is a large item in the common good, since the workers who need union frequently constitute four-fifths of the population. It is now generally conceded by economists, by jurists, and by employers that trade unions are necessary to the interests of these classes.

In the next place, the worst abuses of unionism, as the opposition to machinery, the attempt to prevent young persons from learning a trade, the antagonism to passing from one occupation to another, and lawless violence, tend, with more thorough organization and improved police regulations, to disappear. At any rate, flagrant acts of lawlessness do not belong to the unions as such, but are abuses to be corrected by public opinion and criminal administration. It is not fair to judge the board of trade by the acts of gambling members, nor the church by its corrupt limbs who disgrace it, nor trade unions by the occasional lawlessness of a minority of their members.

It is very often declared that trade unions are the causes of strikes. But strikes have always occurred, whether there were unions or not, and they have been most violent and destructive when they were outlawed. So long as men can freely organize themselves, openly and legally, and thus have a regular discipline and social responsibility, they are not so apt to break forth in acts of desperation. The wiser and steadier heads gain moral influence, and the laws which regulate their conduct, made by themselves, are more likely to be observed under temptation. It is probable that strikes thus carefully planned are more sure of success; but that is because the employers are more certain to be able to meet the demands made upon them by cool and calculating men.

So far as lawless attacks on persons and property are concerned, these are no part of trade-union policy or law. Such acts are provoked among unorganized laborers by the same causes, and they are simply to be classed and treated like other crimes. It is to be regretted that unions do not always formally repudiate such inexcusable deeds as assaults and interference with property or labor, but this is a matter which education and general progress in culture and administration will mend. This same progress in finer and juster sentiment will also make organization more perfect and will diminish the number of those secret and insidious acts of employers which excite men to resentment.

If the unions, by the adoption of a minimum rate of wages, can compel managers to employ none but the more efficient workers and to introduce the most effective machinery of production, the whole community has the benefit of the advance. It seems to be evident that society at large is benefited by having the process of production in the best hands, and by having goods made with the best tools. There is a common agreement of opinion that the unions do compel employers to fill their factories with the higher grades of men and the best of appliances. In China, where wages are extremely low, employers will not use machinery. Wherever human beings are willing to compete with brutes and mill-streams in cheapness, managers will not devise substitutes. Trade unions, by raising the rate of wages, drive the manufacturers to introduce the most recent and perfect methods.

Professor Marshall is by no means the most hopeful advocate of trade unions, but has given a cautious statement[1] of their economic value on the whole favorable.

It is possible to raise general wages if the necessary conditions are met: if they assist in making business easy and certain, so that capital is encouraged to venture on enterprise and is assured of income on investments; if the standard of life is raised, so that men are willing to work steadily and efficiently in order to maintain the standard to which they

[1] *Economics of Industry*, p. 408.

have become accustomed; if the young are assisted to gain increasing skill, so that the business of the country may be enlarged in productivity; if business and technical talent is developed and the cost of superintendence is lowered by a deeper sense of honor among wage-earners; and if conflicts are avoided and life is permitted to move on without serious break and loss. In trades which have a monopoly the workers may secure high wages at the expense of the public, the increased cost being added to the selling price of wares. In ordinary trades there is a flexible margin between the lowest price which the employer would like to make and the highest possible rate which he can afford; the combination may compel the manager to come nearer the possible maximum. If wages are demanded beyond the power of the employer to pay, the trade is killed, since no occupation can be carried on at a loss. Trade unions cannot force the rate above what is permitted by the economic conditions of the community at a given time. The unions have a high value if they train up a body of expert advisers who become thoroughly acquainted with the actual possibilities of each trade, and inform the men when it is possible to make advances of rates and when it is necessary to reduce wages. Strikes would be much more rare if the men knew nearly what the employers could afford; because they would not strike for something impossible to grant, and they would know when the employer would be willing to increase the pay in order to avoid friction or delay. The beginnings of this body of experts representing the unions are found in the so-called "walking delegate," or "business agent"; but it may be many years before the highest type of qualities and training will be more common.

There is an apparent exception to the beneficence of trade unionism: the weak and incapable members of society, who are not able to earn the wage required for efficiency. "Shall these be left to starve, because they cannot get employment at trade-union rates?" This question is often put with the triumphant air of certainty that it settles controversy. It must be admitted that the first effect of enforcing a rate of wages which will support the average family, keep them in health, and give them decent provisions for human existence, must be to cause the discharge of all who cannot earn this rate for the employers. Says Mr. Mulhall: "Whole sections of the wage-earners . . . are habitually crushed down below the level of physiological efficiency." At least 8,000,000 of the population of the United Kingdom — over 1,000,000 in London alone — are adult males who earn under $5 a week. That means starvation or partial dependence on charity. ·The proper method of treating this social residuum must be reserved for the next chapter.

But this is the place to point out that a business which cannot pay full support to its workers must be partly supported by other forms of business, which must carry the underpaid employees. Does it not seem certain that such a business as that is unprofitable to society? Is it prudent for a community to assist in carrying on a business which, if not supported by alms, would cease to exist?

These underpaid persons are really subsidized by society to hang about the necks of capable workmen and make the struggle harder for them. Thus the army of the unemployed, of paupers and of criminals, is augmented by a policy which keeps in reserve a large mob of incapables, who cannot earn enough to support themselves, and whose competition injures the self-respecting men who dread dependence as a scourge.

VI. Social Peace in Industry; Modes of settling Disputes between Managers and Workmen. — The occasions for difference of opinion between directors of industry and wage-receivers are many and various. But they may all be brought under two general heads: those which refer to new contracts about wages, hours, and other conditions of employment, and those which refer to interpretations of contracts already existing.

For both these purposes the trade unions have gradually built up a method of negotiation and administration, which is demanded by the very nature of modern factory industry, where very large numbers of employees are brought under one management, and where it is entirely impossible for the superintendents to deal with individual workmen at every turn.

Conciliation. — There is apparently more room for conciliatory methods than for arbitration. Up to this time no clear way seems open, under ordinary conditions, to compel a set of men to go forward with an employer whom they dislike to serve. On the other side, it seems impossible, on any wide scale, to compel employers to keep their works running on terms which they believe mean impairment of capital, or even loss of profits. Arbitration seems to mean that one of the parties must yield something that he asserts is necessary to a fair wage or a fair profit. Arbitration, which is simply a "splitting of the difference," and comes about to the average of extreme terms possible for both sides to accept, may be practicable; but even then arbitration does not mean that the parties have reasoned their way to a true agreement. They have simply asked an umpire to decide for them a dispute which they confess they cannot settle among themselves. If an agreement can be reached whose reasons have all been explained and argued out, such an understanding has far more moral worth than an arbitrary decree passed by an outsider.

As a matter of fact, the most satisfactory instances of arbitration have been those in which the umpire did not really act as umpire, but as a friend whose character was respected by all, and who had the tact to help both disputants reach a milder temper and a clearer insight into the merits of the case.

> "A peace is of the nature of a conquest;
> For then both parties nobly are subdued,
> And neither party loser." — Part II, *King Henry IV.*

The very general disturbances accompanying strikes of coal miners, gas workers, and especially railroad unions, have so annoyed and injured the general community that men have been eagerly asking if the government should not provide machinery for compelling both parties to go on with work and settle their differences before duly authorized courts. The chief difficulty has been that the corporations have property, and their responsibility can be enforced, while trade unions are not bodies which can be sued, and the individual workmen are too poor to pay fines for breach of contract. It would seem that a body of men driven by force to labor for a company against their own sense of right would be little better than slaves. Thus compulsory arbitration has been rejected by both sides. Experiments are being tried in New Zealand and other British colonies which will be watched by the civilized world; for these recent Acts of the legislatures contain the principle of legal settlement of trade disputes before courts. Similar laws by our Congress and State legislatures give promise of relief. Until the principle has had longer and more extended trial we must suspend judgment, and await the result of the conciliation to which employers and wage-earners may appeal for help in hearing and deciding disputes. Much depends on the fairness, impartiality, and ability of these bodies. In France and Germany, courts are established for the purpose of securing amicable adjustments, and in the last resort the settlement of points in litigation without costly and tedious process. But these courts do not have anything to do with making rates of wages; they go no further than the interpretation and enforcement of existing contracts. Out of all these experiments the industrial world may find the best way. Something may be hoped from the universal growth of education, for intelligence enables men to deliberate, hear all sides with patience, and form reasonable judgments.

The final settlement of economic strife will not come by merely repressive measures, but by increase of intelligence and virtue — both intelligence and virtue. Good impulses without knowledge leave men helpless before astute robbers; while intelligence without increase of regard for social right is merely a tool for selfishness to employ with greater power to harm. Jefferson said that to keep a standing army merely to keep down riots was "setting up a hawk to keep the henhouse in order." He thought that we have no serious need to fear the effects of liberty if we use the means of culture. " Let them take arms. The remedy is to set them right as to facts, pardon and pacify them. What signify a few lives lost in a century or two? The tree of liberty must be refreshed, from time to time, with blood of patriots and tyrants. It is its natural manure." [1] Somewhat extravagant in expression, but sound in its reliance on moral means as opposed to depending entirely on force. Justice and instruction are more powerful to sustain social peace than hireling armies.

[1] T. Jefferson, *Works*, II, p. 265.

VII. Profit Sharing. — Many social students have looked earnestly toward some form of profit sharing as a means of softening the asperities of the relation between employers and employees. It is desirable that our definition should be made precise and accurate, because various writers seem to be arguing for or against very different propositions in discussing what they suppose is meant by the words. Mr. D. F. Schloss[1] thus states the meaning: "A predetermined proportion of profits, divided between employees as partial remuneration of labor in predetermined shares." He claims that this method should be carefully distinguished from other schemes which are often discussed under the same title, as: dividends on stock owned by laborers; extra wages; premiums on efficiency, irrespective of profits; provident funds; bonus-giving, or a distribution among employees of an indeterminate part of profits.

Theoretical writers have very generally recommended this plan, and they have urged very plausible reasons. They have said, that if the workmen knew that they were to have a definite share of the profits they would work harder to produce as much as possible, would drive the machinery to its full capacity, would seek to avoid all waste of material and unnecessary wear and tear of machinery. They have noted the fact that when a man's wages are fixed he has no further direct interest in the business than to keep his place, come up to the minimum demands of his contract, quit as soon as the bell rings, and have no particular concern about the use of materials and tools. The wage-earner must often be kept up to his task by hired drivers or superintendents, whose salaries are a large part of the cost of production. If men worked all the year under the stimulus of hope that they might share the profits, this motive would make them better workmen, more careful and industrious, requiring less superintendence.

To this statement many have added a rather questionable argument, that workmen whose interests are thus made identical with those of the employer will be less devoted to their fellows and take the side of the manager.

It is also urged in favor of profit sharing that it tends to

[1] D. F. Schloss, *Methods of Industrial Remuneration*, 1892.

secure more steady workmen, longer service in one place, because men will not like to leave a situation where certain gain awaits them if they are loyal to the master of the establishment.

To these arguments, which appeal to personal interest, the philanthropists add other considerations. They claim that if employers would divide profits with the workmen there would no longer be a horizontal but a vertical cleavage; that both parties would tend to become joined in interest. All must admit that if this union of sentiment could be cultivated it would be socially desirable, if it does not increase the patronizing airs of employers and the servile, cringing attitude of workmen.

While many of the ablest economists and other theoretical writers have been advocating this plan for many years, it must be confessed that experience has offered comparatively few instances of success; there have been many sad failures; and the majority of practical men, both managers and trade unionists, are either indifferent or hostile. This, in few words, is the present situation. It cannot be said that the movement is a failure, for it may have progressed as rapidly as it was reasonable to expect a novel enterprise to do. There are a few resolute, practical men, of noble purpose and fine ability, who are giving the experiment a fair and honest trial; and such men seem to be able to secure the very kind of results which economists and philanthropists unite in declaring to be desirable. Good and shrewd men are able to succeed with almost any reasonable plan, while the best method fails in the hands of one who is incompetent, harsh, and dishonest. While the scheme is still in the experimental stage, not even specialists in economics can speak with dogmatic certainty as to the issue.

Why do the practical managers of industry object to the profit-sharing scheme? They say that they are already paying the workmen market wages according to agreement; that the men get these wages whether there proves to be any profit or not; that to offer more wages would be to confess that employers are not already dealing justly; that it is unfair to ask capitalists to divide profits in good years unless the workmen are willing to share losses in bad years. Perhaps they are also influenced very much by the fact that the declaration of a dividend of profits involves more publication of the state of their finances than they like to give to their competitors and to the world. They think that a failure to give a dividend would produce as much dissatisfaction as the payments had evoked gratitude; that the custom of paying a certain share would soon come to be regarded as simply justice, as a custom quickly hardens into law. For these and for other reasons the managers of business have generally held aloof from this scheme. "Business is business," they say, and it is not wise to mix accounts of charity and philanthropy with those of profits or loss. They think that the relations of employer and employee should be simply those of any honest and fair-minded dealers in commodities; and that the cultivation of friendly sentiments can go on without obstruction under this arrangement, not only in the shop but also in other associations of life.

If we turn to the trade unions, who are the parties most directly interested in any such scheme, we find them at least very generally suspicious or openly hostile. Profit sharing has now been tried in England for a generation, and the unions have had an opportunity of observing its working. Rightly or wrongly they seem generally agreed in disliking it. If this seems strange to us, we shall come nearer their point of view by considering their argument.

They tell the philanthropist and theorist that they dare not and will not give up their union, and will not do anything to imperil its existence and lessen its power. Experience has taught them that private interest will not protect public interest, and that if they get their own rights they must be combined to maintain them. They see in profit sharing a trick of employers to break up their union and separate them from their natural allies. To them the chief concern is the rate of wages, and next to this, assurance that the length of the day shall not be increased. The bonus offered seldom amounts to very much as compared with the reductions of wages which they suffer if the union is not always presenting a united front all over the country. They are afraid of "bribe participation." The little gain is uncertain, and the loss is great and certain. Many of them will say that the manager has the accounts in his own hand; how do they know that he gives them the share of profits which has been promised? They want nothing to do with a bargain in the dark. And what if they do toil harder to make the winnings larger, if at last loss comes by no fault of their own, as come it often does by some error of the employer?

Perhaps some of the workmen will add that they cannot wait for the introduction of a scheme which depends on the charity or generosity of the employers; that the waiting is likely to be very long and tedious, and the issue uncertain; that they prefer to depend on themselves and on an organization in which they have a voice and a vote.

Many of the economic writers also take up the criticism of this method of industrial remuneration. To the arguments of the trade unionists they add some of their own from an outside standpoint. Since profits depend chiefly on the qualities and conduct of the employer, and not so much on the workmen, the hopes of the latter are built of unknowable elements and share the nature of gambling. This leads to bad morality, since the habit of relying on any event not due to their own conduct educates men to look for gifts of fortune rather than for fruits of personal skill and fidelity. They point to the fact that profit sharing cannot be enforced at law, as wage-paying can be, and that the legal status of the scheme is all in the air.

If the advantage of the manager is sought, this can be secured in a better way, as by piece wage, progressive wage, or collective progressive wage. What most stimulates a workman is not some remote and uncertain share of an uncertain product, but the immediate and certain guarantee of a definite reward for an increased product or diminished waste. The payment of bonus on output is more logical than bonus contingent on profit. By progressive wages is meant a fixed or minimum wage supplemented by a premium paid in respect of efficiency.

Employers — Power and Duty. — Aside from profit sharing the generous employer always has it in his power to improve the conditions of those who sell him their time and energy, who yoke themselves under a wage contract to his establishment of industry. There is a vast difference between managers in this respect.

The first concern of the wage-earner is to receive more wages: he cares more for that than for anything else, and thinks of it before all. Every employer who raises the wages in his factory aids the movement for betterment everywhere. The best men flock to him, and the example of his fairness is used as a lever in other houses far away.

Next to rise of wages the workmen desire shorter hours, and any employer who can give the same wages for less time is assisting the labor movement at a vital point. If the profits of business will permit any advance, it will be more appreciated in these two directions than elsewhere.

The more intelligent workmen appreciate good sanitary conditions in the shops, and some of them feel the difference between æsthetic and ugly surroundings. In this respect we discover that employers differ widely, and the very fact of this difference seems to show that the slower leaders are not doing all that lies in their power. It is probable that those who are able to offer better physical conditions can do so because they are more competent captains, and that they secure better service in return for the increased expenditure. Self-interest and philanthropy are not to be distinguished in effects, if both are really intelligent. Financial ability and the willingness to make better terms for the workmen, are two marks of the most worthy directors of large enterprises.

Even where factory laws give minute directions about sanitation and guarding of dangerous machinery, the character of the manager will come out in the more or less honest way in which he enforces the law. Some employers have voluntarily done more for the physical and moral welfare of their employees than others can be brought to do even with the severest pressure from inspectors appointed by the state.

Personal Treatment of Workingmen by Superintendents. — A practical man, acquainted with the feelings and ways of workingmen, thus lets in light upon the personal relations of managers and employees: —

"No system of management, however good, should be applied in a wooden way. The proper personal relations should always be maintained between the employers and the men; and even the prejudices of the workmen should be considered in dealing with them.

"The employer who goes through his works with kid gloves on, and is never known to dirty his hands or clothes, and who either talks to his men in a condescending or patronizing way, or else not at all, has no chance whatever of ascertaining their real thoughts or feelings.

"Above all, it is desirable that men should be talked to on their own level by those who are over them. Each man should be encouraged to discuss any trouble which he may have, either in the works or outside, with those over him. Men would far rather even be blamed by their bosses, especially if the "tearing out" has a touch of human nature and feeling in it, than to be passed by day after day without a word and with no more notice than if they were part of the machinery.

"It is not the large charities (however generous they may be) that are needed or appreciated by workmen, such as the founding of libraries and starting of workingmen's clubs, so much as small acts of personal kindness and sympathy, which establish a bond of friendly feeling between them and their employers." [1]

Of course these remarks cannot apply in those cases where the managers of the first rank are far removed from the operatives, as are the presidents and directors of railroad corporations and other huge modern enterprises. Even here, the immediate managers and superintendents should be chosen with reference to those human qualities which smooth difficulties and remove causes of social distrust and hatred. Courtesy and fairness are due to all men, without regard to industrial rank, and the superintendent who lacks urbanity, friendliness, and politeness fails so far of doing his duty to the stockholders and to the community.

VIII. Coöperation. — None of the schemes hitherto noticed touch the level of the aspirations of workingmen. They desire to have a share in the control of affairs, and not merely to be the passive recipients of favors which depend on the chances of finding benevolent capitalists. Furthermore, many thousands of working people wish to mingle sociability with business, as in the numerous friendly or mutual benefit lodges which offer insurance to their members.

Coöperation in Partnership Form. — At various periods

[1] F. W. Taylor, *Economic Studies*, p. 126.

during this century, in all modern countries, groups of men have combined to market their own labor by investing their little capitals and joining their efforts in production. It is a long story of moderate and occasional successes with many dismal and pitiful failures. Usually, these associations have either broken in pieces, or have dwindled into mere joint stock partnerships, or have been carried to prosperity by a few of the more able members who soon took control and profit to themselves. It does not seem possible to make much out of this plan, because it has no principle to distinguish it from any other capitalistic enterprise, and therefore has nothing socially new or large to offer. In the type of coöperation under consideration the members are looking out for their own interests, without having any community of interest or sharing of advantages with their neighbors.

Coöperative Shopkeeping. — The famous Rochdale Pioneers, of England, have worked out a method of coöperation which has achieved larger results, and has a wider scope and more certain future. This scheme of coöperation began with a few shillings of money in a very small store. The men who developed the method gradually invented and proved the following principles: that coöperation, in order to succeed, must invite to share its advantages all persons in the town who have any liking for the scheme and wish to benefit by it; that every purchaser must pay cash; that market rates must be maintained, in order to avoid giving unnecessary offence to small shopkeepers; that all customers at the end of the year shall receive a rebate according to the amount of goods purchased by each as registered in the books. Various minor modifications of these rules may be made, but these are central, and mark the highest success wherever they have been strictly carried out.

It was found that goods might be transported by the coöperative shops for themselves, and thus the associations developed contracts with steamships and railroad companies or established their own means of carrying and became owners of ships.

They also discovered that the associations could save much in purchase by joining their accounts, and thus they came to

o

found wholesale branches for the purchase of stocks directly from manufacturers and in large quantities. Here again they saved for the customers.

In the course of further experience they found it to their advantage to grind their own flour and manufacture other kinds of goods sold; and thus the coöperators became managers of factories and mills, and accumulated great funds and possessions. All this has been managed by salaried superintendents and other persons paid wages, as in the case or ordinary merchants and manufacturers. The whole purchasing community are the real owners, and not the small circle of managers and workmen who carry on the business. The humble mechanics of England have thus produced, in these associations, a most democratic form of business in the very heart of a great capitalistic world.

The Limitations of Coöperation. — From these successes many have fondly hoped that all business would gradually come under the sway of the people and be free from the hated rule of the capitalists. It looks so logical and democratic. But logic is not master in the complexity of human affairs. From all that has yet been accomplished we see no tendency to drive the great industry out of such enterprises as shipbuilding, railroad construction and management, and other vast schemes which require the highest order of commercial genius. The groups of modest coöperators would not be willing to pay the salaries which corporations are quite willing to pay, because only high salaries, or hope of large income, will command the best talent. These larger enterprises must at least be started and organized by men who are not merely hired by others, but are masters of the situations which would appal ordinary wage-earners or professional men.

Credit Societies. — The most popular form of credit association in the United States is that called, generally, the Building and Loan Association. There are two kinds of business conducted under this name: the joint stock companies, carried on for the profit of directors and money lenders, and the genuine associations conducted for mutual benefit. These methods are entirely different in principle and should be carefully distinguished by name and legal position. It has been found that associations doing business over a large area must be brought under specially rigid state laws and inspection, in order to prevent designing men from enriching themselves at the cost of the investors or borrowers.

Raiffeisen or Popular Banks. — In order to provide capital for persons of small means, capable and honest, an admirable plan has become quite general in various countries of Europe, which seems well adapted to gardeners and farmers of limited opportunities in this country. It is called by the name of the founder, the Raiffeisen bank, or the popular bank. It is often started by philanthropic persons who wish to help honest cultivators to escape from usurious money lenders. A few hundreds of dollars are placed in a fund and lent at low rates, without other security than the personal liability of the members of the association. These members agree to make good all losses, and they thus secure capital at very low interest. Under this plan almost nothing has ever been lost. But manifestly it would not work on a large scale nor among dishonest partners. It is a plan adapted to a rural community or village where the character of each member is thoroughly known to his neighbors.

Fraternal Insurance Societies. — The spectres which haunt the poor man are dread of sickness, accident, and death of the bread-winner in the home. Where people must live close to the margin of their earnings it is impossible to accumulate property to provide for such emergencies. The little store of the savings bank is soon exhausted, and credit is strained to the point of breaking. Working people of all modern lands are looking about them for some way by which they can provide for the rainy and stormy day, and yet not use up the fund required for reasonable support. Savings made at the expense of health, or even of education, are not economic.

The method of Industrial Insurance has grown to vast proportions. Side by side with this private and capitalistic institution has grown up the voluntary society called the lodge or benevolent society, or the fraternal insurance association. There are many of these bodies in this country as in Great Britain. They are of various kinds and of different degrees of merit. Experience in England and in this country has shown that voluntary associations cannot be trusted to carry on life insurance business without state supervision. Sometimes a society is started by a dishonest company, whose object is to steal the income of the members. More frequently such an association is founded by honest persons who are totally ignorant of actuarial science and art and, therefore, mislead those who join them. These societies offer to carry policies of life insurance at rates so much below those offered by regular companies that they secure many members. So long as these members are young and numerous all seems to go well, and the occasional death losses are easily and promptly paid. But in a few years the older members begin to die, the losses are more frequent, and there is a panic flight from membership. Then comes collapse. Many high authorities believe that these associations can be made useful if they are subject to careful inspection and regulation by competent state boards of administration. Others consider them essentially unsound. State regulation alone can ever give them a reliable basis.

Men are so constituted that they like to act in company. Animals may eat alone, but civilized people enjoy food best at table with others, where jest and story, wit and cheer, make the viands sweet and plain fare appetizing. Sympathy and fellowship are as necessary as insurance. Societies have honors, marks of distinction and appreciation, offices, places for display of abilities; and these are elements of benevolent societies which make strong appeal to many. The capitalistic joint stock companies cannot offer these advantages. Nor can they supply nursing in sickness, the friendly attention in distress, the fraternal features of the assembly, and the countless little services which members of an association render to each other. Men who look at the matter simply as mathematicians and actuaries can never undersand the secret of the growth of fraternal insurance societies in spite of many failures of certain forms of them. If a plan can be devised by which the exact capitalistic management can be combined with the feeling of sociability and mutual assistance, the better method would be welcomed. These associations are likely to exist for a long time, perhaps permanently, and those who are busy with the cares of life cannot inform themselves as to the real financial basis of the societies which solicit their membership.

Those who think that people should be permitted to suffer from their ignorance without interference of government, ignore the fact that the individual citizen is not able to protect himself, and that preventive justice is the highest form of justice. It is far better to avoid cruel losses, which come from the blunders of a vicious plan, than to correct them when thousands have been led blindly into a pit.

IX. Coöperation of the Community; Consumers' Leagues. —
It is highly desirable that the public should study the economic doctrine of consumption as taught in recent discussions. We have long been attentive to the teaching of economics relating to the production of wealth, exchange, and distribution. But of late years very able men have devoted special attention to the direction of the uses of wealth. The buyer of goods does not directly create wealth. Using goods is not by any means equivalent to making them. A very serious fallacy lies in such a paragraph as this: "Near my house the other day there was a barn on fire. When I found that it was well insured I did not weep. Somebody out of a job will get a few days' work and wages. Fire is one remedy for over-production of barns. The shop one of my sons worked in burned down. The result will be a new shop and machinery up-to-date." It is a pity good men should say such wild things. This talk is literally incendiary. It makes arson a virtue. If people really believed it, we should have conflagrations every night. Common sense and the conspiracy of policemen and firemen quell any attempts to carry such economic fallacies into practice.

No less foolish and contrary to sound economic doctrine is the saying that "the vices of the rich are the hope of the poor." Extravagance in the wealthy works misery rather than benefit to wage-workers.

What the buyer and consumer do is to direct the course of production. The consumers have no more to offer than a fixed quantity of goods which they have produced for exchange. Buying does not increase this stock, but it indicates to merchants and manufacturers what the public desires done with machinery and labor. If men buy meat and gems with their wages, they cannot purchase lace and pianos with the same money.

Mr. John Graham Brooks has made a noble and sensible plea for Consumers' Leagues, from which some illustrations are taken to enforce the points suggested. He quotes from the *Forest and Stream* a sound and pathetic passage, good both in economics and morality: —

> "You observed that hat of the lady who walked in front of you down the fashionable part of the main street the other day. . . . You have not noticed, perhaps, that on my lady's hat are some tall, pliant plumes, long as those of the ostrich, but far more beautiful, with delicate filaments as light as frost work on a winter window. These long, filmy plumes on my lady's hat are the plumes of the white egret. Naturally they are pure white, . . . but pure white not being barbaric enough for the use of civilization — though it used to serve Southern Indians who wore these plumes — they are dyed any color of the rainbow, losing thereby none of their gracefulness and only some of their beauty. My lady's hat, if worn too long, will lose its purpose and cease to attract. She must therefore change it. The plumes of the new hat must be of different color. For these new plumes she looks to her milliner. The milliner looks to the great wholesale supply house of the metropolis. The wholesale supply house looks — and with much anxiety these days — to Thomas Jones, market shooter, or, technically speaking, plumage hunter.
>
> "Every egret killed for its plumes is killed when it is helpless through its blind, natural love for its offspring, and when its death means the death of all its helpless young. Does the wholesale man know this? Does he care? Does anybody know or care? Is it not the one thing to be remembered, that my lady must have her plumes? . . . White . . . they are white, these plumes. It is mockery. They should be the blackest sable, and they should stain black the white fingers that caress them."

Too few reflect that the cheap goods they wear frequently come from "sweaters' dens." Clothing made in small rooms at home, where the family is crowded into uncomfortable and ill-ventilated quarters, may be sold at the stores where fashionable people are customers. The wholesale manufacturers give out the cloth ready to sew together; the poor men and women come for their work over long distance with baskets or little hand-carts, and trudge in summer heat or winter cold to their close rooms, where they toil long hours into the night for a miserable wage. When the children are sick with diphtheria or scarlet fever the work must go right on, for life depends on the daily wage. The fact is concealed from the health officials, if possible, so that the source of income, meagre as it is, may not be cut off. In this way the dealer is saved the cost of providing a large and comfortable room for his workmen, and the cost of rent falls on those whose residences are already too small for sound human life.

Against such conditions go up such pitiful and indignant protests as these resolutions, passed in an assembly of journeymen tailors in a great city: "We . . . unite in asking the merchant tailors . . . to fit up upon premises where their goods are sold, or other suitable shop premises, work-rooms in which we may make up these goods; that we will no longer pay rent for our employers, but for ourselves and our families only; that we will no longer be parties to the deceit of the customers of the merchant tailors, but from this time on we will declare to them and to the world that the home shop is insanitary, unnecessary, and those merchant tailors should no longer be patronized who, to increase their own profits, oppress us and deceive their customers." Here is a cry out of the heart of sweated men, who discover to us that we have, as consumers, a direct interest with the producers.

It is true that many employers already provide good shops, and that many workmen prefer to take the material home. But in the interest of the community the small domestic shop must be closely inspected and its work gradually transferred to modernized rooms adapted to the purpose.

What can we do? — Many people are ready to admit the responsibility of the buyer in relation to the producer, and yet are at a loss to know what to do.. They feel, as individuals, so helpless. It surely will not effect any reform to ask the employer or salesman if the offered garment comes from a sweater's den; the response is sure to give no information. Mr. Brooks quotes a cutting and sarcastic passage from the *New York Evening Post*: "What is a lady who goes to the bargain counter and buys cheap things to do in order to help the sewing girl and save her own soul? Is she to refrain from buying? Ought she to go to a dearer shop? Shall she say to the shopkeeper: 'I want to pay double price for all that I buy, on condition that you will pay double wages to all your work people'? We insist that when a man who has acquired the character of a public teacher denounces people for a certain thing (more especially if it is what everybody is doing), he should show them how they ought to mend their ways." The point is well made, and the responsibility for offering a practical method of help may be accepted.

The trade unions have already acted for a long time on a principle which rests on the moral responsibility of the purchaser for conditions of workers. The unions investigate the treatment given by a certain manufacturer to his employees, and finding that he pays standard rates of wages, that he is just and fair in respect to hours and other conditions, they offer him a certain mark for his goods,— the union label. That label is a sign to the buyer that the goods have been made in shops that reach a decent level of humanity. Doubtless the label has been abused, but it is an illustration of a right principle, and it is fairly effective. With the education and the organization of wage-earners it will become still more powerful.

The organization of Consumers' Leagues offers to the general public an opportunity to assist the unions in exacting a humane treatment of producers from manufacturers and merchants. They have this advantage over trade unions, that they are free from the suspicion of having personal ends to serve. They stand for the consumers' welfare.

A Consumers' League may be a special society formed for the purpose, or a charity organization, a woman's club, a civic federation, or any collegiate association willing to stand by the work, to supply necessary funds, and sustain efficient committees.

The Investigating Committee must be composed of honest, cautious, impartial, and intelligent persons, who will not rest until they discover the essential facts, and will not publish a single line unless they have the highest degree of moral evidence.

The League will publish and circulate from time to time, and especially before the Christmas holidays, a "white list," containing the names of firms which give assurance and proof that they are not only conforming to the factory and shop laws of the state, but are introducing humane treatment of their employees beyond the mere demand of the law.

The Investigating Committee will not stop at the mere shop rules and treatment, but will pursue their investigations to the places where the goods are made, and will learn whether the workers are living under conditions which are consistent with health for themselves and the purchasers of their products.

The League will use all possible means of persuading the public to patronize those firms and to ask for those goods which they know have in them no taint of inhumanity. They will carry on a steady and patient campaign of education on the duties of consumers. They will show that commodities may be made cheaply by good machinery, and yet under conditions favorable to the life of the workers. They will make the "white list" plead for kindness to birds and cattle, for women and children and men. They will continue this policy of favoring the firms who sell the right goods and deal uprightly with the wage-workers, until it will become impossible to market garments made in insanitary dens and food prepared in places full of poisonous air and foul with dirt.

X. Utopias. — By Utopias is meant forms of industrial organization or of general social organizations which are at present unrealizable and exist merely in the imagination, hopes, and faith of men. One of the chief Utopias of our time is Socialism. It is said that "Socialism is in the air." True. There is no socialistic state anywhere on earth. There may never be one. But there are multitudes of intelligent, earnest people who strongly believe that there ought to be and will be such a society. This belief itself is a potent social fact, influential, creative, energetic, and one which seeks to realize itself in revolution or in slow and gradual steps of change. It is desirable that we should understand this movement and the grounds which many men have for expecting that their dream will come true.

The most natural thing in the world in the discovery of a widespread social misery is to charge it upon the "present system." It is not difficult to find material for a most pathetic picture of human sorrow, poverty, wretchedness. One does not have to travel far to meet the decrepit, the aged, the sick, the beggar, the criminal, the tramp, and even the honest and industrious man whose children besiege him in vain for food. One must be blind and deaf, must be callous of heart, must refuse to be human, must close his soul against pity, not to know and have compassion for the myriads of people who are having a hard time. Injustice is frequent enough. One could easily fill books with stories of colossal theft, of rank cruelty, of flagrant wrong in places high and low. The socialist finds these facts and charges them to our industrial system. The individualist finds them and charges them to the prevalence of socialistic theory and legislation. The Republican newspapers find plenty of rascality in the Democratic camp, and the Democratic journals relate very damaging accounts of Republican defects. Preachers in pulpits are exposing sins, and judges are trying crimes, while only too many escape unwhipped of both. Injustice is here, and it causes much misery. And error is here. "Man errs so long as he strives." Capitalists make mistakes. They cannot, with all their masterful qualities, command the secrets of the future. Their errors often bankrupt themselves, and as frequently carry down in the ruins many an innocent workingman. In all this wise world no genius has risen to show us how in times of depression we can get willing workers and waiting capital into active partnership. At an hour when children are shivering for coal and women cry for bread, the merchants or manufacturers complain of "over-production," and the mills are shut down. Some awful error is here, some blunder of judgment, which has all the consequences of crime. But no oracle speaks the saving word.

No man doubts the facts on which these severe indictments of our civilization are based. The facts exist. It is natural to charge them to the system in which our industry is organized. That system is before all eyes. It is the "party in power." It is something tangible to strike. But a natural impulse may be false. It seems to be so here. It may be that our industrial system is to be credited for preventing many evils and introducing many benefits. It may be that the evils which are so easy to find are no essential part of the system, but arise from abuses in its working. It may be that the errors are inevitable, because man is not infallible. It may be that, under any system possible to devise, surrender to vicious appetite must bring misery, and that selfishness cannot be turned out by changing the form of government. Perhaps we are expecting more of physical nature than it can give. It is worth while asking whether for some goods we must not wait until time and education and culture have prepared us to win them and use them wisely.

Socialists tell us that we are moving toward their form of government. If we are moving in that direction, it does not prove that it is the right direction. Whole nations have made mistakes and been compelled to turn back or turn aside. It does not follow that because some industries can be socialized, that all industry can thus be made subject to general regulation. Artistic goods, apparently, can never be made by wholesale and machinery.

It is impossible to do justice to the arguments of socialists, or to the considerations against their theory, in a few pages or chapters. More profitable is the attempt to meet the truth in their indictment by seeking immediately practicable measures for correcting the abuses of the present order and bringing out of it increasing good. In this way socialism will gradually come into being, if it is best adapted to the conditions, with the least distress of change. If we must live under the same essential system which we now sustain, it will be more tolerable. In any event, it is our duty to make the best of what we have.

XI. "Practicable Socialism." — Under the discussion of the functions of government we shall study some of the ways in which the community has chosen to use its legal machinery to promote common ends, in which all classes share. In this place we may set down some of the more direct methods of government for protecting and helping the wage-earners.

Health. — The physical condition and vigor of the workmen is the interest of society. The army of war and the army of labor are composed of the same persons, and it is a national concern that they should be strong and sound. All modern nations have adopted the principle of law that the fundamental interest of health shall be the care of law and administration.

Mines, factories, shops, are gradually being brought under these regulations, and as fast as sanitary science makes new demands, legislation is sure to follow and enforce them. It is useless to say that the American citizen is a free man, and that if he chooses to work or sleep in foul air it is his heaven-born right to do as he pleases. That theory has had its trial and its judgment. It meant a feeble and decaying race. The word "freedom" is a mockery under the circumstances of city and factory life, where each man is subject to the conditions around him and utterly powerless to improve them by his individual act. The most direct and effective method of securing the public health is to appoint public officers to see that suitable conditions are maintained. On this point the report of Justice Brown's decision expresses the modern conviction and spirit of legislation, and it marks a great advance. He said that, while he would not pass upon the constitutionality of an eight-hour law in general, he would decide that any measure passed by a state as necessary for health and morals would be upheld as constitutional; and if working in hot, damp places more than eight hours injured health, it was legal to limit the time to eight hours.

The trade unions, as we have already seen, appeal to legislation for protection of health, for regulation of the work of women and children, for enabling legislation, and for legal inspection and supervision. Such legislation is called for by enlightened public opinion in all civilized lands, and is not a mere device of trade unions. It is but natural that those who suffer should be the first to cry out and awaken the conscience and human sympathy of their fellow-citizens. Very likely many "labor laws" are passed by demagogues eager for votes; but this is only the superficial aspect. Labor laws are made in response to the intelligent demands of industrial communities. Mistakes have been made, and will be made; industry will sometimes be retarded and enterprise discouraged; capitalists will be wronged, and the wrong will react injuriously on all classes of the people; but those mistakes are incident to all legislation. We cannot go backward to the old policy of neglect. Our wisest course is to move carefully forward "from precedent to precedent." Life and

limb, health and character, must be the object of the legislator's jealous care and assiduous attention.

Of those measures which affect the dependent members of
society we can speak better at a later point; as, for example,
of the system of public relief, or poor law. The institutions
of education, whose blessings all enjoy, will be given a position of honorable mention. Free libraries and reading-rooms,
parks, municipal music, recreation grounds, are not the peculiar
advantages of wage-earners, but the common wealth of all
citizens.

The care of dwellings, sanitation, clean streets by cities
and by state boards of health, is not a class interest, although
such protection is most of all required by those who are obliged
to occupy rented rooms and houses, over which they have no
control, and in which they may be exposed to unwholesome
conditions.

Compulsory insurance is hardly yet within the range of
practical politics in the United States. The German Empire
has in recent years developed a system of accident, sickness,
and old-age insurance which commands the attention of all
governments, but it has not stood long enough to reveal all
its possibilities. In England several plans of pensions for
the aged poor have been seriously proposed and publicly debated. At present the question has merely theoretical interest
in the United States. Many of us believe that the soldiers of
labor are entitled to a pension in helpless old age, if they have
never received alms and have supported themselves, on the
same principle on which pensions are paid (not "given") to
soldiers of war. As a matter of fact we do pension all helpless, penniless, and friendless old people,— in the country
almshouse. But that cannot be considered a satisfactory treatment for aged persons whose constant industry has helped to
enrich the nation, and who have fallen victims to extreme
poverty in their last days. Why should there not be a separation between the industrious and the vagabond aged poor?
Why should both be supported alike, forced into the same
company, although their previous histories have been widely
different? The plan of paying a pension to the aged poor,
who have supported themselves up to the sixtieth year, is

surely worth considering. It would cost the nation no more than the present plan; it would offer a premium for industry and thrift; and it would separate the merely unfortunate from the vicious and criminal. Any such scheme, however, must be so devised as to offer inducements for self-reliance, thrift, and industry; and none of the plans hitherto tried in Germany, or proposed elsewhere, is quite free from objections on this score. Premiums for negligence, for easy reliance on government, and for self-indulgence in present satisfactions must have a tendency to sap the vitality and moral energy of the race.

The Shorter Work Day. — While trade-union action and the example of progressive employers have assisted the movement for shortening the hours of toil, the advance has not been gained without help of law. In England the law which prohibited excessive hours for women and children helped adult men, since the machinery of certain factories could not run eight or nine hours for one class of workers and eleven or twelve for others. But legislation must move slowly and be firmly supported by public opinion. If the shortening of hours is not accompanied by higher speed and more perfect processes, the country will be poorer, and real wages will suffer. Here, again, we see that improvement for the more capable may turn the slower workers out of employment altogether, or compel them to form a class apart at reduced income.

The methods of improvement discussed in this chapter do not exhaust the list; they are simply illustrations of the vast range of social inventions devoted to the interests of the wage-earners. They reveal the progress of social sympathy, of the power of organization, and of hope of amelioration. It is nothing against these partial measures that they have not abolished poverty and banished misery. Swift machinery, competing employers, and trade unions agree in being *selective of the capable*. They leave multitudes in the morass of deep poverty, hopeless, unambitious, apathetic. Polite society thinks of these as the "unworthy," "incompetent," "unfit," but we do not thus get rid of those we call such hard names. We shall next turn to see if social invention is doing anything for those who are crushed under the chariot wheels of progress.

CHAPTER X

Social Misery, Pauperism, and Crime

(A chapter to be passed over by those who have no pity.)

> "The world . . . look round . . .
> The world, we're come too late, is swollen hard
> With perished generations and their sins:
> The civilizer's spade grinds horribly
> On dead men's bones and cannot turn up soil
> That's otherwise than fetid.   All success
> Proves partial failure: all advance implies
> What's left behind; all triumph, something crushed
> At the chariot-wheels; all government, some wrong.
> Who,
> Being man, Aurora, can stand calmly by,
> And view these things, and never tease his soul
> For some great cure?   No physic for this grief,
> In all the earth and heavens too?"
>
> — E. B. BROWNING, *Aurora Leigh.*

> "Will Fortune never come with both hands full,
> But write her fair words still in foulest letters?
> She either gives a stomach, and no food:
> Such are the poor, in health; or else a feast,
> And takes away the stomach: such are the rich
> That have abundance but enjoy it not."
>
> — *King Henry IV*, IV, iii.

> "To despise
> The barren optimistic sophistries
> Of comfortable moles, whom what they do
> Teaches the limit of the just and true,
> (And for such doing they require not eyes;)
>
> ' If sadness at the long heart-wasting show
> Wherein earth's great ones are disquieted;
> If thoughts, not idle, while before me flow
>
> "The armies of the homeless and unfed —
> If these are yours, if this is what you are,
> Then am I yours, and what you feel, I share."
>
> — MATTHEW ARNOLD, *To a Republican Friend*, 1848.

> " The toad beneath the harrow knows
> Exactly where each tooth-point goes;
> The butterfly upon the road
> Preaches contentment to that toad."
>
> — RUDYARD KIPLING.

THE aim of this chapter will be to show the outline of the
social system of relief and correction. Into the technical
questions of method, the plan of this book forbids us to enter
further than to employ illustrations of principles. The administrators of institutions for the blind, the insane, the feeble-
minded, have developed a literature and body of regulations
for each special class of institutions. The social student seeks
to know first of all the end which is to be met, the nature and
extent of the need, and the proper location of responsibility.
Beyond that point only special students of particular phases
of relief or correction are called to inquire.

I. The Condition of the "Residuum" or Lowest Classes. —
Sir Robert Giffen [1] has made a summary statement of the condition of several classes which, in general terms, may apply to
all modern countries, although it is probable that the situation is better in America than in Europe : —

"The impression left by the evidence as a whole is that among the
more settled and stable population of skilled work people there has, during
the last half century, been considerable and continuous progress in the
general improvement of the conditions of life, side by side with the establishment of strong trade customs adapted to the modern system and scale
of industry. Experience may fairly be said to have shown that this part
of the population possesses in a highly remarkable degree the power of
organization, self-government, and self-help. Work people of this class
earn better wages, work fewer hours, have secured improved conditions
of industrial and domestic life in other respects, and have furthered themselves through trade unions and friendly societies.

"The classes who compose the lower grades of industry, regarded as a
whole, have probably benefited no less than the skilled workers from the
increased efficiency of production, from the advantages conferred by legislation, from the cheapening of food and clothing, and from the opening
of new fields for capital and labor. Of the mass of wholly unskilled labor
a part has been absorbed into higher grades, while the percentage of the
total working population earning bare subsistence wages has been greatly
reduced. . . .

[1] *Royal Commission on Labor*, fifth and final report, Part I, p. 24, quoted by
Levasseur, *L'Ouvrier Américain*, T. i, p. 216.

"There is still a deplorably large residuum of the population chiefly to be found in our large cities who lead wretchedly poor lives and are seldom far removed from the level of starvation; but it would seem that, not only the relative, but perhaps even the actual, numbers of this class also are diminishing."

It is this "residuum" which now concerns us. It is these who are in most pitiable plight and who are the most discouraging element because they show so little signs of helping themselves. The facts already given seem to indicate the ability of the great majority of the population to gain an increasing share in advancing civilization. But here is a large class, composed of many elements, which appear to hang like a millstone about the neck of society—miserable, dangerous, parasitic.

The Influence of Modern Improvements on this Residuum. — In general the conditions of modern life demand, as a security for existence without charity or robbery, that one should have ability of a higher order than was formerly necessary. The stress of competition is more severe. In every calling the applicant or candidate for a position must compete with persons of higher training and education. Machinery is more swift and complicated every year. The modes of transport and communication quicken the pulse and step of the regiments of the industrial army. The trade unions demand that no man be employed unless he is paid a standard rate, a minimum price, and every year they succeed more and more in enforcing this demand. A standard minimum rate is essential to holding the gains they have made. If they yield that demand, they go back to the miserable rates and treatment of a half century ago, and the hard-earned victories of the modern day are given up. But what if a person cannot earn this minimum wage? He cannot get employment. He is thrust out into the army of the "unemployed." It is a harsh process, but it is necessary. Here and there adjustments are made for lower grades of workers, but this is the tendency. It is more and more difficult for weakness, incompetency, stupidity, to find a place in this modern world. Our age offers premiums for progress, not for defect. Without full recognition of this tendency we shall not understand the situation. Business

P

methods, inventions, organized labor, insurance companies, employers, and even public schools are in a tacit league to make it harder and harder for the imbecile, the feeble, and the untrained to find work. Employers and trade unionists alike will help support the feeble by charity, but they will not tolerate their presence in the shop. This is not sentimental, but it is fact. The incompetent get in the way of the swift runners.

"The general fact stands out that the majority of the community is better fed, clothed, and housed than in former times; that education and general knowledge are more widespread; that participation in political power, which is the guarantee against exploitation by other classes, is almost universal; and that the social importance of the working classes is greater than it ever has been before. On the other hand, there is great concentration of capital in the hands of corporations and a few individuals, while a portion of the community seems to be sunk in abject poverty. The stress of civilization is felt in greater opportunity of some and the hopeless submergence of others. Crime is on the increase, except perhaps in England; suicide, vice, and insanity are more manifest than ever." [1]

To the same effect M. E. Levasseur, the French economist, who has recently made a careful study of the situation in the United States, says: —

"The general rate of wages has risen. There are assuredly some exceptions. Wages have not risen for all, because there is a multitude of day laborers who, having nothing but their hands, without trade instruction, are under the yoke of unlimited competition and are exposed to struggle with immigrants of a lower standard of life." [2]

The English statistician Mr. Mulhall says: "Nevertheless, the sufferings of the indigent class in our large towns are greater than ever before; the condition of this class has been aptly described as far worse than that of Hottentots." [3]

II. Analysis of Population according to Economic Condition. — It should be the first effort of a social student to gain a clear and correct knowledge of the community he would help. The conditions of various classes of a community are widely different; the causes of distress vary indefinitely; and

[1] Mayo-Smith, *Statistics and Sociology*, pp. 371, 372.
[2] *L'Ouvrier Américain*, T. i, p. 373.
[3] *Industries and Wealth of Nations*, p. 102.

the modes best adapted to help must be as different as the conditions. To some minds all the "poor" of a great city are alike in distress, in defect, and in social responsibility. In the absence of minute and expensive research, the ordinary notions of the character and needs of a population are apt to be cloudy, partial, and often positively wrong. Those of a hopeful temper are apt to overlook the distress which actually exists, and those who are weary of life and pessimistic are prone to exaggerate the evil aspects. Neither extreme can be corrected without a local study of the real facts in their whole extent. For this purpose every city ought regularly to provide, at public expense, for a minute and scientific investigation of the conditions under which its people live; and the general government, which in our country has already done so much in this field, should provide a perpetual census bureau for the collection of statistics on which reliable judgments may be made. While each city and each state has conditions peculiar to itself, there are some studies of modern communities which are suggestive and instructive. Probably the most gigantic and reliable undertaking of this kind is that made by Mr. Charles Booth of London.[1]

A Standard of Classification. — Mr. Charles Booth, in order to make clear distinctions in securing and presenting his results, made the following classification of the population of the poor district of East London. A. The lowest class of occasional laborers, loafers, and semi-criminals; B. Casual earnings, very poor; C. Intermittent earnings; D. Small, irregular earnings (classes C and D constitute the "poor"); E. Regular standard earnings — above the line of poverty; F. Higher-class labor; G. Lower middle class; H. Upper middle class.

In the district first investigated it was found that of the 900,000 people studied, 64.8 per cent were above the line of poverty and 35.2 per cent were below it. Only about 6000 were inmates of institutions, and over 300,000 were living in poverty in the district. Nearly one-half of these were earning

---

[1] C. Booth, *Life and Labor in East London.* See article by James Mavor, in *Annals of the American Academy,* July, 1893. C. Booth, *A Picture of Pauperism,* and *The Aged Poor.*

regular low wages; about one-fourth were making irregular earnings; about one-third casual earnings; and about 4 per cent of the poor, or one and one-fourth per cent of the whole population, belonged to the lowest class of occasional laborers, loafers, and semi-criminals. It does not follow that just these proportions of the several classes would be found in other districts or cities. That could not be known precisely without local study. But the analysis indicates what, in a general way, may be expected, for in all large communities the same gradation will be met.

Statistics; The Numbers of the Dependents, Defectives, and Criminals in the United States. — Accurate information on this point is not furnished in the census of the nation. The reports in a few of the states are more complete, but an entirely adequate statement cannot be made. Some fragmentary estimates may be formed from such figures as we possess.

The census of 1890 gives the number of paupers wholly supported in poorhouses as 73,045, or 1166.4 per million of the population. This shows a decrease from 1880, when there were 1320 to the million. Some have hastily concluded from this fact that pauperism has diminished; whereas this particular decrease is due chiefly to the fact that the insane, the children, and many of the merely dependent have been removed to other institutions.[1]

Many of the poor are supported or partly supported by public relief in their own homes or in private families. In 1890 "the numerators returned the names of 24,220 outdoor paupers. But it was decided to be impracticable to obtain complete and accurate information concerning this class. They are therefore entirely omitted from the statements contained in the tables of figures herewith submitted" (U. S. Census, 1890). This sentence has been overlooked by many able writers, and the sum mentioned has been set down as the full number of outdoor paupers in this country, that is, about one-fourth of the whole.[2]

[1] Mr. C. D. Wright seems to fall into this error. See his article in *Atlantic Monthly*, referred to in preceding chapter.

[2] This mistake in made by Mr. F. W. Hewes, in an article in the *Outlook*, 26 September, 1896. It was made in the first edition of *Triumphant Democracy*, by Mr. Andrew Carnegie, but modified in the second edition. The statement

The error ought to be corrected because it leads us to underrate the difficulty of the social task before us. Such optimistic use of statistics acts like an opiate on the national conscience. Professor A. G. Warner found that in only six states, with a population of 19,917,082, there were 293,031 relieved outside of almshouses. This is about 1.43 per cent of the population of those states, and at this ratio for the entire country we should have over 1,000,000 persons out of 70,000,000 aided in this way. But such estimates have little value except to correct the bad effects of guesses which give too feeble an impression of the facts.

The census of 1890 gives the number of the pauper insane at 58,866; inmates of benevolent institutions, 111,910; juvenile offenders, 14,846; prisoners, 82,329; inmates of all institutions enumerated, 340,996. But the criminals, rich and poor, who were at large are not numbered.

These cold and lifeless figures do not pretend to be complete. They cannot picture the misery which lurks in them. But in social studies it is our duty to make our conceptions as exact as possible, to recognize the gaps in our knowledge and seek to fill them up as rapidly as we can. If we could learn how many persons are assisted or supported by churches, individuals, and benevolent associations, the numbers would be vastly increased. Indeed, it will never be possible to enumerate all dependent persons.

III. Causes of Social Miseries. — The obstacles in the way of human satisfaction must be either in physical nature or in man and his methods. There is no third party with whom we have power to deal. The defects of a human character may be either in our dispositions and character or in our system of social organization.

So far as nature is concerned, we have already sufficiently blamed our stars and our material environment for their share, and we may not return to that attack. It does no good to grumble at nature, and it makes us unhappy to indulge in criticism of the inevitable. Either we can help ourselves or we cannot. If we are helpless, it is best to be resigned; if

is frequently repeated as evidence that there are very few paupers in our rich land.

we can do anything to utilize such help as nature offers, it is wiser to lose no time in empty threats at clouds and cataracts, at stony soil, floods, prolonged rains and drought. Out of justice and charity to the poor we must never forget that in many places the soil is barren and parsimonious, and that much labor brings scant return.

Defects in the Character and Conduct of Men are to blame for Much Social Trouble, Loss, and Pain. — It is no more than fair to begin with the "better classes." Here the opportunity and responsibility are the greatest. The wrongs done by the rich, powerful, and influential are least excusable and most hurtful. Without seeking to bring an indictment against a whole class or charging the entire group with the sins of a few, it must be admitted at once that the wage-workers have a real grievance when they criticise those who represent to them the control of affairs. They are able to find in the daily newspapers reports of defalcation and embezzlement of public funds. They grow bitter and indignant, not without reason, when they read of heads of corporations who have bribed men of their own election, in state and city legislatures, to give away valuable franchises without remuneration to the community. Their blood boils when they are told by the reporters that a road which cost $7,000,000 pays taxes on $1,000,000 and collects dividends from the public on $15,000,000 of bonds, mostly "water." The small tax payer who is hard pressed to meet his assessment on a little home and a light stock of goods at nearly their full value, feels that justice is violated when he learns that a stock worth $100,000 is assessed at $10,000, and that to secure this low assessment the public officer was bribed by the rich merchant.

In the shop or warehouse the workman feels a dagger go to his heart when the manager looks at him and speaks to him with imperial air of pride and contempt, or issues orders as if courtesy had no place except among members of the "upper ten hundred." He is hurt to the quick when the manager declares that it is beneath his dignity to treat with authorized representatives of his union, elected in a legal and regular way.

The man of scant income is further wounded when he reads

of the money flung to the winds in a single evening of gluttony and display by those who claim to be "Society." Perhaps he does not always wisely distinguish between legitimate and harmful luxury. Perhaps his own narrow experience of the world seals his eyes and understanding to the advantages, even from the largest social view, of expenditures for pictures, statues, elegant residences, and grounds. Granted that popular criticism of the outlay of rich folk is often gross, selfish, and misinformed, and that such outlay does help to "circulate money," yet there is a limit to luxury. This limit is not easily defined, but it may be known by any one who sincerely desires to consider the interests of his fellow-men along with his own true interests. It is very clear that expenditure which debases the taste of the owner himself by its barbarous ostentation, or which produces in him the diseases of voluptuous indolence, must be evil. But it is not enough to consider the influence of luxury on the owner; all other influences and effects must be estimated. It is difficult to preach thrift, self-control, and temperance to the poor when they read of the debauchery and license of wealthy men.

On the other hand, it is just to hear the criticism of wage-workers which come from their own leaders and from the successful classes. First of all we have the enormous drink bill, largely, though by no means exclusively, paid by the men of meagre income. Some of us sincerely think that the vast sum spent on tobacco might be cut down and the saving invested in better houses, pictures, and books, especially when tobacco and liquor give pleasure chiefly to members of the male sex, and little but deprivation, trouble, anxiety, and despair to the women.

Since income must be paid out of product, any habits which diminish the efficiency of machinery must diminish the national ability to pay higher wages. Ignorance, want of skill, neglect, irregularity, dishonesty, and every immoral habit of workers must be part cause of their distress. In many individual instances all acknowledge this to be true.

The population at large has not yet come near the line where the soil will not furnish enough to feed the people. If all who now live could and would work, there is land enough, if the worker could have access to it, to supply the mere necessities of animal existence. But all must see that there are only too many families where the parents bring children into the world when they must know they cannot earn enough to support them. Apparently this tendency is strongest precisely where it does the most mischief. If anything is immoral, this is immoral; and people must learn that the responsible authors of life should be expected by society to support it. In savage times parents who could not supply their offspring with food killed them or sold them as slaves. Modern morality will not tolerate this course, but permits irresponsible parents to abandon their weakling brood to public charity.

The causes of defective constitution and of that mental and physical weakness which unfits for struggle and leads to pauperism are numerous and complex. The parish visitor finds a family very poor and asking for broken food and cast-off clothing. Why do they beg? Because they are hungry and cold. Why are they in want? Because the father cannot earn enough to pay rent and grocery bills. And what is the cause of his inability? Sickness and feebleness. But what is the origin of his sickness? He is a drunkard. What made him a drunkard? His father was a drinking man before him, and the lad grew up in an atmosphere of bad example and foul odors. Vice produces poverty, and poverty tempts to theft and begging. Each factor acts on every other factor, in endless reciprocity.

For some of the causes of vice, crime, and pauperism we must go back several generations. Every error and every injury, every wrong and all neglect in church, school, and state, conspire to crush and debase those who are already low down in the scale of energy and moral fibre.

IV. What are we Doing to help these Helpless Ones in the United States ? — Every citizen should know the modes of public relief of his own state and county or city in order to direct the destitute and to make the improvement of methods his own constant care. The system of relief differs somewhat in the various states of the Union.[1]

---

[1] I follow here the arrangement of material used in my article in *Jahr-buecher fuer Nationaloekonomie und Statistik*, 3te Folge, 1898.

A "pauper" is a person who, on account of poverty, needs relief. The epithet does not imply that the person is good or bad, worthy or unworthy, but simply that he cannot support himself and has no friends who can or will take care of him. It is a common theory of our poor-laws that a resident of a county or town is entitled to receive assistance in destitution, while strangers have no claims. But this theory does not work in practice, and all states make some kind of provision for those who need, whatever be their origin or the cause of their distress.

The state legislatures have the power to determine the methods to be used by towns, counties, and cities for local relief. These local governments have many different methods of performing this duty. Sometimes the county authorities administer the fund directly; sometimes the township or town or city erects machinery for this end; sometimes the state supports a class of paupers who have no legal claims on local authorities. In certain parts of the country the authorities can make contracts with private families to board the dependents at public expense. A very common practice is to build a poorhouse for those who are utterly friendless and alone, and to give aid in their homes to those who can partly support themselves.

Provision is generally made for the sick poor by the public system, a physician being paid to care for those who cannot pay, and medicines being furnished without cost. Large communities, towns and cities, either build hospitals or make contracts with private hospitals for the care of the sick poor.

For a long time it was only too common to place little homeless children in county poorhouses, where they mingled with old paupers and criminals and learned vice of them. This wicked policy is now condemned by enlightened public opinion, and in the more progressive states it has been made illegal. The legislatures have made various kinds of provision for orphans and other homeless children: provide for binding-out and apprenticing; or for boarding them in families at public expense until they are adopted or come of age.

The feeble-minded, in the more advanced states, are cared for in separate schools and asylums, public and private. The better opinion commends this method and pleads for life-long custody of those who are irresponsible. Idiotic and imbecile children should never, under any circumstances, be brought up with other children. Adult feeble-minded men and women ought not to be left free to wander about, the sport of thoughtless boys, victims of the vicious and reckless. Irresponsible girls and women should not be permitted to go in and out of poorhouses at their pleasure, because they are almost certain to have illegitimate children who inherit their weakness and augment the great army of incompetents and criminals. Several of the states have led in the advance movement to segregate all such cases, to treat them with firm kindness, and to remove them all their lives from the danger to which their defects expose them.

The states almost always provide for the education of the blind in special institutions, on the principle that all citizens are entitled to an education, and that those who cannot be taught in the ordinary schools should be taught in special schools suited to their needs. As there are usually not enough of this class in a county or town to justify a local school, the state takes upon itself the duty for all. The deaf mutes are educated and cared for on the same principles. But all deaf mutes should be educated, so far as possible, with normal children, and should not be a separate class.

The insane, whether dependent or not, are cared for by the states. Private establishments under rigid state control may also protect and treat the insane, and wealthy persons frequently choose to send their insane to such places. In some states the friends or estates of the well-to-do insane may be charged with the cost of their care. But no one is excluded.

It is not generally understood that the epileptics are a very large class in every land, and that they require a special treatment. They should not be placed with the insane nor with the feeble-minded, as a rule, but should have homes in the country, in colonies, where they may labor for their living in the intervals of paroxysms and be kept apart from the stress and pressure of public life.

The confirmed inebriates have furnished a problem of public care which is not yet solved. Certain localities have made experiments with special institutions for their treatment. The methods thus far tried have been only moderately encouraging. It is clear that the present neglect of this class cannot long be tolerated by enlightened public opinion.

Private Charity. — In addition to this legal or public system of relief there is a vast and growing system of institutions supported by benevolent associations, endowments, and private persons, dedicated to the sacred service of charity for all kinds of distress. Voluntary gifts and services have made possible the care of the sick in numerous hospitals; nurses are trained for visiting the homes of the poor or for nursing them in the hospitals; orphan asylums are multiplied; funds are raised to keep the unemployed from starving in times of special depression; lodging-houses are opened for the homeless wanderers, men and women; child-saving societies are busy everywhere guarding the interests of the young; social settlements bring the means of æsthetic and scientific enjoyment to the very door of the poor; and invention busies itself with devising some way of comfort or help for every kind of need.

In spite of all these appliances misery continues, and, in many places, increases. Charity is at best a mitigation of the evils of poverty, and it is often administered in such a way as to positively increase misery. If charity educates people to depend upon others, if it trains them to idleness and beggary, if it offers premiums upon unthrift, then charity does the work of hate and evil. It debases the moral nature, and finally raises up so large an army of the unfit that all the product of the industrious laborers cannot support the burden. Therefore the method of distributing relief is one of the most serious problems of our civilization.

State Boards of Charity and Correction. — The various states are gradually, but all too slowly, establishing boards of representative men and women for the purpose of visiting and inspecting the institutions of charity and correction. They are able to expose and correct abuses, to protect the poor, and to suggest advanced methods to inexperienced officials.

In every town and city there should be a society composed of delegates or representatives of all benevolent associations, churches, and civic bodies, whose purpose it should be to maintain a good understanding and a common plan of harmonious action on behalf of the dependent and those in peril of falling into need. A confidential record of all persons and families applying for relief should be kept, so as to give wise direction to charity and prevent imposture. Children in vicious homes should be rescued. Assistance should be given on the basis of work. Thrift and self-help should be encouraged. Educational and sanitary improvements should be carried forward by united action.

The National Conference of Charities and Corrections, the National Prison Association, and local organizations with similar scope and aim have been formed by practical workers and students for the purpose of comparison of views, discussion of important questions, encouragement of reformers, and the introduction of the best methods.

V. The Problem of the Unemployed. — Into a few paragraphs must be condensed the suggestions which require far more elaboration. We should distinguish between the unemployed and the unemployable, to use a happy distinction of Mr. Webb. Consider first what might be done for the *capable* unemployed. The social demand is for more regular industry, production free from the fever-and-ague fits of occasional high pressure alternating with periods of idleness. One cannot pretend to foresee how this difficulty will be removed, if it can be removed. Socialists tell us that private control of industry can never regulate industry, and that production should be governed by state officials in one grand system, so that no capable workman should ever be idle, and none ever be hurried to severe strain. Here we are in the region of conjecture and prophecy. They may be right, but we do not know. The change of system might be our ruin, and it is so far off as to bring no good to our generation. Under the present system of private direction can society lessen the evils of fluctuation and irregular employment?

Employers might do something to cure the evil by making their plans to keep their works going more steadily and avoid the rush of specially active seasons. The consumers of goods have it in their power, by concerted action, to distribute their purchases over a larger portion of the year. Spasmodic demand compels spasmodic activity of shops and factories. A great social event on which hundreds of thousands of dollars are spent may give momentary employment to a large number of persons, even beyond their powers of endurance, and then leave these same persons idle and without income for many months. It is not altogether possible to avoid these vicissitudes of demand, but generally intelligence and reflection might modify the customs of society in the right direction. Consumers' Leagues urge persons of leisure to do their shopping in the morning and not to defer holiday purchases until the last moment, and they are beginning to improve the holiday customs. Trade unions have diminished the irregularity of employment by discouraging "over-time," excessively long hours, and by insisting on steady occupation of those who are actually hired.

Legislation may by cautious measures help to secure more uniformity of hours and business methods. All such considerations belong to political economy and to practical statesmanship.

VI. The Unemployable. — It should be made distinct and clear that in passing from the capable to the unemployable we are dealing with entirely different elements. We cannot treat minor children on the same legal principles as adults. The feeble-minded, the insane, and all anti-social persons must be regarded and treated according to their nature, capacity, and attitude to society. Justice and benevolence must make the distinctions and take on adapted and suitable forms. The doctrine of free contract applies only to free beings, liberated from dependence by maturity of power and education. The idea of liberty to choose place, calling, and employer does not have any meaning in the case of defectives. The great majority of workmen in past ages were slaves or serfs. In later times, through increased intelligence and moral mastery, they have gained the place of personal responsibility. A small class of adults remain unable to use this freedom, and society must deal with them as with persons still under tutelage. But every effort should be made to educate for freedom and self-direction, not toward hopeless dependence and parasitic habits.

The first step is to organize the unorganized working men and women. Poor sewing-girls, tailors, and a multitude of persons engaged in various unskilled occupations are competing against each other and driving each other in herds down the slope of misery and pauperism. They are like sheep without a shepherd, and the Master certainly pities them. They are without education, without hope, without self-respect or aspiration. When they strike, it is to be defeated, because they have no funds to support them and no experience in bargaining as a body with keen employers. Indeed, their employers are frequently as poor and anxious as themselves. In union there would be hope, education, light, influence, and public thought. Artisans and mechanics of the factory type are more easily brought into efficient association; it is these scattered and largely unskilled people who need help from without to make them feel the utility of combination. Philanthropy could do a thousand times more for this class by organizing them than by casting alms into their laps. It is not necessary to fill them with aimless discontent, to stir them to hate and bitterness, to arouse them to wrath against the rich. All this is useless and hurtful. Appeal can be made to the same motive which merchants and manufacturers and corporations employ when they offer partnerships or sell stocks and bonds, thus increasing the number of shareholders and the resources of the enterprise.

Women's clubs, social settlements, and philanthropic societies should direct their efforts for those on the lower margin of self-support in this way. Thus the dock laborers of England were assisted to combine and secure important improvements in their conditions, which had been so utterly hopeless and wretched before.

Tests. — Each year, but especially in very "bad times," the cities are troubled with the presence of a large number of wandering men who cannot find employment, or who pretend that it cannot be found. The honest laborer and the drunken tramp, the workman out of a job and the vagabond who trembles lest work be offered him, the adventurous youth and the hardened thief, are mingled and crowded in the cheap lodging-houses, and even on the floors of police stations, with nothing but a sheet of newspaper, perhaps, for a bed on the stone pavement. These men beg on the streets or knock at the kitchen door. They swarm in places where free soup is offered, and sometimes form mobs to threaten the banks and public authorities. Bread riots are frequent in some countries and have occurred in this country.

Now the first public duty is to sift this mass and classify the mixed material of which it is composed. The only reliable test is work. Each community should provide for such a work test, under the careful direction of the mayor or other chief head of local government.[1] The wages promised should not be equal to those of ordinary wage-earners, because no inducement should be made to keep men from accepting the best employment that ordinary business can afford. Nor should the products of this work come into competition with those of ordinary industry in such a way that those who are employed shall suffer a reduction of wages and be driven to beg. This is a nice and difficult task, and demands ability of high order. In small towns or cities a stone-yard may answer the purpose.

One of the first effects of the work test is to induce weak and wavering men who are playing at the trade of mendicancy to go to work, when employment can be obtained. The next effect is to distinguish the willing from the lazy.

But this sifting process is only a beginning, and it must be related to a complete and adequate system, of which it is only one factor. It would be simply heartless and cruel to test men as in a mere scientific experiment, without any intention of helping them humanely until our resources of wisdom and means are exhausted.

In the course of applying the work test it would usually be found that a large number of young men and of women entirely willing and able to work had become mixed up with the other classes through want of early and special training. Thrown upon their own resources, without having learned any form of skilled labor, they are the last to be employed and the first to be discharged. Indeed, the employers find it impossible to use their service because it is so awkward and inefficient. At this stage the state or the city should provide a system of farm

[1] Article by Mr. Homer Folks, *Charities' Review*, March, 1898.

colonies and shops, to which the capable and willing should be sent, at their own choice, for the purpose of training them to do some useful work. Some of them could be taught farm work; others, various processes of manufacturing. Nor would this be a new thing for the government, since the policy has already been adopted for one class of wayward citizens,— the prisoners. It has long been the declared policy of all modern states to train the criminal for a life of usefulness, because it has been discovered everywhere that young men often follow the trade of crime because society has never taught them any other. But why should society wait for a young man to get the habits of crime before it gives him the opportunity of making himself a productive and useful member of the group? Vagrants fall into the habit of wandering and begging because they have no other habits, and they hardly know why they are not employed.

The same work test, under careful management and watchful supervision, would classify others as not capable of being trained to take care of themselves. It is dangerous to permit them to wander about as vagrants. It is a wrong to self-supporting wage-earners to permit them to compete with the independent poor and reduce them to pauperism. For these incapables the community should furnish a farm colony, where they might be supported at public expense, but not in idleness nor with freedom to discharge themselves on the first fine spring days, to prey on indiscriminate charity. Society is even now supporting them and permitting them to produce children as feeble, incompetent, and diseased as themselves. It is not a question of whether society shall keep them alive, but of whether they shall be kept alive by a method which degrades them, injures those just above them in ability, and burdens the next generation with a larger number of incompetents and degenerates. For a part of these incapables the custodial asylums of the feeble-minded are the appropriate places. For others, somewhat stronger, better provision would be special farm colonies under rigid supervision, to which admission is gained by choice or by judicial warrant or by certificate of poor-authorities, but from which discharge comes only by special act of the poor-authorities, under careful legal definitions.

Such custodial institutions, when once provided with land and cheap buildings, may be made almost, if not quite, self-supporting, through the directed and organized labor of the men and women.   Thousands of persons can work well enough under command who cannot find work in a competitive labor market.

There is another class of vagrants who cannot be managed so easily as those just mentioned; they are the confirmed tramps, often criminal in disposition and with a criminal record under various names.   They are the terror of farmers and farmers' wives.   They are the "sturdy beggars" of English story, known in every country during all the mediæval times, and surviving in our own age as a reminder of the "good old times" when robbery and highway callings were legitimate industries.   These men are venal voters in the slum wards of cities.   They are loathsome with physical and moral disease and the corrupters of all with whom they come in contact.   Among them are swarms of persons, men and women, who spend their lives in the invention of new modes of begging.

Here again the farm colony, under still more rigid conditions, is the best social treatment.   This need not be severe or harsh, except as all discipline and deprivation of liberty are hard for men who detest regularity and hard work.

After all the measures suggested, we should still have the discharged prisoner to handle.   To this subject a few sentences must be devoted.

VII. The Criminal. — Society has established from very early times a system of ciminal law, procedure, and punishment.   It is one of the primary functions of government to protect the lives and property of citizens against fraud and violence in all their forms.

Legislatures define the acts which constitute crimes.   The courts are established to hear complaints and the evidence of accusers, and to pronounce sentence.   Police officers are provided to detect, arrest, and bring to the courts for trial.   Sheriffs and prison officials are employed to carry the sentence of the courts into execution.

What is the object of all this elaborate social machinery?

Q

To protect the members of society against the injurious acts of the anti-social man. This is the primary purpose. But the anti-social man is also a member of society, with rights and interests. His character and conduct are the concern of all. As a human being he is entitled to our pity and care. If society can, in the very act of protecting itself, reform the criminal and so educate him as to make him conform to the right modes of life, there is a clear gain for all.

It is so difficult for a man who has once been imprisoned to rise in the respect of others and to respect himself, that we should avoid imprisonment as far as possible without encouraging crime. England has been making a vast experiment with the plan of substituting fines for imprisonment. Many thousands of youths have thus been saved from associating with old criminals. It is urged by high authorities that a man who has damaged the property of another, or hurt him by act of violence, should be compelled to make pecuniary restitution by labor. This would be a severe lesson, would be a substantial recompense to the injured person, and would save certain men of hot tempers, who are by no means criminal in disposition and habit, from the degrading influences of the prison. Some new offenders could be saved by placing them under the responsible guardianship of good citizens under suspended sentence, without sending them to jail.

In all modern countries societies for aiding discharged prisoners have been formed, and in individual cases have done much good. The case of a friendless man at the moment he goes forth from the prison gate is pitiful in the extreme. His record is against him; he has formed the acquaintance of thieves; even if he desires to reform, the world sets up a wall in his face.

Attempts have been made to form colonies of such men, free for them to come and go as they like. Excellent religious persons, supported by philanthropy, have hoped to influence such men by religious appeals and by rewards of industry. Unfortunately, there is a constant danger of colonies of this kind becoming dens of thieves, haunts of robbers, starting-points for raids upon society.

A better method is that used by Mr. Z. R. Brockway and

other heads of reformatories and prisons where the "indeterminate sentence" is legal. A few weeks before the time for discharge on parole, the superintendent finds a place of employment for the young offender, preferably in the very community where his crime was committed. The chief of police or sheriff becomes interested in him and watches over him during the period of his sentence, and until he gives evidence of being able to hold himself upright. The advantage of this method is that the offender knows that if he does not keep his word and act according to the rules, he will be taken back to prison and subjected to still harder conditions. A private religious society has no such control over the discharged man. The legal method does not exclude religious work on his behalf, but it affords the help which most such weak characters require for a long time, the assurance that they will have work and the fear that if they refuse to work regularly they will be again incarcerated.

After all, the most encouraging and necessary effort is that directed to the proper education of wayward youth. Prevention is the true policy of nations. It is not likely that crime can ever be entirely prevented, but it can be greatly reduced by caring for endangered children at an age before the stress of temptation begins. Education, mental, moral, spiritual, is the chief means of restoring the wanderer, and it is the only way of turning childhood and youth from the downward path to ruin.

CHAPTER XI

The School and its Social Service

" We confront the dangers of suffrage by the blessings of universal education." — PRESIDENT J. A. GARFIELD.

" Science, the arts, and every form of human knowledge await the coming of one who shall link and unite them all in a single idea of civilization, and concentrate them all in one sole aim. They await his coming, and he is destined to appear. With him the anarchy that now torments intelligence will cease; and of arts — the proper place and rank assigned to each, the vital power of each fortified by the vital power of all, and sanctified by the exercise of a mission — will once more flourish with harmonious union, immortal and revered." — MAZZINI, 1833, as quoted by F. W. PARKER, *Talks on Pedagogics.*

" I call, therefore, a complete and generous education, that which fits a man to perform justly, skilfully, and magnanimously all the offices, both private and public, of peace and war. . . . The end, then, of learning is to repair the ruins of our first parents by regaining to know God aright, and out of that knowledge to love him, to imitate him, to be like him, as we may the nearest by possessing our souls of true virtue, which, being united to the heavenly grace of faith, makes up the highest perfection. But because our understanding cannot in this body form itself but on sensible things, nor arrive so clearly to the knowledge of God and things invisible, as by orderly conning over this visible and inferior custom, the same method is necessarily to be followed in all discreet teaching. And seeing every nation affords not experience and tradition enough for all kind of learning, therefore we are chiefly taught the languages of those people who have at any time been most industrious after wisdom; so that language is but the instrument conveying to us things useful to be known. And though a linguist should pride himself to have all the tongues that Babel cleft the world into, yet if he have not studied the solid things in them as well as the words and lexicons, he were nothing so much to be esteemed a learned man, as any yeoman or tradesman competently wise in his mother dialect only. . . . Learn the substance of good things, and parts in due order." . . . — MILTON, *Of Education.*

" Man am I grown, a man's work must I do.
Follow the deer? follow the Christ, the king,
Live pure, speak true, right wrong, follow the King."
—TENNYSON.

I. The Institutions of Education. — We follow the method already made familiar in past chapters: the method of approaching the soul by the gate of bodily appearances. No man ever yet discovered a soul except as it made signs to us through some physical medium. Thoughts, emotions, purposes, are interpreted to us through glances of the eyes, cording of the brow, lifting of the hand in threat or promise, spoken words, written messages, of papers and books. The school system of the United States is outwardly a vast and impressive physical fact. In city and village, "along the quiet waters, in niches of the hill," by boulevard and roadside, in granite and marble, or in logs and clay, this great system finds its visible homes, its material embodiments.

Imagine the army of teachers, janitors, superintendents, book agents, publishing houses, school boards, trustees, committees who belong to this complicated institution. Watch the children coming home from school, looking in at all sorts of open doors, ready for all kinds of enterprises. Millions of money are spent on the building of edifices, the payment of teachers, and all the other expenses of the system. This cost is increasing every year, with growing population and wealth. In our day the school budget is one of the largest for which city authorities must provide. Every family must reckon with the cost in taxes and bills for books.

In addition to the public schools there are many parochial or church schools and many private establishments, since many of our citizens exercise the freedom of the land in paying for the style of goods which they most fancy, even if it is already paid for by the public. Often this additional burden is the price paid to keep a good conscience and perform what is thought to be parental duty.

There are many state and private colleges and universities in which education may be carried further than is possible in the elementary schools, and these institutions are part of the national means of instruction. Through lecture courses and classes even those who have entered their callings at an early age are often enabled to continue their favorite studies far into life.

II. This Vast and Costly System is the Expression of the National Estimate of the Value of Education. — In a general way these institutions manifest the popular conviction as to what schools should aim to be. After making sufficient allowance for the limitation of financial resources, for the errors of official judgment, and the defects in administration, this great institution does yet tell the world that the people believe in the value of knowledge, in mental development, in the superiority of intelligence, and in the formation of social habits.

In a nation composed of so many millions of persons, and these of all shades of belief and grades of culture, it is surprising that there should be such a universal, cordial, and progressive support of free public schools. Since the Civil War the South has joined the East, the North, the Middle, and the Western states in providing free and universal means of learning.

It is not claimed by the best friends of this system that it is perfect. There is not and never can be absolute agreement in details as to the courses of study and methods of instruction and discipline. Such unanimity is not possible in the support of any general measure, and it is not desirable. Entire unanimity would mean ossification and death. A ship at sea is always keeping its carpenters and engineers busy repairing it; but the ship does not stop in mid-ocean merely to splice a spar. The human body works and mends its bruises and lesions while it lives, and by living. The public school expresses great common convictions shared by the controlling spirits of the people, and criticism serves merely to correct errors and improve methods of an institution which, even as it is, commands our universal admiration and loyal support.

A people can form an opinion, reach an agreement, and vote on a national or commonwealth policy, but it cannot vote intelligently on a system of administration which only a corps of trained professional persons can carry into effect in millions of details. With practical unanimity, after bitter controversy, long opposition, and tentative experiments, the people of the United States have covenanted to establish and maintain a free school for every child in the land. That of itself is a conception so vast and sublime that it is enough to unite and ennoble a nation.

III. What Society has a Right to ask from its Schools. — The student of social welfare formulates social needs and looks about for the appropriate organ by which the need can best be supplied. He does not dictate the policy of the institution, but calls upon it for a service. Those who have specialized training and skill are the proper persons to carry out the measures and perfect the agencies. Society assigns the cure of disease and the direction of sanitation to physicians; the formulation of laws to jurists; the leadership of the church to theologians and pastors; the management of finance to bankers; the care of trains to a hierarchy of railroad men, experts in their way. Society knows fairly well what it wants, and it learns to assign particular tasks to different bodies of servants. Thus the task of education, in all its details, falls to the teaching profession. It is the social function of this profession to study the nature of the human soul; to understand its interests, modes of development, and methods of helping it to realize its own inherent powers.

This chapter will not trespass on the ground of the teaching profession, save to borrow a few illustrations, with the kind permission of the specialists. We have to do here with the attitude of the good average citizen and tax-payer who wishes well to his country and wants to get all he can for his money; from the standpoint of the parent, who loves his children and desires to have them enjoy the services of artists rather than of bungling hirelings; from the standpoint of the sociologist, who surveys the various institutions which make up the resources of the civilizing process, and discovers that if the public school fail, the entire structure must become a crumbling ruin. Perhaps the teacher thus questioned and stimulated from without will see somewhat more clearly, and feel a little more deeply, the solemn grandeur of his task and the immensity of the interests which depend upon his efficiency.

Society asks of its schools that they should assist each citizen to live his best life, in all that makes a truly human life.

In the chapter on the Individual we have endeavored to indicate what this implies.

The teacher and the social student meet upon the same ground and traverse the same field. This is natural and inevitable, because society is all about the schoolhouse and comes to its very door. Parents and statesmen, employers and artists, are urging upon the school the claims of civil life and asking for help.

Society has for its end the development of personality, the attainment of ideal freedom. It is great only as its members are developed. Social life is the sum of coöperating persons, and all that society is must be found in its persons and nowhere else. There is not and cannot be any real difference of interest between society and its component parts. Therefore, social welfare requires the largest possible enrichment of the mental and moral being of all. In the school is found the most universal and direct agency of society for developing personal quality. This end is not to be compassed in a phrase, in a verbal abstraction.

It requires all philosophies to unfold the infinite meaning of the human spirit; all poetry to image the rich and manifold contents of life in its experiences and its aspirations; all churches to voice its wonder and reverence; all industries and arts to embody its inventions; all literature to express in fiction and noble prose the revelations of the boundless divinity in man; all history of all nations to display as in one connected and endless panorama the procession of ever-growing souls; all life to hint at the possibilities which await us. The teacher must be a student of these various forms of expression. The personal and social ideal as stated in text-books of psychology or ethics is apt to be devoid of interest, a ghost, perhaps a skeleton. Science represents only the framework of this inner world, and reduces all to hard and juiceless formulas of speech. This is suitable to the "dry light" of exact and solid science. But the inspirer of the soul must also have help from poet and orator, musician and artist, in order not only to understand but to personally share the abounding and exuberant life of the human species. For great books of the master minds there is no substitute, and the school should ever keep before the pupils the choicest literary products of all ages.

Take a few of the philosophical statements of the end of life and teaching, and it will be seen how these abstractions, accurate and deep though they are, need the fresh pictures of literature to give them inspiring quality.

"An end to serve as a standard must be a comprehensive end for all acts of an individual, and an end comprehending the activities of various individuals — a common good. The moral end must be that for the sake of which all conduct occurs — the organizing principle of conduct — a totality, a system. The moral end must also include the ends of the various agents who make up society. It must be capable of constituting a social system out of the acts of various agents, as well as an individual system out of the various acts of one agent; or, more simply, the moral end must be not only the good for all the particular acts of the individual, but must be a common good — a good which in satisfying one satisfies others." [1]

"The fundamental necessities of life constitute ends than which none worthier can be conceived, or made the objects of education." These ends are explained to be health, knowledge, adaptation to social intercourse. "Every child is born into some social environment, and is therefore a member of some social whole. A recognition of this fact, an understanding of what it involves of personal right and personal service, a feeling of what social life is, and what social ostracism or social suicide means to the individual and to the social whole — these are necessary to an intelligent preservation of, and an effort to perfect, the social aspect of being as an end of human existence." [2]

Mastery of Nature. — Society, having charged itself, in the last resort, with the care of all its citizens, is interested in having them able to help themselves in contact with nature. The ignorant and unskilful man cannot protect himself against the destructive agencies of the external world. Its miasmas, its dangerous gas, its venomous serpents, its poison

[1] J. Dewey, *Outlines of Ethics*, p. 31.
[2] Alling-Aber, *An Experiment in Education*, pp. 83–95.

ivy and deadly mushrooms, its microscopic bacteria, and all the swarming, flying, creeping, insinuating foes of health and strength find easy victims in the untaught and undisciplined.

But the mastery of nature through science and skill is more than protective; it makes utilization of matter and force possible. The vast majority of men have capacity enough to wrest from the surrounding earth all they require to support themselves and their families, if only they know how to employ available means to the best advantage. Utilization implies more than knowledge of the laws of chemistry and physics, of the laws of plant and animal life; it requires some practical training in the direction of these elements to the supply of human wants.

The process of acquiring such necessary knowledge and skill expands the faculties of the mind, gives each man greater command of himself. It is essential not only to give citizens a knowledge of certain facts, but the power to learn other facts as they arise in experience, and to understand them and make personal adjustments to them.

Nature studies have a value in making more perfect beings. Where science is pursued by right methods the memory is crowded with delightful images. Two educational interests are thus served, taste or appreciation of beautiful objects is cultivated, and the creative activities are brought into use. Under the microscope colors and forms and wondrous combinations are discovered by the eye, and through drawing and color painting kept on record. Artistic power is thus evoked. New sources of rational satisfaction are awakened.

Nature studies, rightly conducted by competent teachers, awaken in the mind convictions that this is an orderly world, in which law, order, system, are at the basis of all things, and discoverable by the patient student.

The careful and well-directed study of nature trains the mind to love of truth for its own sake; makes exactness of seeing and saying a habit; and gives valuable discipline in mental honesty, veracity, and coöperation with others. The art of truth-telling is based on the difficult science of truth-knowing. "Easy as lying," is a proverb.

Without intending it, such studies gradually build up in the mind a conviction as to the unity, order, fidelity, rationality, and goodness which command matter and rule force. The mystery of life, manifesting itself under the eye, compels reflection on the spiritual significance of things. This result is not far away from religion.

Society desires that each citizen should be taught and disciplined to make some contribution to progress, to discovery of new facts and truths, and to useful invention or the creation of worthy and beautiful objects. Out of a sense of indebtedness to the past will grow a desire to improve the future. It is possible to make of every human being an inventor and discoverer. Every child is a creative being unless he is actually discouraged and repressed. Old knowledge can be acquired by such a method, and in such a spirit of investigation, that intellectual curiosity will become habitual. When all the members of society are thus alert and keen to observe and probe, science will advance far more rapidly than at present, when only a few are seeking new knowledge. Thus, also, old arts and ways may be so taught that the students will become habitually artists, designers, inventors. It is wonderful how many valuable designs are produced by mere children and artisans of only average capacity when they are wisely taught. Society asks that its schools so instruct its future citizens that the world may be better for every life.

But the environment in which citizens are living, and are to live, is not merely the physical world about us. Physical science is not the only science which deals with reality. Unless we actually identify physiology and psychology, matter and mind, and beg the whole question for materialism, there is still nearer to us than nature a world of spirits, of thinking beings. It is the thoughts, feelings, volitions, whims, heroisms, beliefs, prejudices, and desires of our fellow-men which most sharply affect us. There is not only an astronomical and chemical order, but there is a social order. The observance of this order by all citizens is indispensable to their happiness and growth and prosperity. Here again both knowledge and discipline are necessary, since many persons know very well what they should do but are not trained in habits suitable to community life. We have been studying the various elements of this social order; the modes of human association and coöperation; the customs and laws and beliefs in respect to family, neighborhood, industry, and friendly intercourse which regulate conduct. The supreme expression of this order is found in the state, its laws and its administration. Certainly it is socially desirable that citizens should know what society expects of them. It is hardly necessary to show how all suffer when a person is ignorant of his legal rights or duties and is swindled by those more shrewd and intelligent. If we are to have obedience to law, we must have universal knowledge of law in its principles and of the institutions through which it is administered.

Society cannot hold together without a sense of obligation on the part of each individual. The school is called upon, in the interest of order, to create reverence for all that makes our present lives rich, happy, and hopeful. In all possible ways it is desirable to show children and youth how much they are indebted to their forefathers and to their contemporaries. This recognition of debt to others is a basis of morality.

It is proper to expect from the schools that they will so teach and train the children that in them will grow up a sentiment and habit of thought favorable to socialization. The good citizen will have reverence for the benefactors of the country in the past, a strong sense of obligation to his contemporaries, and a willingness to make sacrifices for his town and for his land. The school is under obligation to foster these elements of good citizenship.

President Eliot gives a hint as to one practical method of enforcing the conviction of social dependence: —

"Another mode of implanting this sentiment is to trace in history the obligations of the present generation to many former generations. These obligations can be easily pointed out in things material, such as highways, water-works, fences, houses, and barns, and, in New England at least, the stone walls and piles of stone gathered from the arable fields by the patient labor of predecessors on the family farm; but it may also be exhibited to the pupils of secondary schools, and in some measure to the pupils of elementary schools, in the burdens and sufferings which former generations have borne for the establishment of freedom of conscience and of speech, and of toleration in religion and for the development of the institutions of public justice.

"By merely teaching children whence comes their food, drink, clothing, and means of getting light and heat, and how these materials are supplied through the labors of many individuals of many races scattered all over the world, the school may illustrate and enforce this doctrine of intricate inter-dependence, which really underlies modern democracy — a doctrine never more clearly expressed than in these two Christian sentences, 'No man liveth to himself,' and 'We are every one members one of another.' The dependence of every family, and indeed every person, on the habitual fidelity of mechanics, purveyors, railroad servants, corps, and nurses can easily be brought home to children."

The ends of society should be made a part of the conscious aims of the child.

"It may be presumed that the more conscious he is of these ends, the more perfectly he will adapt to them the means which come to his hand. At present the educational means of bringing these ends to consciousness as ends are mostly reserved for the higher institutions of learning, and even then they are not adequate. If they be true fundamental ends of human learning, every child, in his measure, has a right to them; and the primal duty of education is to bring them to consciousness in every child. . . . These ends are worthy ones, whose pursuit makes of living an art, desirable for its own sake; and this being true, these ends become the guiding lines for all educational processes, — an aid to the determination of all subject-matter to be taught, and of all methods to be used in teaching that subject-matter." [1]

One aspect of the ends of education is sometimes expressed by the assertion that the school should fit youth for the social environment. But the saying must not be accepted without an understanding of the meaning.

Environment means more than society, and that in two directions. Part of our environment is the physical world and its materials and forces. The spirit also is believed to live in the Father, in the world of religion which transcends human society though in it. If "social environment" is meant to include these lower and higher elements, it may be accepted.

"Environment" is sometimes taken to mean something fixed and stable; but education really prepares us to outgrow the present fixed conditions, to draw upon the unrealized, to invent, protest, reform, and advance. If this growing factor is implied in the definition, we may remove objection.

[1] *An Experiment in Education*, p. 103.

"Environment" may be taken to mean something merely external to the person. But education develops personality within, and does not rest with making the man a convenient tool and means of others. If the definition of environment carries the idea that the person is himself a social being, who realizes himself in social service and coöperation, this difficulty is removed.

Then we must not confine the word "environment" to the workshop and the vocation. Education does not stop with teaching a special craft, but leads to the fulness of life. Education is more than the training of blacksmiths, weavers, preachers, doctors, and actors; it is the development of men.

The demand for teaching social relations is recognized by leading educators everywhere.

"No one lives to adult years in however favorable conditions without having felt the influence of these differentiated groups upon his life — now furthering, now hindering his purposes; making his path broad and inviting, or duty paved and forbidding; elsewhere and again setting up insurmountable barriers.

"The great questions of the day are social questions belonging to this group of relations. The education of youth, compulsory school attendance, the higher culture of women and girls, the economic and moral rights of children, the existence and public treatment of a large leisure class both among the well-to-do and the needy, the conflicting rights and responsibilities of the employing and employed classes, the public care of the defectives and dependents, public manners and morals, the policing of highways and places of general resort, the punishment of criminals, their reform and nurturing, the prevention of crime, the community and institutional responsibility for crime, and the movements toward making universal or common the culture and skill and foresight which are now the possession of experts only: these are at once the great questions of the pulpit, the press, and the platform, and the vital school question."[1]

IV. What Knowledge is of Most Worth? — What teacher or parent has not asked that question? A visit to a library, or the study of a college curriculum, or a glance at the columns of magazines and newspapers with their wealth of subjects, must raise the inquiry in every thoughtful mind. In the vast accumulation of books and other expressions of knowledge

[1] President R. G. Boone, State Normal School of Michigan, in the *University Record*, Feb. 25, 1898.

we stand aghast, wondering, overwhelmed.   Yet we must choose, we must select, and we desire to secure some principle of selection.   We have already tried to show that all forms of knowledge are desirable; but some kinds are more valuable than others and should be given more emphasis. The survey of social interests already outlined may assist in making the choice.   Something must be deferred, but life is on us.   That cannot be deferred.   How to live a human life, to resist the deadly forces and utilize the powers of nature, to coöperate with our fellows in orderly ways, and to advance human welfare to a higher point, — these are matters that must not be postponed.   For meeting these needs we must have knowledge of certain facts and laws.   We are ignorant at our peril; if we are untrained and helpless, it is to the injury of our fellows.   The principle of selection of studies according to their relative worth and importance is given in the study of society, its modes of being, its problems, its wants.

Social ideals must be ever held above transient means.

> " Men who might
> Do greatly in a universe that breaks
> And burns, must ever know before they do.
> Courage and patience are but sacrifice;
> A sacrifice is offered for and to
> Something conceived of.   Each man pays a price
> For what himself counts precious, whether true
> Or false the appreciation it implies.
>   Who blames
> A crooked course, when not a goal is in them
> To round the fervid striving of the games?
> An ignorance of means may minister
> To greatness, but an ignorance of aims
> Makes it impossible to be great at all." [1]

V.   The Order of Studies and Arrangement of Programmes and Courses. — The survey of social expectations will throw light on another educational question which has long disturbed teachers and programme-makers: What is the true order of studies?   Into the controversial and disputed points it is not necessary to enter.   Nature, man, society, are here, pressing

[1] E. B. Browning, *Casa Guidi Windows*, II.

daily upon us. Literature, art, worship, are lifting up before us daily the light which beckons onward. Every day each human being, from cradle to grave, is beset by this environment. Daily does experience widen the circle of knowledge and push back the bounding horizon of vision. The question is answered clearly by the duty of every hour, by the fact of the unity of nature and life in one environment. Sitting at the dining-table every bite brings up a chemical problem, a question of physical properties and values. One cannot lift his fork to his mouth without observing or trampling upon a rule of etiquette. The very plates suggest art. Life cannot be cut up into artificial sections and taken point by point. It is all down upon us at once, in the fulness and largeness of its meaning. The school, which is initial society, and not a mere preparation for future life, must confront all the world at once. In the nursery the mother runs around the whole circle of the world with the omnivorous infant; and she is teaching chemistry, physics, arithmetic, geometry, botany, zoölogy, astronomy, poetry, music, all the day to her little brood. In the universities there are no longer universal scholars; it is an extinct species in the realm of the learned. But the mother is a universal genius, because she is companion of a human being who claims the earth, the moon, the stars, and all that is in reach of hand or eye or mouth. And the primary teacher is simply in the next stage of the process, specializing to some extent, but still the companion of the young poets who glance from earth to heaven, from heaven to earth, and whose possibilities are limitless. The diameter of the circle in the elementary and secondary school is somewhat longer, and the circumference more extended, but still teachers must go around that range of nature, man, and the laws which these reveal.

The selection of reading matter, pictures, casts, music, noble prose, is one of the most delicate duties of the parent and of school authorities. Fortunately, the literature intelligible and interesting to the young is rapidly growing, and is already very large and valuable. The material must be graded rather according to individual tastes and development than according to age.

Each day is a complete chapter of life and should have its full rights. From infancy to the transition from adolescence, life should be presented constantly in its integrity, as a whole and not as a chaotic mass of unrelated experiences. Goethe declared that every man should have before him each day a beautiful statue and picture, hear a little good music, and speak one bright sentence. Bacon declared that reading makes a full man, conversation a ready man, and writing an exact man. There is no reason why any person should not be full, ready, and exact. Life will be what is presented to the young soul and wrought into its very fibre by habitual action. Parents and teachers have this problem of presentations before them for a daily task. A child has little power of discrimination. He is omnivorous and not at all fastidious. If the matter presented is interesting, he will take it down with relish, but he is like those game fish which will bite only at "live bait." He will rise only to what is moving, active, forceful, and that he will devour without waiting to taste it. Subsequent life will reproduce just what is stored away in memory, be it evil and debasing or sublime and inspiring.

It is entirely practicable for teachers and parents, during the period of childhood and early youth, to present some significant portion of life every day to every child. In the chapter on nature the value of the physical sciences has been discussed. It is here insisted that some aspect of the external world can be and should be directly brought to the attention of child or youth every day.

Thus also each day some connected portion of the actions and works of mankind should be surveyed.

We have seen the function of art in general and the limitations and specific values of each particular art. Music should be heard and produced, as an expression of fellowship and aspiration, by every human being every day. It is entirely possible both at work and play, and the homes and schools and churches should make it a national custom. Much of the toil of sailors, farmers, laborers, drivers, and other workers is even assisted by a song. Hours of leisure should often be filled with delightful, cheerful, and noble choruses.

From earliest childhood pupils should be accustomed to

R

rhythmic action in concert with others, with or without musical accompaniment. Some parents will have objections to teaching dancing, but none will object to calisthenic exercises, motion songs, marching movements, by which action is socialized. Immorality is selfish and inharmonious, unsocial conduct; and one cure of it is unselfish and coöperative action made habitual and customary. The meaning will be felt by the child and interpreted later in life, when reflection begins. The words of the songs which accompany the rhythmic action may suggest the thought which the play symbolizes. The words of affection tend to awaken affection.

Poetry should form an element in daily habit, a part of social custom in home, school, and church. It should be the duty of each member of each family to contribute some perfect expression of fine thought at the table, so that the act of eating shall be associated in thought with the highest ideals of the race. This is one point in favor of free dinners, nicely served, at school. Out of the stores of memory each member of the school should be required to bring at regular and frequent intervals some "quoted ode or jewel five words long" for the common pleasure. Thus also passages of perfect prose, worthy expression of some master of the race, should be read and recited, not merely as a means of training the facial muscles, but to give social pleasure of the first order. On the walls of all homes and schools and Sunday Schools should be hung copies of the works of great artists, photographs, and plaster casts, so that the eye, even in its casual wanderings and turns of resting, should alight upon an object of beauty. All the designing and artistic gifts of school and home should be called upon to make blackboards beautiful with color and graceful forms. If without the sky and clouds and landscape are beautiful, the teacher can call attention to the glorious display. Even in the gloomy and narrow streets of crowded cities the desk of the teachers and the sill of the window may shine with flowers. All the better if trips to the open country enable the teacher to develop the taste of the pupils for natural beauty.

Conduct itself may be made a fine art. The ordinary routine of home and school may be so cheerful, systematic, harmonious, as to be a discipline in moral conduct. By a moderate exercise of invention the educator of childhood may find ways of training the young to think of the needs and interests, the feelings and desires, of those outside their circle of house and playground, and introduce them, with thoughts and purposes of good, to the wide, wide world.

Professor G. E. Vincent[1] has made an admirable study of the scheme of study for a college course based on the social demands of the age; and from this recent investigation we may here profit.

It is true that a formal course of study for a college is adapted to those who are mature enough to consciously and intentionally seek an integration or correlation of the different matters of knowledge and of practice. At this advanced stage of culture, it is proper to follow out special lines of investigation according to the division of labor used in the world of science and literature. Thus in college it is desirable to make a special class for chemistry, for botany, or for civil government. The mature teacher or parent may look forward to this scheme and catch some prophetic hints of the direction in which it will be wise to direct and encourage even the child in the kindergarten. For the baby faces toward the university, or rather to that noble life which the university serves, from the moment it opens its eyes to the light. "I have urged," says one of the inventive and inspiring teachers of our land, "that all subjects taught in any university shall be begun in an elementary way with the little child of six years of age, and that exercises in all the modes of expression shall be continued or imitated."[2]

If we divide the "studies" into four main classes, we have a tentative and suggestive arrangement something like the following scheme, which shows the outline of college work and the connection of one topic with the others:

(*a*) Formal and instrumental studies,— mathematics and language; the famous "Three R's," reading, writing, arithmetic, being examples. These are not to be learned merely for their own sake and before anything else is learned, but in

1 *The Social Mind and Education*, p. 126.
2 F. W. Parker, *Talks on Pedagogics*, p. 388.

the process of learning something felt to be desirable for its own sake, and as means of expression. It is not here implied that "formal" studies have no intrinsic value and interest.

(*b*) The physical conditions of social life,— nature studies. (1) The sciences of the inorganic,— physics, chemistry, astronomy. (2) The sciences of the organic, of life,— biology, botany, zoölogy. (3) Physical geography.

(*c*) The human person. (1) Physiology,— closely connected with the life sciences and geography. (2) Psychology. (3) Ideals,— art, literature (as a form of art), biography, ethics, religion.

(*d*) Men in society. (1) Domestic institutions. (2) The arts. (3) Industry and business (economics). (4) Politics (civil government) and law. (5) Literature (as one expression of historical growth). (6) History. (7) Sociology and social ethics.

Specialization. — There is indeed a necessity for specialization, if we heed the lesson of social life. Specialization is necessary for an educational reason, and also for a social reason. The interests of education require that each person learn one thing so thoroughly that he will ever have in his mind a high and critical standard of perfect work. The social reason is that we must learn to trust experts and to respect them, if they are competent. These lessons must be impressed in school during the plastic years.

One important cause of popular opposition to "civil-service reform" in our country lies in the fact that our education has not sufficiently taught the people to respect specialists. We think any person can soon learn to do anything just as well as another. Why should a man not pass at once from being an engineer to be statistician of the city or commonwealth? Why should we not elect a person skilful in managing primaries to be postmaster? Why should not a successful distiller become superintendent of an asylum for the insane? Perhaps in coming years, when our schools have been careful to require each child to learn some particular thing thoroughly, whatever else is done superficially, we shall have a citizenship with more exacting demands upon public servants.

There is nothing inconsistent in giving pupils a broad culture while we give them at the same time discipline in some one subject until perfection is attained. It is one advantage of the sloyd and manual training methods that accuracy and finish can be at once tested and measured at every step by the child himself. A boy who has failed twenty times in trying to fashion a perfect foot rule out of a bit of box wood, and at last reaches the moment of triumph with his masterpiece, has a lesson in absolute standards of veracity, justice, sound learning, and thoroughness which he will never forget. From that moment he has a standard of completeness which he can apply to all studies and all labors. He becomes intolerant of sham, of half-way knowledge, of hypocrisy in every form.

President Eliot has emphasized this idea of specialization. "In some small field each child should acquire a capacity for exact observation, exact description, and power to draw a justly limited inference from observed facts." [1]

VI. Illustrations of Methods. — Up to this point we have been looking at the school simply as one of the social institutions which compose the entire system of society. We have been trying to make clear what society must require of its schools. This is all the scope of this work demands. It is not the duty of the writer on society to go beyond his field into the realm of teachers and instruct them in their art. The division of scientific and professional labor requires us to lay the entire responsibility of method on pedagogy and pedagogues, and there it must rest. It is not proposed to trespass on the preserves of the teaching profession and the normal school.

But for many years there has been a growing conviction on the part of the more advanced teachers that social life must determine the means to be used in the school. The literature of education is now teeming with suggestions and reports of experiments, some of them crude enough, but many of them indicating a rapid and wholesome improvement in theory and practice.

It will make some of the points already discussed still more clear and impressive if a few of these experimental methods be outlined. The teaching devices here given are not intended

[1] *The Outlook*, Nov. 6, 1897, p. 570.

to be systematic and exhaustive, but suggestive and aphoristic. It is useless to insist upon a principle of social duty without showing, by pertinent illustrations, that it is within range of practice.

Children come to school at the age of five or six, or even to the kindergarten, with a social experience and memory. They have learned by imitation how to walk, talk, make and interpret gestures. They have heard music and become familiar with family life,— its industries, economics, thrift, saving, technical processes of cooking and housekeeping, coöperation in work, sociable converse, worship, and insistence on moral order of duties and virtues. The child has known law and government, and thus does not arrive at the school a mere blank paper to be written over with the teacher's own egotism. The possession of language is a treasure and the key to a greater treasury.

The school itself, even without any conscious plan of imitating society at large, is a miniature social organization. There is government, order, preferred qualities and habits, ideals to be admired and followed, and the discipline of coöperating actions.

The neighborhood furnishes new social experiences, and the road to school affords incidents for instruction in the social order. There is property in apples and flowers by the way, to be protected by the social conscience. There are the rules of highway and pavement to be learned and respected. There is the awful legend over the bridge, "Five dollars fine for riding or driving faster than a walk."

The children have had social experience at Sunday School and church, and have formed some dim provisional notion of the ecclesiastical organization about them, and the peculiarity of its purposes.

The problem of the teacher is to utilize all these experiences so as to secure an orderly arrangement of the images in the child's mind. Manifestly the teacher must first secure such a conception of the relations of social institutions as will make direction possible. The teacher must, as guide, know the world about the school, and have a large, exact, clear, and systematic view of the structure and relations of the members of the community. This does not require that each teacher must be a social philosopher and master of culture history and student of the dawn of time. All that is necessary is a true, complete, and intelligent conception of the institutions near at hand, a keen interest in their purpose and working, and a living curiosity to follow out the lines which run from the cross-road store to the tea plantations of dusky Chinamen and to the iron mines of Michigan.

By the aid of sand charts and maps, pictures, globes, and stories, the paths of thought and fancy will lead to the ends of the world; and the little schoolhouse will be populous with images of societies of a hundred different types. Thus the mental horizon will expand and the affections and reverence of the children will make them kin to all mankind.

Many teachers are actually organizing the school itself into various forms of association like those into which the lives of the children are to flow at maturity. And here the play instincts come to the aid of the ingenious teacher.

Play is not merely the overflow of exuberant animal spirits. Nor is it merely the imitation of the serious work of mature persons. Play is both these and more. By a useful and interesting instinct children are actually trained by their plays to learn the callings of adult life.[1] Every game of this kind is part of an apprenticeship to a trade or calling. All is free, unconstrained, pleasure-giving, and yet directly adapted to practice in useful habits. The teacher has a right to take advantage of these functions of play activity and direct it to an educational end.

Wise Plato had a clear view of the significance of play in education. "And the education must begin with their plays. The spirit of law must be imparted to them in music, and the spirit of order, instead of disorder, will attend them in all their actions, and make them grow, and if there be any part of the State which has fallen down, will raise that up again."

Let us apply the suggestion to the imitation and study of industrial and business institutions. It would be easy to find a clerk who could show how to organize the entire body of pupils into a bank, with its clerks and customers. A visit to

[1] Baldwin, *Social and Ethical Interpretations*, p. 139.

a bank would give the children not only a more definite conception of the modes of business, but would lead them to inquire further about the social use of the banker. Every school, perhaps, ought to be itself a branch of the savings-bank system. When a savings department is added to our postal system, this will be easier to arrange. Knowledge would be gained, skill in accounts, the habit of foresight and thrift, the inclination to save and provide for future events, — qualities which lift the child above momentary animal and savage impulse.

Dr. Elisha Gray, the famous inventor, gives us a delightful parable of the law of power through use and exercise : —

"I have said that the permanent magnet would hold its charge after once having been magnetized. This is only true in a sense and under favorable conditions. If made of the best of steel for the purpose, and hardened and tempered in just the right way, it will hold its charge *if it is given something to do.* If a piece of iron is placed across its poles it also becomes a magnet, and its molecules turn and work in harmony with those of the mother magnet. These magnetic lines of force reach around in a circuit. Even before the iron, or 'keeper,' as it is called, is put across its poles, there are lines of force reaching around through the air or ether from one pole to another. This is called the field of the magnet, and when the iron is placed in this field the lines of force pass through it in a closed circuit, and if the 'keeper' is large enough to take care of all the lines of force in the field, the magnet will not attract other bodies, because its attraction is satisfied. As long as we give our magnet something to do, up to the measure of its capacity, it will keep up its power. We may make other magnets with it, thousands, yea millions, of them, and it not only does not lose its power but may be even stronger for having done this work. If, however, we hang it up without its 'keeper,' and give it nothing to do, it gradually returns to its natural condition in the home circle of molecular rings. Little by little the coercive force is overcome by the constant tendency of the molecule to go back to its natural position among its fellows."

In many schools it has been found practicable to give the older pupils some actual share in the instruction, management, and even government of the school. It is by action that we are led to reflection. The school itself, as one of the most precious institutions of the land, should become the object of study by the pupils. Its purpose should be made clear; its cost should be understood, and the expectations of its founders should be rehearsed.

The school may become the material for study of political institutions and of legal administration. At the time of a primary or regular election the teacher may take advantage of the natural interest of the pupils and help them to go through the forms with which all citizens should be more familiar. The issues may be discussed under the guidance of a discreet leader.

In relation to streets and roads, the children are sometimes organized into brigades for reporting defects to the authorities, to keep a short bit of highway ideally clean and beautiful as a rebuke to the neglected sections. Conduct is more educative than lectures.

There is an immediate advantage in organizing the children into a fire department. Military history can be illustrated in a way never to be forgotten if the boys are asked, when the snow falls, to fortify a field, just as their fathers prepared for the battle of Bunker Hill or Gettysburg. Snow is plastic and good material for projectiles and for constructing the plans of foreign cities, palaces, and halls of legislature.

In many neighborhoods there will be occasion for organizing the children into relief societies for helping poor families. Hospitals may be remembered, and gentle deeds be done in neglected poorhouses where aged people pine and droop unnoticed and forgotten. The chorus of children may be permitted to sing their joyous glees and carols for those whose declining day is clouded by sorrow and poverty. Thus, by action, the three forms of reverence taught by Goethe in *Wilhelm Meister* are woven into the habits of the soul and the customs of the town.

In a certain city vacation school there was organized a "Clean City League." The older pupils received instruction in regard to city ordinances governing the cleaning of streets, alleys, yards, and garbage boxes. The members of the league were asked to observe the condition of the neighborhood and to bring in formal complaints of all violation of the ordinances. These complaints were sent to the city hall and received prompt attention from the authorities. The members were also taught that each citizen should help the authorities by not making dirt or throwing papers or rubbish in the streets. In this school every morning all of the teachers and pupils gathered in the school hall for opening exercises. They sang a patriotic hymn, saluted the American flag, and repeated the following Civic Creed: —

"God hath made of one blood all nations of men, and we are his children, brothers and sisters all. We are citizens of these United States, and we believe our flag stands for self-sacrifice for the good of all the people. We want, therefore, to be true citizens of our great city, and will show our love for her by our works.

"Our city does not ask us to die for her welfare; she asks us to live for her, and so to live and so to act that her government may be pure, her officers honest, and every corner of her territory shall be a place fit to grow the best men and women who shall rule over her."

The Gill School City. — Mr. Wilson L. Gill, of New York, has worked out a plan for the organization of children in the public schools into a miniature municipality or "school city." The plan was successfully carried out during the months of July and August with the twelve hundred children in a vacation school in the east side of the city of New York. The children were organized into a perfect miniature municipality, governed exactly like large cities, with a mayor, aldermen, police, street-cleaning, and health departments. The officers were elected or appointed as they are in New York, and they performed their duties under the rules of the several departments of the municipal government of that city. The plan not only solves the questions of discipline and control within the school, and of keeping the school buildings and grounds in sanitary condition, but is of the greatest value in teaching, by "doing," the duties of citizenship. The plan is now being introduced into two or three of New York's schools and into the Hoffman School of Philadelphia. It is hoped to extend it to the schools of all the large cities of the country (*Public Opinion*, Aug. 26, 1897).

To Mr. W. A. Millis, Attica, Indiana, I owe the following illustrations of methods in actual use: —

"In the ordinary school activities various and many devices are resorted to to secure coöperative work, — decoration of rooms; committee work in care of property, distribution of materials, criticism of work, etc. The pupils are made responsible as a body for as much as possible of the mechanism. In the many ways offered to a bright sympathetic teacher she endeavors to awaken and mould a healthy social consciousness. The method of procedure may be illustrated with the study of the bank in the sixth grade. By discussions, excursions, and reading the pupils work out the province of the bank, as place of safety deposit, means of easy and safe exchange, the local clearing house, as a promoter of business, as the good neighbor that helps the business man over the tide, etc. The pupils are taken to a bank, its workings explained, depositing, checking out, buying exchange, loans; and particularly pupils are made to feel at least, and understand if possible, the 'disinterested honesty' of the bank as a public servant. We want them to get acquainted with and become friends with the bank as an institution."

Another interesting experiment is the University Elementary School, Rosalie Court, Chicago : —

" *Grading.*— In order that the pupils may receive individual attention, each of the younger groups is limited to eight children; after the age of twelve to fifteen, as circumstances prove advisable. At present the children are arranged in eight groups, the youngest children being five and six, the oldest eleven and twelve. The grading is flexible, the children being classified, not according to technical attainments, but according to intellectual maturity and capacity for work. Children in the same group do varying amounts of work along the same general line, thus combining community of aim and material with variety of individual execution. Children are advanced from one group to another whenever they show signs of requiring the stimulus of more difficult work. No examinations are held, nor marks given.

" *The Programme.* — The programme is arranged on the basis of providing a balance between active (manual training, gymnasium, cooking, sewing, etc.) and more strictly intellectual work. Each group has physical culture daily. Each group has field work, or visits some museum, gallery, etc., weekly. With the younger children the active factor predominates; and work in science, history, number, etc., is kept in strict connection with the constructive activities of cooking, sewing, and carpentering. Differentiation is gradually introduced as the children mature, till (as with Groups VI–VIII at present) distinctively intellectual problems are introduced. Books are neither made a fetich nor excluded. Lessons specially prepared, records of work done, etc., are printed for the smaller children, and this work will be carried much further as soon as the school has a printing-press — a great need at present. Books are used with older groups not as set texts, but for reference, as convenient summaries and as guides to the matter under discussion. Owing to limitation of funds, art work at present save in music is scantily provided for. It is hoped that this will speedily be remedied.

"*Moral Aims.* — Genuine, as distinct from artificial, moral growth is measured by the extent to which children practically recognize in the school the same moral motives and relations that obtain outside. This can be secured only when the school contains the social conditions, and presents the flexible, informal relations that prevail in every-day life. When school duties and responsibilities are of a sort found only in the school, comparatively little aid is secured for the all-round, healthy development of character. When school conditions are so rigid and formal as not to parallel anything outside the school, external order and decorum may be secured, but there is no guarantee of right growth in directions demanded by the ordinary walks of life. When what is expected of children is based on the requirements of school lessons and school order as laid down by text-books or teacher, not by work of positive value to those doing it, external habits of attention and restraint may be formed, but not power of initiative and direction nor moral self-control.

" Hence the emphasis in the school laid upon social occupations which continue and reinforce those of life outside the school, and the comparative freedom and informality accorded the children. These are means, not an end. Moral responsibility is secured only by corresponding freedom. Hence the school work on the moral side is to be judged not by passing, external occurrences, but by its efficiency in promoting healthy growth of character, which is slow, not sudden; and a general modification of disposition and motive, not an external bearing or attitude.

"*Intellectual Aims. The Question of Motive.* — For genuine intellectual development, it is impossible to separate the attainment of knowledge from its application. The divorce between learning and its use is the most serious defect in our existing education. Without the consciousness of application, 'learning' has no motive to the child. Material thus 'learned' is separated from the actual conditions of the child's life; and a fatal split is introduced between school learning and vital experience — a split which reflects itself in the child's whole mental and moral attitude. The emphasis in the school upon constructive and so-called manual work is due largely to the fact that such occupations connect themselves easily and naturally with the child's every-day environment, create natural motives for the acquiring of information and the mastery of related methods through the problems which they introduce.

"*The Question of Method.* — As to methods, the aim is to keep alive and direct the active, inquiring attitude of the child, and to subordinate the amassing of facts and principles to the development of intellectual self-control, — power to conceive and solve problems. Immense damage is done wherever the getting of a certain quantity of information or covering a certain amount of ground is made the end, at the expense of mastery of methods of inquiry and reflection. If children can retain their natural investigating tendencies unimpaired, gradually organizing them into definite methods of work, when they reach the proper age they can master the required amount of facts and generalizations much more effectively than when the latter are forced upon them at so early a period as to crush

the natural interest in searching out new truths. Acquiring tends to re-
place inquiring.

"*The Question of Subject-Matter.* — Statistics show that, in our existing
school system, from sixty to eighty per cent of the time of the first two or
three years of school life is spent upon mastery of the technical forms
of knowledge, learning to make and recognize written and printed forms
and manipulate number symbols. If these same ends can be accomplished
(even if somewhat later than at present), and the child at the same time
brought in contact with fields of experience which have a positive value
of their own, there can be no doubt of the great gain. Accordingly reading, writing, spelling, composition, figuring, etc., are not introduced as
ends in themselves. They come in as records of what has been done, and
as helps in connection with the positive subject-matter found in history,
literature, and science. So far as experience goes, it demonstrates that
the relative loss in the amount gone over in the first two or three years, is
much more than made up for in ability to use intelligently what is got, to
say nothing of the inestimable advantage of substitution of intrinsically
valuable facts and ideas for the trivialities of ordinary reading and writing
lessons, etc." — *The University Record*, Jan., 1898. $\mathcal{t_o}$ $\mathcal{here}$

VII. Betterment of Rural Schools. — Order and progress,
peace and vigorous life, in the United States depend, in very
great degree, on the condition and work of the rural schools.
The subject is of vital importance to the entire nation and
to mankind. Already these schools have done a splendid
work. Multitudes of strong men and women, leaders in the
centres of industrial and political life, professors in colleges,
editors of wide influence, have been educated in their early
life by these modest institutions. Some of our greatest statesmen have had no other regular instruction. At this hour the
rural school is quietly sending forward a noble army of
healthy, sensible, and patriotic students, many of whom are
to be in the front rank of society in years to come.

But we must advance. The achievements of the past can
be maintained only by virtue of progress. The tree must send
out new buds and leaves or it must perish. The economic
condition of the world is rapidly changing. Wasteful methods
are more ruinous than when we had plenty of free and virgin
soil. The modern means of transportation have made the
farmer of to-day in Missouri or Minnesota the competitor of
the cheap laborer of India or of Siberia. Necessity goads to
invention, and invention demands educated minds. Worn
soils will not be restored to their productive powers without

knowledge and application of chemistry. Farmers will not know what crops to raise in due proportion without knowledge of the demands of foreign countries and the markets of manufacturing cities. Men must farm with their mental powers as well as with their hands, and thought must direct muscle. The competitions of the world market have come down upon us to compel us to be wise and skilful and educated.

There are in some quarters of our country very deplorable facts which demand serious thought and effort. The tendency to city life provoked by the increase of manufactures, stimulated by the spectacle of large fortunes, incited by the desire to live in the centres of motion, culture, and interest, has drawn away many farmers and their families from certain districts, and population has thus diminished. Frequently, the character of the population has changed for the worse, and the tenant immigrants have not had the same ideals as those of the earlier residents. Roads and schools and churches under these conditions have grown worse. The very regions which have most need of good schools are often too poor to support them, and as the means of education become inferior the very desire for culture diminishes. Reports from many parts of the Union reveal the fact that the schools are too small to permit necessary grading of classes and furnish enough pupils to be inspiring and encouraging to teacher and pupil. Where numbers are so small the salaries are too low to induce competent teachers to give themselves to the task.

This is not an indictment against the rural schools in general. The statement applies only where the conditions described actually exist. But there they apply in their full force. The nation cannot afford to leave any portion of its population in circumstances which tend to barbarism. Each human being affects the life of all.

What is required? What means of reformation are advisable? On this subject we have the verdict of experts, in the "Report of the Committee of Twelve on Rural Schools,"[1] made to the National Educational Association in 1897. Some

---

[1] Published separately by the University of Chicago Press. See the discussions on the subject in *Proceedings of National Educational Association*, Milwaukee, 1897.

of the principal points of agreement may here be set down by way of illustration. I use the language of Mr. Henry Sabin, the chairman : (1) "For purposes of organization, maintenance, or supervision, nothing should be recognized as the unit smaller than the township or the county; the school district is the most undesirable unit possible. (2) Every community should be required to raise a certain sum for the support of its schools as a prerequisite for receiving its share of public money. A certain definite sum should be appropriated to each school out of the state funds, and the remainder should be divided in accordance with some fixed and established rule, a discrimination being made in favor of townships most willing to tax themselves for school purposes. (3) One of the great hindrances to the improvement of the rural school lies in its isolation, and its inability to furnish the pupil that stimulative influence which comes from contact with others of his own age and advancement. The committee, therefore, recommends collecting pupils from small schools into larger, and paying, from the public funds, for their transportation, believing that in this way better teachers can be provided, more rational methods of instruction adopted, and at the same time the expense of the schools can be materially lessened. (4) There is a tendency to fill the rural schools with untrained, immature teachers. The establishment of normal training schools, under competent instructors, with short courses, each year of which shall be complete in itself, would do much to remedy this evil. The extension and adjustment of the courses and terms of the state normal schools so as to constitute a continuous session would enable them to contribute more directly than now to the improvement of the teachers of rural schools. The state would then be justified in demanding some degree of professional training from every teacher in the rural as well as in the city schools. (5) The establishment of libraries, the prosecution of the work of school extension by lectures and other means, the introduction of such studies as will have a tendency to connect the school and the home, especially those having a direct bearing upon the every-day life of the community, and the necessity of applying the laws of sanitation to the construction of rural schoolhouses, demand immediate attention. (6) The rural schools are suffering from the want of official and intelligent supervision. In every state some standard of qualifications, moral and intellectual, with some amount of actual experience, should be demanded by law from those who aspire to fill the office of superintendent or supervisor of schools. (7) Good morals and good manners constitute an essential part of an educational equipment. The inculcation of patriotism, of respect for law and order, of whatever tends to make a good citizen, is of as much importance in a small as in a larger school. Regularity, punctuality, obedience, industry, self-control, are as necessary in the country as in the city school. Country school teachers should call to their aid the beautiful things in nature, that with reverential spirit they may lead the children to reverence Him who hath made all things good in their season."

One reform helps another forward. In the Report already quoted, we find this example of the principle of social solidarity: "School consolidation turns largely upon means of cheap, safe, and easy communication throughout the school area. Here we touch a question intimately relating to social progress — the improvement of roads. Those who have been promoting this movement have not probably regarded it as a measure of educational reform; but such it is. Perhaps there is no rural interest of a social nature that would be more decidedly enhanced by good roads than the educational interest. The people of some of the towns of Ohio, where the new plan is being tried, claim this as a decided advantage, that the drivers of the omnibuses serve as carriers for the mails between the farmhouses and the post offices, thus promoting the diffusion of intelligence in still another way."

In illustration of the principle that the school should be related closely to the daily home life and the probable life interest of the child, an important suggestion is made, and that on the basis of successful experiments. The normal schools should fit teachers of rural schools to give instruction in horticulture and agriculture. The school garden should be a feature of every school, as a means of education in the elements of physical science, as chemistry and biology, and as a direct agency for training children for their future life work.

By connecting the daily labor with the study of beauty and of science, the ordinary occupation of the community comes to be associated in the mind, not with servile drudgery, but with the accomplishments and dignified pursuits of the soul.[1]

The township system of rural schools should not be content with a plan of elementary instruction; it should be itself a comprehensive system of education for persons of all classes and all ages. The entire community should be united in enthusiastic devotion to constant study. There is no end to knowledge and to the need of knowledge. The brain loses its power unless it is busy with fresh thought. Common pursuit of ideal goods elevates the standard of thought and binds together the people in a worthy fellowship. Political thought and action become more serious, effective, and helpful when all citizens are reading the same books and discussing the topics thus introduced. Church life becomes broader, kinder, more practical and generous with influx of new forms of knowledge. Home life is made more attractive, purer, more wholesome by the perpetual supply of fresh inspirations, noble literature, and interchange of ideas among neighbors. Country society comes to have some of the advantages of city life, its variety of interest, its intellectual stimulus, its broader outlook; with this advantage over city life that there is more quiet and leisure for reflection and meditation during the winter season.

The supervisor of the school system of a township may well be the leader in such a large and hopeful work; he may act with the state reading circle, with county school authorities, and with educated persons to frame plans of reading, to arrange meetings for discussion, debate, and entertainment, and to give certificates of work done upon the basis of careful

---

[1] "A series of text-books have been prepared for school and home use. Professor Bailey, of Cornell University, has written *Plant-Breeding: a Horticulturist's Rule Book*. Professor King has given us a good book on the Soil. Professor Voorhees, of the New Jersey Agricultural College, a *Manual of Agriculture*. Professor Shaler, of Harvard, Professor Waldo, Professor Tarr of Cornell, and Professor Spaulding, on geology, botany, entomology, chemistry, and meteorology in their applied forms, as well as physical geography, adapted to the use of children on the farms." — *E. P. Powell, in the Independent*, Jan. 20, 1898.

A list of books is given on pp. 190–193, *Rep. Com. on Rural Schools*.

s

records. He will be the responsible officer to care for the
local library, see that it is replenished with new publications,
and that the volumes are worn out by actual use, since to be
used up in usefulness is the end of books and of good people.

VIII. The Duty of Society to the School. — If education is
for social life, and the imperative condition of order, happiness, and progress, then we have determined for us the duty
of the state in relation to education.   We know the function
of government as the organ of the universal will.   Society has
no other instrument through which the entire community can
protect its interests, promote its welfare, and secure its good.
If it is true that education, of the right sort, is a universal
necessity, then the agency of the universal will must provide
for it.   Society cannot risk this essential in the hands of private parties and irresponsible bodies.   That which is vital to
order and progress must be provided for beyond the possibility of failure through caprice and fashion.   The state must
provide schools for all and require the attendance of all the
growing community.

This does not mean that private and parochial schools
should be suppressed.   It is even an advantage to have a kind
of competition in methods.   Perhaps all schools are better
for a degree of rivalry.   Perhaps any institution might become
formal, bureaucratic, and dead, in the absence of varied and
competing institutions.

But it is a fair inference that the state must guarantee a certain minimum of education to every child, and make higher
culture and research work possible in every branch of science.
There is no logical limit to the state function in education, if
all are left free.   Its work reaches from the primary school to
the university.   And as the process of education is endless,
each community should provide, by means of voluntary associations, classes, conferences of teachers, and citizens, for
adult study.   For this advanced work the schoolrooms are the
natural place of assembly, where all citizens feel they have a
right to be.   The educational functions of the government
do not end even with university graduates.

CHAPTER XII

Socialized Idealism. Religion and the Church

" God is in all that liberates and lifts,
In all that humbles, sweetens, and consoles."
— J. R. LOWELL, *The Cathedral.*

" Pomp and ostentation of reading is admired among the vulgar, but
doubtless in matter of religion he is learnedest who is plainest. The brev-
ity I use, not exceeding a small manual, will not therefore, I suppose, be
thought the less considerable, unless with them perhaps who think that
great books only can determine great matters. I rather choose the common rule, not to make much ado, where less may serve. Which in controversies, and those especially of religion, would make them less tedious,
and by consequence read oftener by many men, and with more benefit."
— JOHN MILTON, *A Treatise of Civil Power.*

" Religion's all or nothing; it's no mere smile
O' contentment, sigh of aspiration, Sir —
Rather, stuff
O' the very stuff, life of life, and self of self."
— R. BROWNING.

" The life of Christ was lived to inspire, not to confuse. Little things
are restless; the great repose. Scholars are tenacious of details, for they
hold the values of accuracy in their keeping. But Christian scholars are
generous in feeling, for they hold the treasures of faith in trust. They may
contend about the unimportant. On the essential they will agree. . . .
The important things — all that any of us need, all that most of us care
for — are few, clear, and unquestionable. Jesus Christ lived and died, and
lived again after death. He lived a life explicable upon no other view of
it than his. He founded a faith comprehensible upon no other interpretation of it than his own. He himself is Christianity. He is the greatest
force in civilization : the highest motive power in philosophy, in art, in
poetry, in science, in faith. He is the centre of human brotherhood. To
apprehend him is to open the only way that has yet been found out of the
trap of human misery. His personality is the best explanation yet given

259

of the mystery of human life. It offers the only assurance we have of a life to come. . . . The butterflies of immortal hope are delicate organisms, easily impaled by sceptical naturalists, and eagerly catalogued with other lost ideals. . . . Men are many, and scholars are few. It is with more confidence in the warm, human world outside of books, that this one hopes to find its friends.

"There has come to me, during the time given to the growth of this work, an experience always full of wonder and of charm. Often, on waking in the morning, after days of the most absorbing and affectionate study of the Great Life, the first conscious thought has been, 'Who was with me yesterday? What noble being entered this door? In what delightful, in what high society, have I been? I felt as if I had made a new, a supreme acquaintance. . . . I pass over this feeling to those who can understand it, or who may share it, and wish it, from my heart, for those who do not."

— ELIZABETH STUART PHELPS, *The Story of Jesus Christ.*

"But what we seek is association.

"How shall we realize this securely, unless among brothers, believing in the same ruling principle, united in the same faith, and bearing witness by the same name?

"What we seek is education.

"How shall we give or receive it, unless in virtue of a principle, that sums up and expresses our common belief as to the origin, the aim, and the law of the life of mankind upon earth?

"We seek a common education.

"How shall we give or receive it without belief in a common faith and a common duty?

"And whence can we deduce a common duty, if not from the idea we form of God and our relation to Him?"

"Doubtless universal suffrage is an excellent thing. It is the only legal means by which a people may govern itself without risk of continual violent crises. Universal suffrage in a country governed by a common faith is the expression of the national will; but in a country deprived of a common belief, what can it be but the mere expression of the interests of those numerically the stronger, to the oppression of all the rest?

"All the political reforms achieved in countries either irreligious or indifferent to religion have lasted as long as interest allowed — no longer. On this point the experience of political movements in Europe during the last fifty years has taught us lessons enough.

"To those who speak to you of heaven, and seek to separate it from earth, you will say that heaven and earth are one, even as the way and the goal are one. Tell us not that the earth is of clay. The earth is of God. God created it as the medium through which we may ascend to Him. The earth is not a mere sojourn of temptation or of expiation; it is the appointed dwelling-place wherein we are bound to work out our own im-

provement and development and advance towards a higher stage of existence. God created us not to contemplate, but to act. He created us in
His own image, and He is Thought and Action, or rather, in Him there is
no Thought which is not simultaneous Action.

"You tell us to despise all worldly things, to trample under foot our terrestrial life, in order to concern ourselves solely with the Celestial; but
what is our terrestrial life save a prelude to the Celestial, — a step towards
it? See you not that while sanctifying the last step of the ladder by which
we must all ascend, by thus declaring the first accursed you arrest us on
the way?" — MAZZINI, *The Duties of Man.*

I. We may follow our uniform method thus far and begin
with recalling to our minds the *visible institutions* and *social
manifestations* of religion. It is always desirable to collect
some unquestionable facts and deal with reality at first hand.
That religion is actually a mighty force in society no one
doubts, and the marks and outward revelations of that force
are everywhere manifest in edifices, associations, assemblies,
congregations, conventions, numbering many thousands, census returns of membership, reports of work, deeds of beneficence, devotion of money and life in furtherance of religious
ends.

It is well for us to approach the social study of religion
without prejudice, as far as possible. Social theory does not
consider whether creeds are true or false. That work belongs
to metaphysicians, theologians, preachers. There must be
division of mental labor, and sociology does not inquire into
the grounds for the various beliefs of mankind, nor seek to
criticise or reconcile the warring tenets of creeds.

But the student of society has no right to ignore any solid
fact which bears upon the explanation of institutions and
associated movements. Even if one detests a doctrine in
finance, politics, art, or religion, he must not pass it over in
giving a history of an age. One must be impartial and never
close his mind's door in face of any factor which helps to
explain life. Therefore we must notice the fact of religion.
It will readily be understood that the word "church" is used
here as the common and well-understood designation of all
institutions of religion. Into the particular definitions given
in ecclesiastical and theological controversies this is not the
place to enter.

II. The Immediate Causes of the Church. — Certain beliefs, convictions, hopes, affections, and determinations, shared by a vast number of the members of society, and affecting all members in some degree, explain the church. These beliefs relate to the "ground of being," to the hope of future life, to present duty, to the nature of man and his spiritual origin. Religion, like all interests of mankind, has three aspects,— rational, emotional, and active. It is a certain mode of thinking, a mass of feeling and sentiment, an attitude of will, and a course of conduct.

Because religion is human, it must be imperfect in its earthly manifestations. There is no perfect music, painting, architecture, oratory, government. Science is always outgrowing its clothes and bursting its seams. Philosophy is ever increasing in compass and clearness. All that is human is a becoming, something in process of growth. Earth has no complete circles, only arcs that suggest vast circles. Our souls are narrow. "God's fruit of justice ripens slow." Each new book is a confession of the sins of ancestors and an appeal to the mercy of posterity. Newton and Galileo, if they were now alive, would admit the imperfections of their great work. There is no use to quarrel with our destiny. Volumes have been written filled with criticism of the church, its creeds, its acts, its superstitions. The criticism was necessary, for it is only by revelations of error that we advance to larger truths.

The church has no monopoly of bigotry. A French free-thinker writes: "Formerly, when a city was attacked by some scourge, the first care of the notable inhabitants, of the chiefs of the city, was to order public prayers; to-day the practical means for battling with epidemics and other scourges are better known, but nevertheless, in 1885, when there was cholera in Marseilles, the municipal council devoted its attention almost singly to removing the religious mottoes from the walls of the public schools; it is a remarkable example of what one may call a counter-superstition."[1]

> "Man is not God, but hath God's end to serve,
> A master to obey, a course to take,
> Somewhat to cast off, somewhat to become?

[1] Guyau, *Non-Religion of the Future*, p. 18.

> Grant this, then man must pass from old to new.
> From vain to real, from mistake to fact,
> From what once seemed good to what now proves best.
>
> *   *   *   *   *   *   *   *
>
> While man knows partly but conceives beside,
> Creeps ever on from fancies to the fact,
> And in this striving, this converting air
> Into a solid he may grasp and use,
> Finds progress, man's distinctive mark alone,
> Not God's and not the beasts'; God is, they are,
> Man partly is and wholly hopes to be." — R. BROWNING.

Man cannot rise above his own thought; it is his duty and right to help his thought to grow more complete, more adequate.

> "Each age must worship its own thought of God,
> More or less earthy, clarifying still
> With subsidence continuous of dregs."
>
> — J. R. LOWELL, *The Cathedral.*

Social consciousness of the imperfection of all things human brings with it sweet reasonableness and tolerance or charity of judgment.   "It is said that John Huss, when tied to the stake at Constance, wore a smile of supreme joy when he perceived a peasant in the crowd, bringing straw from the roof of his hut to light the fire. . . .   The martyr recognized in this man a brother in sincerity; he was glad to find himself in the presence of a *disinterested conviction*."[1]   Each of us is working out some aspect of truth; others are toiling away at some other aspect.   The time may come for us to compare notes, to exchange results, to widen our mental horizon by accepting the discoveries of our neighbors.   We often learn more from opponents than from allies.   Controversy and debate are often sorry affairs and leave the members on each side certain that its champion has triumphed.   But both go home to meditate, and, finally, unconsciously to themselves, to absorb and assimilate the element of truth advanced by the opposition.

Religion is an aspiration after ideal goodness, beauty, and truth.   It is never complete attainment.   Indeed, to say of a man that he is "finished," is to say he is a corpse.   When one imagines himself complete, he is already bankrupt.

[1] Guyau, *The Non-Religion of the Future,* p. 18.

Religion, being human, is real. It is not something manufactured, like those Japanese artificial water flowers, which seem to grow when put in water, but really only swell out and simulate growth. Religion is not the cunning contrivance of priestly castes bent on gain and power. No doubt greed for gain and influence, with many other bad motives, has affected ecclesiastical development, but superstition and avarice are not full explanations. Humanity is weak, imperfect, and sinful, but it is not so easily duped as the theory of fraud implies. It is nearer the truth to say that religion makes pastors and priests. The marks of the imperfect tools are on them.

Love of art builds museums and establishes schools of drawing, painting, and sculpture. Justice erects court-houses and maintains police. Love of learning endows schools of teaching and research. All great institutions are the products of man's desires, aspirations, wills. The explanation by dupery and superstition is too simple and too shallow. Men may be in error, and they often have been grossly in error. But they have sought truth and searched for the divine, and the quest has been real. This quest is religion, worship, even if it find no tongue, even if it be of "the silent sort."

III. Religion has a History. — If we turn from the immediate causes of religious institutions to the history of religion, and ask the past to help us interpret the present, we shall have before us one of the most interesting, difficult, and noble of intellectual pursuits. Students of comparative and historical religion are busy with this inquiry. They have studied the worship of the lowest savage tribes; unearthed the altars of the earliest human beings who have left monuments of their devotions; translated the sacred books of India, China, Japan, Persia, Babylonia, Egypt; interpreted the sagas of our European ancestors; and they are now busy arranging the vast material so as to make out the meaning of this strange and eventful history of man's deepest thoughts and desires.

Religion and its institutions are of great antiquity. Science cannot yet tell, perhaps never will be able to tell, the dates of its origin. We must long be content with more modest statements. We may believe that real human beings have always had some kind of thought about the Unseen, the higher powers.

Certainly as far back as authentic knowledge extends some childish faith has manifested itself.

Practically religion has been a universal interest of man. Here, again, we may not speak too confidently where data are lacking.   The gaps in reliable evidence are very wide.   But it seems only fair and reasonable to think that, since almost all men have a religious faith, all have.

It must be admitted that religion must have a very wide and rather vague definition if we are to declare its universality.   All the high thoughts of men about science, art, law, and worship began with very humble germs, and grew larger, more definite, more adequate, with time and toil.   Religion is no exception.

Religion has been a powerful influence in forming the family. The earliest worship seems to have been closely connected with the graves of the dead.   Certainly ancestor worship was very common, if not universal, among all early peoples whose annals have come down to us.   As the father was feared, loved, obeyed, trusted, and was the protector of the family in his life, so he seemed still to be near the family after his death.   Therefore savages imagine the spirit of the dead to hover near the last place where the strong one was seen.   They think he ought to have food and weapons, as he had in life.   It is pathetic to see how this faith is realized in burial customs, where rude pottery, once filled with the accustomed viands, are found by the bones of the warriors, dead ages ago.   This custom of making offerings at the grave transformed it into an altar, a shrine of adoration.   And thus family life became closely connected with worship, and the ghost of the ancestor was the representative of the awful and mysterious Unseen.   This domestic worship bound brothers to brothers and generation to generation.   It was the sanction of domestic morality, and the will of the dead ancestor was the first form of law within the narrow limits of the family.   The grave became the door to the future life.

But as the family expanded into the clan or tribe, perhaps from the first being faintly distinguished from the clan, the common ancestor became the common deity, and thus all the beliefs and sentiments of a larger group helped to cement them in a common life.

It was in the tribe that the medicine man, weather prophet, sage acquaintance of the departed, laid the foundation for a special class in society, the priestly class. He was the first representative of leisure and reflection. It was the priests' class who first developed each of the sciences, the social arts, and the laws.

It was in religious creeds that the earliest ethics found expression and formal statement.

It was in religious thinking and action that law and government had their rise. For many ages religious and civil or criminal law were not distinguished. In the Old Testament, as in all ancient writings, all codes are mingled confusedly, — sanitary, ethical, criminal, commercial, political, and ceremonial.

The priestly class laid the foundations of science. Other men were toiling or fighting. It was necessary to have a group of men devoted to meditation in order to make a fair beginning in the systematic observation of nature and life.

The fine arts were long under the control of those who originated them or carried them to their heights. Dancing, music, architecture, poetry, and all other arts were for ages upon ages cultivated almost exclusively for religious ends. Only gradually did each art become separate from the ecclesiastical rule and begin to lead a life of its own.

The useful arts and professional training have been largely monopolized and developed by the priestly class and in the service of religion.

It is needless to go over the confession of the sins of the priestly guilds, their selfishness, and their obstruction of later advances. It was but natural that a profession should cling to age-long privileges which gave them influence and power. The story of persecution of scientific men by the church leaders is full of sickening horrors, and it should be read in order to prevent us from slaying the living prophets while we decorate the tombs of those who have already won a triumph over bigotry and ambition.

If social progress is the debtor of religion, it is also true that religion owes much to the general progress of mankind. Social obligations are reciprocal. Two sayings have been set over against each other as if they were exclusive: "An honest man is the noblest work of God," and "An honest God is the noblest work of man." Sober reflection will reconcile the element of truth in each of these very partial statements. Out of the infinite springs of original creative energy of goodness man's best principles arise, and his progress is ever fed afresh from this well of eternal life. And it is also true that a man's thoughts about nature and life expand with his experience and investigation, that his conceptions of God become larger, more moral, more useful, more beautiful and sublime. The word "God" is like a great ship, which stops at many ports in its course and takes in cargoes of all kinds at each point of contact with new marts and communities.

From the long history of the family, religion has come to think out the meaning of its universal prayer, "Our Father which art in heaven."

From a varied political life and development of states, with the expansion of tribes into city states, and of city states into empires, the other part of the great petition becomes clearer and grander, "Thy kingdom come, thy will be done." The act of devotion is domestic and political.

From its heroic struggle for the material means of existence, its tedious contest with parsimonious nature, its constant facing of starvation, its awful uncertainty as to the economic to-morrow, the Son of Man has learned and taught us to say, "Give us day by day our daily bread." Bread will not keep long. Industry and hope must live on daily renewed decisions and gifts. Religion and industry ask for fresh manna, while prayer and labor go to the field together, not begging for release from constant exertion which ennobles, but for a return in fruit for all painful planting.

Each science has made its contribution to religious thought and feeling. Geology has taken the idea of God and enlarged it in time. Our thought of the Creator is affected by our knowledge of creation. Geology has studied this creation, unfolded leaf by leaf the mighty books in the vast library of the earth, and discovered footprints "of the Creator" back in more and more remote ages. A few years ago the creation was a story of six thousand years, a mere speck in the infinity of time.   Now the college lad is made familiar with æons and cycles of time during which the solemn procession of creative events moves before the reverent mind.   Each stratum is a revelation of the Eternal.

Astronomy does for our thought of space what geology does for our conception of time.   The idea of immensity is helped by study of the starry depths.   The revelations of the telescope lift the mind far above those childish pictures of a universe only a few miles high and wide.   The Ruler of the universe is measured for our intellect by the largeness of our knowledge of the universe.   And astronomy has been a direct contribution to religious imagination by its opening up new systems of worlds, until our solar system, that once seemed all, now appears to be a small colony in the mighty empire of the sidereal heavens.   Chemistry and physics have coöperated with astronomy in this contribution to religious faith, for they have given us the spectroscope, which demonstrates the fact that all belong to the same system of laws.   Thus the chemist may feel that his knowledge of the materials of the earth will equip him for further laboratory investigations in some other world to which he may be transferred when his labors here are suspended for a moment by death.

A feeling of kinship with wider circles of being, a foreboding that this life is "but a suburb of the life Elysian," a prophetic hope that the range of thought and affection means more than this brief existence between cradle and grave, seem to be reasonable in the light of modern discovery.

Thus also religion grows more beautiful with art and offers a finer service, if not more sincere.

The social function of religious institutions is the unification of mankind on the most exalted levels; or rather the unification of mankind in an upward movement in which the divine attractions of the Perfect Life are at once the bond of affection, the object of faith, and the inspiration to unceasing creative energy of goodness.

Public worship may be defined, from the present point of view, as the socialized act of approach to God, a united effort of men to assist each other to realize worthy thoughts of the Divine.   Public worship can do for men what private devotions cannot do. In the great congregation thought and reverence swell into grander expansion. The large objects of noble architecture, multitudes, chorus of mighty music, assist the imagination to form worthier conceptions of the unspeakably sublime topics of religious meditation. The experience of mankind approves the custom. Public worship is a social institution which thrives where freedom is perfect, where compulsion is out of the question.

Public reading and preaching are the symbols through which the divine thought enters the social mind or is intensified and glorified there.

The discipline of the church, expressed in admonitions, personal warnings, pastoral visits, personal attentions, criticism of immorality, exclusion from communion for unworthy conduct, is one of the social means of moral purification. Its social importance is beyond valuation.

> " What is a holy church, unless she awes
> The times down from their sins? Did Christ select
> Such amiable times? The whole world were wrecked
> If every mere great man, who lives to reach
> A little leaf of popular respect,
> Attained not simply by some procedure
> In thought and act, which, having proved him higher
> Than those he lived with, proved his competence
> In helping them to wonder and aspire." [1]

Social unification is a function of the church. "That they all may be one," was the prayer of the Founder to the Father of all. Like all ideals which grow with life, this ideal of unity seems remote. But the thought of it has arrived and is at work. All of us feel it.

The church ought to seek the most perfect unity in order that it may more perfectly fulfil this function. "Religion being the chief bond of human society, it is a happy thing when itself is well contained within the true bond of unity." [2]

The sociologist, therefore, must regard with hope the recent tendencies toward greater courtesy and spirit of harmonious labor on behalf of humanity. He must look with pleasure

---

[1] E. B. Browning, *Casa Guidi Windows.*
[2] Bacon, *Essays, Of Unity in Religion.*

upon movements to secure comity of action between missionaries in our own frontier towns and on the foreign field. He
must take satisfaction as a student and reformer in the movements to consolidate sections of the church into compact
bodies, with larger resources and fewer impediments.

" To the sociologist, what keeps the church most alive is its power to fit
human beings for harmonious social life. The church is a brotherhood,
but it is something more. It is a union for service, a bit of philanthropic
machinery, a transmitter of opinion, but it is more even than these. It
is, in the last analysis, the repository of certain related ideas, convictions,
symbols, and appeals which are admitted to have more efficacy in socializing the human heart than any other group of influences known to Western
civilization." [1]

It seems worth while to quote more at length this statement
of a thoughtful, honest, and free-thinking teacher, who feels
scorn at mere clericalism, and perhaps even too much impatience with some of the doctrines of Christianity.

"Does the human heart need socializing? Moralists and
reformers from the days of Rousseau and Godwin have insisted
on the goodness of human nature, and found the root of all
evil in bad social institutions. But the sociologist can take
no such rosy view. Whatever his origin, man has undoubtedly
come up. Social order, instead of being spontaneous, is the
formation of thousands of years. The self-restraints implied
in social life have been slowly acquired. It is the social, not
unsocial, in character that needs explaining; not evil, but
goodness, presents the greater problem. Rejecting, of course,
the dogma of total depravity, we must still recognize that man
brought to the beginnings of society only the feeble altruism
developed in the relation of parents to offspring, and that
even to-day social character is painfully dependent on influences which are unnoticed simply because so unfamiliar.
People need to be trained or developed to the self-restraints,
sacrifices, unselfishness, and helpfulness that must abound in
the members of society if social life is to go on smoothly.
Without space to prove, we can only lay down the proposition

[1] Professor E. A. Ross, *The Outlook*, Aug. 28, 1897. Reprints may be procured
of the Educational Church Board, No. 139 S. Pine Avenue, Albany, N.Y.
Price, each, twenty-five cents.

that the harmony we actually enjoy is for the most part due
neither to the coercion of law or public opinion, nor to the
inborn goodness of men, but to extensive changes wrought in
character, especially during the early years."

Further he declares, on the strength of much evidence from
biology and history, that "we dare not rest the future on a
flabby faith that goodness once acquired is transmitted by
inheritance to offspring. Family and church must always
work, with energy and unremitting patience, at this hard task
of fitting human beings for social coöperation and harmony."
The same writer asserts that the church possesses equipment
for this task in its religious belief in the fatherhood of God,
its ideals of ethical perfection, its union in worship, its historic ceremonies, its music. "There is no other single environment which collects within itself so much that has proven
efficacious in the regeneration of men and women as the
church."

IV. What will be the *future* of Religion? Is it to be
among the permanent social forces or is it an evanescent
dream? Was it useful once with savages, and will more civilized men dispense with it? Has it been entirely necessary
to bring mankind thus far, and can we now afford to dismiss
it with compliments and thanks for its past services, with some
satirical references to its mistakes? Now that the temple of
social order has been reared are we about to find religion a
piece of scaffolding which should be taken down as unsightly
and a rude screen in the way of our enjoyment?

There are very learned men who predict that religion has
seen its best days, and that science or patriotism or humanita-
rian sentiment or philosophy will take its place and turn
churches into laboratories or halls of amusement or arenas for
political discussion.

If religion has always been a human trait, it is probable that
in some form it will be a permanent trait of human nature.
Its power to grow with all other growths is evidence of its
vitality. And, furthermore, the occasions which gave it rise
and maintained interest in it remain. All science is of the
defined, the limited, the near. But science itself is always
turning up evidence of an inner power and life. Science is

forever enlarging our conception of the word "infinite." Science itself leads man out more and more where faith and hope and boundless affection and sublime resolves seem more than ever fit for man.

"Psychologically, the bond of union in society and the state is not law in a legal or judicial sense, much less force. It is love. . . . The highest product of the interest of man in man is the church. This brings into explicit consciousness the elements involved in all social organization. It requires love as the supreme obligation, and it brings to light the relation of this love to the perfect and universal personality, God" (Professor John Dewey, *Psychology*, p. 343).

Science requires religious conceptions as uniting idea and principle, and in this it is one with practical life. The Roman Emperor, Marcus Antoninus, said: "As physicians have always their instruments and knives ready for cases which suddenly require their skill, so do those have principles ready for understanding of things divine and human, and for doing everything, even the smallest, with a recollection of the bond which unites divine and human to one another. For neither wilt thou do anything well which pertains to man without at the same time having a reference to things divine, nor the contrary."

Tennyson gives us a picture of a sceptical doctor moving through the childrens' hospital, muttering half under breath:

"All is very well — but the good Lord Jesus has had His day."

The nurse who watches with divine love over the sick weaklings, washes their sores, ministers to their wants, bears with the repulsive sights and sounds, answers out of deep instincts:

"Had? has it come? It has only dawned. It will come by and by.
O how could I serve in the wards if the hope of the world were a lie?
How could I bear with the sights and the loathsome smells of disease
But that He said, 'Ye do it to me, when ye do it to these'?"

To the soul which has trusted the Eternal, found life and strength and joy in Him, the very question as to the permanence of religion seems unreasonable. Marriage for a limited season is founded on infidelity. At its very beginning there is an element of distrust and suspicion which makes all uncertain. To doubt the permanence of religion is to doubt its essence, for it has to do with the eternal. It is from the everlasting.[1] It is easy to bear the idea that theologies will change: —

> " Our little systems have their day;
> They have their day and cease to be."

But the life which theology seeks to explain has its roots in the Reality, which is in all reality. Sciences improve, but the world abides.

Religion may seem to be a smaller part of human life in our day because the outward institutions of the church are not, relatively, so much thought of by most men. Modern life has a greater variety of interests and of legitimate interests than former ages. Business is on a vaster scale; cares are multiplied; art presents its attractions and requires time for appreciation and creation; newspapers and libraries bring a torrent of ideas to the mind; social enjoyments are multiplied by recent inventions; political questions ask service of citizens. There is neither need nor time for protracted sermons and repetitious prayers.

But does this indicate that religion is disappearing from among men? Rather does it not mean that religion is sinking deeper into life? It was never intended that this element of our being should be an isolated thing, apart from human uses. The Master compared faith to leaven which was "hid" in the meal. If only the very spirit and essence of faith and love can permeate and transfigure all duties and relations, then has the divine factor done its perfect work. The spring that wells softly forth "and wandering steeps the roots of half the mighty forest," and goes into fibre and flower, "tells no tale of all the good it does."

It seems altogether probable that our age has not given itself enough time for meditation and devotion, and in this it has the defects and commits the sins of an active and busy age. Doubtless we shall find after some unhappy experiences that

[1] Here study the sublime images of the 90th Psalm.

T

the contemplative life is necessary to feed our active life and save it from shallowness and hollowness. But better far the useful, energetic life than one given over to droning forms and endless prayers to heaven for individual salvation. Better far to spend life for the good of fatherland and the poor, for education and patriotic service, than to dream dreams and avoid the burdens of social duty.

V. The Social Claims of Religion. — Religion cannot ask any man to profess what he does not believe. It must not ask for blind faith. It must not check criticism of fallible leaders and erring institutions. It must not be thought of as repelling suggestions of improvement, for life and betterment are of its eternal essence. But for its achievements and its sublime range of thought, religion seems to deserve reverent treatment, thoughtfulness, and sympathy.

Sociology has a certain relation to religion and theology. Religion is the popular mode of realizing the unity of man and his environment. Theology and philosophy are the constructions of learned men given to systematic reflection. Sociology seeks to attain and give a unified conception of a portion of this universe, human society, beginning with some local community and extending the range of its view until at last mankind will be compassed by its theory. The completion of this task is far off in the future. But our studies have already helped to make the idea of solidarity, unity, communion familiar to our thought. It suggests the hope that with advancing knowledge we shall secure ampler evidence for the prophetic belief on which we already act by instinct, that the entire universe is one and under the law of one Intelligence, one righteous Ruler, one supreme Friend.

Philosophy expresses this belief in this form: "A single, active, self-conscious principle, by whatever name it be called, is necessary to constitute such a world, as the condition under which alone phenomena, *i.e.* appearances to consciousness, can be related to each other in a single universe." [1]

Coleridge joins with Berkeley in affirming the demand for a divine foundation for social order and personal dignity. "Whatever the world may opine, he who hath not much medi-

[1] T. H. Green, *Prolegomena to Ethics*, p. 40.

tated upon God, the human mind, and the highest good, may possibly make a thriving earthworm, but will most indubitably make a blundering patriot and a sorry statesman. . . . To God, as the reality of the conscience and the source of all obligation, to free will, as the power of the human being to maintain the obedience which God through conscience has commanded, against all the might of nature, and to the immortality of the soul, as a state in which the weal and woe of man shall be proportioned to his moral worth, with this faith all nature,

> ' all the mighty world
> Of eye and ear,'

presents itself to us, now as the aggregated material of duty, and now as a vision of the Most High revealing to us the mode and time of realizing and applying that universal rule, preëstablished in the heart of our reason."

CHAPTER XIII

The Natural and Spiritual Bonds of a People

MODERN nations have grown by the union and coalescence of smaller groups. The earliest of our ancestors known to us lived in clans and tribes, occasionally joining forces under a leader for war. Out of the federation of the towns and surrounding country grew provinces, and provinces united to form kingdoms, and kingdoms have been consolidated, as in Germany, into a mighty empire.

This process is not merely something of the past, for we may observe it in our own experience. Each member of society is early conscious of connection with his narrow domestic circle, and later comes to care for his neighborhood, his club, his lodge, his friendly correspondents, his church, his country.

I. Likenesses and Connections in Society. — It will not be difficult, with some reflection and observation, to find illustrations of the distinctions which are now to be described. Millions of threads run up, down, and across the community, weaving all together in firm and enduring tissue. The student will strive to realize the fact suggested; will seek to understand what it means; out of what motives and causes it has grown; to what duties it leads.

The social connections are partly spontaneous and partly selective and voluntary. But these constantly flow across the boundary and mingle with each other.

(A) Spontaneous. — The "family stock" may first be taken for investigation, since it primarily grows out of the fact of common physical descent, but at a later stage becomes a purely mental representation. It is true that this bond is not so strong with us as it is in China, where some of the poor

276

peasants have pedigree tablets which enable them to trace back their ancestors many hundreds of years. In the Old Testament we have preserved several such tables of the ancient Hebrews. Our Aryan ancestors, the early Greeks and Romans, maintained a worship of their departed fathers; and this domestic worship linked one generation to the next and held clan and tribe in close relations of common duties of defence and friendship. We no longer depend on those who bear the same name for support and protection; and yet, even in this youthful country, where memory is short and individualism is so strong, we often collect and publish family genealogies. Sometimes this search for a common ancestor is disappointing. The path may graze the gallows or run back to a founder who was not a man to be proud of. "My ancestor came into Britain with William the Conqueror," boasted a certain noble lord. And a noble commoner tartly asked, "Did he or his descendants ever do anything beside?" The pride of stock manifests itself in many ways, some of them ludicrous, others serious. There are assemblies of related families and correspondence between persons of the same blood who never see each other. In modern times this tie has been weakened by migration, by the dispersion of members of the same lineage, by the reluctance of moderns to give honors merely on the ground of descent, and by the demand that each person prove his own worth and value by his own service. So far as there is a survival of the feeling, it is based on a degree of belief that "blood will tell," a belief which is made more rational by modern biology. It is presumed that honorable qualities will, in some degree, follow hereditary lines. The inheritance of estates, titles, libraries, heirlooms, and traditions of achievement helps to keep the feeling alive. Perhaps the tracing of genealogies may have some social value by acting as an incentive in the individual to preserve the honor of the name in times of temptation and at moments when heroic sacrifices are required.

The *neighborhood sentiment* may begin with a physical fact, that of proximity in the same region. Families who have no kinship, who differ in religious creeds, languages, political opinions, business aptitudes and callings, find themselves inhabiting the same space, farm joining to farm. Juxtaposition leads to relations of dependence. In harvest neighbors assist each other. Utensils and books are borrowed. Children go to the same school. The followers of diverse creeds attend certain union services, regularly or occasionally, as at funerals, weddings, and holidays. This external happening to be together is the basis for a weaving of reciprocal influences, an exchange of ideas and sentiments, for contracts and agreements. People thus brought face to face learn from each other, copy each other, adopt common ways of doing things, and thus, on a physical foundation arises a spiritual edifice joined by invisible forces and attractions.

An interesting manifestation of the neighborhood feeling is seen in a colony of persons from the same country who agree to move into a frontier state and settle in the same locality. Thus, in a northern state may be found to this day a "Kentucky settlement," a colony of descendants of men who moved north together before the abolition of slavery.

This neighborhood tie has great social value. It is the beginning of patriotism. The neighborhood has natural boundaries and interests special to the locality. In cities it is especially desirable to intensify this neighborhood sentiment and make the most of its attachments. Coöperation is prevented primarily by want of acquaintance among persons who have been drawn to one spot from the ends of the earth. Only in direct social intercourse does the face light up with the smile of recognition, and the look of care and distrust fade away. Social settlements have won some of their best triumphs by building squarely on this real fact of a neighborhood interest.

Churches, missions, public schools, town meetings, political assemblies, amusements, recreations, and all acts of coöperation assist in the strengthening of this connection.

(*B*) *Voluntary, Selective.*

Trade Connections.— There are relationships which grow naturally out of business and trade. The customers of a wholesale or retail dealer, the clients of a lawyer, the fellow-craftsmen in the same trade, the solicitors of the same line of business, are brought into contact with each other through economic interests, and friendships spring out of these financial relations which may cross seas and endure the test of adversity.

Classes. — It is the common boast in America that we have no social classes. Certainly, democracy has been carried further here than in feudal lands, but the fact of stratification exists. It does not appear in any official way. Our law ignores it. Geographies cannot bound it, north, south, east, or west. But every one feels it. Many are embittered by it. The fact may give pain or pleasure, may be disliked or greeted with favor: it is impossible to ignore it, thoroughly artificial and accidental though it be.

In older countries social classes or ranks are inherited by families or social position may be fixed by royal decrees or acts of legislatures. Perhaps the origin of social distinctions was in conquest. Those who belonged to the conquering race held others in subjection and contempt, ruled over them, despised them. But conquest itself usually implied some sort of physical and mental superiority, which was recognized by the inferior peoples. There were natural causes for the primary classification, and the advantages were inherited from generation to generation. Unquestionably these advantages have produced, in the long course of ages, a type of "gentlemen" who have furnished some of the finest elements of modern life. We cannot account for their long lease of power as "ruling classes" unless they had, on the whole, some gifts as rulers. The modern world is finding the exceptions so numerous, and the selfishness and injustice of the feudal rule so great, that, with universal suffrage, the yoke is being shaken off. Henceforth all classes are to compete for political power, but on the basis of individual desert and fitness. Still the classes will long continue, with their pretensions on one side and the lackey-spirit of descendants of serfs on the other, till the antiquated and artificial elements fade out.

Social classification in America rests on different grounds, chiefly on wealth and occupation. Those who are relatively rich and can command fine houses, indulge in luxuries, and cultivate fine manners, separate themselves from others. Their claims are more or less acknowledged by those who look upon them from afar, sometimes with admiration, sometimes with envy or hate. The manifestations of the classification are in the choice of the best residence districts in cities; in the exhibition of equipages, dress, and jewels; in attendance at the finest churches and the renting of the most desirable pews; in the selection of the best boxes at balls, operas, and horse shows; and in marriage alliances.

If we seek for causes of this fact, we may find them in both natural and conventional differences. The standards vary according to local circumstances. In a purely commercial community wealth is far more essential than in a city where great educational establishments have long raised the respect for learning and culture. Traditions have great power. But even if the artificial and offensive marks of distinction could be effaced the differences would exist. They seem to increase with civilization, because progress implies variation. Such differences will always show themselves. It will always be true that superior power and faculty will secure superior advantages, and that these advantages will have their effects in personal character and situation. People who are congenial will live together and have companionship. People who have little in common will prefer to seek their homes and companies apart. If attachment to one's class unfits him for cordial participation in the life of the community, in its educational, political, and religious enterprises, then that attachment is wrong in degree or direction. If class spirit conceals from one the highest values of humanity as seen in the poor and the manual worker; if it leads one to regard dress, fashion, styles, amusements, and conventional etiquette as more worthy of time, effort, and consideration than useful labor, intelligence, and ideal aims, then the class spirit has transgressed the bounds of social right, and stands self-condemned.

If President Garfield did not describe a constant reality he certainly did express a noble American ideal when he wrote: "There is no horizontal stratification of society in this country like the rocks in the earth, that hold one class down below forevermore, and let another come to the surface and stay there forever. Our stratification is like the ocean, where, from the depths of the mighty deep, any drop may come up to glitter on the highest wave that rolls." This is a sparkling bit of autobiography, for its author began life as driver on a canal tow-path and closed his career as President of the United States.

Friendship between the members of various social circles and classes shoot golden threads through the social fabric. Friendship has no organization, needs no constitution, is not limited by political lines, sends its messages across the continent and around the world. It exists between members of different ranks, opposed parties, conflicting creeds. When a certain belief or interest threatens to divide a community along the line of some partisan difference these fibres of friendships bind up the cut and give it a chance to heal.

There are *schools* or *tendencies* of thought and taste, of conviction and belief. There are similarities and attractions of persons in relation to art, science, literature, theology, and politics. For example, one may find "Hegelians" in philosophy all over the world; "Herbartians" in psychology and pedagogy; Single-taxers in economics and politics; Socialists in theory, apart from all organizations. There may or may not be any association or correspondence. The bond is entirely psychical and needs no physical expression to make it more real, although all spiritual forces tend to embody themselves in some institution.

Very closely akin to the "school" of thought is the *sect* and *party* feeling and attraction. Waves of belief pass over a great community from individuals or influential centres, or spring up in response to common interests. We are inclined to regard those as wise and worthy who agree with us. Our sentiments and beliefs return to us, reflected and reverberated in other minds, with tenfold force, because they are approved by many. We feel more secure in our positions and more confident in our plans when we belong to a party.

The members of the same *race* are attached to each other quite apart from distinctions among them, and especially if they are in a land of strangers. The beginning of the distinction lies in the common origin and physical descent. But the physical facts are the basis and occasion of prejudices, affections, fears, ambitions, which become powerful social factors. American states present the "race question" in its most interesting forms, for here are the African, Indian, Chinese, Japanese, and many other races.

There is a *national* bond. For example, the Africans in America boast of their citizenship in the United States and have shown their patriotic affection on many bloody fields of battle. We have Austrians whose patriotism transcends the race differences between Germans and Slavs. One cannot tell the race of a Briton by his citizenship.

Those who speak the same *language* are drawn to each other, as we see in our cities. Wise statesmanship must take account of this bond where the population is composite, as it is with us. We have noticed already that business connections, denominational creeds, art interests, philosophical studies, may connect the members of various nations and constitute true *international* bonds. As the submarine telegraph supplies electrical communication between nations, so the fraternity of ideas draws men of all nations into an invisible federation which seems to foretell the parliament of mankind.

> "For mankind are one in spirit, and an instinct bears along,
> Round the earth's electric circle, the swift flash of right or wrong;
> Whether conscious or unconscious, yet Humanity's vast frame
> Through its ocean-sundered fibres feels the gush of joy or shame, —
> In the gain or loss of one race all the rest have equal claim."
> — J. R. LOWELL, *The Present Crisis.*

We are enabled by this sketch to understand how varied and numerous are the bracing and consolidating elements of a great community. A rope of many strands twisted together is a faint symbol of the cords which hold the souls of men and tend to make them one. If a single fibre should be broken, the others may hold. And these threads are living, growing realities, becoming more intricate and extended.

There is a discussion among sociologists over the questions: What constitutes society? What is its one essential element? Many answers have been given, as economic interest, common descent, sympathy, coercion of the individual by the group, imitation, consciousness of kind. At a later stage we may give more attention to these solutions. But let us imagine the controversy settled and ended. Let us admit that some one of these forces should be shown to be the peculiar and singular mark of human society. Still it would remain true that this force would be a mere abstraction, meaningless and powerless save as it grew out into all the forms of attraction which we have been studying and as it transfigured them. These bonds are real. The cement of society is a combination, as all cements are, of various elements. To give a full account of social organization, to state all the causes of co-operation, we must take in all motives, from lowest appetite to highest aspiration. All that is common to a large part of the community helps to advance fellowship.

The attempt to simplify life may destroy it, as the attempt to reduce all thinking to one idea results in the absolute,— Nothing.

The People. General Conception

Within the geographical area marked off on the map of the world as the United States there are living about 70,000,000 persons, men, women, and children, of various ages, classes, races, and stages of intelligence. These people have many modes of organization, as families, associations, churches, trades, corporations, unions, clubs, societies. In spite of all these differences, this People has much in common and constitutes one great society or community. It is in possession and enjoyment of one undivided territory to the exclusion of all the rest of the world. It is bound together by common commercial interests more closely than to other portions of mankind. It has a system of communication which connects all parts by ties of quick intelligence. It has common memories of struggles and triumphs, common days of celebration and holidays unknown to other peoples. It has one language, everywhere instantly intelligible to all its citizens. This People is a reality and not a mere fancy. It is a vast and impressive fact, worthy of study and consideration. As this very fact of the existence of a people or a society has been denied with contempt and scorn as a mere invention of literary theorists and metaphysicians, it is worth while to present evidence that we are dealing with the most real and fundamental of all actualities. Of course if there is no such reality as society, there is not and never can be a social science, for we cannot know what does not exist. It has been said that a society is simply a name for a population living on a certain territory, and composed of persons and associations, classes and ranks, whose interests are at perpetual war. In such an aggregation of conflicting persons, with no common bond for all, a community is unthinkable. One great writer, who denies the reality of a society as a unified association of persons in agreement, affirms the reality of the *state*, that mighty institution which holds these jarring, warring contestants together, prevents them from eating each other, and makes life between seas tolerable. Let us examine this notion thoroughly, and see whether a society thus eternally and essentially a mass of mutually repulsive persons could ever produce a state.

Men who have lived under absolutism in government are prone to see in the king or the law the sole fount and origin of social life. In the imperial diet a great statesman asserts that a constitution was a present from the ruler to his people! To us Americans this language is unintelligible. Government with us is from the people, and it is only one of the instruments of the character and will of the people. When it is said that social life is base, lucre-loving, voluptuous, and degrading, we hear a voice of a distant age, a dying voice, a fainting echo. It is near the truth to say that the great ideas originate among the choicest spirits of the people, are propagated until they become popular and, at last, after many experiments and defeats, become a part of the government.

Grounds of the Belief that there is such a Reality as a Society or People which creates and maintains the State. — There is the solid substantial state itself as a witness. All admit that it is a unified organization of human beings or families occupying the same space. It is the work of persons, not the product of blind natural forces, like the sand dune of the coast, or the channel ploughed by a glacier, or the mountain built out of coral. Is it credible that a society whose characteristic is strife, antagonism, cannibalism, could produce this majestic spiritual pile, the state, with its unity, firmness, and common glory?

We have a right to turn to the words of men who have modern minds; who are not under the spell of the traditions of absolutism; who are accustomed to see a nation act in concert, even when divided in opinion about some themes. We have a right to select the weighty words of Abraham Lincoln, one who had a profound knowledge of the very springs of our life and prophetic insight into the dominant forces of democratic countries. In the classic Gettysburg speech this noble seer said: "Fourscore and seven years ago, our fathers brought forth upon this continent a new nation, conceived in liberty, and dedicated to the proposition that all men are created equal. . . . That we here highly resolve that these dead shall not have died in vain; that the nation shall, under God, have a new birth of freedom; and that government of the people, by the people, and for the people shall not perish from the earth." Plain men, unused to refinements of theory, understood what he meant and felt its power. The words "nation" and "people" meant something, some one great thing, to them, as it does to us all. And again, in February, 1861: "I must rely upon you, upon the people of the whole country, for their support; and, with their sustaining aid, even I, humble as I am, cannot fail to carry the ship of state safely through the storm." And again: "Why should there not be a patient confidence in the ultimate justice of the people?"

The occupation of a common territory is the physical basis of a united society, a Folk. Occupation of the same plain or valley would not mean society with plants or animals, for the capacity for social community is not in them. A mass, a herd, a swarm, are not yet full society. But when a people dwells in a space and covers a land, all objects become touched with a new feeling. Our national hymn makes this appeal clear and beautiful:

> "I love thy rocks and rills,
> Thy woods and templed hills."

There are the houses where our loved and our honored were born and reared. Under the oaks and willows of our cemeteries rest the ashes of our dead. In hallowed places gray-headed comrades recite the story of battles won for great convictions. To such memories Lincoln appealed in his first inaugural, before the irrevocable step was taken which plunged the nation into war : " I am loath to close. We are not enemies, but friends. We must not be enemies. Though passion may have strained, it must not break our bonds of affection. The mystic cord of memory, stretching from every battle-field and patriot grave to every living heart and hearthstone all over this broad land, will yet swell the chorus of the Union, when again touched, as surely they will be, by the better angels of our nature." Years have passed, and now, without severity of judgment, with bonds of affection renewed, verdure clothes the patriot graves and tender hands lay flowers on all alike, whether of blue or gray. War was a spasm of error and passion; union is the deeper fact, the enduring reality, and every hill and farm witnesses to some common heritage. The very earth is humanized, socialized, by the presence of a people.

Economic interests seem to be an exception and to present the spectacle of a war of all against all. Of this we have spoken in the proper place, but even here let us notice that competition is not the only fact in business, though it is one. We must admit that between persons and classes these differences of interest are real, terrible, and provocative of antagonisms bitter and relentless. This conflict for possessions and power seems rooted in all forms of living beings. All devices proposed to remove the necessity of struggle and rivalry seem to promise stagnation, loss of energy and faculty. Let us admit the fact of tragic conflict, and admit it to be, for all practical purposes, permanent. Certainly it will endure our time through. But antagonism does not exclude unity, contract, and coöperation. Reason sits supreme even at the jousts. Not here are we pleading for an unrealized and pious wish to be fulfilled, for something millennial and remote. Here is a contemporary fact, one that may be observed of all and which is full of promise of better things akin. Lawyers are competitors, and not always lovely fighters at the bar. Yet even there, arrayed on opposing sides, contending for vast moneyed interests, for honor and for success, they seldom forget to call each other "brother." It is not all form. Physicians are competitors for business; and yet they have clubs and associations where their science and their professional art make them forget the meaner instincts of rivalry. Wageworkers are competitors for places, and yet they are building up great societies for mutual benefit. The famous "bears" and "bulls" on 'Change are reported as being in perpetual strife, and yet their board holds them to a common agreement on the strength of a few marks on a card. They may fight, but it is according to rules formed by agreement preceding the competitive acts and made by themselves.

If we look at the large outlines of economic affairs over a great territory, the aspect of antagonism almost disappears from sight, and nothing remains visible but a huge organization of industry and trade to serve the wants of the people.

It is hardly necessary to repeat in detail all that has been said of the vast network of bonds of every kind which knit this people of the United States in a community. Our government itself is only one of the institutions in which this community is declared.

Family ties are braided into this mighty cable of affection and interest. In New England dwell the parents of the makers of Chicago and Minneapolis and Denver.

Language is a common bond of deepest import. It is true that many languages are spoken among us, tolerated with wise patience, and even taught in our schools. We can afford to admit variety. Our English tongue will enrich itself from the spoils of other forms of speech, as it has ever done. A composite people will require for the expression of their many-sided life a full vocabulary drawn from all sources. But practically all comprehend each other through the English, the tongue of Shakespeare and Milton. And to understand each other is to "come to an understanding."

We have already a great literature which voices our common ideals. It is not inhospitable, but full of praise for Goethe, Dante, and Hugo. Borrowing from all older literature, our own is living and growing, moving toward something vast and noble, worthy of our race, and creative of new modes of higher living.

It is true that the church is divided into many branches and does not seem to stand for union. It must be confessed that here also are strange, mysterious, and tragic contradictions. But after all, a few sublime and simple ideas and impulses are actually common and serve to bind all hearts together. In two directions it is an interest which passes the boundaries of the state; for it stretches its influences and organizations across the seas, a truly international bond, and it makes the hope of immortality a social bond even with the dead. The church cannot take the place of the state. In some respects it is more narrow. But it is also deeper and larger, and serves to draw out other social threads, finer than silk and stronger than steel.

A threefold cord is not easily broken. What shall we expect, then, of a bond which is composed of millions and millions of cables,— material and ideal interests, hopes, ambitions, and affections, all woven together in the large space of national life?

The People is a reality. It has common thoughts, ideals, wishes, will, and power. It can follow traditions and imitate examples, as a person can. It can also invent. In our Constitution both elements are present; the body of the document provides for the usual order, while the last article anticipates progress, improvement, by suggesting the way of amendment. The People is one reality, therefore they can do a great work. It creates the state. The state is not the original source of those millions of vital and spiritual bonds of the Folk. The Folk created the state, upholds it, uses it for its own varied interests, educates as it protects itself by this grand instrument. What we make reacts upon us.

The Communities of the People and their Organization. — The life of the Folk organized itself by communities, which vary in size, complexity, and various local characteristics. The social student should cultivate the power and habit of observing the working of the social forces under the varying conditions of place and history. For the present purpose we notice certain forms of community life,— the Family, the Village, the Town, the Commonwealth, and the Nation.

Of the Family something has been said. This is the smallest community. In this group the personal relations are most intimate and enduring. The most intense social spirit is felt where there is a natural tie of inheritance, instinctive sympathies, mutual dependence, prolonged acquaintance, legal and economic interest, and religious agreement. The relation may be weakened by separation, but need not be broken; and frequently by correspondence the family feeling may remain strong and influential although brothers and sisters are far apart and can seldom meet. Migration from city to city, from land to land, and change of language and citizenship, forge new ties of love and loyalty. The family group does not depend on location.

The Village is a familiar group. Here the social relations rest primarily on occupation of the same territory, and location is important. In the settlement of this country many families have drifted to certain desirable locations on account of the fertility of the soil, the beauty of the scenery, the convenience of a harbor, the salubrity of the climate, or the opportunity of purchasing cheap land. In many cases the settlers were not acquainted with each other at the beginning, and the only bond of interest was locality. But out of this juxtaposition grew up other ties, as of industrial interest, friendship, religion, and politics.

The study of such a group would begin with a careful gathering and arrangement of the facts about the natural environment, as soil, climate, vegetation, animals, and all the physical forces and influences which help or hinder human life and enjoyment.

In the next step the history of the people should be studied and written. What has this community done in connection with the great events and movements of the state or nation? what monuments has it built to its soldiers? what share has it had in developing the material resources and the educational system of the commonwealth?

Here should be collected, as far as possible, all facts relating to births, deaths, marriages, migrations, races represented, and the causes of any of these phenomena. The economic and other social changes of the past should also be carefully searched out and described.

The student who desires practice in social observation may,

U

with a convenient outline before him, make for himself a series of local maps in which are represented in various colors the location and character of all the visible products of human art and industry. The maps should be accompanied by a careful description of the systems into which the social activities of the village have been organized, as transportation, communication, protection, industry and business, education, regulation, government, religion, philanthropy and reform, voluntary associations for improving conditions and advancing the better life of the population.[1]

After a long, patient, and painstaking survey of the history and present conditions has been made, the student may venture to propose to himself for thought and inquiry the subject of defects and of reforms. The smallest rural village will present social problems of surpassing interest and importance. It is not necessary to travel to London or take residence in a social settlement of a town in order to find a field for investigation and reflection. Our own little world is a miniature of the wide world, and he who thinks great thoughts for his neighbors is walking in sympathy with statesmen and prophets of all ages and all lands.

The Town or City is a community with a character determined by the extent of territory occupied and by the density of population. It may be studied according to a plan similar to that used in case of the village, only that the increasing complexity of city life demands a corresponding intricacy of the forms of investigation.

It is common to think and speak of a "city" as a certain form of government. This is natural enough, because the government is, along with the common territory, the chief common possession of the population. But it is inherently false and vicious to consider the town merely from the political standpoint. The community is first of all an economic community, with its members working in the same region for the attainment of the means by which all life can be supported. The industrial system of the community is not created by the municipal government, and its primary motives and forces do

---

[1] A convenient summary for this purpose may be found in *Catechism for Social Observation*, by the author of this book. See Appendix.

not proceed from law or its ministers. This industrial system is only in small part organized by or into the government. This is also true of the system of transportation and of protection, since these agencies are organized in a measure by private enterprise. While a great part of the educational system of a city is managed by the municipal government, very much is done by parishes, by individuals, and corporations. It is a serious error to regard a community as entirely lost and absorbed in its political life, important as that is. Indeed, the tasks of the government itself are set for it by the mighty currents of popular desires and aspirations which have their origin elsewhere.

What is true of the City is also true of the Commonwealth, the next largest community. The government here defines the geographical limits and political divisions of the social life, and business, schools, and churches find it convenient, in large measure, to follow these lines of demarkation and boundaries. But there is a very real common life of the people of a state which is not taken up into the law or realized by political institutions.

The Nation is the largest community which has the legal forms of unity. But here again a nation is something far deeper than what appears in laws, legislatures, and governments. There is a depth and a height of popular being and feeling, of thought and motive, which political institutions cannot express, create, or regulate. In some directions governments are taking on more of the functions of social work, as in schools, colossal economic enterprises, and research. In other directions governments are leaving social organization more free than in the past, as in the case of religion, sociable assemblies, and all the finer and more personal manifestations of spiritual activities. The fact that the only universal and visible institution of the whole Nation is its government should not blind us to the truth that the Nation is more than its government.

CHAPTER XIV

The State and the Government

"The state, if once started well, goes on with accumulating force like a wheel. For good nurture and education implant good constitutions, and these good constitutions, having their root in a good education, improve more and more, and this improvement affects the breed in man as in other animals." — PLATO, *Republic*, Book IV.

"Force cannot give right. . . . The great principles of right and wrong are legible to every reader; to pursue them requires not the aid of many counsellors. The whole art of government consists in the art of being honest. Only aim to do your duty, and mankind will give you credit when you fail." — T. JEFFERSON, *Works*, I, 141.

"Universal suffrage may give the power of unmaking Order by making laws. Our federal system gives us a safeguard, however, that is wanting in more centralized governments. Should one state choose to make the experiment of mending its watch by taking out the mainspring, the others can meanwhile look on and take warning by the result." — J. R. LOWELL, *The Progress of the World.*

"We have no arbitrary power to give, because arbitrary power is a thing which neither any man can hold nor any man can give. . . . We are all born in subjection, all born equally, high and low, governors and governed, in subjection to one great, immutable, preëxistent law, prior to all our devices, and prior to all our sensations, antecedent to our very existence, by which we are knit and connected in the eternal frame of the universe, out of which we cannot stir.

"This great law does not arise from our conventions and compacts; on the contrary, it gives to our conventions and compacts all the force and sanction they can have; — it does not arise from our vain institutions. Every good gift is of God; all power is of God; — and he, who has given the power, and from whom alone it originates, will never suffer the exercise of it to be practised upon any less solid foundation than the power itself. . . . Name me a magistrate and I will name property; name me power, and I will name protection. . . . In every patent of office the duty is included. For what else does a magistrate exist? To suppose for power is an absurdity in idea. Judges are guided and governed by the eternal laws of justice, to

which we are all subject. We may bite our chains if we will, but we shall
be made to know ourselves, and be taught, that man is born to be governed
by law; and he that will substitute will in the place of it, is an enemy of
God." — EDMUND BURKE, *Speech on the Trial of Warren Hastings.*

"Here, then, is one point at which danger may be expected. The
question recurs, 'How shall we fortify against it?' The answer is simple.
Let every American, every lover of liberty, every well-wisher to his posterity, swear by the blood of the Revolution never to violate in the least particular the laws of the country, and never to tolerate their violation by others.
As the patriots of '76 did to the support of the Declaration of Independence,
so to the support of the Constitution and laws let every American pledge
his life, his property, and his sacred honor; let every man remember that
to violate the law is to trample on the blood of his father, and to tear the
charter of his own and his children's liberty. Let reverence for the laws
be breathed by every American mother to the lisping babe that prattles on
her lap; let it be taught in schools, in seminaries, and in colleges; let it
be written in primers, spelling-books, and in almanacs; let it be preached
from the pulpit, proclaimed in legislative halls, and enforced in courts of
justice. And, in short, let it become the political religion of the nation;
and let the old and the young, the rich and the poor, the grave and the
gay of all sexes and tongues and colors and conditions sacrifice unceasingly
upon its altars." — A. LINCOLN.

"Find in any country the ablest man that exists there, raise him to the
supreme place, and loyally reverence him; you have a perfect government
for that country; no ballot-box, parliamentary eloquence, voting, constitu-
tion-building, or other machinery whatsoever can improve it a whit. It is
in the perfect state; an ideal country. The ablest man; he means also
the truest-hearted, justest, the noblest man; what he tells us to do must be
precisely the wisest, fittest, that we could anywhere or anyhow learn; the
thing which it will in all ways behoove us, with right loyal thankfulness,
and nothing doubting, to do. Our doing and life were then, so far as government could regulate it, well regulated; that were the ideal of constitutions." — T. CARLYLE.

"The next removal must be to the study of politics; to know the beginning, end, and reasons of political societies; that they may not in a
dangerous fit of the commonwealth be such poor, shaken, uncertain reeds,
of such a tottering conscience, as many of our great counsellors have lately
shown themselves, but steadfast pillars of the state." — JOHN MILTON,
Of Education.

THE form in which political facts come to our daily attention
in the newspapers may be illustrated by the following extracts
taken almost at random from reports which appeared during the
writing of this chapter. If they appear disjointed and unintelligible at first sight, this is because all events seem to us

unrelated until we learn to relate them in our own mental system of knowledge and thinking. It is not the purpose in these pages to offer a treatise on political science, but to show the place of facts of the political order in the general scheme of society. From this general survey, which will assist the power of comprehension, one must descend into the particular discussions of civil government, law, administration, and international law. It is hoped that by presenting the relations of these subjects, readers may be stimulated and encouraged to give themselves to the further study of political institutions. The reader should collect many more facts of the political kind and classify them from day to day until the instinct of classification has been firmly seated in habit.

All through this book we are seeking the essence of the inner life of our own society by a study of its institutions and enduring relations. This method has been used and distinctly approved by a very important writer on politics. "I shall simply take the peculiar political institution which each of these races has produced and to which it has clung, as expressive of its innermost political life in all the periods of its development; and from this I shall attempt to lead up to a recognition of the political ideals peculiar to each race. It seems to me that in this manner we shall gain a surer foothold and shall be less likely to substitute fancy for fact." [1]

From neighborhood gossip or from the local papers the student hears that the township trustee has recently made an appointment of a certain teacher in a school district; and in the same day has refused poor relief to the family of a drunkard. Complaints having been made against the superintendent of the county poorhouse, the commissioners institute an inquiry. The records of the same meeting report that they closed a contract with a city firm for the building of a new steel bridge over the creek. These reports compel one to form an image of local administration of township and county.

One morning the people of a city read in the newspaper an item to this effect: "Last night the council passed an ordinance voting themselves extra salary on a 'grab' motion, and passed it over the mayor's veto by a majority of 48 to 16."

[1] Burgess, *Political Science and Constitutional Law*, I, 30.

What is a grab bill? It is a vote of legislators to raise their own salary after taking office, it being understood at the time of their election that the salary of the office was a well-known sum. This sort of an item brings up the questions of the powers and duties of aldermen, of the mayor, of the courts which decide such matters in law. It suggests the study of ordinances and their relations to a city charter and to state legislation; the nature of a veto and the reason that it can be overborne only by a large majority vote. If, when one reads such an item, he at once learns thoroughly the meaning of every term, he will, the next time he sees such a sentence, understand it at once and exactly. Still better is it to master the subject of civil government, and then all similar bits of news will drop into their proper place without hasty and unsatisfactory inquiry on each occasion. He who knows government in general will be able to interpret the meaning of any particular act.

In mid-winter it is made public that the governor, upon the petition of many citizens, has concluded to call an extra session of the legislature to act upon various matters which must be decided at once and which cannot wait for the regular biennial session. In these fragments of fact the young citizen has his attention called to the government of the commonwealth. In a regular place in the newspaper there appear news items about decisions of state and county courts, civil and criminal cases being described with fulness of details, and these accounts of arrests, lawsuits, and final decision direct thought upon the judiciary of state and nation.

While Congress is in session at Washington the daily talk of voters runs upon the speeches relating to tariff, supplies for army and navy, and the prospects of wars.

Discussions of the affairs of Spain, Cuba, and Hawaii compel people to think of treaties and diplomacy, or international relations and law.

It is in connection with these daily topics of conversation that interest in politics and government is awakened. The wise citizen will take advantage of his own curiosity at such a time to gain a more systematic and thorough view of the meaning and relations of these isolated facts which come to his notice. And the wise teacher will seize upon them at school to arouse and direct study of the great subjects of civil government and the history of the age.

I. The People. — Having already studied the meaning of this august word and found that it carries with it the entire contents of social existence, we now turn to the most distinct and commanding mode of the action of the People — the State; and the particular organ of the State — the Government.

The State does not absorb into itself all the energies and interests of the People, though it watches over and protects all. The People is more than a political organization, and its laws touch chiefly the overt acts and outward conduct of the popular life.

The family, business, manufacturing, travel, arts, schools, culture associations, religion, are other forms of the existence of the People, and are often independent of the State. Their freedom from State control is guaranteed by common conviction and belief, and the most solemn guarantees of the Constitution itself prevent the organ of the commonwealth from disturbing some of the most important functions of daily life.

It is very dangerous to completely identify the People with their State, because this creates the impression that nothing can be done by free invention and enterprise until it has been offered by some superior power and comes from without and from above.

It leads to intellectual confusion to identify the State with the People and to make the State the primal origin of family and business and art; for thus we must fail to see that there are boundless creative energies in man which the State should leave in liberty, merely regulating those extravagant displays of force which tend to injure the community. One who lives under a government which leaves little liberty to the people is very apt to think no other mode of associated action can be important. Students devoted to political science are prone to betray a bias in this direction. Their intensity of interest in a specialty may keep vital elements of force and welfare out of the range of their mental vision.

II. The State. — Among the forms of organization which this People possesses is its Political Organization, which in its

most general form we may call here the State. And this form
of institution is so complex, so wide, so difficult to comprehend that we must give it special attention. Since the
authorities are not yet agreed on definitions, we must accept
a definition provisionally, giving full permission to any one
to frame a better statement for himself. By State let us
understand that particular social institution of the entire
People which represents its supreme power within the territory
which belongs to it. The State is the People acting and living in a certain way, that way being expressed in Law. It is
not some body of persons above and outside of the People,
but just the People declaring its will and asserting its right
and its might.

Since this general statement is likely to seem vague, we
must make it more distinct by particular definitions and illustrations.

Heinrich von Treitschke (*Politik*, S. 13) says: "The State
is the united People legally organized as an independent
power."

He proceeds to show that it is not the totality of the People,
and the People does not lose itself entirely in the State; but
the State rules the external life of the People on all sides. The
State does not ask about the disposition and inclination of
men, but demands obedience, and its laws must be observed
whether willingly or unwillingly. In this respect it differs
essentially from the Church, for this institution deals with the
motives and dispositions of men, and in its view mere outward
conformity to rule is nothing without inward acceptance and
inclination. The State uses force, if necessary; the Church
cannot suggest force without contradicting its essential aim
and purpose.

Characteristics of the State. — "The State is *all-comprehen-
sive*. Its organization embraces all persons, natural or legal,
and all associations of persons. Political science and public
law do not recognize in principle the existence of any state-
less persons within the territory of the State. The State is
exclusive. Political science and public law do not recognize
the existence of an *imperium in imperio*.

"The State is *permanent*. It does not lie within the power

of men to create it to-day and destroy it to-morrow, as caprice may move them.

"The state is *sovereign*. This is its most essential principle. Sovereignty means original, absolute, unlimited, universal power over the individual subject and over all associations of subjects (Burgess)."

The Ends of the State. — First, the *assurance of order*. Without security for life and property there can be no social development, for the ordinary creative activities of life would be absorbed in individual struggles against encroachment. The unscrupulous strong would disturb the weak in the possession and enjoyment of their wealth. The powerful and well-organized peoples outside of the nation would take possession of territory. The State exists in order that men may not be perpetually uncertain about the issue of their toils. Second, the State exists that men may *enjoy liberty* of action. Liberty was not the natural state of primitive men, but it has been painfully acquired by the slow formation of states. Third, the State exists in order to *promote any interest common to all the people*. It not merely protects associations formed to secure certain advantages for their members and for the public, but it authorizes organizations of its own for the attainment of any good which may be enjoyed by all. Fourth, the State tends to *promote the welfare and perfection of mankind*. At present the widest organization of political life is the national State, but the time may come when there will be a parliament of man, a federation of the world. Of that distant day we can only hope and dream, but already the various states are coöperating to advance liberty, security, peace, enlightenment, and justice in the whole world.

The following condensed summary of the aims of a good popular government is worthy of careful consideration : —

"The modes of equality that enter into the modern democratic ideal, and that, on grounds of sociological theory, are necessary to the success of the democratic experiment, are the following : —

" 1. Political equality; universal and equal suffrage.

" 2. Equality before the law; neither wealth nor privilege, nor vice, nor ignorance, to control legislation or to receive consideration in the courts.

" 3. Equality of opportunity to serve the public according to the measure of ability; men of equal ability to have absolutely equal chances of appointment to office under impartial civil service rules, irrespective of party service or allegiance.

" 4. Equality of rights in public places and in public conveyances.

" 5. Equality of sanitary conditions; all streets to be equally cleaned and cared for; tenement houses to be made decent and wholesome.

" 6. Equality of opportunity to enjoy certain means of recreation and culture; in public parks, libraries, museums, and galleries of art.

" 7. Equality of elementary educational opportunities, through a well-administered public-school system.

" 8. Equality of fair play; especially in all bargaining between employer and employee, and in the relations of workingmen to one another." [1]

The Manifestations of the State. — We are familiar with the idea of a written constitution for the State. Back of all governments is the supreme law of the land. Governors, presidents, legislatures, courts, and all officials of government look up to that document as absolute over all. Its authorized interpreters are the judges of the land.

Not all the will of the People is expressed in any document. Much of it is formulated in a less definite way. But higher than all legislatures is the will of the People — the organized State.

The government is a partial manifestation of the popular will and power, under the constitution. It is created by and according to the directions and limitations of the constitution. To the government, therefore, let us turn for a brief study. In books on civil government, law, and political art one will find detailed descriptions and explanations.

III. The Government. — Having distinguished the People from the State and the State from the government, we may now consider the particular uses or ends of government. In reality the government is the institution created and maintained by the State to carry out its purposes; that is, to protect order, to

[1] F. H. Giddings, *The Theory of Socialization*, p. 35.

defend liberty, to promote welfare of the People, and to advance the civilization of mankind. The person who represented early law in olden times was he who

> " Sent a thousand men
> To till the wastes, and moving everywhere
> Cleared the dark places and let in the law."

The Functions of Government. — It costs much money, hard-earned wealth, gathered as taxes, paid out to officials, kept back from direct expenditures on desired objects of enjoyment, to support the State. Why should men endure this cost? Why should not the people abolish government and govern themselves without the army of tax-eating senators, congressmen, governors, legislators, justices, policemen, judges, clerks, and this whole army of locusts? People are asking this question, often with plain declarations that they think all government is injustice, waste of life and wealth and energy that might be more usefully employed. It is desirable that the use and usefulness of government should be soberly and intelligently considered by all teachers of youth in these days of fearless and unlimited criticism of all that exists. There is no reason to fear that a reasonable institution will fail to make good its claim. It might be well for the people who decry all legal constraint to reflect that up to this time the whole human race has found it, for some reason, convenient and necessary to found and mantain some form of regulative apparatus. Of course this antiquity would not justify us in retaining a burdensome and antiquated institution. But a fact so ancient, so general, so universal, deserves at least consideration.

The Value of Rules. — If we look more closely into the actual reasons for government, we shall discover one that strikes us at once as worth weighing: the need of a common understanding about ways of doing things. Coöperation demands a rule of expectation, and sometimes almost any method that may be counted on is better than the absence of all rule. It does not matter whether we go to the right or the left when we cross a bridge, but it is desirable that we know what to expect. Ships on the sea or in channels might pass each other just as well in some other order than that which is legal, and they might exchange the green light for the red; but collisions happen because rules are broken. Pilots and captains of vessels willingly follow an arbitrary code of signals, fixed by maritime laws, because they know that safety lies in a common rule. The gold dollar might weigh a grain more or less just as well, but the chief thing is to know in advance exactly what it weighs. In China the bankers adhere to the old custom of cutting off pieces of silver from a mass, and it is claimed that the customer seldom gets more ounces than his bill calls for, and he usually receives less. One function of government, therefore, is to define terms of exchange and methods of doing daily acts.

We need a government to *settle disputes*. Burns would not say that "men are villains a'." But he did say: —

> " When self the wavering balance shakes,
> 'Tis rarely right adjusted."

We require an impartial tribunal, of persons not directly interested in our disputes, to adjust the wavering balance. Instead of standing up with pistols and clubs to define our rights by our mights, we ask our sober and trained judges to define the just in the case in question, and we go about our business while they are weighing the matter for the disputants and for the millions of other citizens. A case decided thus for one party is good for the entire nation. We get a rule and we know how to manage our affairs.

Government is required to *curb the antisocial members of the community*. There are very hopeful and generous men, mixed up with others who fret at the restraints of law, who tell us that human nature is so good and wise and kind that if we left all men to do their liking we should have no thieves, no burglars, no outbursts of brutal appetite and revenge. Is there a shadow of reason for us to try this wild theory? On the frontier, before society has time to erect its courts and jails, and provide its detectives and laws, we hear of robbery and nameless crimes. It is not long before the most abandoned men see the necessity for checking the selfishness of their fellows by some means. In fact, from the beginning the com-

munity is an armed camp, every man being his own army,
legislature, court, and sheriff.   This method of government is
soon found to be too costly and hazardous, not to say uncomfortable.   Division of labor follows, and certain persons are
set apart to perform this special duty for those who desire to
go about their farming, fishing, and mining undisturbed, and
who prefer to pay a part of their earnings that they may sleep
soundly at nights.   It is ignorance of history which gives
credence to the sentimental theory that human nature needs
no bit and bridle.

"Tiberius Gracchus erected a temple in honor of liberty,
with a sum obtained from fines.   If the fines were just, there
was no inconsistency in thus making penal justice build a
temple of freedom; for liberty demands security and order,
and, therefore, penal justice." [1]

The government is an *instrument of producing goods and
rendering services*.   All civilized peoples with developed governments put them to other uses, more positive and creative
than those just mentioned.   The government is the tool or
machine of all society.   The shop, the store, the church, are
private institutions, supported on a voluntary basis by those
who belong to them.   But we are all born to the duties and
rights of government.   It is not something over us, but of us
and in us.   The courthouse belongs to all citizens.   The governor is the chief servant of the commonwealth.   The president of the nation is the chief servant of the United States.
If we choose to employ our public servants, who are supported
out of our taxes, and hired to perform certain tasks, to do
what all tax-payers desire to have done, we have chosen a
proper function of government.   If a county desires to have
better roads, its people elect officers who will make roads.   If
a city thinks it can supply water for drinking, cooking, and
sanitation at a cheaper rate than corporations are willing or
able to do, that is a wise use of government.   There is absolutely nothing which the whole community wants which it has
not a right to obtain by State means.   It is highly desirable
that this idea of government should be generally held, as it is
coming to be, because nothing can make it so acceptable and

[1] F. Lieber, *Civil Liberty*, Ch. VII, p. 74.

reasonable to all.   If men are in the habit of thinking of government merely as an instrument of repression and punishment, as a giant holding a club over their heads, they can never so love and adore it as if they regard the State as their friend, their own common means of attaining the good things of life.   The "night watchman theory" of government makes it hateful when it should be loved and trusted.

Government is the organ of all, not of a part of the community.   It follows from this principle that government should not be used to supply the wants of a few.   Indeed, it is usually impracticable to establish or maintain any branch of government at common expense unless it ministers to at least a majority of the people.   There are forms of entertainment, perfectly innocent in themselves, which ought not to be, and will not be, provided at public expense, because they are not desired by all.   For example, while only a few persons care for good music it will not be supported by the municipal council.   But when the demand is general we may expect to hear a public band discoursing classic compositions in the parks.   On the same ground, if for no other reason, the government must not support sectarian establishments, because these are not common to all and are under control of parties in the State.

Outline of our Government Organization. — The social student coming to the border of this great territory of government is like a captain entering a port, who takes on board a pilot better acquainted with that particular coast and harbor; or like a Livingstone who, in the exploration of the continent of Africa, employed a native guide upon reaching the confines of a new realm.   The modern specialization of the sciences has assigned the province of government to the professors of political science, administration, jurisprudence, and various subdivisions of these.   Those charged with the practical direction of government are politicians, statesmen, lawyers, judges, legislators, and administrative officers of all ranks. The student of society accepts with gratitude the service of all these specialists, and learns from them the more important and essential elements of the political and legal organization. In turn he seeks to show how society, in the breadth and fulness of its being, creates problems and makes demands. Details of scientific explanation must be surrendered to the specialists, but every intelligent citizen ought to seek to master the essential features of government and its place in the great social system of which it constitutes one very significant element.

The order of investigation may be outlined in some such way as that which here follows. Without going down into the spiritual and eternal source of being we may for the moment begin with the *will of the people*. Philosophically, that will itself must be explained. Historically, it might be traced to antecedent causes more or less fully known. But politically the will or mind of the people in our own time is ultimate. The will of the people includes all that can properly be called common in their thought, wish, and purpose. A part of this purpose, though by no means all, is expressed in the Constitution, a word which may be here taken to mean not only the printed document to which the Supreme Court appeals in its final decisions, but also those well-understood traditions and beliefs which no government would dare to contradict. The Constitution of the United States is a document produced in the course of our history, and which provides for the national government, creates that government in three departments of equal dignity, but with different social ends,— the Legislative, the Executive, and the Judiciary.

The Constitution of each commonwealth provides in a similar way for the government of the restricted territory. Each state has its three departments,— the Legislative, the Executive, and the Judiciary,— with the necessary administrative officers to carry out the details of each department — military, civil, criminal, educational, and all the others as they arise. The government of a state is subordinate to the national laws and constitution. In the later chapter on Social Order some further illustrations from law will be given.

Local government is represented in the political organization of cities, counties, towns, townships, and districts for elections, schools, roads, and other purposes.

Every citizen should study this organization, its laws, its modes of operation, and his duties in relation to it; but this belongs to the sciences already mentioned, and this outline must suffice for our present sketch.

This brief survey should be taken in connection with all the subjects of previous chapters. In geography one of the first steps in the mastery of topics is to "bound" a country or a state, on the north, the south, the east, and the west. The science of society enables us to "bound" the science of politics by describing the various orders of association which are related to government. No man understands his own language thoroughly who knows only one language. No person can appreciate the value of political science who considers nothing but government and the legal system. The grist mill is understood best by those who have studied the wheat which supplies the materials and the bread which is the end of both grain-raising and grain-grinding. By these illustrations it is sought to suggest the relations of sociology to political science.

He who makes a wheel helps to make a watch, and so do those assist who polish the gems, paint the dial, shape the hands, coil the spring, and set the posts. But he also is useful who, though he makes not one of the separate parts, yet "assembles" them all and fixes the place and duty of each one in relation to the others.

Government is a merely arbitrary conception, and practically it becomes antiquated tyranny, unless it is kept at every moment in living contact with those social forces, wishes, hopes, beliefs, wants, which rise up outside the cabinets of presidents and governors, far away from the noisy halls of legislation.

The government is in close and organic relations with all other social institutions. This must be so, because it is only one of the ways by which the same persons act who are living their lives in factory, banks, mines, homes, and temples. We should also notice the reciprocity of this relation, for each institution is at once giver and recipient of advantages.

In other places we have seen that each social organization is provided with its own government, and that it attends to part of the training of citizens for their public duties. But as individuals require a final court of appeals before which all selfish elements may be struck out and the common right be chosen and asserted, so all institutions require a place of resort

x

where their differences may be adjusted. As the final test of
conduct is its adaptation to the common interest, therefore
the organ of the common interest and will must determine the
right where question arises.

It is not proper here to attempt a systematic discussion of
the particular regulations made by governments for the myriads
of associations which spring up in all free countries, and it
will be enough to select a few illustrations of the way in which
government affects and controls other modes of united action.

The domestic institution is not the creature of law, but it
springs from the most powerful physical and psychical forces.
Love, esteem, sociability, economic interests and advantages,
religion, and many other motives cause the family to arise and
furnish the incentives to its support and activity. There would
be some sort of domestic institution without law or penalty.
Probably many persons overestimate the power of government
in directing, regulating, and improving the customs of the
home, parental and filial relations. Most people are not influenced by the fact that divorce is easily procured, for they are
held together by affection and care of offspring. Others take
divorces without regard to law, and separate even in face of
severe penalties. Law can do little to kindle and sustain those
delicate bonds of sympathy which are the real cement of
household union.

Yet the law has a very important function, and social interest
demands that government regulate those exceptional and ruinous acts which tend to disturb public order, corrupt morality,
and leave weak women and tender children without the fostering support of the men who are responsible for their existence.
The law represents, as against brutal excess and caprice,
against avarice and selfishness, the supremacy of the common
good over individual egoism. The government cannot create
happy homes, and must leave that to nature and reason and
religion; but it can and must prevent the worst effects of anti-
social actions. And this threat of penalty has its effects deep
in the disposition, since it compels the reckless savage, the
impulsive youth, the passionate victim of undisciplined indul-
gence, to reflect and consider before he yields to impulse and
appetite.

In a similar way the government does not create industry, nor set flowing the springs of economic enterprise. Natural desires, ambitions, the demands of every hunger and thirst of man's soul, feed the fires of industry and sustain the energies of commerce. It is not necessary to pass laws urging men to plant and till, to build railroads and to mine ores. But here again government is necessary to direct the selfish forces of individuals, to curb excesses, to protect the weak from being trampled in the eager throng, and to point out the limits of aggressive trade and competition. Sometimes huge enterprises, too vast for private means, may be undertaken by a nation or a commonwealth, in which case the government becomes itself a great business manager and employer.

The government does not create the incentives of culture. The desire to know truth and reality is not the effect of law. Here also government may, by wise provision and by careful direction, make it possible to advance the cause of learning and to diffuse the knowledge of discovery and invention.

Most of all is religion above the power of governments, and it flourishes only where there is no constraint and no bribery of conscience. Hypocrisy may be purchased, and cowardice is cheap; but faith is sincere only when it is voluntary. Experience shows us that governments, by their attempts to sustain the Church, are really impertinent and tyrannical. In no country in the world is religion so richly supported as in the United States, and here our Constitution forbids gifts to the ecclesiastical bodies out of taxation. And yet the government renders indirectly a noble service to the ends of the Church by protecting the peace of worshipping assemblies, by guaranteeing defence against personal constraint, and by defining and enforcing the great primal duties of civil relations.

Thus examples might be taken from every one of the associated enterprises of the human spirit, and it would be seen that government is everywhere present with beneficent direction and protection. All human works are imperfect, but law is one of the most sublime and divine expressions of the reason which dwells in our race. The famous passage of Bishop Hooker cannot too often be repeated: "Of law there can no less be acknowledged, than that her seat is the bosom of God, her voice the harmony of the world: all things in heaven and earth do her homage, the very least as feeling her care, and the greatest as not exempted from her power: both angels and men, and creatures of what condition soever, though each in different sort and manner, yet all with uniform consent, admiring her as the mother of their peace and joy."[1]

IV. Reforms. — A series of political reform movements is engaging the attention of thoughtful citizens in this country. It is clearly seen that the democratic movement tends to enlarge the duties of local and general governments. Gradually city governments are charging themselves with functions formerly performed by individual citizens or business firms. Not long ago each family could draw water from its own well, but now this is impossible, and the water must be brought many miles at cost of millions of dollars. Formerly each family could dispose of its own garbage by feeding to swine, burning, or burying; but in a large town the waste must be carried away a long distance, and the city government must supervise this function. Our fathers carried lanterns to light their evening walks, but in cities lighting must be furnished by the organ of the whole community. Our ancestors rode in their own wagons, but very few people can keep horses in a city; they must rely on public means of conveyance. Thus, also, schools are seldom private, and the city is burdened with the institutions of education. The municipal government must supervise the height of houses, the drainage of alleys, the conditions of cellars and plumbing. Innumerable tasks have been thrown upon the public authorities, and the end is not yet. Many of the demands of the socialists have been quietly accepted by millions of people who never think of socialism as a theory.

It is seen that this increase of governmental tasks requires a superior kind of officers and organization, and hitherto the most conspicuous failure of American cities was at this very point. The reform spirit is rising. Democracy itself is in peril in our cities. If self-government fails here, it writes its own doom.

Electoral Reform. — The "Australian ballot system" has been one of the important steps in securing purity of conduct

---

[1] Richard Hooker, *Ecclesiastical Polity*, I, 16.

at the general elections. Under the older methods it was common for the partisan bullies in cities to watch and intimidate voters at the polls, and there were corruptionists to bribe them. There was a crowd about the place for this purpose in certain of the lower wards. The new plan includes a printed ballot furnished by the public authorities, independent of the party. The voter is protected in his act of voting without the presence of any other person to discover how he marks his ticket.

Primary Election Reform. — Gradually a similar method is being introduced in the nominating elections of each party, so that the independent members of a party may not be forced to nominate any person whom the rings of managers choose to print upon the tickets. Slowly but surely the people are seeking to emancipate themselves from the grasp of professional politicians, who prostitute suffrage to their own private gains. It was natural and logical that the government should follow its management of ordinary elections by recognizing the party movement as one stage in the expression of the common will, and not a mere private matter which may be left to chance and to the struggles of partisan despots intent on personal profit. Under the more recent primary election laws it has become possible for good citizens who do not like the barbarous methods of saloon politicians to concentrate their votes upon candidates of their own choice, without being compelled to wrestle and fight with ruffians in dark and questionable resorts. There seems to be hope in the near future of having primary elections which will be as honestly managed as the regular elections are conducted. Under these happier conditions the conscientious and patriotic citizen will attend the caucus of his party, or will seek the coöperation of like-minded men in bringing forward independent candidates of the highest order of ability and character. Whether this shall be through some form of a direct ballot for nomination, or through the selection of delegates to nominating conventions, is a point yet in dispute, and must, with other special problems, be debated, and the best way found by trial and experiment with different methods.

It has been found that more stringent and minute regulations are necessary in the crowded cities than in the rural neighborhoods, because the throngs of towns make it easier for a rabble to gain control of a caucus and practically drive away or cheat citizens who will not resort to the means which are natural to corrupt and vicious men intent on victory at any cost. The state law for primaries should be adapted to the differing conditions in the commonwealth.

The Corrupt Practices Act. — The election of important officers has always been attended with more or less of bribery, improper modes of influence, intimidation of voters, treating, and similar evils. It is manifest that such practices tend to debase character, to pervert the opinions of the people, and to lift into places of power the worst sort of candidates. England has succeeded in suppressing these acts, at least in a high degree, by laws which punish these offences with great severity, and which compel candidates to keep an accurate and itemized account of all expenditures connected with their campaigns, and to return this account to the proper officials for investigation, supporting their statements with their oath. The states of this country are gradually introducing similar legislation. When they have become general, we may hope for diminution of temptation to deeds which must deprave all who share in them. Law cannot absolutely and directly prevent immorality and crime, but it can help to make dishonesty difficult and can open for virtue the path of least resistance.

On the *Civil Service Reform or Merit System* I have already published some sentences, which may here be repeated, as the need for them is still everywhere apparent.[1]

The "merit system" is a mode of social rational selection to assist the rough process of natural selection to weed out the unfit, the incompetent. It is a moral invention of the age as truly as the electric motor is a mechanical technical invention. The merit system is an intellectual relative of the steam threshing-machine. Its function is to exterminate egoistic parasites. It is offered as a substitute for the spoils system, whose chief function is to honor the lovers of themselves and the enemies of mankind, and to heap rewards and emoluments

[1] *Proceedings of the National Conference of Charities and Correction*, 1896, p. 382.

upon the treacherous and the incapable. We have many competent and honorable public officials even under the spoils system; but that is in spite of the spoils system and not in consequence of its legitimate work. Healthy and vigorous people are sometimes found surviving in malarious districts, but malaria did not produce health. To define the merit system is to recommend it. To define the spoils system is to damn it. Society is required by its interest and its sympathy to support defectives and delinquents in its institutions, but it is not under obligation to put defectives and delinquents in charge of its institutions as a reward for treasonable services rendered to unscrupulous politicians. The "spoils system" has a tendency to pick out the men who disgrace municipal politics and reward their unclean and selfish industry with titles and salaries. The merit system aims (1) to examine candidates and apply tests which exclude at one stroke a mass of impudence, greed, ignorance, and imbecility; (2) to subject the novitiates to a probation which will bolt out the bran which is left, even after chaff and weeds have been winnowed away by the examination; (3) to offer inducements to public servants to do their very best through hope of recognition and promotion; (4) to enable them by security of tenure to give their entire and undistracted thought to the technical duties of their office, undisturbed by the hurly-burly of local politics; (5) to open the service to the poor and to the rich, to the entire people without partiality for social position, sect, or party. The spoils system tends to demoralize the public by the display of honors given to the unfit for treachery to the public, and it diverts attention from the chief moral reason for office-holding, that it is an opportunity for serving the common weal. So long as the head of a public department must be constantly looking after votes and wire-pulling schemes, he cannot have time and strength for his duties. The merit system is demanded by our national honor before the civilized world. The spoils system is practically unknown in a great part of Europe and has been nearly suppressed within one generation in England. The worst abuses of municipal politics come from the fact that incompetent men can hope to secure important positions, not by preparation for their duties, but by doing mean and degrading work for the "bosses." This state of affairs is profoundly immoral, and it disgraces us before the world.

Charter Reforms in Cities. — Perhaps the chief difficulty in the working of our democratic institutions of government lies in adjusting the relations of city to state government. All over the United States there is vast confusion on this point. Charter reforms innumerable have been proposed, and all seem to contain conflicting elements. Our cities have grown so rapidly, and our national experience has been so long chiefly that connected with rural life or small towns, that our huge heterogeneous people has not yet worked out a consistent and adequate theory of city government. It would seem that we must find out what duties of a local character should be entrusted to local authorities, so as to encourage local public spirit and give scope to community enterprise; and that, on the other hand, the functions of more general government should be controlled by the State, through suitable and permanent bodies of administrative officers.

All these reforms depend for their ultimate success upon the character and intelligence of the voters. There is no cunning device, no mechanical contrivance, no rearrangement of political methods, which will secure the return of the honest, capable, and high-minded candidate from a ward or precinct where the people admire another type of man and choose the corrupt bribe-taker. It is sheer blindness in us to suppose that the people always desire the best men. It is not true. Democracy is on trial, and has not yet fully won a permanent place. If democracy fails, as in places it has miserably and disgracefully failed, it will be because education has failed. If we believe in the ultimate triumph of popular rule, we must "educate our masters." None but a mere demagogue, ignorant or dishonest, will flatter the crowd by telling them that they are always right. Misery and loss will teach them something, but conscious educative methods give more hope. Why should men be left altogether to the bitter and costly process of experience to learn over in each generation the lessons which history has already in store for those who can and will read and weigh?

Nor can it be said that the disinclination to elect the best men is confined to the "poor wards" of cities, for this also would be a piece of pharisaism and self-righteousness which blinds eyes like a bribe. Wealthy men are often the worst sinners; and it is at least commonly believed that great corporations and real-estate speculators have systematically corrupted caucuses and electors, as well as legislators and aldermen of cities, in order to secure valuable franchises and other privileges at low cost to themselves. In individual cases such charges are always hard to prove, but it is impossible that common rumor and multiplied circumstantial evidence should be altogether at fault. Our education, therefore, must not merely be directed to the slums, but to the homes and offices of powerful magnates in business life, some of whom are honored in polite society, flattered and worshipped by those who seek their favors, and are even praised and ʼexalted in churches. It is so easy for us to think of looking down into cottages and tenement houses when we go hunting for the causes of social evils, and we often miss finding the largest game of all because we do not go where silks rustle and music charms the ear. This is not intended to attract more popular lightning against the rich, but rather to remove excuses and show the solidarity of interest and of guilt in all society.

This practical education should begin in the public schools. In the chapter on the School some suggestions are made on this point.

The Function of the Voluntary Association in Political Reform. — It is often asserted that associations of private citizens are impertinent, and that legal and political matters are the business of elected and appointed officials. It is said that the people choose those whom they wish to represent them, and that no body of ordinary citizens has any right to interfere, nor to assume any of the functions of government. At this point it is highly desirable that citizens should gain clear and definite conceptions of the proper functions and limits of the voluntary society in relation to the constituted authorities.

It should be strongly asserted that the officers of law should enforce the law, according to their oath of office. Prosecutors should prosecute; mayors should see that the ordinances are kept alive; policemen should be compelled by their superiors to do their duty without fear or favor.

But suppose there is failure and neglect? Is the private citizen to sit down and fold his hands and murmur in secret or wait for something to happen? Rather should he not move upon the sworn officers of law by direct appeal, by trial suits, by legal complaints, by reporting neglect, by public notice, by every means of reaching the sensitive spot in every official, until the wrong is righted and the neglect repaired? This is not only to prosper, but it is the duty of every citizen. But if this is the duty of each citizen, then he may perform his duty in the most effective way, that is by association with others of like mind. The voluntary association has been recognized and legalized from the beginning of our republic. It has the support of law, of custom, and of enlightened experience. A united band of good citizens can secure information where a single citizen would fail; can correct the errors of the isolated thinker and agitator; can promote more deliberate, and therefore more prudent, measures; can secure attention of the public; can guarantee that the movement is unselfish and directed by competent and responsible citizens; can provide adequate funds for necessary expenses; can persist where the individual alone would grow weary and exhausted. All the reasons which demand that each citizen should watch his government apply with more than double force to the voluntary association. This cry against the "reformers" is often raised by men who are themselves working by secret combinations to corrupt the public officers and throw dust in the eyes of the public. Such men, especially if they have long enjoyed a wicked monopoly of political control, are likely to imagine that they own the entire political machinery and administrative system. There is absolute need of voluntary action, persistent and united. The spoils system would have gone on corrupting and debasing our country if it had not been for the union of such men as Mr. George William Curtis and Mr. Carl Schurz in the Civil Service Reform League, who are honored for the enemies they have made. Primary election laws were formulated and pushed through legislatures by such voluntary associations. There is hardly an important movement for betterment which has not been started, fostered, and watched over by this form of social machinery all through the history of our nation.

V. Positive Programme of Betterment. — All the reforms of machinery just mentioned are simply preparatory to making the governments directly and positively helpful to the people who support them, whether they be national, state, or municipal governments. We desire honest and capable officials, in order that the true work of political and administrative management of affairs may advance the security, order, health, intelligence, morality, and happiness of all members of the various communities. The engineer does not oil and polish his locomotive merely to have its photograph taken. Of national government we desire an efficient agency of protection against foreign aggression and insult, regulation of interstate commerce, defence against gigantic aggregate greed and internal conflict, watchful attention to the conditions of manufacture and trade in other countries, fostering care of ocean and inland commerce and navigation.

Of our commonwealth governments we demand the most efficient civil and criminal codes, the most perfect methods of administration, the care of state charges among the destitute and feeble, the supervision and upbuilding of our great public-school system, "from gutter to university," the regulation of local affairs by efficient administrative boards.

Of our municipal governments we ask more services, because they are nearest to us and deal with a multitude of daily wants and needs. First of all we demand the preservation of order and protection of persons and property by a carefully selected and thoroughly disciplined police force. We ask that city governments should take care that every rented house is in good sanitary condition, and that the poor are not left to the mercy of landlords in such vital matters as plumbing, drainage, ventilation, and light. Cities should provide agencies for compulsory vaccination, that we may not be exposed to periodical invasion of small-pox, as our fathers were. Foods should be inspected, adulterated and poisonous meats, vegetables, and bread condemned, and the sellers punished. Parks, playgrounds, and places of recreation should be provided, that all men may have a chance to build up healthy bodies. Cities should maintain schools for every child, and see to it that all the young are sent to school, that they may not grow up enemies of the republic. Schools for manual training, science, art, music, should meet the varied wants of men; while museums and libraries should serve the most advanced taste of cultivated cities and lure the dullest to finer things.

The streets should be clean in all quarters, and not merely in boulevard districts and along the avenues. Transportation should be so directed that it will be as convenient and cheap as possible, and should not return extravagant income to promoters. Pure water should be furnished at minimum cost and for all inhabitants.

The defective, the blind, the deaf, the slow-minded, the criminal, and the exposed waif should not be forgotten by our paternal and fraternal city governments. We are not afraid to use the word "paternal," for it is a good word,— almost as good as "maternal," — and entirely suitable to express that friendly and helpful relation of the government to all its children which tends to excite in them patriotic devotion and boundless affection. American "paternalism" is merely fraternal coöperation.

It is true that governments are not yet fitted to perform all public services, and that we must beware of adding public functions until the corporation of cities breaks down under the weight of taxation and difficult administrative tasks. There is a natural limit to the power even of these mightiest agencies of society, the limits of wealth, of productive force, and of directing ability. Many functions can always be best performed by private parties or firms. Each case must be decided on its merits, for the particular locality; but no community should be frightened from securing for itself the appliances or a higher civilization by the spectre of some theory of "individualism" or by the taunting epithet of "socialism." Arguments for progress are not answered by flinging out a hard name that happens to be unpopular with many. In fact, the word "socialism" is coming to be rather popular than the contrary with multitudes of workingmen and educated persons in every modern land. We have no right or reason to pre-judge a measure merely because some heretic has been its advocate.

Rational Patriotism. — Let it be engraved in the memory of every young citizen that the government is simply, at a given time, the embodiment of our morality, our intelligence, our will, our character, and that it is not an automatic machine, run by perpetual motion, without need of our coöperation and sacrifice. It is pitiful and discouraging that a well-informed man should feel obliged to write: "Great communities of wealthy people, removing their homes from the bustle and din of the working world, build up stately rows of palaces, or fill great parks with their splendid villas. There is a single town in Massachusetts rich enough in men of education and re-sources to lead a score of colonies such as established the Commonwealth in the beginning. The fathers or grandfathers of these men were natural leaders, cheerfully carrying civil responsibilities in a hundred New England towns. But this well-to-do class to-day, so largely endowed with all the capaci-ties to make responsible leaders for the city, the state, the nation, are merely private citizens, often too careless of their civil duties to take the trouble to vote. Youths grow up in the wealthy homes of Beacon Street and Fifth Avenue on whom no serious burdens rest, who believe that their chief function in life is to be ornamental, to travel abroad, to sail yachts, to discover pleasure. There was a Greek word *idiotes*, which meant one that counted for nothing in the state. Our word 'idiot' comes from the old root."[1] It is the duty of all teachers and students to "count for something in the state."

[1] *The Coming People* (p. 114), by C. F. Dole.

PART IV

SOCIAL PSYCHOLOGY, ORDER, AND PROGRESS

———•◦•———

CHAPTER XV

Some Problems of Social Psychology

" I love to believe that no heroic sacrifice is ever lost; that the characters of men are moulded and inspired by what their fathers have done;
that, treasured up in American souls are all the unconscious influences
of the great deeds of the Anglo-Saxon race, from Agincourt to Bunker
Hill." — PRESIDENT GARFIELD.

LET us recall what occurs when a cry of alarm startles a
village at the discovery of a fire. The excited shout rings
through the short street; there is a quick response of thought
as the terrible meaning of the signal is understood by many
householders in a few moments; there is interest, fright, eager
curiosity, pity, sympathy — a flood of emotions; and almost
at the same moment come resolves and action. Men hurry
to the place with pails of water and are ready to coöperate to
assist extinguish the flames and aid the refugees move their
furniture to a comfortable shelter. Or we may reflect on the
order of events when it is announced in a rural neighborhood that a horse has been stolen. The news travels along
the highway, that a lock has been broken and a valuable animal has been taken away. There is an assembly of citizens, a
hot discussion, gestures, and speeches indicating anger and
resentment, a hurried conference as to ways and means, an
agreement as to action, followed by the forming of parties sent
in pursuit of the criminal. The event leads to the discussion
of new legislation relating to rural police and regular detective

force, and to state intervention when local authorities are terrorized by a band of ruffians. Thus the local interest becomes a topic for the people of an entire state and of adjoining states, for no one knows when his turn will come to be robbed.

Select an event which has a wider and more permanent interest — the meeting of a state teachers' association, now so well known in this country about Christmas week. Various topics are brought forward and discussed, in committees and in general assemblies. Interest is aroused; a common agreement is finally reached among those best informed; memorials are presented to the legislature; new laws are debated and passed; new officers are appointed or the administrative machinery is modified in some other way.

Widen the scope of thought and recall what happens when some great and honored man is killed. Remember the rush of thought, the torrents and floods of emotion which followed the death of Lincoln and of Garfield. In less sensational ways, and still with deep and prolonged effects, the entire people of the nation and many of foreign nations, follow the discussion of a monetary conference or the introduction of a financial bill in Congress.

The news from Cuba and China awakens thought and feeling in respect to Spain, Germany, and Great Britain. There are debates in literary societies, speeches in conventions, resolutions of representative bodies, perhaps some further action of committees or diplomatic agents of government. That wonderful arrangement of social forces called the Associated Press, praised and blamed in the same breath, serves up news for the breakfast table with our hot coffee. It makes it possible for persons in Liverpool and San Francisco to be considering the same facts at the same hour.

Thus, by illustrations drawn from life we begin to understand how the members of society actually have the same knowledge, share the same feelings, resolve upon the same line of conduct at the same time. It is this aspect of society in its interior essence to which this chapter is devoted.

We have been studying particular forms or institutions, the more external aspects of various associations and societies;

and now we seek the very soul of the totality, of society itself, without regarding the special modes of manifestation. This more abstract and difficult task has been reserved until the reader has become accustomed to observe in visible, tangible, and familiar modes of expression the working of the invisible forces.

I. Problems of this Chapter on Social Mental Life. — We are seeking to state to ourselves the essential spiritual elements of energy which have created and which perpetually sustain the social institutions which have hitherto engaged our attention. Each institution has some peculiar end or purpose, some special combination of mental forces which called it into being. Now we wish to survey the entire field and see what features are common to all. We are ready to inquire whether there is any reality corresponding to such phrases as "the social consciousness." What are the contents of the social mind? How are spiritual possessions socialized? What is the causal connection between these inner experiences and their external manifestation in institutions? Is there a common human nature in which this unity exists, a universal reason and character to which all human beings are essentially related? What is the best explanation of such phenomena as social influence, imitation, mobs, regular social agreements, and other modes of coöperation? Are there spiritual peculiarities which characterize entire nations and races? Such are some of the topics which are discussed in a "social psychology."

II. Conditions of Community of Ideas, Emotions, and Purposes. — Occupation of the same region favors the beginning of association. Coëxistence within the same territory is the primary condition of fellowship. Persons separated from each other by impassable barriers, living in different planets, or divided by mountains or oceans which they have not wit to cross, are incapable of association. Living together is not so necessary after means of communication are extended. There are firms of bankers, publishers, and merchants whose members have offices on both sides of the Atlantic; and this is made possible by the telegraphic cables and steamships. If there were people like us in the moon, and if there were a system of signals between us, a society of corresponding astronomers might soon spring up.

Common descent and crossing have been physical means of connecting peoples. It is still an open question in biology and ethnology whether the human race has descended from one centre or from several centres. The origins of the race are hidden from the methods of science in impenetrable mists, perhaps never to be lifted. But there is no doubt that common descent has been a very large and important factor in creating a common basis for thought and sympathy. A common physical descent, while favorable to the realization of common nature and to association, could not account for the unity and likeness of the soul's life in men. That is not a physical fact, nor does it spring from physical elements.

Association requires physical means of communication of thoughts. Living upon the same territory, even if the persons are descended from the same ancestors, does not insure association. There must be a possibility of actual exchange of ideas. And there must be an actual system of active communication provided by human art, with outward symbols which bear the same meaning for all. The existence of such a system of symbols, even in a family or horde, already implies at least the beginnings of association. Here appear the significance and the value of language, means of transportation, communication, newspapers, libraries, and all the lines on which thoughts may radiate from the centre of their birth to the outermost members of the groups.

III. The Essential Psychical Forces of Social Organization. — What is the real nature of the influences which bring human beings to combine in family, industry, state, church, and in other social institutions?

Men acting as human, rational, and free beings, act with a purpose. Their object, in general terms, is something they value or prefer. The particular objects of desire become more and more numerous and varied with the development of human faculty by culture.

Classification of the Objects of Human Desire and Preference. — There are two grand divisions of these objects corresponding to the dual nature of man — those which appeal to

Y

his physical nature, and those which appeal to his psychical nature. But it is impossible to separate one from the other in any absolute way.

The works on physiology and psychology treat fully the objects which excite and gratify the bodily appetites of hunger, thirst, sex, and the feelings of filial and parental emotion which men share with animals of the higher orders. The desires are directed toward certain specific things or persons.

There are other objects which excite and gratify our more distinctly human interests: beautiful works of art; external phenomena and forms of knowledge; social meetings for fellowship; worship; persons in suffering who appeal to pity.

Why do men value these objects? What is it in men that causes them to move toward the attainment of the means of satisfying physical appetites or the higher wants of the æsthetic, religious, and intellectual nature?

Many writers are extremely confident in instantly replying: men seek such objects for pleasing sensations, for happiness.

It is affirmed that we desire nothing else but to enjoy pleasure and to avoid pain; that we have this purpose in mind when we take measures to get possession of viands, houses, wines, clothes, books, pictures, churches.

But many others, including at least some of the profoundest thinkers of the race, repudiate this statement. They point to the martyrs and patriots who have preferred pain to comfort and luxury; to scholars who choose to live on crusts that they might proceed with their absorbing investigations; to hosts of self-forgetting mothers who devote themselves to their children, not counting the pain nor reckoning on agreeable sensations.

If it be said by the defenders of the pleasure theory that these persons also are seeking pleasures, only those of a higher kind, more intense and prolonged, perhaps eternal, this is denied on two grounds: first, that it is contrary to the very essence of self-devotion, and also that it is contrary to the memory of experience. When a scholar is intent on a chemical analysis, or pursuing an insect, or dissecting a brain, or digging up a Hebrew root, he is not thinking of pleasure, but of chemicals, roots, insects. His object is a discovery, and

nothing else.   Pain and pleasure are indifferent to him.   He
is absorbed.   If he should stop to think of pleasure, his insect
would get away from him, and happiness itself would fly.

> " Pleasures are like poppies spread;
> You seize the flower, the bloom is shed;
> Or, like the snow-fall in the river,
> A moment white, then melts forever.
> Or, like the borealis race,
> That flit ere you can point their place;
> Or, like the rainbow's lovely form,
> Evanishing amid the storm."

We do not prefer an object because it gives us pleasure, but
we have pleasure in it because we prefer it.   Only objects
which we value can give us enjoyment.

Has pleasure no part in the motives of men?   Is the dread
of pain no factor in social forces?   This cannot be affirmed.
Sensations and feelings of varying degrees accompany all acts
of body and mind, and we do remember what has given satisfaction and tends toward it; we do remember the sensations
of discomfort or pain which attend a certain act, and we
naturally shrink from a repetition of it.

Among the reasons properly given for avoiding war with a
foreign nation would be, that it would certainly cause much
positive suffering and deprivation of happiness.   No one
would think of disputing that fact.   But multitudes of brave
and patriotic persons would say that there were other considerations, and that such words as justice, honor, humanity,
civilization are not empty words, nor goods that could by any
logical trick be analyzed into agreeable sensations.

Contrast these psychical or "moral" forces with merely
physical causes.   The explosion of a keg of gunpowder is an
example of a happening caused by a purely physical cause, the
union of fire with a certain chemical compound which easily
ignites and produces a rapid expansion of gas in the process
of combustion.   Here the cause is a physical contact of parti-
cles of matter of a certain constitution.   There is no thought,
reflection, or choice in the process.

The meeting of a city council is an example of the acting of
psychical forces.   The members of the town legislature have

information of the purpose of the meeting; they come together from choice and with varying purposes; and their deed is the result of deliberation, of desire to accomplish certain things and with ultimate prospect, perhaps, of enjoyments to be secured.

In the case of a social force there is a thought of end and of means, a deliberation more or less prolonged, and a determination to select one among several possible courses. The object desired is pictured to the imagination; it is held up before the mind of several persons as desirable; and the consequent conduct is chosen by all participants after weighing many conflicting considerations.

Social causes, in the strict sense, are thus to be carefully distinguished from physical causes. Natural and social science deal with different modes of force. It is possible that they may be shown at last to be one force, but at present we must treat them as of entirely different essence because they manifest themselves in such different ways. It produces confusion to treat them as identical. If a man is shot out of a cannon across a bay, that is physical causation; if, at command of the general, he takes his life in his hand and swims across in face of the enemy, for duty or glory, that is psychical causation and comes from spiritual motives.

Social Results of Acting on the Desires. — Each special kind of desire has a different effect, although there are combinations of desires and corresponding complexity of results.

We may begin with the lower appetites shared with animals, the two appetites of hunger and sex. The one desire leads to securing food which is essential to maintaining the life of the individual. Nutrition makes propagation possible, and the appetite of sex issues in offspring, which continue the existence of the race. These two results are the vital necessities. Without individual preservation there is no propagation; without propagation the race perishes. These cravings are the lowest, but they are the foundation of all higher possibilities. Now that they have come under the control of reason, have been associated with art, religion, poetry, reflective patriotism, and all the purely spiritual qualities of humanity, they are no more merely animal.

The psychical desires, æsthetic, religious, intellectual, and sociable, result in the arts, worship, associations, literature, and all the strictly human and spiritual activities of mankind.

Are these results of satisfying desires *intended* by men? Are they a part of the plan of individuals and of societies? Certainly there is little evidence that animals have any such foresight and purpose, although the habit of nest-making before the young are born seems to reveal a half-conscious presentiment of the race meaning of sexual union among the feathered tribes. The lower races of men are chiefly moved by immediate appetite, without much control of higher interests and without great powers of foresight and deliberate considerations of consequences. But as human beings gain larger views, as civilization advances, and reflective faculties are cultivated, every instinct, passion, desire, and interest is viewed in the light of all consequences to the individual, the family, and the larger self of society. Even marriage has been entered among peoples given to ancestor worship, under the distinct law that every man ought to provide a legal heir to perpetuate the domestic worship. Marriages of noblemen, princes, and rich men have certainly been influenced by a purpose which included these considerations. Leaders of French society, frightened at the decrease of population caused by selfish love of ease, entreat the people to give to their country larger families as a patriotic duty; while economists urge the people in too densely populated districts to limit their numbers so that distressing poverty may not oppress them.

In the case of the higher and more spiritual pursuits the results are surely part of the purpose. The young man goes to college or takes costly journeys in lands of ancient art, just because he has in mind some conception of "culture" as a desirable and honorable state to attain. The formation of a character with the traits of justice, benevolence, veracity, and courage is distinctly set before millions of fine natures as an object of a definite value and a result which is consciously sought for its own sake. The continuance of life, the advantage of the human race are, therefore, not only the results, but actually part of the plans of civilized and socialized men and women. This conscious purpose may grow more definite, intelligent, and powerful until it becomes dominant in society.

The question whether there is any such intention or design in *nature* is one which does not belong directly to social psychology to answer, but rather to philosophy or metaphysics. Strictly speaking, nature itself, as a system of unconscious forces and matter, designs nothing. Only a moral personality, a conscious intelligence, can entertain a purpose. Nature is the material with which intelligence may work its designs, but nothing of intention originates in nature.

Nature may reveal design, not its own, but that of the Intelligence and Will, of which nature is the creature and the servant. This seems to be the truth. Our own experience in working as souls pervading bodies and acting with design upon the matter and forces of nature, helps us to understand that a superior and creative Intelligence may work in a similar way to its ends. This inquiry belongs to theology and philosophy. We must admit that our comprehension of the divine intentions disclosed in nature and in history is very narrow and imperfect, and in particular instances we must think of our interpretations of that design with modesty and humility.

What is the *function of intelligence* in relation to social forces? The process and the product of our knowing powers are desired. We wish not only to know facts, truth, laws, but we find delight even in the pursuit of knowledge. When discovery follows discovery, when the meaning of some natural phenomenon or of some deep author flashes on our minds, we rejoice with a pure and noble joy. Study becomes with many people a necessity of daily life. When a new law is found the birds sing in the heart. The desire for knowledge, whether seen in the infant school or in the university laboratory, becomes a social force.

The intelligence comprehends ends of life and apprehends the means of their attainment. It passes judgment on the pursuits of men and also finds a way to reach the objects desired.

Intelligence comprehending the ends of existence is wisdom. Intelligence apprehending the means of realizing the purpose of the soul is science and art.

The will, in all its stages of development, from spontaneous and reflex motions up to the most deliberate covenants of national ambassadors of states, is the immediate social force. It is in acts of will that human spirits touch the border line between the inner and the outer world. In the choice of ends and means the soul of man puts forth its last effort, and submits its selection to the unthinking forces of nature.

Thus far we have dealt with no element which is not known in the individual consciousness and known to be a part of individual experience. But we cannot pause here without neglecting most vital factors. We are to see how these elements behave themselves in society.

In the chapter on the Social Person or Individual we have already given a brief summary of the equipment for social life possessed by every human being. We have analyzed the various aspects of soul life,— sensations, cognitions, sentiments, volitions,— and the deep fund of character which results from habitual conduct. We have seen the vast network of influences which bind each man to the past of the race and to his contemporaries. Each person is made by society, and therefore bears the social image. But society is nothing more than an association of persons, and there is nothing in society which is not in persons and embodied in their institutions. Therefore, if we follow the order of analysis of persons, we have the characteristics of the social mind. Indeed, we have but to interrogate our own mental experiences to know what is passing in the minds of other persons. It is the duty of the psychologist to give a detailed description and explanation of thought, feeling, and volitions, as a preparation for understanding the organization of society.

Pursuing this hint, we may study the social mind under various aspects, always remembering that it is one reality with which we are making so free in our artificial divisions,— divisions which are necessary to secure a complete analysis and discovery of social energies.

IV. What is the Real Nature and Essence of Association? — What is a society? What characterizes a society and distinguishes it from other modes of aggregation and collection? Here are fundamental questions. It is important to understand them for many reasons, and first of all in order that we may know the true limits of the science of society. For a special science must have some matter peculiar to itself. Chemistry deals with the combinations of atoms of matter. Physics deals with masses and forces of matter. Astronomy treats of systems of bodies and their constitution and motions. Psychology deals with the spiritual elements of human nature and their laws. Economics has for its field the phenomena of the market. Politics can fairly claim the sphere of legal and governmental activities. Sociology ought to have a distinct field in the facts and laws of human association, since society is a complex of relations in which association is the common element, present everywhere, and running through all forms of conduct, economic, political, and educational.

Is there such a reality as a "social mind"? Some affirm and some deny. We may form our judgment without much disturbance from the controversy. We have seen already many times in this book that various groups of persons do share the same thoughts, emotions, sentiments, and volitions, and so are able to act together. There is nothing obscure or difficult to understand thus far. One has only to watch a game of football, or the motions of a militia company, or the crew of a boat, to have evidence of something general and social in thinking and willing.

Is there, then, some common social *brain*, such as each man has, in which these general notions and decisions are formed? Certainly no such mass of nervous matter within one case of bone has yet been discovered by anatomists or explorers. To all particular nervous systems and spinal cords society does not add others for the collective use.

Is there any "social will," *outside* of all the members of society, which dictates to them, coerces them, instructs them, makes laws for them? No psychologist or phrenologist has ever yet discovered such a mythical creature.

The plain, simple, every-day fact is easy of comprehension: society is composed of social persons who are, with some differences, much alike, capable of communication and of communion, and who actually do share in some degree the same thoughts, emotions, and choices. There is nothing at all mysterious or remote about this spiritual community, and any one can give evidence of it at any moment. That is what we may call the "social mind," or the "soul of society," or the "spiritual life of society," or we may call it by any other title which will suggest the fact.

But this fact is so very important, so rich in contents, so practically interesting, that we should give it more attention. Here is a comparatively fresh field of investigation, and so it offers the charm of novelty. Not that it is absolutely new, but that more particular attention is now concentrated on it than ever before, and with all the recent improvements in scientific method and instruments of research.

There may be simply community of intelligence, as when the same information is published not only through a nation but in all the civilized world. This may exist without deep personal interest or sympathy. For example, the Associated Press may telegraph any morning the failure of some great railroad or copper mining company which has been paying large dividends. This will be read by most readers of journals with languid attention and soon forgotten, and also by investors with a keen anxiety which may lead to calling meetings of bondholders from three continents to consider what should be done to protect personal interests.

Community of feeling goes deeper. When interests and affections are touched, the common information arouses the creative and moving energies of great populations. Such feeling implies previous connections of race, language, religion, and the emotional qualities which accompany such relations. Thus the news of the cruel treatment of Armenians by the Turks awakened resentment among their fellow Christians in Europe and America, and the murder of missionaries in China, when announced in these countries, awakened not only wide interest but deep feeling.

It is sometimes said that "conflict" belongs to association. But so far as there is conflict there is not true association, but isolation and separation. The declaration of war can hardly be called association, although it may lead to some agreements afterwards, as the subjugation and enslavement of the Africans in this country led to association of the alien peoples living in the same territory. Collision can occur only between those who have by some means come to interchange ideas. We may thus admit that association, in a weak sense of the word, is evidenced and even promoted by antagonisms. Antagonism as such is not the phenomenon we are studying, but it may, like the lightning flash, reveal possibilities of likeness and agreement. Unless we abuse common language and use words in a sense which is opposed to that generally understood, we cannot call conflict association. Sympathy is a true sign of real human community.

And what is sympathy? It is a final element of consciousness, and cannot be defined in any simpler terms. It is ultimate. He who knows sympathy in any of its forms, as affection for his wife or child or neighbor, understands the meaning without further attempts at definition. Poetry may set it forth in images, music may sing its praise and stir its chords, but only experience can interpret its essence to any man. Happily the readers of these lines will have abundant memories from which to explain what is meant. Sympathy is the emotional side of the social bond. Where it exists, as it has ever existed since there were mothers and fathers, there is an association. It may be small, narrow, provincial, but it is real; it is a beginning for the rising temple of humanity.

When common information thus arouses deep affections and appeals to large interests, it tends to unite societies in community of action. In this the fact of solidarity asserts itself in its intense manifestation. Examples may be found of the declarations of war by the authorities of a people moved by a common impulse of revenge or justice or humanity. In the past, war has been the chief cause of fusing the thoughts, emotions, and decisions of great societies into one mighty plan of action.

But there are other examples of united volitions consequent on deliberation and discussion. National and state legislation are sometimes evidences of the convictions and determinations of a people. Tariffs have been made upon the general demand after long debate. Schools have been founded and fixed in law by the popular vote. A great church may be induced to raise millions of dollars for some vast missionary or educational or philanthropic enterprise.

With the increase of intelligence and the means of communication and education, it is reasonable to expect that towns, cities, states, and nations will more and more bring industrial affairs, educational establishments, and other common interests, under the control of the organ of the common will. This is the psychological meaning of what is vaguely called "Socialism"; the expectation that in some way, by the government or by other modes of associated action, the whole people will come to think and feel and act in concert, and not be subject to the secret schemes, the tricks, the dishonesty and oppression, and the covert betrayal of the common interest of a few who are in position of advantage.

It may be permitted to use the phrase "social self-consciousness" to designate the state of social thinking when the comparison of views leads to agreement, when the entire community of persons acts as one man. Formerly this was possible only in a very small population. The ancient city of Athens was composed of a few thousand citizens, who discussed state affairs in the public town meeting and voted after discussion for the measures which were approved by the majority. Now it is possible for the inhabitants of a wide continent to act in concert and to be moved by the sense of a common obligation or passion or ambition. This is the grandest known form of social soul life. It is essentially an act or state of faith in persons, based on knowledge of their character, and going out into deeds on the strength of this trust. It is a manifestation of prudence, of illuminated self-interest, when the necessity for coöperation is discerned. It may be a manifestation of sympathy, of devotion to an ideal relation.

"A social organism of any sort whatever, large or small, is what it is because each member proceeds to his own duty with a trust that the other members will simultaneously do theirs. Wherever a desired result is achieved by the coöperation of many independent persons, its existence as a fact is a pure consequence of the precursive faith in one another of those immediately concerned. A government, an army, a commercial system, a ship, a college, an athletic team, all exist on this condition, without which not only is nothing achieved, but nothing is even attempted." [1]

Human association is not complete except so far as there is a common determination. The will side of every man is

[1] James, *The Will to Believe*, p. 24.

present in all the acts of collective man. Association is an act. It is not something done to man, but something made by men working together. If ten thousand men of all tribes and kindreds were forced at the point of the bayonet into an inclosure,— strangers, enemies, saints, criminals, aliens in language and religion,— that would not be an association. By a miracle of spiritual union it might become an association, but the mere fact of being forced into a pen would not make them one.[1]

This community of ideas, sympathies, and choices which is human association has many degrees. Some races and peoples are much more closely and intimately bound together in thought, understanding, and action than others. In the most intimate unions of persons, conflicting and alienating factors may exist and subtract so much from the strength and happiness of the relation. The geographical range of an association may be very narrow at first and afterward be extended. Indeed, this is one of the marks of moral progress, the widening of the realm of knowledge and sympathy and agreement.

Perhaps we require a word of less intense meaning than "association" to designate the more general fact of a social organization which includes conflicting members. We must admit that all communities recognize the citizenship and membership even of criminals, the antisocial class. Deeper than any conventional contracts, agreements, and covenants there is a solidarity which resides in society even when it is theoretically and practically denied. The idiot, utterly unconscious of human qualities, is, merely as human, protected by the shield of law, fostered tenderly by ministers of the nursing goodness of states. The Civil War was fought for the principle that this nation is one and that secession is void, impossible. Even when the Federal armies fronted the southern hosts in dreadful battle, it was to assert the fact that we are one people, and to realize that truth, even against armed resistance.

The amnesty which swiftly followed the laying down of dis-

[1] The text discusses chiefly rational and deliberate coöperation. The intensifying efforts of a " crowd " upon the impulsive and instinctive emotions of its members are treated by Le Bon, *The Crowd*.

union arms was not a different policy from that embodied in forts and monitors; it was simply the glad recognition that the price of blood and treasure had not been expended in vain. Society may exist when the process of socialization is imperfect, when conflict lingers. Society maintains its control over its criminal citizens at the very moment it is seeking to "reform" them; that is, prepare them for freedom in a voluntary and not enforced coöperation.

In other words, society is constantly socializing its members, reducing the dissensions, universalizing its highest knowledge and its best sympathies. Society is never altogether socialized. Its ideals are never fully realized. Its best life is not a fact, but a becoming, a striving,— but a striving which is creative of some part of the ideal at every moment.

A Reconciliation of Theories. — I have spoken of the controversy among social students in relation to the real characteristic of human association. Have we succeeded in making it clear that there is a union of elements in a unity? All the higher forms of unity are thus composed. A grain of sand may be a unit, but it is not a unity. An atom must seek company before it can combine into something larger and higher.

Various definitions of the essential factor of society have been offered, and in examining them in a certain order we may see that each has an element of truth, and that all are needed in a complete analysis.

Let us take up those definitions which seem to select the *cognitive element* in association and make that conspicuous if not exclusive.

The economic idea of community life is that of a perception of common interests. Men work together because they can produce goods to better advantage. So do ants, beavers, monkeys, and herds of buffaloes. The perception of a common interest is one component element in the cement of society. But lime alone will not make mortar, nor sand alone; both are necessary. The perception of a common economic interest is one of the thought elements in association. It is only one, though it is very strong. It is a rational motive.

Professor Giddings has emphasized the definition "the con-

sciousness of kind." In the word "consciousness" the cognitive element seems to be uppermost. The perception and
belief that we belong to the same species or stock and have
much alike in our composition, from nature and inheritance,
are powerful and fundamental elements in association. M.
Fouillee's "*idée force*" seems to bring forward this intellectual
side of the social bond.

Next take up the definition which indicates the element of
emotion and *sentiment*.

The characteristic of association has been declared to be
"sympathy," and this enters into Professor Giddings' later
definitions of the "consciousness of kind," in which he
includes a "perception of resemblance, sympathy, and liking,
and a desire for recognition." Unquestionably the sentiments
and affections enter the social bond.

There is an element of *will* in the principle of association.
There must be, or nothing would be done. There must be,
or association would not be a work of man. Man is will.

Here we may place the important contribution of M. Durk-
heim, who insists that it is the social will which coerces men
to coöperate. Certainly men do many things together because
they are required to do it, perhaps forced to do it, by their
fellows. Men go to prison because they feel the hand of a
powerful will upon them. Men go into armies, being drafted,
because society demands it of them. This factor of will is
very manifest everywhere.

But the will of associated men also manifests itself in actions
voluntarily chosen, in free contracts and agreements. This is
the side of the matter brought out by De Greef.

As men advance in civilization they are more capable of
voluntary coöperation, less in need of some coercive control
in order to secure effort.

What is the uniting agent? What assurance have we that
ideas, emotions, affections, wills, may not run off, north,
south, east, west, scampering in all directions, without ability
to congregate and accomplish common action? Just the same
assurance that we have that a person will not from a blow on
his head instantly fly into sections labelled "Intellect,"
"Heart," "Free Will," like the parts of a joint snake.

Man's rational nature is one, and each individual derives his essential being from one kindred source. Back to this conclusion we are forced by every attempt to explain the facts of continuous habits and memories in persons, and especially in associations of persons. Here we are at the line where psychology passes into philosophy.

V. The Psychical Process. — What is the *method* or *process* by which this psychical state of union is produced? Does it not seem to include many stages or phases, although all of them may be observed at once, as buds, blossoms, and fruit may be seen on one orange tree?

There must be a *common presentation* of the symbols of knowledge and ideas to a number of persons, two or more up to millions. Ideas are not communicated as sun-rays or waves of force are made to travel. Nor do ideas descend by physical generation, as plants grow out of seeds, produce new seeds, and send them flying with the winds and birds to start colonies of their kind. Ideas pass from mind to mind by some method of presentation. The mother shows her child how to sew by doing the act before her eyes. The teacher wishes a child to learn to draw or fashion a form in plastic clay, and achieves the desired result by placing the materials, models, and process before the eyes.

Suggestion and Imitation. — It has been claimed that the process of socialization or society-making is explained by imitation. It has been represented that the learner imports something from his neighbor's mind and so lays in a stock for himself, and that this process goes on between multitudes of individuals until all are in possession of the spiritual goods.

The fact of suggestion and imitation has long been observed and its significance noted, but of late it has come into great prominence, and has been declared to be the full and entire explanation of the communication of ideas in widening circles of knowledge and agreement. The child and the man do unquestionably receive information and spiritual stimuli from their companions and fellow-citizens, through gestures, sounds, pictures, printed words, poems, and novels. It is easy to watch this process going forward in any family, kindergarten, or university class-room. In large and crowded assemblies, under the spell of a magnetic orator, something mesmeric, hypnotizing, seems to radiate from a commanding personality to enchant or intoxicate the auditors.

But there is grave danger that we shall miss the essential spiritual facts in the observation of the outward form and media of the process. We may persuade ourselves that by collecting many examples of imitation in response to suggestion that we have explained the mental process of assimilation and unification which is the essence of association. The mere conveyance on a raft of words or gestures of foreign wares from one person to another is the husk of the process, not its central truth. A deeper and a truer representation is that *suggestion gives a hint to a self-active and creative mind of its own native and original but yet unawakened powers. Imitation is the reaction upon suggestion, the sign that the hint has entered the soul and set it to the work of self-development.*

It is not enough to tell us that there has been imitation of something; we must further inquire whence came the thing imitated and the faculty for understanding and responding to the mediating symbol.

If the English people had not had a moral nature akin to the best in Edmund Burke, they never could have understood his lofty appeals. Gladstone was brother and unit of the same race, and the vibration of his soul set harmonious chords to thrill with the same emotions and convictions which aroused him to eloquence. Social communication is not the manufacture outright of a totally new article, but the expansion and development of a common nature.

The essence of the process of socialization, the formation of a social organization, is not in some mechanical and passive reception like that of the image on a sensitized photographic plate. It is the discovery of a vital kinship, of an actual fraternity which is psychical and not of the flesh.

Plato's doctrine of reminiscence hints at a more profound verity, fanciful as it may seem, than the purely outward notion of imitation as something ultimate. Wordsworth has symbolized this deeper truth in the famous Ode: —

> " Our birth is but a sleep and a forgetting:
> The Soul that rises with us, our life's Star,
> Hath had elsewhere its setting,
> And cometh from afar:
> Not in entire forgetfulness,
> And not in utter nakedness,
> But trailing clouds of glory, do we come
> From God, who is our home."

Learning is recognition of one's own being. No material atoms pass over from teacher to pupil; nothing is lost from the former, and nothing is piled upon the latter. At the moment of communication there may be the flash of vision and the birth-cry of a new-born power. Suggestions are far from being the ultimate psychological explanations of the process of communication. They are the mediating methods by which the soul comes to its own and finds its true self in fellowship and not in isolation.

The purpose of teaching by imitation is to elevate men above the slavery of imitation. Mere copying is not the last and noblest fruit of culture. Rather do we seek to evolve free, self-conscious, self-governing personalities. "What is fashion, with its apparently capricious changes, but the method of emancipating individuals from the tyranny of old customs and usages that insist on minute punctilios in matters that are unimportant except as symbols of our membership in the social whole? Thus one kind of imitation supplants another as more progressive. The fashions of the semi-civilized and savage people last without change from generation to generation — and, indeed, it is likely for hundreds and even for thousands of years — because the savage intellect cannot as yet attain the strength to discriminate between moral and indifferent actions. The savage has only two kinds of deeds, moral and immoral; while the civilized man has three kinds, moral, immoral, and unmoral. Thus that form of imitation which we all despise as mere fashion has significance as the means of emancipating us from that heavy yoke of ceremonial that once prescribed the forms of our indifferent actions as though they were of moral or religious import."[1]

[1] W. T. Harris, *Psychologic Foundations*, p. 300.

z

Invention accompanies imitation. It introduces new factors into the symbols of expression. Invention, however, does not differ essentially from imitation, for man does not create absolutely new objects; he only combines and composes what he has seen. These new compositions of image, tricks of doing and making, enter by imitation into the common life. What is discovered passes in ever-widening circles from man to man, from group to group, until the wave of knowledge breaks against some Chinese wall of exclusion, obduracy, prejudice, custom hardened into vice, degradation, and ignorance. There it rolls back only to accumulate wave upon wave of renewed energy sufficient at last to overthrow the barrier and flow onward.

This whole process of imitation is a grand system and interlacing network of interchange. Thoughts travel in a luminous and heated atmosphere of emotions of all kinds, as meteors take fire and blaze in passing through the air of our earth. They combine and recombine in decisions, contracts, agreements, laws, institutions, until all that is desirable becomes the possession of mankind.

The process is ever renewed, never absolutely finished. New ideas are started on a journey around the world, meet friends on the way, form caravans, and partnerships, grow richer in their wanderings, and return, scarcely recognizable, after their world-embracing voyages.[1]

VI. The Testing Process. — All the contents of the social mind are forever subjected to a trial. The struggle for existence seems to be carried up from the world of brute life to the "powers of the air," good as well as bad. As in the ancient dream of battle, when night fell and the earthly combatants sank weary on the earth, the gods took up the strife and continued the war in the heavens.

> " The clashing of creeds and the strife
> Of many beliefs that in vain
> Perplex man's heart and brain,
> Are nought but the rustle of leaves
> When the breath of God upheaves
> The boughs of the tree of life."

[1] Read Tennyson's *Ulysses*.

This is the significance of controversy in theology, philosophy, science, and art, that theories are brought to trial by the competent, error is winnowed out, the wheat remains on the threshing-floor. The bad passions of men, their vanity, jealousy, and pride, make it certain that no discovery shall pass into current thought without a challenge. Even if the disputes of men of science and politics become somewhat more urbane and gentle, there will still be a rigorous demand for demonstration of hypotheses and plausible speculations. The unlearned public has in this process its best guarantee that it is not imposed upon by pretended experts. No legal censorship can ever be half so effective in the suppression of incompetency as the censorship which scholars and rivals exercise in academic life, in publication, and in political rivalries.

The founders of our republic, instructed by the wisdom of the centuries, wisely provided for deliberation in the formation of public opinion and the enactment of laws. They provided that there should be two chambers in the national legislature, so that the people would have time for consideration and reflection, and thus be able to fix at last on the ripened results of investigation and meditation. It was not out of distrust of the people, but from familiarity with the only method by which truth can be discovered, for truth is "the daughter of time and of discussion." We may be impatient with this tedious process, but the alternative is practically mob rule, and that is inconsistent with both order and progress.

In the same way they gave us, out of long historic experience, a judicial system which, though often vexing for its proverbial delays and sometimes perverted by criminals, is yet the safeguard of judgment and of the rights of individuals.

VII. The Conservation or Capitalization of the Spiritual Fund. — That which is learned by the son from the father or by the apprentice from the master is stored in an individual memory. Much of device and knowledge has thus been preserved for long periods. Imitative customs and fashions take up and hold many of the inventions which have added valuable elements to the thought of mankind. But it is in written and printed documents and books, in works of useful or beautiful art, and in the permanent institutions of men that the contents of the social mind, including all the truths and principles reached by investigation and experience, are preserved from loss. Not that this magnificent heritage of knowledge can ever be mastered by every citizen, but that all of it and each part is accessible to all. No one man ever read all the books in the British Museum or the Congressional library; but any scholar can use any item which finds a home in those wonderful collections.

Knowledge is ordinarily preserved chiefly by use. It is true that monuments and records may for ages keep the thoughts entrusted to them, but forgotten and idle knowledge is only too apt to perish. In the living traditions, the beloved songs, the controlling and administered laws, wisdom is most securely enshrined.

VIII. Transmission of Ideas. — The ordinary means of preservation are also the ordinary vehicles of transmission of knowledge. Influences and emotions will not carry across oceans or ages. But the symbols of thinking register and convey the knowledge, the ideas which have the magic power of kindling emotion long after the composer, the poet, or the orator has become dust. There are no "dead languages." The Assyrian inscriptions probably kindled at their resurrection and decipherment more interest than they did with the contemporaries of the writers. Cathedrals are not dead; for the visitors and worshippers to-day hear the chants of mediæval monks reverberated in the solemn aisles.

The methods of transmission are various as the situations of mankind. The most direct method is that of personal tradition in presence, as in conversation, teaching, or the public address before an assembly.

But with advance in the arts of writing, printing, publication, transportation, and distribution, widely separated peoples receive the same thought at nearly the same time. It is already quite possible for audiences separated by a thousand miles to hear a speaker during the moments of utterance. But still more important is the method of printed publication and telegraphic communication.

Our successors in time, the children of our posterity, will

become the heirs of our enlarging fund of knowledge through books, papers, and libraries. Not only contemporaries but even following generations are helped to enter into the enjoyment of the spiritual treasures of any age, and thus a psychical union is effected which makes mankind one.

"The perpetuity by generation is common to beasts, but memory, merit, and noble works are proper to men — and surely a man shall see the noblest works and foundations have proceeded from childless men, which have sought to express the images of their minds, when those of their bodies have failed — so the care of posterity is most in them that have no posterity." [1]

IX. The *formation of a socialized character* in individuals, we may hope, is a tendency of our race development. Of the future we cannot speak with the same confidence which we use in speaking of what is already accomplished. But if we can reason from experience and history, if we can form any estimate of what is to come from the prevalence of known forces, then we have reasonable ground for thinking that egoism will yield to justice and to generosity; that persons will discover that their real individuality is found only in service and fellowship. "The ultimate man will be one whose private requirements coincide with public ones. He will be that manner of man who, in spontaneously fulfilling his own nature, incidentally performs the functions of a social unit; and yet is only enabled to fulfil his own nature by all others doing the like." [2]

In the competitions of life the honest, kind, polite, humane man is more and more in request. The cowboy yields to the careful dairyman, the rough and brutal driver to the patient and cautious coachman who treats his fine horses as if they had rights and feelings. Less and less is it possible for a coarse and immoral physician to gain practice. Competition compels a churlish salesman to learn to tell good stories and greet customers with a smile. Every manufacturer, even if he is somewhat tricky himself, demands honesty of his clerks. Habits thus acquired tend to become fixed and, perhaps, are transmitted to posterity with accumulating force.

[1] Bacon, *Of Parents and Children.*
[2] Spencer, *Social Statics.*

CHAPTER XVI

Harmony with the Present Order

> "Self-reverence, self-knowledge, self-control,
> These three alone lead life to sovereign power.
> Yet not for power (power of herself
> Would come uncalled for), but to live by law,
> Acting the law we live by without fear;
> And, because right is right, to follow right
> Were wisdom in the scorn of consequence."
> — TENNYSON.

"The science which deals with social welfare may always be regarded as a master science in human studies, not indeed in the sense that, like Logic, it regulates their principles, but in the sense that it determines their worth. It is worth while to know Social Philosophy, because, until we know that, we do not know what else it is worth while to know."
> — MACKENZIE, *Social Philosophy.*

"Two things move me to ever greater awe: the starry heaven above me and the moral law within me. Duty! Words so sublime and full of meaning, whence art thou, and what origin is worthy of thee? Thou dost not appeal to us through the persuasiveness of passion; not by threats dost thou seek to stir our wills; thou wouldst not have us shrink from thee in fear and terror. But thou settest up a law which is of our own souls: to this law thou exactest unconditional submission. Before the law we bow in awe, even though not always in obedience; all feelings retire before it in silence, even though they may seek to evade its decrees."
> — IMMANUEL KANT.

"How to fill a breach
With olive branches; how to quench a lie with truth, and smite a foe upon the cheek
With Christ's most conquering kiss!" — E. B. BROWNING.

> "In a state where men are tempted still
> To evil for a guard against worse ill:
> And what in quality or act is best
> Doth seldom on a right foundation rest,
> Fixes his good on good alone, and owes
> To virtue every triumph that he knows."
> — WORDSWORTH.

"Thus some, in consideration of the pretended rights of the individual, have organized, or rather disorganized, society by founding it upon the sole basis of unlimited freedom of competition; while others, merely regarding social unity, would give the government the monopoly of all the productive forces of the State. The first of these conceptions has resulted in all the evils of anarchy. The second would result in immobility and all the evils of tyranny.

"God has given you both the consent of your fellow men and your own conscience, even as two wings wherewith to elevate yourselves towards Him. Why persist in cutting off one of them? Wherefore either isolate yourselves from, or absorb yourselves in, the world? Why seek to stifle either the voice of the individual or of the human race? Both are sacred. God speaks through each. Whensoever they agree, whensoever the cry of your own conscience is ratified by the consent of Humanity, God is there. Then you are certain of having found the truth, for the one is the verification of the other.

"If your duties were merely negative, if they merely consisted in not doing evil, in not injuring your brother man, perhaps, even in the stage of development which the least educated among you have reached, the voice of conscience might suffice you for a guide. You are born with a tendency towards good, and every time you commit what mankind has agreed to name sin, there is a something within you that condemns you, a cry of reproval which you may conceal from others, but cannot from yourselves.

"But your most important duties are positive. It is not enough not to do. You are bound to act." — MAZZINI.

LIFE is a series of problems, and all involve some moral element. The question "What ought I to do?" stares us in the face at the turn of every corner. Take examples. A gentleman came, no matter how, to believe sincerely that we ought not to call physicians for the sick, nor to administer medicines, nor use the results of experience, science, and art; and that we should have "faith," deny the reality of sickness, ignore pain, and believe that health will certainly follow. This theory led the gentleman to refuse to call a physician when, as common mortals thought, his daughter was desperately ill. She died, and learned men said that any doctor of ordinary skill could have saved her life. In such a case what should the community think? What should health boards and sanitary police do?

Turn to a different problem. The Mormons thought they had a heavenly revelation commanding each man to take two or more wives. The Gentiles drove them out from place to place, and, finally, the federal government prohibited them from practising according to their religious creed in Utah. On what ethical ground was this act of repression exercised?

A shopkeeper persists in extending his establishment over the sidewalk, much to the inconvenience of the public. Why should he not do as he chooses? A young man claims the right to drive over the left side of a double bridge and meets a wagon in the dark. Who has right of way? Ordinary experience will suggest and supply thousands of concrete problems in which the question arises, What is right? Why is one act right and another wrong? What motives are commendable and what are to be censured?

It is not proposed here to give a treatise on ethics, but to show that ethics and sociology are connected; that they deal from different sides with the same elements, the same life; and that in starting with either study we are compelled to regard the lessons of the other. If we begin with the study of the spirit, we discover the sense of obligation, duty, conscience. The nature of the moral person testifies to the existence of a moral order. It is in the social world, however, that the full meaning of these ethical claims becomes apparent. It is in social contact and experience that the moral nature is stirred to life. It is in fixed institutions that the regulation of conduct is formally manifested. It is by social conditions that particular duties are determined. It is by their final effect on social welfare that modes of action are judged.

I. The Purpose or End of Order. — It is generally agreed that the purpose of maintaining order and harmony of conduct is to secure and promote the common good. If one should say the object of social systems is to make men generally miserable and wicked the thought would be rejected by all without exception. If any one who had power or influence declared it to be his purpose to disturb the peace, the unity, and the prosperous occupations of society, he would at once be hurled from his seat of control. Vice, selfishness, and avarice, when they intend to seek benefits at the cost of the community, always pay to virtue the compliment of assuming her dress, tone, and voice. There never was a "boss" in city hall, or a perjured stock-jobber, or an unscrupulous franchise thief, who did not accomplish his selfish purposes by loud and repeated proclamations of serving the dear public. Saints and sinners agree that the general welfare is the end of right conduct.

The appeal here must be to our own nature as moral persons. We have seen that nature gives us no certain ethical ideal, for it seems utterly indifferent to moral distinctions and to differences of character, smiting saint and sinner with the same thunderbolt or summer heat. But in moral persons we discover just the revelation of right and wrong, of good and evil, which makes us think of moral order. If our own nature is irrational or devoid of reason, then it is vain to seek any reasonable end of life and conduct. Assuming, as we must assume if we take one step toward the discovery of the meaning of our being, that our nature is rational, we may conclude that the realization of personality is the supreme purpose of our being and striving. The same end has been stated by different writers in different words. Thus it has been affirmed that the end of being is to realize ideal freedom, or to attain perfection, or to develop all the powers of our nature in harmonious relations. In the discussion of the Social Member or Person a brief analysis was made of the essential elements of the Person, of the psychical life, as powers of knowing, of feeling, and of will. It is evident that the highest good must include the activity and normal growth of all these modes of the soul's life.

But we have also seen that this Person is a social nature; that his faculties cannot grow without social help; the contents of his knowledge, feeling, and volition are derived from contact with society; the treasures of mental riches are the complex product of all the past experiences and inquiries and triumphs of mankind; only by loving sympathy with others can our affections be warmed into consciousness; only by the support of social influences is our will sustained in the choice of the right and the worthy. The realization of our own nature, therefore, cannot exclude but must include a sharing of life with our fellows, persons of our kind. This sharing must not only be a receiving, but also active, creative, giving. Only in reciprocity does our rational nature unfold.

Nature is part of our world, and the arts are the means of bringing this realm of being into due subordination to man and society. It is partly in learning the forces, laws, and possibilities of nature that man develops his powers of knowing; by his useful arts he not only brings these forces to serve his wants, but becomes master of himself. In the arts of beauty man brings the objects of nature into the sphere of his æsthetic life and satisfies and educates that life in the creation or appreciation of works of style. And as, in this quest of truth and this active making of useful and beautiful objects, men must combine and agree, the fellowship of the race is cultivated, men realize their own powers in their sympathies; and the individual's narrow self expands into a wider, spiritual, social self.

Two subjects remain to be discussed: the social order, which at any given time or place is the condition of realizing personality in the individual and the community, and last of all the movement of the race toward higher ideals and richer realization of personality. We may, in other words, consider humanity in camp, drilling under discipline with a view to struggle, and then humanity on the march, by regiments and divisions, toward new victories. In each case the goal is the same, the persons are the same; only the point of view is different. In this chapter we are to consider the conditions essential to self-realization in the order of society; in the next and last chapter the conditions of discovery and realization of a growing ideal of the good. The mastery of nature, the provision of a social organization, and the adjustment to new conditions and relations are all subordinate factors as means of the grand end — the more complete realization of our rational nature.

Mackenzie (*Social Philosophy*, 2d ed., pp. 260, 261) has thus stated the social ideal: —

"It is enough for us here to observe that, in so far as we come into relations to other human beings in the world, we are attaining to a partial realization of the ideal which our rational nature sets before us. And there is no other way by which we come to such realization. In so far as the world is merely material, it remains foreign and unintelligible to us. It is only in the lives of other human beings that we find a world in which we can be at home. Now in this fact we obviously find a much deeper significance for the organic nature of society than any we have yet reached. For we see that the society of other human beings is not merely a means of bringing our own rational nature to clearness, but is the only object in relation to which such clearness can be attained. It may be asked, indeed, — Why should such clearness be taken as our end at all? May we not rest satisfied with the mere animal life, or with some partial attainment of clearness, such as we find in the working out of some particular science? The answer obviously is that, from the very nature of our rational being, we cannot possibly be so satisfied. We cannot become mere animals, however much we may desire it; and there is no halting place between the pure animal consciousness and attainment of our highest ideal. Every step we take in the way of seeing our world as a universe and being at home in it inevitably urges on to a step beyond. It is our nature to seek to make such advances, just as it is the nature of an animal being to satisfy its animal wants.

"Here, then, we seem at last to have found out what the true nature of man's end is; and we see that end is by its very nature a social one. It is clear too that the end which we have now defined includes everything which we 'divine' as belonging to the highest good. . . . It includes what we have described as the objective ends, — the realization of Reason, Order, and Beauty in the world: for the realization of them is part of our work in making our world intelligible and clear to ourselves. It includes also the realization of Life: for it is the fulfilment of that toward which our lives as rational beings strive: and in the fulfilment of this for ourselves there is involved also the realization of the lives of other intelligent beings: since it is only in the fulfilment of their intelligent nature that our own can receive fulfilment. It includes the perfection of Knowledge and Wisdom, since it is the clearing up of our world and the making it into an intelligible system. It includes the perfection of Will: for it is the devotion of all the energies of our nature to that end which we recognize as our highest ideal. It includes the perfection of Feeling: for it is the attainment of that in which our nature as rational beings would find full satisfaction. And, so far as we can judge, it may also be described as the fulfilment of the divine purpose in the world: for it is the attainment of that which is necessarily taken as an end by every intelligent being, and which is consequently the only end at which we can suppose a Supreme Intelligence to aim. . . ."

Happiness cannot be the immediate and direct end of living, acting, and of social organization.

The great utilitarian philosopher, J. S. Mill (*Autobiography,* Chap. IV), said: —

"I never, indeed, wavered in the conviction that happiness is the test of all rules of conduct and the end of life. But I now thought that this end was only to be attained by not making it the direct end. Those only are happy (I thought) who have their minds fixed on some object other than their own happiness; on the happiness of others, on the improvement of mankind, even on some art or pursuit, followed not as a means, but as itself an ideal end. Aiming at something else, they find happiness by the way. The enjoyments of life (such was now my theory) are sufficient to make it a pleasant thing, when they are taken *en passant*, without being made a principal object. Once make them so, and they are immediately felt to be inefficient. They will not bear a scrutinizing examination. Ask yourself whether you are happy, and you cease to be so. The only chance is to treat, not happiness, but some end external to it, as the purpose of life. Let your self-consciousness, your scrutiny, your self-interrogation, exhaust themselves on that; and if otherwise fortunately circumstanced you will inhale happiness with the air you breathe, without dwelling on it, or thinking about it, without either forestalling it in imagination, or putting it to flight by fatal questioning. This theory now became the basis of my philosophy of life. And I still hold to it as the best theory for all those who have but a moderate degree of sensibility and of capacity for enjoyment; that is, for the great majority of mankind."

This passage sounds much like a demonstration of the bankruptcy of the proposed creed as a complete account of the highest good.

This statement of the supreme end of good has already been brought to our attention as we noticed, one by one, the various institutions of society. Especially did we find it necessary to anticipate this discussion when we were considering the aim and the social task of the school and of the other agencies of education. The fact is that all institutions have one supreme purpose, that of society, and they promote this purpose by fulfilling some special task, by furnishing some peculiar and characteristic element in the good of being, in the unfolding of our many-sided nature. Indeed, it is only by studying these various modes of social life that we escape from the barren and vague definition of the spirit and discover how boundless and varied are the contents of our souls. Nothing short of the world itself can satisfy the least of mortals. Aspiration and want are infinite.

II. The Belief in a Right Order. — There is a large practical agreement that there is a certain system and order of society which is adapted to promote this common good. Men do not agree on all points, especially in matters of detail.

There are extreme cases of dissent, men of genius and sanctity, lunatics, martyrs, fools, madmen, and criminals. Some are too good to live, some too bad and unwise. But the vast bulk of conduct is measured and judged according to the code of the time, the community, or the class.

As men grow older and read history they see that conditions slowly change, and that conduct which was once helpful and sane becomes wrong and painful and injurious. New conditions call for new kinds of action. When the street of a city is crowded, it is not right to drive rapidly, as it would be when few carriages pass over it. This proves no more than that the complexity of relations is recognized in definitions of the best system of conduct. For example, the method of management of a rolling-mill includes such different elements as the place and duties of superintendents, puddlers, helpers, porters, and boys who carry water to the workmen.

If there were not some degree of practical agreement on the conduct which is required and expected of all citizens in a given time and place, it would be impossible to go on with the business of life.

The ordinary working of every-day affairs in cities, factories, church, travel, school, rests on this belief, although only reflecting and educated persons consciously yield to the custom of the age on this ground. Most persons act by imitation, without considering why they follow the usual modes of conduct. If any one moves out of the ordinary path, and crosses the way of others, or does anything irregular, he is apt to clash with his fellows, who count on his following the rule of the place.

III. An Order implies Institutions which are Parts of One System. — The good state of things for a given time and country implies a certain set of institutions and authorized customs, recognized as suitable by the community. There is not only a general belief in a right order, but this belief is founded on reality, on the actual order into which every human being is born. The individual does not invent, does not create, this system of conduct, but is encompassed by it from his first breath. The family, the school, the customs of the street, the factory, the police, are parts of an established and powerful system which touches life at every point, and never relaxes its claims.

It is believed in this country that social welfare demands that no man shall marry more than one wife, and the domestic institutions are all constructed on that plan, and no others are openly and legally tolerated.

In industrial relations there is a general belief that wages should be high enough for men to support their families as human beings, with something above mere animal wants; that the hours of labor and the intensity of toil should not prematurely sap the sources of physical strength and unfit men for the duties and responsibilities of existence. It is further required by this general belief that wages should be paid promptly at regular intervals not far apart. It is commonly believed that each man should be free in the peaceful possession of his property, that he should go where he likes and engage in any occupation which is agreeable to him, so long as he does not bring damage to others. Person, property, freedom, and good name are protected by this belief, and without such security it is impossible to see how work and the pursuit of happiness could be safely carried on. The description of social institutions already given reflects, in a partial way, that order of things and conduct which is generally believed to be conducive to the community welfare.

The Various Definitions of "Law." — It is desirable at this point to indicate the fact that the word "law" is used in various meanings, which should be carefully distinguished. (1) Law may mean an observed uniformity of events. For example, there is the law of the tides, which rise and fall so regularly that a table of them is made by astronomers months in advance. There is a regular order of occurrence of eclipses of sun and moon; a regular order of seasons; of the flowering of various species of plants, and of the migration and nest-making of birds. (2) There is the positive law of the statute-books of civilized countries, a code which forbids certain actions and permits or requires others, according to social relations. (3) There is the moral code, which tells us what we ought to do or avoid doing, whether the statute requires it or not, and it even goes down into our motives. (4) There is a law of well-being, whether we yet see it or not, whether we command it or not, deep in the nature of the world and of man. All our moral and legal codes are attempts, more or less successful, to state for us all what conduct is suitable in view of this fact of nature and life taken in the widest sense.

Statute law and moral codes cover the same ground, although they do not coincide in their whole extent. For example, both the moral and the legal codes forbid murder, theft, adultery, arson, and other overt acts. But morality goes further on one side to forbid ingratitude, misleading language, careless tattle, and ten thousand feelings and acts which the coarse machinery of laws and courts could not manage. On the other hand the positive statute may command conduct about matters which might in themselves be morally indifferent, as the directions relating to driving over bridges and along boulevards, entering omnibuses or railroad cars.

Statute Law. — The most formal statement of this social belief is the law of the land and of each commonwealth, civil and criminal. Here one may find a careful definition of acts which are forbidden, and directions as to the method and way by which men must proceed in their dealings with each other. The government is the institution by which these laws are made, interpreted in courts, and administered by executive officials of all grades.

The common and statute law, recognized by courts and executive officers, enforced by the machinery of governments, covers the various relations of men in civil life; defines the rights and duties of husband and wife, of parent and child, of guardian and ward; fixes the conditions on which marriage may be contracted or dissolved; specifies the kind and amount of education to which minor children are entitled; provides for the guardianship of imbecile or insane persons; defines the obligations and liabilities of members of corporations and of partnerships.

The ordinary state law also fixes the rights of property; the mode of inheriting estates or of making wills; the rights of joint owners; the powers of debtors and of creditors; the method of transferring property by devise, purchase, or descent; the nature and obligations of various kinds of contracts.

There is also a law of crimes, defining those acts which are regarded by the community as hurtful to private persons or as disturbing the public peace and order, or as weakening the authority of the state itself.

What is called international law is made up of a large number of principles which are recognized by modern civilized governments as proper regulations of nations in peace and in war.

The complete presentation of this code and of the political machinery for stating, interpreting, and executing the law belongs to the study of the sciences of jurisprudence, politics, and administration.

Morality in Conduct. — There is another code, which cannot be so exactly and fully formulated, the "code of ethics." In works of morality, sermons, didactic essays of duty, poetry, orations, and in common conversation the moral code is declared, interpreted, applied to passing events and acts of public and private persons. Editorials, when they lash a culprit or expose a sinner, either clergyman, bank swindler, or "esteemed contemporary," assume that there is in the minds of their readers a law unwritten but authoritative.

In order that every person may do his duty and adjust himself easily and quickly to the motions of his comrades, and in order to avoid endless disputes without a fixed standard of appeal, it is necessary to have the regulative laws and customs formulated and made definite and public. It is not enough to leave duties, especially important rules, to a general and vague understanding. Very much of our daily duty must be regulated by specific and minute directions.

"I have already referred to the mischief and danger that may arise from customs which have outlived their use, but fixed customs . . . are essential in keeping society together, and, as all scientific students of ethics have come to see, morality is dependent upon institutions. We may have to fight against custom to get a hearing for new ideas, but we must make use of custom to get them realized. Ideas can only be productive of their full benefit, if they are fixed in institutions. We cannot build up anything on a mere shifting basis of opinion."[1]

[1] D. G. Ritchie, *Darwinism and Politics*.

IV. Habits and Actions under the Social Code. — The code of a community requires certain habits and actions of persons regulated by accepted codes of morality, positive law, and customs of convenience. It seems probable that savages living in small groups and with very limited knowledge of the world, with coarse intellectual and emotional natures, are most apt to think of certain definite deeds which hurt the members of the group. These they forbid and prevent by means customary among savages. It must not be thought that early men and modern savages have no sympathies, no sense of common welfare. They do manifest those affections which even animals developed before men. Long before there were written languages there must have been an understanding among the small groups of rude primitive men to use certain words and signs in a uniform sense, and thus some rudimentary kind of veracity must have become recognized. It would not do for a man to beat his wife and children too hard, or to kill a member of his clan, for then he might be left alone with tigers and bloodthirsty neighbors. Obedience to the head men must have been required in order to hold the group intact and make it strong to resist the incursions of strangers.

Boys in playgrounds develop a moral code of actions which consists in a series of demands laid upon each member of the group, and which require definite conduct. In playing marbles or ball they will be heard shouting, "That is not fair," — a direct appeal to a rule which all understand.

Each profession and calling has its own code of ethical conduct, its statutes of permissible acts and of prohibited conduct. The various schools of medicine have drawn up these laws and printed them in manuals, and they have means of punishing one who transgresses. For example, they brand with shame one who spreads his advertisements in the newspaper. Stock exchanges and some other bodies of men in business have their rules of admission, dealing, and discipline, and they find ways of punishing those who sit upon the 'curbstone" to play at the same game. Bar associations of lawyers have a system of principles by which they admit or exclude from the privilege of pleading causes in the courts. Horse racers and gamblers have built up a set of principles which regulate the

2 A

"events" of the turf or of the faro banks. In contests of base-ball, foot-ball, and bicycle sports a code is rapidly evolved defining the acceptable methods of winning and losing games. None are crowned unless they strive lawfully.

V. The Social Virtues. — In the higher stages of ethical development we not only require of ourselves and others specific actions and outward habits, but also certain dispositions and types of inward character.

It is the duty of the psychologist and of the ethical philosopher to treat these virtues in detail. We have a right to borrow from them here in order to round out our survey of the elements and conditions of social order. Harmony in society, if it reach deeper than mere external quiet enforced by physical powers, means inward grace, spiritual acceptance, and voluntary, cordial adoption of those personal dispositions which make intercourse sincere, reliable, and fruitful of welfare.

The virtues have been discussed by many philosophers, prophets, and reformers from the first days of reflective thought on human life. One of the most important interpretations of the Greek wisdom is that which has come down to us from the genius of Plato. The Great Teacher of goodness, Jesus, has left an entirely independent statement of his own, which strikes home to the very core of moral reality. In an age that had many rules and commandments, an age lost in nice distinctions and formalities He summed up all righteousness and goodness in the two commandments of love to God and love to man, and His entire career was a living illustration of this law of the Father, this central moral principle on which the rational universe is built. From this single fountain flow many streams, and on their banks flourish many varieties of beautiful trees with healing leaves and wholesome fruits.

It is in this interior life that we find the sources of genuine and lasting social order.

> " In every government though terrors reign,
> Though tyrant kings or tyrant laws restrain,
> How small of all that human hearts endure,
> That part which laws or kings can cause or cure."

Professor Dewey thus states the organic connection of the cardinal virtues : —

" Love is justice brought to self-consciousness, justice with a full, instead of partial, standard of value; justice with a dynamic, instead of static, scale of equivalency. Psychologically, then, love as justice is not simply the supreme virtue; it is virtue. It is the fulfilling of the law — the law of self. Love is the complete identification of subject and object, of agent and function, and, therefore, is complete in every phase. It is complete interest in, full attention to, the objects of life, and thus insures responsibility. It provides the channels which give the fullest outlet to self, which stirs up the powers and keeps them at their fullest tension and thus guarantees, or is, freedom, adequate self-expression. It alone is wisdom, for anything but love fails to penetrate to the reality, the individuality of self in every act, and thus comes short in its estimates of values. It alone is courage, for, in its complete identification with its object, obstacles exist only as stimuli to renewed action. It alone is temperance, for it alone provides an object of devotion adequate to keep the agent in balance and power. It alone is justice, dealing with every object, aim, and circumstance according to its rights as a constituent, a member, an organ of self — the sole ultimate and absolute." [1]

Courage is an element or phase of love. The timid mother, out of affection for her endangered child, will suddenly discover a heroic and sublime indifference to the wrath of a mob, the demonic flames of conflagration, the perils of the jungle and the tiger's lair. Sweet and modest spirits have gone with hymns to the martyr's death by flood or stake, for love of God. Philanthropists who would naturally shrink from the foulness of prisons and lazarettos, pluck up courage, for the sake of the suffering, to visit the pitiful objects of their compassion in the noisome dungeon and the pestilential cell. Perfect love casts out fear.

Temperance, self-control, is an element in love. Unselfish affection makes self-restraint and self-denial easy, even a luxury. For the sake of the loved wife or child the voluptuary tightens the reins upon appetite, and places a strong bit in the mouth of his desires. In order to provide for the little ones, the strong man denies himself tobacco, stimulants, and other indulgences. He is strong because others need him to be his own master.

The all-comprehending virtue includes widsom, the practical judgment of ends and means, and it seeks all possible truth and knowledge. Only too frequently it is suggested that

[1] *Study of Ethics*, p. 150.

if the disposition is right, ignorance may be excused; but the disposition is not right when one rests satisfied in ignorance when he might by effort find out a better way. Cupid may be blind, but Christian love "rejoices in the truth," and adds knowledge to faith and temperance, and "a wise man's eyes are in his head."

" The modern ' I have followed my conviction ' finds substantiality only in the ancient ' wisdom is the guarantee of all virtues.' There is and can be no duty of living up to conviction till we have some surety as to the rationality of conviction; no duty of ' obeying conscience ' till we have taken pains to have an instructed conscience. Moral education requires a shifting of the centre of obligation, locating it less in the mere doing of what seems to be right and more in the habit of searching for what is really right." [1]

And the famous English critic says: —

"There is a view in which all the love of our neighbor, the impulses towards action, help, and beneficence, the desire for removing human error, clearing human confusion, and diminishing human misery, the noble aspiration to leave the world better and happier than we found it, — motives eminently such as are called social, — come in as a part of the grounds of culture, and the main and preëminent part. . . . It moves by the force, not merely or primarily of the scientific passion for pure knowledge, but also of the moral and social passion for doing good. As, in the first view of it, we took for its worthy motto Montesquieu's words, ' To render an intelligent being yet more intelligent ! ' so, in the second view of it there is no better motto which it can have than these words of Bishop Wilson : ' To make reason and the will of God prevail ! ' Only, whereas the passion for doing is apt to be overhasty in determining what reason and the will of God say, because its turn is for acting rather than thinking and it wants to be beginning to act; and whereas it is apt to take its own conceptions, which proceed from its own state of development and share in all the imperfections and immaturities of this, for a basis of action; what distinguishes culture is, that it is possessed by the scientific passion as well as by the passion of doing good; that it demands worthy notions of reason and the will of God, and does not suffer its own crude conceptions to substitute themselves for them. And knowing that no action or institution can be salutary and stable which are not based on reason and the will of God, it is not so bent on acting and instituting, even with the great aim of diminishing human error and misery ever before its thoughts, but that it can remember that acting and instituting are of little use, unless we know what we ought to act and to institute." [2]

Justice is one aspect of love. A wise love seeks to give to each man his due; to pay obligations before buying a reputa-

[1] J. Dewey, *The Study of Ethics*, p. 150.
[2] Matthew Arnold, *Culture and Anarchy*, p. 7–9.

tion for philanthropy; to raise the wages of employees before bestowing liberal alms on the idle; to favor honest and equal assessments before subscribing to missions and founding asylums; to demand rectitude in a legislator, rather than "loyalty" to henchmen and "heelers"; to keep promises more than to parade piety.

Benevolence is a manifestation of love; and, combined with wisdom, is beneficence. The good man is just, and never imagines that he can do more than his duty. He will not claim merit with God nor boast his virtue before men. But he will go beyond the strict letter of the statute and his contract; he will not exact the bond to the cutting away of the pound of flesh; he will temper his own demand with pity; his hand will overflow with deeds of kindness prompted by gentleness and amiable disposition.

If we go inward more deeply from the consideration of the external machinery of control, we may discover the spiritual life of the social body. Usages, laws, constitutions, are the coarse shell of the real forces which maintain order and hold men to duty. In the principles of art, understood and accepted by the members of society, are the real regulators of matters of taste. The system of moral sentiments, the beliefs of the community in reference to virtues and duties, surround us all with an atmosphere of bracing convictions. Government becomes less necessary as taste, refinement of feeling, regard for the rights of others, come to sway conduct.

VI. The Enlargement of the Moral Field. — Moral maturity is marked by the extension of the code of conduct and of virtues to widening spheres. The savage may be very kind to his own family, or at least careful not to inflict destructive pains upon them. He keeps his word with his clan, even at cost of life. Tortured in fire, the Indian would not beg for mercy nor reveal the trail of his tribesmen. Toward all others he was treacherous, cruel, unfeeling as a tiger, to man.

There is honor among thieves, though they show none toward the public. Gamblers are said to pay their "debts of honor" even if grocer and laundress suffer, and the green "lamb" is shorn and left shivering.

There is a tribal morality which recognizes all the cardinal virtues analyzed and praised by Plato, but only for "home consumption." Foreigners have no rights. Like a sacred secret this domestic virtue must not be vulgarized by ordinary exposure to wear. People of the same nationality or language may be honest and charitable among themselves, but hostile to others. Where employers and employees come to regard each other as belonging to different castes, there a sense of obligation to veracity, kindness, and honesty is weakened. Then we have the singular limitation of the cardinal virtues which consists in excusing crimes done to others, especially to people we dislike, on account of some gracious act done to ourselves. This also is akin to tribal morality. The fact is, that in both cases the instinct which is followed is sound, only that it lacks breadth of application, and is often very short-sighted.

Moral ripeness is marked on an ascending scale of qualities which are approved. Savages, bullies, and prize fighters call one a "good man" who can strike hard and endure blows; they adore physical power. At a little higher level of enlightenment cunning and craft command honor. In reaction against sensuality and voluptuousness the virtues of self-denial and asceticism are reverenced. With advanced culture a symmetrical and many-sided character, rich in all virtues and endowments, wins social esteem.

A remarkably keen analysis of a ward politician, made by Miss Jane Adams, will illustrate, as in a portrait from life, what is meant by provincial or tribal morality, as distinguished from social morality. Her contention is, that the poor people of her ward vote for this politician and give him power for his narrow good qualities which hide from them the subtle and hidden evil acts whose stories float to them as mere rumors. They know little of any other public save their own neighborhood, and in the great outside world they seem to discern the looming forms of their alien oppressors. Only when the "better classes" prove by real deeds of kindness that there is a city to care for them will they be able to expand their sentiments of justice to consider this larger scope of city morality.

"To say that all the men who vote for him are equally corrupt, or that they approve of his dealings, is manifestly unfair." The people admire and revere simple goodness, and the corrupt politician seizes upon this trait. At one time he had twenty-six hundred men, a third of the entire ward vote, on the public pay rolls. He bailed the men out of the police station, helped a man escape the bridewell and go back to support his family, found them jobs, gave presents at weddings and christenings, patronized church bazaars, gave away loads of Christmas turkeys, and was always a kind, sympathetic, and helpful friend at funerals. These poor people are not shocked to hear that the politician gets his money from bribes, for they imagine that it comes from the rich and goes to the poor. Many think their alderman is like others in securing boodle, but unlike them in giving a share of the spoils to his constituency. "The sense of just dealing comes apparently much later than the desire for protection and kindness. The alderman is really elected because he is a good friend and neighbor. He is corrupt, of course, but he is not elected because he is corrupt, but rather in spite of it. His standard suits his constituents. He exemplifies and exaggerates the popular type of a good man." They admire this kind of man also because he is successful, and the ward is full of lads who admire him and intend, when they are grown up, to copy his ways. "This lowering of the standards, this setting of an ideal, is perhaps the worst of the situation, for daily, by our actions and decisions, we not only determine ideals for ourselves, but largely for each other. We are all involved in this political corruption, and, as members of the community, stand indicted. This is the penalty of a democracy,— that we are bound to move forward or retrograde together. None of us can stand aside, for our feet are mired in the same soil and our lungs breathe the same air. . . . If the so-called more enlightened members of the community accept public gifts from the man who buys up the council, and the so-called less enlightened members accept individual gifts from the man who sells out the council, we surely must take our punishment together."

As to the thing first to be done, no deeper word has been uttered than this: " If we discover that men of low ideals and corrupt practice are forming popular political standards, simply because such men stand by and for and with the people, so

that the sense of identification overbalances the sense of out-
raged ethics, then nothing remains for us but to obtain that
sense of identification before we can hope to modify the
ethics. . . . We forget what Mazzini so many times told us,
that the great word of the century is association. A neighborhood of less sophisticated people has one advantage, that
when a dramatized truth does reach them, it excites at the
same time hero worship and their disposition to follow. They
thus balance their opinions by living; and it is conceivable
that their big emotional ethics, just because they constantly
result in activity, have in them a possibility for a higher and
wider life than the ethics of those of us who are content to
hold them merely as a possession. . . . We may learn to
trust our huge and uncouth democracy in its ethics, as we are
coming to trust it in other directions, for by slow degrees the
law emerges. That conduct which opposes the ends of the
common weal must finally give way to conduct which furthers
those ends."

VII. Modes of Social Control. — At a given hour in the life
of a social group or nation there is a mode of living, or order
of coöperative action, which is essential to its very existence.
The beliefs and ideals of the members of the group in respect
to this order are expressed in their ethical system and teachings. The ultimate test of these beliefs lies, not in the feelings
and thoughts of men alone, but in the fact of persistence of
the group. A people which does not survive in the struggles
of life can do nothing; its thoughts come to nothing; its
civilization perishes with its members. Survival may not be
the highest mark of the worth of a social ideal, but it is
an essential mark. The Indians in this country, even when
protected, have not been able to conform themselves to the
external conditions of existence, and their inflexibility has
destroyed them; they are passing away. The natives of various islands of the Pacific are dropping out of sight in the same
way. Whole peoples have thus been blotted out. If a nation
makes a mistake, it pays the penalty with its life. Sometimes
a group may not become extinct, but simply becomes subject
and tributary to a stronger race or class and lives with it as
burden-bearer. There is infinite variety of types and classes,

adapted to an ever-varying and developing environment. It is not one quality, but many, which insure survival. The proportion of qualities is also an element in power to endure the test of existence.

In this sense there is a "natural" or "normal" type of conduct which is absolutely imperative for every man and for every social organization. It is not the earliest mode of being, as the savage; it is not an unchanging and unvarying mode; but one, rich, endlessly diversified, and growing. We can, however, think of the group at a single moment and declare that above its will, independent of its choices, master of its ideals, is a right way, a system of conduct, a mode of being and doing, which it must observe, or perish. Call it fate, or providence, or moral law, what you will; it is here, and we must know it and conform or die. Ignorance and neglect are deadly.

It is the purpose of sociology to find what this order is in our age, and it is necessary to make this study for every country, and even for limited communities. For while there are certain very general conditions and principles which are wide and permanent, as the cardinal virtues, there are specific conditions true only of a nation or a commonwealth, or even of a township. A nation which should breathe excess of carbonic dioxide or should become thoroughly dishonest must disappear anywhere. But a negro can live in a climate which would destroy a white man, and the form of government suitable for Massachusetts would ruin Mississippi.

The test of survival may be called the minimum test. It was the sole measure of conduct for plants and animals, and savage men seem to live near the margin of bare existence. The higher societies of men have attained a nobler standard of the right mode of conduct, and they insist on conditions not only of *being* but of *well-being*. The "economic man" might be satisfied if laborers received enough wages to live, work, and breed more human drudges; but the socialized employer seeks conditions favorable to the advancement of personality and happiness through culture and free activities. Society no longer leaves survival to be determined by coarse physical struggle, in which not the best endure, but the mere average and toughest.

We come now to the question of the enforcement of a current belief about the order which nature declares necessary for our being, and experience and reason tell us are desirable for our well-being. In earlier ages men hit the right way by accident or waited for the external pressure of immediate and obvious need. In modern civilized society ends and ways become the subject of much more reflection, deliberation, forethought, and planning.

Unconscious influence is active and passive, creative and receptive. There is a social control which is exercised without devices, unconsciously. We no more think of it than we think of the air we breathe until some one mentions the fact that we are taking in air every minute. Primarily the law is supported by the social nature of each person. He is born with a capacity for coöperation, and from his first breath he takes and gives in a social atmosphere. Most of the useful acts of life are done instinctively, unreflectingly, by those who catch the spirit and breathe the motives of their domestic and industrial and political environment. We have already seen how the inner nature of each individual is shaped and inspired by the community in which he is reared. The product of this process is a social being in whose heart are written the modes of desire and volition of neighbors. Society is constantly, steadily pressing its members into the moulds of traditional forms, and without conscious purpose or directed effort, modifying the outward acts and inner nature of all. The unconscious influence of teacher, parent, sage, as well as of custom and public opinion, produces results in this way.

There is also need of *conscious effort* to secure conformity to the best order. It is very evident that the right conduct and disposition, those most conducive to common welfare, do not come to perfection without direct effort on the part of society. Our ancestors were savages. The word "savage" carries us back to the time when it was thought right to love the near neighbor a little and to regard the tribe who lived across the river or over the mountain as a natural enemy. The pictures of idyllic innocence and gentle manners of the "state of nature," which were so popular in the last century, have no meaning for us.

And if we turn to our contemporaries, and regard them without prejudice, we must admit their inheritance of disrupting and conflicting tendencies. " Be good and you will be lonesome " is a hard and cynical phrase of wit, but it has only too much justification in actual experience. Parents and school teachers are under no illusion on this subject. The most optimistic man of affairs may be very fortunate if he is not exasperated on hot days with present ways of acting. It is not necessary to go to penitentiaries to discover refractory materials of human nature.

We shall not attempt to measure the relative power of selfishness and benevolence in common life. Altruism and egoism grow up side by side. In some soils the sensitive leaves of gentleness and consideration are quickly withered in the hot sun of trial, while elsewhere self-devotion is carried to excess. All that is necessary for our present purpose is the full and candid admission that weeds will grow in any garden to the exclusion of flowers and edible vegetables, unless the gardener takes the side of the latter and champions their cause.

If we believe half of what great editors say about each other; of what politicians declare about rivals in the heat of campaigns; of what jealous men and women set afloat in gossip; of what sectaries affirm of heretics in the moments of wrathful love of truth; of what idle rumor hisses down every wind,— we can see that this rebellious human nature of ours sadly needs training.

Who shall control? — The actual determining factor is the common will. That will may be driven by passion, may be blind with prejudice, cruel as the grave, and urge the mass of the nation straight on to destruction; but there is no appeal from the majority, even under a despotism. The people have the supreme power, subject only to the Power above all. If they are wrong, their only salvation is somehow to be set right.

There is usually a more enlightened minority who see the better way, at least more clearly than their contemporaries. Happy the people which has such leaders in school, church, and state, men who can read the signs of the times and interpret the demands of nature, the law of welfare.

" A people is but the attempt of many
　　To rise to the completer life of one;
　　And those who live as models for the mass
　　Are singly of more value than they all." — R. BROWNING.

There are also in every social group vigorous but narrow and selfish leaders who seek power and control. They debauch the public mind. They purchase newspapers and use them to pervert and blind the voters. They bribe electors and circulate tons of misinformation. They cover brutal and selfish schemes with the cloak of charity, and recommend poisonous nostrums under the labels of justice, freedom, and science.

The practical result is a compromise of all these forces. It is at best rough justice, and it can never be said with clear certainty, that "the voice of the people is the voice of God." But we must somehow stagger on and move with such guidance as we can secure. Life will not stop; hunger must be appeased; industry cannot wait for absolute right and infallible wisdom; religion does its service with only a balance of evidence in its favor; and room for a doubt is everywhere. So men agree, in a rough way, and find a mode of stilling controversy long enough to accomplish at least a part of the mission of existence. If they select the worst leaders, they find it out by suffering, increase of disease, poverty, mortality, and even extinction.

The determination of social leadership is made in this part of the endless struggle and competition of ideals. Those who wish to influence men for good must prepare for a long contest in which physical powers of endurance, tenacity, and aggressiveness are joined to superior intellectual resources. The weakling must stay in his corner.

The organs of control are all the institutions of society, since every one of them has, as part of its constitution, the means of directing the conduct of its members. From the hod-carrier's family in the hovel up to the Senate of the United States, housed in splendor and clothed with national authority, every social organization takes part in this great task of bringing social members into what is supposed to be the right order.

Proceeding inward from the outward fact, the visible embodiment of social regulation, along the line of our personal memories, we come first upon family government. From the earliest moments of life the infant is subject to the control of the mother and could not exist without it. The rhythm of each day, answering to the physical rhythm of tides, dawns, hunger, heart-beats, sleep, and waking, is directed by mother-rule. The citizen takes his first lessons in obedience in the cradle. Law begins to write its commands upon the speechless babe and shape his habits long before he can reason. If his impulsive cries are heeded and his caprices fostered, he is a rebel before he can name a cat or articulate his mother's name. Regularity of habit fits him to the motions of the stars, the trains, the bells of shops, the calls of duty. The alphabet of civic virtue and duty is learned in infancy.

Our next memories of government are those of teachers, schoolmasters. They "deliver us to laws." They have rules, rods, sanctions, laws, penalties, inducements to obedience. School management is a part of the governmental machinery of the universe. It is a function of kings and queens, of parliaments and parents, of councils and senates. The teacher, in the direction of conduct, is sharing the office with presidents and governors, is a personal factor in social control. School and family government are not merely preparation for participation in the general regulation of society; they are themselves part of the means created by society for the direction of individual conduct. "God could not be everywhere, so He made mothers," said the Talmud. The government of the world is farmed out, and its offices filled by the heads of departments, domestic, educational, and others. Only imagine the task of a legislature having directly to manage a troop of bootblacks in a waifs' mission, or a crowd of urchins at a picnic! The institutions of control must be everywhere, because human beings are everywhere, and each group must set up its system of administration.

Enter a factory where a thousand men are busy manufacturing steel rails or machinery. There, also, is a local form of government, from president and superintendent down to the boy who carries the messages. There are rules which touch every act: rules governing the time of beginning, dinner, closing; rules as to quality and quantity of products; fines for neglect or awkwardness; threats of discharge for incompetence or dishonesty always hanging over the heads of employees; foremen to see that the rules are followed and law-breakers brought to account. As soon as boy, man, or girl accepts a place for wages the pressure of laws begins to be felt, a will outside of the personal will, and sometimes in collision with it.

Customs and fashions are petty tyrants which chastise us into social conformity, even the most reluctant. Customs are more ancient and seated, as the custom of dress, of eating at a table, of observing certain holidays, of keeping to the right on a public road. Fashions are just as imperative but more fleeting. Yesterday it was duty, in the eye of fashion, to wear a long coat; to-day it is sin. Short tails are demanded on the ground of "right"; but again the fashion plates are changed, no one knows where, and short tails are criminal. One hangs his head, after a voyage around the world, because his waistcoat should have been sent to the museum rather than worn to the reception. Dame Fashion reigns but a single day, but she is cruel while she holds the sword.

Censorship is another whip which society wields to "haud the wretch in order." Gossip sits upon the front steps and scans the passers-by. Her judgments are final and her darts are mortal. She may be ugly herself, but beauty dreads her tongue. Gossip chills with a blast of frost more severe than a blizzard from the north pole, burns with fire hotter than steel just out of the fiery furnace, sounds a note of warning which may be heard above the ocean's surf.

The Devices of Social Control. — The ruling factors or agents in each of these institutions must adopt various modes of influence or power to conform to the rule of life. These devices are so numerous and various that it is difficult to give a complete account of them or even to classify them.

Tentatively the devices for securing conformity to the approved order may be classified as *educative, coercive,* and *suppressive.*

The Educational Devices of Social Control. — In order to bring conduct into line with the requirements of social harmony the leader, or those ambitious to become leaders, must gain possession of the instruments of forming the opinions of men. One of the most striking illustrations of the power of influencing conduct by persistent presentation of an idea is found in the advertising methods of vendors of patent medicines. The land is deluged with notices in newspapers, with pamphlets and pictures sent to hundreds of thousands of persons through the post-office, and almanacs are given away by the million. These notices are served up in sensational form, seasoned with wit, spiced with pungent threats of death, puffed with glowing promises of health, fortified by the certificates of clergymen and lawyers and other persons whose opinions on such subjects are not those of experts. Some of these medicines are good; some are harmless; others are deadly poison and made of cheap whiskey and bitter weeds; but persistent advertising produces widespread belief in their virtues, and millions of dollars annually are spent upon them in witness of the sincerity of these beliefs. Those who survive live at least long enough to give their testimony and their photographs, — and the dead are silent.

Processes. — Conduct is formed by influences directed to secure habitual choices. The will is the man, and oft-repeated volitions in a given direction shape the will. Thoughts which occupy consciousness tend to become exclusive, and acts which are steadily accompanied by pleasure and satisfaction are most apt to be repeated. Society can secure conformity to its standards by interesting the citizen in its ends and by investing duty with memories of enjoyments. Reluctance is overcome by offering higher satisfactions or more intense pleasures. Take for an illustration the raising of money for a great exposition or for an emergency fund in time of financial distress. People who are already aroused head the list with liberal subscriptions, and others are "whipped into line" by appeals and threats, which are as effective as bludgeons. The air is filled with the project; the newspapers give space to nothing else; unbelievers are silenced by rebuke or sarcasm; the stingy are cajoled, bribed, flattered, honored, according to the demand of the moment. Advantages are painted in vivid colors, losses are concealed. Contagion takes charge of the enterprise, and at last all congratulate themselves on the grand achievement.

Other devices of education, the school, the platform, the

press,— are subsidized or employed to propagate a belief. Witness the introduction of temperance teaching in the public schools of many states, and instruction as to the effects of tobacco and other poisonous substances. It is an educational device to secure social control, to enforce an idea.

The kings of England sought to mould public opinion by "tuning the pulpit" in the ancient times of union of church and state. The preacher is still, in spite of newspaper competition, one of the educative agencies in the formation of a social policy. Reformers have always sought to set ministers talking, Sunday after Sunday, upon their theme.

The Devices of Coercion. — Social control is secured not only by instruction and persuasion, that is, by the production of conviction and personal choice, but also by devices which constrain action even in the absence of consent of will and judgment. It must be admitted that the dividing line between educational and coercive devices is not very distinctly marked, but we can readily distinguish extreme cases of each kind. For example, so long as John Brown sought by speech-making to persuade the American people to abolish slavery he was an educator; but when he placed himself at the head of a little army and invaded a state where slavery existed as by law established, he passed from an educative to a coercive device. It is the difference between inviting an intruding boy to descend from an apple tree and throwing stones at him to make his position uncomfortable and dangerous. Coercion is of all degrees of stress and pressure, and is applied in all organizations: in family and school by bribe or censure; in the factory by threat of discharge; in the state by police and prison.

The Device of Suppression. — Suppression is the most summary process. A head that is full of rebellion must be cut off. That is "capital" punishment. In former ages it was the most popular and reasonable form of correcting eccentricities of conduct. It was very fashionable in England not very long ago. Fine ladies and gentlemen went to a hanging as we go to an exposition. The high roads were ornamented with the dead bodies of persons who liked not the golden mean of regularity. So-called witches confessed the sins of other people and died for their own. Dissenters were fortunate if they escaped with whipping and banishment. Murderers, thieves, traitors, rich Jews, and dreaming pilgrims like Bunyan were treated to similar diet.

Our reasonable tolerance and our power of discrimination have somewhat improved in these bright days of science and philanthropy, but we are not yet beyond the need of prisons, asylums for those unfit to become parents, and other modes of eliminating the waste products of the civilizing process. The genius of government is persistently seeking ways of extirpating human weeds, of breaking the line of inheritance of qualities and characters which disturb society.

The method of extirpation has narrow scope. It does not produce order, but merely gets rid of the most troublesome factors of revolt. The worst use we can make of a human being is to hang him, if it is possible to do anything else with him. The alternatives of capital punishment and banishment are control or education.

Order is a Condition of Progress, not merely preserving Past Gains. — The problem of a bicycle is twofold, keeping the balance and moving forward. The rider cannot do the one without doing the other at the same moment. If he does not preserve his equilibrium, he comes to a full stop; if he thinks to rest in order to keep his balance, he falls. He preserves his balance precisely because he is moving forward. Society is also a "moving equilibrium." The ship of state does not respond to its rudder unless it is sailing. Momentum and guidance are parts of one life and cannot be separated.

This consideration opens the theme of our closing chapter, as that is intended to reveal an endless vista of possible achievements, a boundless horizon whose margin fades forever as we move.

2 B

CHAPTER XVII

Social Progress

"He who thinks we are to pitch our tent here, and have attained the utmost prospect of reformation, that the mortal glass wherein we contemplate can show us, till we come to beatific vision; that man by this very opinion declares, that he is yet far short of truth. The light which we have gained, was given us, not to be ever staring on, but by it to discover onward things more remote from our knowledge." — MILTON.

> " ' Have patience,' I replied; ' ourselves are full
> Of social wrong, and maybe wildest dreams
> Are but the needful preludes of the truth:
> For me, the genial day, the happy crowd,
> The sport half-science fill me with a faith,
> This fine old world of ours is but a child
> Yet in the go-cart. Patience! Give it time
> To learn its limbs; there is a hand that guides.' "
> — TENNYSON, *The Princess.*

> " His soul is still engaged upon this world —
> Man's praise can forward it, man's prayer suspend,
> For is not God all-mighty?" — R. BROWNING.

"The life of a soul is sacred in every stage of its existence, as sacred in the earthly stage as in those which are to follow. Each stage must be made a preparation for the next; every temporary advance must aid the gradual ascending progress of that immortal life breathed into us all by God Himself, as well as the progress of the great Entity — Humanity — which is developed through the labor of each and every individual.

"God has placed you here upon this earth. He has surrounded you with myriads of fellow-beings whose minds receive aliment from your own, whose life is fecundated by your own. In order to preserve you from the dangers of isolation, He has given you desires which you are incapable of satisfying alone, and those dominating social instincts which distinguish you from the brute creation, in which they are dormant. He has spread around you a material world, magnificent in beauty and pregnant with life; a life — be it ever remembered — which, though it reveal itself by divine impulse, yet everywhere awaits your labor, and modifies its manifestations through you, increasing in power and vigor in proportion to your increased activity.

"God has given you certain sympathies which are inextinguishable. Such are pity for those that mourn, and joy for those that rejoice; anger against those who oppress their fellow-creatures; a ceaseless yearning after truth; admiration for the genius; enthusiasm for those who reduce it to beneficial action upon mankind; and religious veneration for those, who, failing to achieve its triumph, yet bear witness to it with their blood, and die in martyrdom: and you deny and reject all the indications of your mission which God has thus clustered around you, when you cry anathema on the work of His hand, and call upon us to concentrate all our faculties on a work of mere inward purification, necessarily imperfect, nay impossible, if sought alone.

"Does not God punish those who strive to do this? Is not the slave degraded? Is not one-half of the soul of the poor day-laborer (doomed to consume the light divine in a series of physical acts unrelieved by a gleam of education) buried beneath its animal appetites, in those blind instincts which you name material?

"'Where the Spirit of the Lord is, there is Liberty,' has been declared by one of the most powerful apostles the world has known, and the religion he preached decreed the abolition of slavery. Who that crouches at the foot of the creature can rightly know and worship the Creator? Yours is not a Religion. It is a sect of men who have forgotten their origin, forgotten the battles which their fathers fought against a corrupt society and the victories they gained in transforming the world which you despise, O men of contemplation!

"The first real, earnest religious Faith that shall arise upon the ruins of the old worn-out creeds will transform the whole of our actual social organization, because every strong and earnest faith tends to apply itself to every branch of human activity; because in every epoch of its existence the Earth has ever tended to conform itself to the Heaven in which it then believed, and because the whole history of Humanity is but the repetition — in form and degree varying according to the diversity of the times — of the words of the Dominical Christian Prayer: 'Thy Kingdom come, on earth as it is in heaven.'

"'Thy Kingdom come, on earth as it is in heaven.' Let these words — better understood and better applied than in the past — be the utterance of your faith, your prayer, O my brothers! Repeat them, and strive to fulfil them.

"Workingmen! Brothers! When Christ came, and changed the face of the world, he spoke not of rights to the rich, who needed not to achieve them; nor to the poor, who would doubtless have abused them in imitation of the rich; he spoke not of utility nor of interest to a people whom interest and utility had corrupted; he spoke of Duty, he spoke of Love, of Sacrifice, and of Faith; and he said that they should be first among all who had contributed most of their labor to the good of all.

"And the words of Christ, breathed in the ear of a society in which all

true life was extinct, recalled it to existence, conquered the millions, conquered the world, and caused the education of the human race to ascend
one degree on the scale of progress.

"Workingmen! We live in an epoch similar to that of Christ. We
live in the midst of a society as corrupt as that of the Roman Empire,
feeling in our inmost soul the need of reanimating and transforming it, and
of uniting all its various members in one sole faith, beneath one sole law,
in one sole aim, — free and progressive development of all the faculties
of which God has given the germ to His creatures. We seek the Kingdom
of God on earth as it is in Heaven, or rather, that earth may become
a preparation for Heaven, and society an endeavor after the progressive
realization of the Divine Idea." — MAZZINI, *Duties of Man.*

I. Definition. — The conception of progress is too large and
complex to shut up in a little formula of words. Yet we may give
it abstract expression, and proceed to make the contents more
real to ourselves by particular details. In its negative form,
progress implies a relative decrease of the number of defective
human beings, and a diminution of misery. Always our eye
must be kept on the rational and sentient beings who constitute our kind. The lower animals, since they are related to us
by many bonds, and are capable of pain and pleasure, cannot
be excluded from consideration. Their suffering and enjoyment enter into the consciousness and the duty of mankind.
Human persons are capable of suffering and happiness, of
goodness and crime. Progress would mean nothing to us, or
mean something bad and discouraging, if it implied increase of
the vile, the debased, the miserable.

In its positive form, we mean by progress increase of well-
being in all its elements, and over the widest possible area.
All life becomes full of significance to us, not as we read about
it, but as we dip into it, as we live. No man standing on the
shore can know the joy of the strong swimmers buffeting the
waves with laughter, and exulting in the invigorating sea-water.
We realize the meaning of progress in general, only as we are
ourselves advancing from day to day, as we can look back at
our own inferior past, and think of increase of power, intelligence, enjoyment, and feel ourselves related to a wider range of
objects in nature, and of persons in society.

Any definition of progress must bring us face to face with the
ancient question of all thoughtful minds : what is good ? what

is worth striving to gain? what is the end of action and struggle? The good we seek as the end of Order, is the good we seek as the end of Progress; for in all we do, human welfare is the purpose of all conduct.

If anything is good, life is good. To be sure, many people, who can hardly be called insane, declare that life is not a good, but evil. It is difficult to get common ground for argument with those who are sick of the world. But we have a right to judge of beliefs by facts which test their genuineness. Suicides are not yet so numerous as large families. Population grows even in countries where the creed seems to make annihilation equivalent to heaven. The pessimists on principle are always illogical, or they would take poison and remove their murmurs from the hearing of healthy men. If we can judge faith by works, the vast majority of men have voted life to be a good, for any of them could quit it, at any moment, by opening any one of a hundred doors. We must start somewhere, and we may assume the value of life. Illogical pessimists should be left out of a logical argument, and the logical pessimists are all dead.

Life is a good. Then all that furthers and fosters life is good: sound physical conditions, vigor, power, strong limbs, and organs of digestion which do their duty without attracting too much notice. In heroic moments and exceptional circumstances, it is "sweet and beautiful to die for one's country," but in ordinary conditions it is both more difficult and more useful to live for fatherland, and plough deep. But that is just because the life of the fatherland is, on the whole, both beautiful and sweet.

As there is controversy over the meaning of the word we are using, we may begin where all competent persons will at once agree: progress means increase of power over things and over men. Is there any question that European peoples have advanced beyond the hordes of African forests or the miserable natives of Australia? Brought to the test of power, we see the inferior races disappear before the arms and the strategy of the educated invaders or bow to serve them. The Australian may excel the Englishman in throwing a boomerang, but that art is useless to a man who knows the rifle.

The civilized races have more numerous and plentiful means of happiness. There is no comparison in this respect between the nations we call advanced or enlightened and the backward peoples. Illustrations by the thousand could be offered in every department of life. Prof. S. N. Patten tells us we are passing from a "pain economy" to a "pleasure economy." In former ages inferior races spent life in turning from pain; we spend life adding to pleasure.

But all this involves a progress in inner and spiritual qualities, without which superior power over nature and inferior men could not exist. The civilized races control natural forces and compel them to serve because they have improved in intelligence, in actual knowledge, in methods of communicating knowledge and skill to their children, and in preserving the discoveries of progressive minds and making them available for all.

This increase of intelligence implies larger social coöperation over wider areas. In the lower and earlier races of mankind, each member of the small group could use only the discoveries of his neighbors, low in the scale of intelligence like himself, while the poorest laborer in civilized lands daily employs devices and methods which have been picked out of the best patents of the civilized world.

The mechanic at his lathe is an heir of past ages and a partner of millions who are engaged in similar employments. A man may not know all the arts and sciences, but any competent man can, by diligence, find out any one fact or device which is in his day anywhere known in Europe or America. Instead of the coöperation of a narrow and restricted horde each man is in correspondence with millions of vigorous and progressive men. A modern nation is an example of social coöperation on a scale vast and impressive, and each citizen is strong with the might of all the multitudes who live under the same flag.

But this coöperation could not exist without progress in sympathy, larger and finer morality. The rise of international commerce compels the growth of international morality and law, a recognition of the practical solidarity of mankind, a surrender, slowly but surely, of the merely national morality of former ages. The ideal of a moral law for mankind is far from being realized in diplomacy and conduct, but it is working to leaven the world's life, and usher in the age when

"Man to man shall brothers be, o'er all the world."

A finer, broader morality goes with a philanthropic religion, a "fortifying" faith. Progress of the lower kind is helped by this higher factor, and reacts to increase its sway. As Professor Giddings says : "Christianity became the most tremendous power in history. Gradually it has been realizing its ideal, until, to-day, a Christian philanthropy and a Christian missionary enterprise, rapidly outgrowing the esoteric sentimentalism of their youth, and devoting themselves to the diffusion of knowledge, to the improvement of conditions, and to the up-building of character, are uniting the classes and the races of men in a spiritual humanity."

Progress, in the strictest sense, does not mean the mere multiplication of goods and processes already known, but new devices, new qualities, discoveries, combinations, revelations of insight. It is very desirable, for example, when a sewing-machine is invented, that it should be manufactured, cheapened in price, placed in the homes of the people. But the invention is the new starting-point ; all the rest is mere copying and transportation. The invention of the linotype has revolutionized the business of printing within a few years ; but the transition was determined as by a destiny from the hour when the novel idea of the machine was born in the mind of the inventor. Thereafter merely mechanical minds could communicate and vulgarize the process. In commercial enterprise, as in the consolidation of railroads into a system or the laying of the first cable, the first successful application of the principle requires genius ; the details can be administered and the plan developed by less gifted men.

II. Causes of Progress. — We cannot think of curses or blessings as coming causeless into being. As every event and fact is in time and space, so every event has a cause, even if we cannot at once find it. Social progress is a fact observed, and the human mind is impelled by its very nature to seek explanation.

First we may look for the causes of progress in the whole vast movement of the universe about us, the movement which has written its history in the fossils of the rocks which geology is reading off. Nature-history offers revelations of advance from inorganic to organic, from matter without feeling to humble creatures sensitive to heat and light and touch, and from these upward by slow degrees to man with his material body and his spiritual powers of sensation, thought, reasoning, and worship.

Up to the appearance of man upon the earth, the movement from lower to higher forms of life was due to causes independent of plans of the participants. " Natural selection," the result of struggle, steadily chose higher and more complex types. Even in the history of mankind our race has been brought forward by similar means, without the foresight or intention of human beings.

The directly human causes of progress are more clearly seen. To understand the causes of progress in general, we may well begin with facts under our eyes. The family and the schoolroom are themselves miniature worlds, and the processes there enacted are suggestions of universal principles. How does the family, how does the school, advance life? Answer that, and you have a hint of the great, wide world and its way upward. In home and school, in bank and shop, in field and factory, the cause of progress lies first of all in inventions. Some one finds a better way of doing things than was known before. No matter just now where or how this inventor came by his improved method : he has it. The man who does a thing better than we have been doing, stands at the head of his line as truly as did Adam. The invention may be a mere trifle, but if it is new it becomes a creative force for mankind. In the United States there are inventors in all parts of the country. Read the lists of patents granted at Washington for all sorts of machines and processes. A new one is announced almost daily in the newspapers. These inventions are found in every sphere of human interests, in houses, furniture, tools, machines, and every appliance of comfort and learning. The list of copyrighted books and pamphlets shows invention in another realm. Of course not all copyrighted matter is original and new. But here and there, even in dull books and compilations of old matter, a bright and fresh discovery may be found. Humble men and women may in hours of special inspiration utter words which men of genius themselves will appropriate. Some of the proverbs of Solomon and Jesus were started by unknown men. George Eliot has woven into her great novels many a saying which she caught from persons in narrow conditions; and she has not grudged to give humble folk credit for the wit which graces her pages. Most people are dull and imitative most of their lives, but one who mingles freely with Irish laborers will pick up witty and suggestive phrases which would make a page of Shakespeare sparkle, and give lustre to a volume of Thackeray. The folk-lore which has made the name of Grimm famous was gathered in the cottages of peasants whose traditions had preserved the inventions of forgotten generations.

Social progress is not the result of mere blind, brute matters of fact, pushing upward and outward like frost or sap; but it is also and now chiefly the result of imitation of ideals, conceptions of a good yet unrealized but practicable. We are not to think of progress as the mere effect of climate, food, dress, but also of ideals of what we ought to be and do. These beliefs, warm with desire, are real social causes of advance.

"If there is to be a competition for scientific recognition, the world without us must yield to the undoubted existence of the spirit within us. Our own hopes and wishes and determinations are the most undoubted phenomena within the sphere of consciousness. If men do, act, feel, and live as if they were not merely the brief products of a casual conjunction of atoms, but the instruments of a far-reaching purpose, are we to record all other phenomena and pass over these? We investigate the instincts of the ant and the bee and the beaver, and discover that they are led by an inscrutable agency to work towards a distant purpose. Let us be faithful to our scientific method, and investigate also those instincts of the human mind, by which man is led to work as if the approval of a Higher Being were the aim of life." [1]

That nation is most favored and advances with most rapid strides which has the largest number of persons of genius, whose varied gifts enrich life in all directions.[2] There is a

---

[1] W. S. Jevons, *The Principles of Science*, Vol. II, p. 470.
[2] W. H. Mallock, *Aristocracy and Evolution.*

legitimate place for hero-worship. "Arnold Toynbee once asserted that changes can be accomplished only by two things : first, an ideal which arouses interest and kindles the imagination, and, second, a definite, intelligent plan for carrying that ideal out into practice." This ideal must first be formed, this plan must be laid by a superior person. When such a leader appears, then —

> "A better day's begun —
> And soon this leader, teacher, will stand plain,
> And build the golden pipes and synthesize
> This people-organ for a holier strain."

The spheres of invention are as numerous as the forms of genius and the wants of mankind. In the advancement of science we have examples in Newton, Darwin, Galileo ; in fine arts, Angelo, Raphael, Titian ; in philosophy, Kant, Leibnitz, Hegel ; in poetic insight, Goethe, Shakespeare ; in statecraft, Cromwell, Gladstone ; in commercial enterprise and organization of trade and industry, those men of genius who have produced a system which has carried forward modern nations more rapidly than any others the world has known ; in religion, Moses, prophets, sages of the Orient, and One whose name cannot be classed on a level with theirs.

" In strictness, the vital refinements are the moral and intellectual steps. The appearance of the Hebrew Moses, of the Indian Buddh, — in Greece, of the Seven Wise Masters, of the acute and upright Socrates, and of the Stoic Zeno, — in Judea, the advent of Jesus, — and in modern Christendom, of the realists Huss, Savonarola, and Luther, are causal facts which carry forward races to new convictions, and elevate the rule of life. In the presence of these agencies, it is frivolous to insist on the invention of printing or gunpowder or gas-light, percussion caps and rubber shoes, which are toys thrown off from that security, freedom, and exhilaration which a healthy morality creates in society. These arts add a comfort and smoothness to house and street life; but a purer morality, which kindles genius, civilizes civilization, casts backward all that we hold sacred in the profane, as the flame of oil throws a shadow when shined upon by the flame of the Bude-Light. Not the less the popular measures of progress will ever be the arts and the laws." — EMERSON.

The time seems to be rapidly approaching when great societies will consciously coöperate to bring forth inventions in all spheres of discovery and desire. Society is beginning to build up its own system of education, and does not wait for the initiative of a few and the slow processes of competition to give the blessings of culture to the poorest of her children. Society is moving forward in all modern countries to direct industrial and commercial enterprises in such a way that the weak shall not be crushed by the strong, and the ignorant citizen outwitted by the few who are in position of advantage. This process is certain to go much further as the social consciousness widens and becomes more intelligent. But while the world stands, the actual inventions and discoveries will not be made by the mass, but by the few. It is inconceivable that a people numbering seventy millions or a hundred millions can ever set itself to the task of improving a microscope, a telephone, or to create a new epic poem. Such deeds must always come from single minds, although these will borrow materials from their age and from all the past. A man of genius is himself a social product, and ought to pay his ancestors for their gifts to him by bestowing something valuable on posterity. But a community advances by selecting specialists and then taking possession of their works and diffusing them. The debt and the service are reciprocal, and the highest soul owes the largest duties to mankind and becomes great only as he imparts and communicates. The isolated genius is nothing, — a bell in an exhausted receiver.

> " God's light organized
> In some high soul, crowned capable to lead
> The conscious people, — conscious and advised, —
> For if we lift a people like mere clay,
> It falls the same."

Preservation of Useful Inventions. — The imagination of vigorous minds is full of fancies, swarms and teems with suggestions and compositions according to the previous education and experience of the favored son of nature. Some of these trooping ideas are mere vagaries, some of them frivolous quips and cranks, some of them flashes of light which illumine the path of science, or art, or philosophy, for a hundred years in advance. The new device, the poem, the burst of eloquence in moments of impassioned speech, the draft of a law, the working hypothesis of a biologist, the theory of the mathematician to account for perturbations in the course of a comet or planet, are subjected at once to the test of experiment more or less scientific. Just as the tree blossoms with millions of flowers, only a part of which comes to fruit, while all the rest are frost-bitten or shaken off by winds, so the guesses of great minds are sifted and tried in the stern experiences of life. Only that which fits the situation can endure this test. All that is false, mere seeming, plausible, must sometime be found weak and unworthy by the inventor himself or by his critics. Ideas struggle for place in controversy and in practical life, just as ancient beasts and savage men fought for place and food, the strongest surviving. Thoughts, devices, new ideas, come into the fierce conflicts of competition. The temper of the edge is tested on real life.

Illustrations may be found by comparing the models of machines in the patent office with those which have been found practicable. Most have failed at some points, — have been too costly, or have broken down when put to strain required in actual shop-work. In all large libraries may be found books which are never read, and which are buried in dust, never to be resurrected. They did not fit. Some quality was lacking. But Homer lives in his poems. Milton composed lines which the world cannot permit to die. Shakespeare sings for all thoughtful people. The odes of Horace are a monument more enduring than bronze. Time, which weighs all things, decides what shall remain, and drowns in her flood all that is weak, vain, false, unfit, useless for some human end.

III. Propagation of Inventions. — The familiar story of Columbus brings vividly before us the thought that common men can easily do a thing over, which only a man of genius could do the first time. Men who had mocked at the possibility of crossing the ocean and finding a new continent thought it an easy task after it had been done, and their stupidity was rebuked by the dramatic lesson of making an egg stand on end. When the ship has been built and launched, then imitation takes charge of its voyage around the world. There are great centres of thought, from which, as from a sun, rays of light move out in illuminated circles to the farthest parts of the earth.

This method may be witnessed in operation in family, school, and factory, in the daily process of learning. The teacher is always setting a copy. The pupil is always watching, studying tone, gesture, accent, writing, and inmost temper and disposition. The picture, word, or thought is turned over in the child's apprentice mind, and, perhaps with other elements mixed in, finds expression in an act of the learner.

The renowned painter gives the world a splendid picture, and soon Europe and America are flooded with photographic and sun-type copies of it in the illustrated magazines.

> " Read my little fable;
> He that runs may read.
> Most can raise the flowers now,
> For all have got the seed."

There are three orders of force, — physical, vital, and social, — including in the last all intellectual and moral activities. M. Tarde thus summarizes the mode of action peculiar to these different ranks of forces. Physical energy moves outward from the centre in connected waves, as light, heat, and electricity. Vital forces are communicated by generation, as the inheritance of qualities, the spread of epidemics. Social forces move from their centres by imitation, and actual contact is not necessary if the process is served by literary symbols, as books, letters, pictures. Social forces act almost instantly between Liverpool and Pekin, while heredity acts slowly and by long intervals.

Ideals incarnate in the best men tend to become general. " Far off as seems such a state, yet every one of the factors counted on to produce it may already be traced in operation among those of highest natures. What now in them is occasional and feeble may be expected with further evolution to become habitual and strong, and what now characterizes the exceptionally high may be expected, eventually, to characterize all. For that which the highest human nature is capable of is within the reach of human nature at large" (H. Spencer).

IV. Laws of Progress. — Throughout the known world all things move according to some method. Our hope of constructing a science rests on belief in an order which runs through all acts and events. By "law," in this connection, we do not mean the command of some legislature or emperor, nor any ethical requirement confirmed by the conscience, but solely an observed order or method. Can we yet discover any hints of orderly movement in the facts of social progress?

Probably the world must wait many a year before all the uniformities of society and its life can be formulated; and multitudes of students must contribute to this task. At present we must cheer our quest by partially successful attempts at formulating, in very general terms, some of the more obvious instances of uniformity.

We may first give the law of evolution as stated by Mr. Spencer : " Evolution is an integration of matter and concomitant dissipation of motion ; during which the matter passes from an indefinite, incoherent homogeneity to a definite coherent heterogeneity ; and during which the retained motion undergoes a parallel transformation." (*First Principles*, § 145.) This sentence is for most persons a " hard nut to crack."

We are still a long way from being able to formulate laws of social progress which will be at once comprehensive and yet serve to express clearly and intelligibly the essential nature of the process. The statement of evolution made by Mr. Spencer is and was designed to be an expression of the most general principles, applicable not only to society but to the physical universe. The law which applies to a spiritual organization must contain distinctively spiritual elements, but must not ignore the presence of the matter-of-fact world.

Evolution includes not only progress but *degeneration*, — all the phenomena of our existence, — while progress is our present study. We are now asking : What are the laws of evolution so far as social human progress can be discerned?

Among the apparently well-ascertained lines of uniformity we may indicate this one : There is an ascending order of ends of social choices.

" This dominant law do we not detect in that conscious scale of worth and authority on which our springs of action dispose themselves? There are four types of human life, well marked in the course of its personal or social ascent, viz. (1) that of instinctive appetite and passion, in which there is the least remove from the condition of other animals; (2) that of self-conscious pursuit of personal or social ends, involving the first exercise of will; (3) that of conscience, in which these ends are taken, not as we like, but as we ought; (4) that of Faith, in which the conflict is transcended between what we like and what we ought, and duty becomes Divine." [1]

This ascending scale of ends may be seen in the history of peoples as well as in the biography of individuals. The mercantile conquests of the Phœnicians superseded lower barbaric tastes and customs; the Roman self-restraint and respect for the ideal of law subdued the lower force; Greek culture, even when it issued from a conquered land, took possession of the conquerors; and Christianity overcame both Greek and Roman because it appealed to deeper elements and offered a higher good. The ages give the field to the best, not to mere physical might. Mighty mastodons are extinct, and man is nature's choice, though inferior in physical power.

Professor Giddings states his "first law of social choice" as follows: "In all social choice the most influential ideal is that of personal force, or of virtue in the original sense; the second in influence is the hedonistic or utilitarian ideal; the third is integrity; the least influential is the ideal of self-realization; but if mental and moral evolution continues, the higher ideals must become increasingly influential." [2]

The law of progress means a social choice of more varied and more harmonious interests.

The law of progress implies a higher degree of rationality in choice of both ends and means.

In the lowest stages of culture men move directly and impulsively toward the objects of desire. The rule of imitation sways conduct. The persons who compose society are conscious in their acts, but not purposeful.

Professor Giddings sums up the laws of imitation, after

---

[1] J. Martineau, *A Study of Religion*, II, 119. Cf. M. Baldwin, *Social Interpretations*, p. 510 ff.

[2] *Principles of Sociology*, pp. 408, 411.

M. Tarde, in these two principles, (1) in the absence of interference, imitations spread in a geometrical progression; (2) imitations are refracted by their media. This stage is what Dr. Ward calls "genetic" progress.

Progress by rational intention, — what Dr. Ward calls "telic" progress. By this we mean that the members and the administrative representatives of communities increasingly direct their associated actions according to plans. They are not content to fumble and grope in the dark, but light the lamps of science to find the way and the objects of desire.

There is an increasing command over the environment of mankind, due to this application of intelligence to the conditions. It is seen and recognized that unless the choices and preferences of a people conform to the conditions of survival they will produce feebleness, suffering, and extinction. So the very choices of society come under this regulative principle.

With the diffusion of intelligence and the formation of customs and character suitable to the conditions of survival and of well-being mankind becomes more truly free. Constraint is less necessary, because the likings and preferences of men more nearly correspond to the demands of life and the ways to happiness. The time is not yet ripe for a codification of the laws of social progress; but the grand trunk lines of the direction and tendency of the progressive movement are suggested by a survey of history and a minute investigation of individual development.

V. Petrifaction and Retrogression.— Observation shows us that progress, as defined above, is by no means necessary or universal. Our view of life, to be true, must take into its survey the facts of decay, stagnation, and ruin. We know that large numbers of persons cannot keep step with the advancing host. Crippled by inherited weakness or acquired vice, they straggle in the rear and sink at last under the burdens of existence. They seem to add nothing to the sum of good and to be themselves dead weight upon the strong. We have in all civilized lands to support a mixed multitude of indolent, slow, defective, stupid, vicious, and criminal people. Entire nations, like the Chinese, seem to reach a fairly high level of culture and then cease to make additions to inventions, ideas, and inspiring thoughts. Other peoples seem to go backward until they perish, as tribes of Indians have done, and the natives of the Sandwich Islands. We need to consider these facts because they are realities, part of the sum of reality with which society must deal. There is a sort of immoral optimism which looks on the struggle of life as a game where humanity is doomed to win without sacrifice and effort, without self-discipline, without strenuous toil. Progress is, in their view, secured by some fatal process which does not consult the choices of mankind. But an honest and intelligent study of the facts of stagnation, parasitism, vice, crime, and selfish injury should dispel all such shallow hopes.

VI. The Prospects of Social Progress. — We have already emphasized the fact that the future is not for our sight. There we must walk by faith. If we are to see the coming day as it must be, and if we are to help realize our own vision of good, we must pass beyond the limits of rigid science and construct our hopes out of the same materials as those which compose the foundations of science itself. We are not fully equipped for making the hoped good become a reality until we attain two convictions; that at the heart of the universe is everlasting rectitude, goodness, and veracity; and, secondly, that we ourselves should give our choice to that theory of existence and commit our very lives to that hypothesis.

We may find it impossible to verify this theory, to make it clear to sceptical neighbors, to prove it by what is called scientific argument; but every step we take in that direction we help to make sure that our venture was wise and fair. If all good men band themselves together to make the world better, sustained and directed by belief that they ought to try, they may in the end prove beyond a cavil that they were right, demonstrating the truth of their theory by the visible institutions of wisdom, knowledge, and love which never could have been built save by those whom faith made faithful. Nor is this a mere blind belief, a desperate plunge into a dark abyss; it is the rational act of human beings following with fidelity the best sentiments and highest interests of mankind. Faith is to the spiritual adventurer what courage is to the soldier in battle; his very shout of determination and hope is part of the means

2 C

of victory. Theoretically it may be imagined possible that the universe will make dupes of good men and mock them with defeat and eternal death. Theoretically it may be imagined possible that the pessimist is right, and that existence is an evil; that all we count good is weak and helpless; that there is no divine event of love toward which the whole creation moves. Those who believe that way and act logically, will help to make a world of blackness and darkness which will verify their dismal and wicked theory. All the more important is it that there shall be others who will not believe that faith in good is wrong, and who will make sacrifices and efforts to justify their creed of light and justice. It is hard to argue with the other kind of reasoners. Fortunately we are not required by any canon of morality to pass judgment on them. Their lives are often better than their logic. But an immoral logic, whose natural tendency and effect is to poison the fountains of energy and enfeeble the soul that strives for perfection, we may and ought to judge and rob it of influence if we can.

> " Cast leaves and feathers rot in last year's nest,
> The winged brood, flown hence, new dwellings plan;
> The serf of his own past is not a man;
> To change and change is life, to move and never rest; —
> Not what we are, but what we hope, is best."

VII. What is Next to be Done ? — In connection with the discussion of each particular social institution we have considered various suggestions of betterment. Social progress depends on a multitude of special works carried on by multitudes of individuals, each filled with the desire to promote the welfare of others, each endowed with some faculty of special service held in trust for his fellows.

But there is a great advantage in surveying these specific efforts from a more general standpoint. Society is advancing to the position where the thought of one person soon becomes the thought of many or of all. With our modern system of communication and transportation thoughts travel quickly from centres of influence to the remotest corners of the civilized world. Trade between towns, states, cities, and nations diffuses ideas and unites interests, or at least compels one people to feel quickly anything which affects other peoples. A good example is the effect of an outbreak of fever in Cuba upon the health and trade of the Southern States. The failure of a wheat crop in Siberia or South America or India affects the purchasing power of Minnesota farmers. Society is rapidly gaining a true common consciousness. Men know their common interests and are prepared to act together.

It is natural that society should begin to consider the law of common action in reference to the advancement of the common welfare, and that men should consciously discuss and agree upon definite plans for betterment, and not leave the dearest interests of society to accident and the rough play of selfish struggles.

In each part of the discussion we have sought to bring out the truth that human welfare is not some one simple, abstract thing, but the very wealth of life itself. For the intellect, it is knowledge ; for the feelings, it is the varied world of beautiful and agreeable objects and experiences ; for the moral nature, it is goodness and justice ; and for society as a whole, it is the sharing of all the infinite richness of life by all members of the community.

The human race may be improved, we hope will be improved more and more, in the same way in which varieties of grains and fruits, and breeds of horses and cattle are perfected, — by selection of parents and favoring conditions of rearing. Plato saw this method clearly, and proposed a plan of producing the best citizens under strict governmental control. But his theory was never adopted, and seems further from acceptance than ever. We can see, however, some slight steps in this direction when the State separates the feeble-minded and other defectives, and thus prevents them from reproducing their defects. It is possible to extend this measure to some extent, but not very far. The amount of interference with liberty and the possibility of cruel injustice will restrict such direct governmental breeding process within narrow limits.

We may look for some improvement in the human type from growth of intelligence and morality. Consumptives and other diseased persons will voluntarily refrain from marriage or from reproduction. But we cannot expect much from this direction for a long time, perhaps for ages. Those who are weak in body are likely to be weak in mind and will, short-sighted, impulsive.

We must depend more on education, and for two reasons : If social selection is to be promoted on a large and effective scale, it will be only by the growth and diffusion of intelligence and increase of moral self-control. If the general type is to improve, it can be only by the adoption of a universal system of education which will develop body, intellect, and character.

Progress implies not only an improvement in man himself, but also in his resources, his control over nature, and his better social organization. Social selection must, therefore, aim at amelioration of outward conditions as well as of the human type. The two elements constantly react upon each other.

The Limitations of Direct Effort.— A little reflection will show that direct commands, laws, and efforts go but a little way toward securing these goods of social life. Personal character does not spring up instantly in response to our individual acts of will, or in answer to the edicts of legislatures and emperors. Nor can we by saying to ourselves " let us will to be joyous and happy, contented and peaceful," be so on the instant ; for the feelings are not thus at our command, and the will of an empire, expressed in law, cannot make one bootblack happy. Beauty, wealth, goodness, happiness, knowledge, are not thus to be gained by direct attack. Reforms built on this haste to secure the ends of life by direct action come to bitter grief and sore disappointment. The pleasure-seeker never finds the object of his quest, but his pursuit ends in disgust, *ennui*. Pleasure comes with agreeable occupation. Knowledge issues from mental toil suitably directed according to the laws of learning. Wealth arises at the end of a long series of prudent actions. The satisfactions of our æsthetic nature spring from the presence of statues, pictures, poems, which are the fruits of continuous discipline and prolonged labor.

The Place of Beliefs. — Actions, which form habits when repeated and lead to character at last, are themselves the results of certain convictions. Social actions are the effects of beliefs or convictions shared by many or by all. Beliefs of a community are embodied and exhibited in social institutions, and these several institutions express special beliefs and forms of conviction, as schools, governments, industries, languages, customs, fashions.

Ideas are the cause of beliefs and convictions, feelings, and volitions. We may use these general words, ideas, and thoughts, to include all the forms of knowledge, thinking, imagination, sentiments, ideals which take possession of the mind. We may extend it to all presentations brought before the intelligence ; impressions from nature, knowledge of external reality and of human character and achievement ; all pictures, statues, casts, edifices, dress, forms of animals and of men, poems, — all which supplies materials for the intellect. What we desire to see come out in emotion, character, and conduct must first be offered as presentation. We cannot directly cause feeling or produce devices. All we can do is to bring ideas, images, knowledge, before the soul. The logic of the soul takes charge of these suggestions. If we could absolutely exclude hurtful impressions, and keep the whole sky, horizon, and landscape of the mind full of beauty, truth, and goodness, there would be no alternatives of choice. The suggestion of the perfect would have the field without a base rival. This entire possession of the mental range being impossible, we must strive to approximate it.

The Introduction of Ideas into the Social Mind. — We are not here considering the first origin of knowledge, its primary discovery in some individual minds, but its beginning as a common possession of a community. We are seeking to answer the question, how do thoughts become a common possession, and thence a common cause of social action, of social beliefs, and so of social conduct, character, and happiness? The most obvious answer is that ideas must be presented in some way to the minds of the members of a community, must be transmitted from the centres of origin, and somehow set before the thought of all.

What Presentations ? — The two great questions here are What? and How? And, first, consider, as a brief summary of the scattered suggestions of this volume already given, what presentations are desirable in order to secure the actions, habits, and conduct which lead to social welfare. Certainly all will see that knowledge is necessary, — knowledge of the two great worlds which press upon us all, the worlds of nature and of humanity. Every chapter of this treatise has brought out the subjects of human concern, and given reasons for the study of particular fields of investigation.

But if man is to appreciate, create, and enjoy beauty, then objects of beauty, in nature and in art, must be presented to all men. In homes and galleries, in streets and parks, in museums accessible to all citizens, in music halls and churches, in schoolrooms, in the forms and adornments of public buildings, in the green fringe of roadsides and the calm of cemeteries, in dress and gestures, in polite graces and sweet speech, in handwriting and etiquette, in table manners and public greetings, — everywhere, and in all objects and acts, the imagination must have presented to it the finished and perfect forms of things and actions.

But beyond all knowledge and beyond all objects of beauty is the Person who transcends our knowledge, and yet whom we must assume as existing, if we are to have any rational ground for our science or our art. God is the object of our Faith. Complete living implies the constant presentation of the thought of the Perfect One, perfect wisdom, beauty, goodness.

Thus we come to the presentation of ideals of character and personality, and of social coöperation. Professor E. A. Ross has classified these ideals as follows: " The church has a heritage of ethical types so nobly conceived and so graciously put as to have wonderful power of exciting love and admiration. But whatever in conduct or character we admire we strive to become. The admired becomes the ideal — the goal toward which we press. Now, the church is the custodian of many fragrant and precious ideals, framed to the idea of fraternity. These are collective ideals, such as the transfigured society designated as 'the kingdom of heaven'; abstract ideals, such as that of purity or forgiveness; specific ideals, such as Paul's portrait of the Christian; concrete ideals, such as the transcendent figure of Jesus. The effect of holding up such pattern lives, characters, qualities, or virtues, as they are imbedded in the tradition of the church, and set forth so entrancingly in narrative, example, parable and saying, is to inspire for them a love and admiration that may become the formative force of life." [1]

By What Social Means is this Presentation Effected? — Somehow knowledge, wisdom, grace and superior character have found their way into human history, and become embodied in individuals of lofty form, in literature, in text-books, in various institutions. But so long as these spiritual goods are unknown they are dead to mankind. Books unread, pictures unseen, characters hidden, lie cold and stark as in a mausoleum. Only by popularizing a truth or a work of art does it become a social power. Those who are in possession of these elements of good are responsible trustees on behalf of mankind.

The Public School System. — The only organ of the entire community for the transmission of knowledge, the exhibition of ideals of character, and desirable instruction and training is the free and "compulsory" public school system. This is the only institution which belongs to the whole society, which is created and governed directly by its administration, and which is available to bring the growing community of youth under the best influences which can be offered by the present adult mind and heart. If society is to make education possible for all, it must provide the means of instruction for all. And since nearly all children would neglect the opportunity until too late, and since many parents, through ignorance, indolence, greed, or poverty would fail in their parental duty, therefore the State is obliged to require all parents to send their children to some school for a certain minimum period. "Compulsory" education, as it is generally and unhappily called, is the necessary and logical expression of the social conviction that every citizen should be fitted by knowledge and discipline for his place in society. The requirement that every child should go to some school is compulsory only as parental requirement is compulsory. Family discipline usually calls for more or less exercise of the power and authority of parents over their young children in order to avoid physical and moral injury. The State simply directs parents to see that this authority and power are exercised in the manner judged to be necessary to the safety and propriety of the people of the State.

[1] *The Outlook*, Aug. 18, 1897.

But compulsory education does not imply that private and parochial schools shall be forbidden. The State may properly require that every child be sent to school for a certain period, and may so inspect all schools as to make certain that their instruction is of suitable quality, without in the least interfering with the liberty of parents to establish schools of their own if they choose to support them at private cost. And this is exactly the principle on which our governments in this country usually act.

Society is not identical with the State. The government is only one organ through which society may act to gain its ends. The family, the church, the voluntary association, the club, the lodge, are other forms of organization by means of which groups of persons may give instruction and transmit culture. The voluntary association has often been the pioneer of education when the majority of the people were either hostile or indifferent. The various branches of the church established schools of all grades before public sentiment generally supported the movement for free public schools. It was these denominational and private schools which cultivated a taste and produced a hunger for universal provision for education.

And when the State neglects its duty, private agency is again left free to push into new fields of enterprise. If the State should suppress competing schools, its own institutions might be in danger of petrification. By permitting full freedom to all competent persons, and by requiring all to prove to inspectors that their intellectual work is of proper quality, the State schools are always kept up to the highest standard of efficiency. No private rights are invaded. No injustice is done. No reasonable consciences are wounded.

There is always room for individual acts of generosity to promising scholars. The Scotch village schoolmaster in *Beside the Bonnie Brier Bush* was roused to eloquence in his plea with the rich laird to assist a bright young scholar at the university: "Ye think that a'm asking a great thing when I plead for a pickle notes to give a puir laddie a college education. I tell ye, man, a'm honorin' ye and givin' ye the fairest chance ye'll ever hae a' winning wealth. Give ye store the money ye hae scrapit by mony a hard bargain, some heir ye never saw'll gar it flee in chambering and wantoness. Give ye hed the heart to spend it on a lad o' pairts like Geordie Hoo, ye wud hae twa rewards nae man could tak frae ye. Ane wud be the honest gratitude o' a laddie whose desire for knowledge ye had sateesfied, and the second would be this — anither scholar in the land; and a'm thinking with auld John Knox that ilka scholar is something added to the riches of the common-wealth." Domsie gained his point.

The question of the provision for religious education is one of vast moment. Most citizens recognize the fact that education which omits the religious factor is incomplete. In some countries the public schools do teach religious doctrines, as was formerly true in this country. Indeed, religion has by no means disappeared from our state-supported schools and colleges and universities. So long as most teachers share the faith of the community which has produced them, it will be impossible to take this influence out of the establishments of education. Formal lessons may properly be prohibited and excluded. Denominational teaching may be and should be left to family and church. But so long as incarnated religion, ideals, and faiths embodied in personalities and good deeds, are the clearest and mightiest expression of worship, so long religion will be taught in public schools. Patriotism, good nature, kind charity, and wise statesmanship will be able to adjust the claims of different elements of the community, so that all interests will be justly treated and the highest factors of culture find a place in every soul.

In Goethe's *Faust* the hero tries learning, lust, power, ambition, — all. In his old age he turns to the task of rescuing a barren tract from salt sea waves, and giving it over to happy homes and fertile gardens; and in this addition to the sum of human good he finds the climax of his joy:

> " Below the hills a marshy plain
> Infects what I so long have been retiring.
> This stagnant pool likewise to drain
> Were now my latest and my best achieving.
> To many millions let me furnish soil,
> Though not secure, yet free to active toil;
> Green, fertile fields, where men and herds go forth

At once, with comfort, on the newest earth,
And swiftly settled on the hill's firm base,
Created by the bold, industrious race.
A land like Paradise here, round about:
Up to the brink the tide may roar without.
And though it gnaw, to burst with force the limit,
By common impulse all unite to hem it.
Yes! to this thought I hold with firm persistence;
The last result of wisdom stamps it true:
He only earns his freedom and existence,
Who daily conquers them anew.
Thus here, by dangers girt, shall glide away,
Of childhood, manhood, age, the vigorous day;
And such a throng I fain would see, —
Stand on free soil among a people free!
Then dared I hail the moment fleeing:
'Ah, still delay — thou art so fair!'
The traces cannot, of mine earthly being,
In æons perish, — they are there! —
In proud free feeling of such lofty bliss,
I now enjoy the highest moment, — this."

Angels (bearing to heaven the immortal part of Faust) sing:

" The noble spirit now is free,
And saved from evil scheming:
Whoe'er aspires unweariedly
Is not beyond redeeming.
And if he feels the grace of Love
That from on High is given,
The Blessed Hosts, that wait above,
Shall welcome him to heaven."

APPENDIX

———◆◇◆———

DIRECTIONS FOR LOCAL STUDIES

" The art of asking questions is not so easy as some think. It is much more the art of a master than of a pupil. One must already have learned much in order to know how to ask what he does not know. An Indian proverb says: 'The learned man knows and inquires, but the ignorant person does not even know enough to set him inquiring.' " — ROUSSEAU, *La Nouvelle Héloise.*

Make your own maps. Do not be content with looking at those made by others, although they may be more beautiful and perfect than those you may make. Drawing is a creative act, not mere passive reception of impressions, soon forgotten. Make many different kinds of maps, with records of different sets of facts of interest to the common welfare. The maps given herewith are merely illustrations and suggestions.

SUGGESTIONS FOR THE STUDY OF A TOWN: MAPS AND DESCRIPTION

I. The Physical Environment. The basis of social study is geography.

Draw a map of the *state* in order to show the location of the town in relation to the commonwealth. The natural features can be indicated as in ordinary maps. The reports of the state geologists, botanists, etc., and the local histories will furnish materials. Indicate on the maps, as far as possible, the following facts, and write down information in accompanying descriptions and explanations.

Soil; elevations and depressions; mineral products; streams. Draw maps of the county and of the township, with more details. Climate: describe seasons, rainfall, temperature, and their influence on food, clothing, houses. Describe the vegetable productions of the county, native and exotic. Give an account of native and domesticated animals.

II. The Sources of the Population.

1. The early settlers.
2. The immigrants, at various dates.
3. The present elements of population.
4. The population of the county and state.

In description, state in regard to each of above classes :

1. Their former residence (country, race, language).
2. Their reasons for emigration.
3. Their reasons for selecting this particular location. These reasons may be economic, political, family, religion, education, etc.
4. Map showing distribution of population ; as, neighborhoods of negroes, or some other race element.

III. The Buildings of the Town.

On large outline maps, draw the location of buildings at different stages of growth : (1) the early village settlement ; (2) the first town incorporation ; (3) the present city. Distinguish by color or other marks : (1) the residences ; (2) the hotels ; (3) the places of manufacture ; (4) the places of wholesale and retail trade ; (5) banks ; (6) government buildings, — national, state, county, city ; (7) schools ; (8) churches ; (9) public halls ; (10) saloons ; (11) other buildings. Describe height and materials of buildings.

IV. The Works of the Community for Protection, Health, Convenience, Comfort.

1. Means of transportation. Draw a map of the town and surrounding country to show navigable streams, canals, roads, railroads, electric lines.

Draw map of streets, alleys ; indicate pavements, walks ; describe the system of transportation, extent, ownership, fares, accommodation.

2. Means of communication. Map showing telegraph, telephone, postal lines and offices ; describe system ; map showing the houses and offices of subscribers to the most popular newspaper.

3. Protection. Map of offices, houses, districts of (*a*) police department, (*b*) militia, (*c*) fire department ; describe each system.

4. Map of lighting system, extent, cost. Describe business organization.

5. Sanitary. Map of (*a*) drainage and sewers ; (*b*) water system, pumping stations, reservoirs, pipes ; (*c*) low and insanitary places. Describe each system, cost, extent, defects, and its business organization, whether private or public.

6. Parks, drives, and boulevards.
7. Cemeteries.

V. *Industrial and Commercial Organizations.*

Map showing (1) location of all shops and factories; (2) wholesale and retail stores; (3) banks.

Describe conditions: Members engaged in each occupation; capital invested in each occupation; product, quantity, and value; organization of each industry, household, capitalistic, or coöperative; describe the process of one or more industries, step by step; set down the number of adults and children (under 16) in each place; the hours of labor, per day, per week; the wages paid, per day, per year; average days of employment, idleness, regularity, and causes; Sunday work, how general, how regarded by workmen; physical and moral conditions of the shop; mental and spiritual effects of the work on employees; ownership and lease of lands and buildings; commercial property: capital invested in various forms of business; amount of yearly sales; banks: capital and business; trade unions: names, objects, membership; how regarded by employers and others; tendencies towards socialism, single-tax, etc.; coöperative enterprises: describe methods and extent of business; corporations: capital invested, dividends paid, influence on local business; competitions of large cities with local trade, and local opinion about it.

Friendly societies for mutual benefit, so-called "benevolent" associations, lodges, fraternities: memberships, fees, benefits (sick, accident, burial, death, etc.).

VI. *Institutions of Culture.*

Map showing location of buildings devoted to the following purposes:

Schools, with accompanying description and statistics of edifices, rooms, studies, physical conditions, apparatus, libraries, teachers (men and women), system of supervision, normal instruction. Give an account of private schools and compare with public schools.

Museums and collections of art or science.

Libraries: number of volumes, method of distributing books, work with the schools and affiliation with clubs, kinds and numbers of books read.

Book clubs.

Methods of learning trades and arts.

Literary, art, musical, debating societies, membership, character of work, effects and influences.

Entertainments, kinds and influence. Public sentiment.

Gymnastic classes.

The use of Sunday for art, sociability, study, lectures, and action on public sentiment.

VII. *Regulative Agencies.*

Map showing buildings devoted to city, county, state, or national offices; political divisions (wards, voting precincts, etc.).

Describe the government of the state, county, city, town; titles of officers, duties, mode of election or appointment, terms of office, salaries and incomes from fees, efficiency; assessment and taxation, rate, modes, principles, abuses, efforts to regulate and reform.

Make a brief outline or digest of important state laws relating to the family, to business, factories, schools, crime, poor relief, sanitation, sale of liquor, Sunday laws, landlord and tenant, apprenticeship.

Describe customs, sentiments, fashion, and etiquette relating to domestic affairs, intellectual and artistic life, industry and trade, churches, politics, funerals, ornaments, dress, salutation, public assemblies, religion, and church.

Describe the kind and degree of influence exercised by local "leaders" in business, fashions, church, medical matters, politics, etc.

VIII. *Churches.*

Map showing location of buildings; houses of members by denominations.

Describe value, seating capacity, rooms for social purposes; church, houses, and halls; attendance (men, women, children), at morning and evening services; Sunday school, attendance, teachers.

Ministers, — salaries, college and divinity school graduates.

Sectarian strife, union efforts, etc.

Other religious organizations; Y. M. C. A. and Y. W. C. A.; their income, membership, departments of work, methods, influence.

IX. *Philanthropic Associations.*

Public charities. Map showing offices of relief, and residences of persons assisted. Describe law and method; number aided; amount given, — for support, medical care, rent, burial; condition of receiving, need, "settlement." Number of residents sent to state institutions; blind, deaf-mutes, feeble-minded, insane, epileptic. Describe (from visit) conditions and management of county or town poor-houses.

Church charities; members helped; amounts given.

Private and benevolent societies; numbers helped; amounts given.

X. *Institutions of Vice and of Punishment and Correction.*

Map showing saloons; also offices of justices, jail, lock-up, prison. Describe (from visit) the jail, etc.

Local magistrates, duties and character.

Number of arrests, — by sex, age, offences; number in jail, reform school, prisons, from this community.

XI. Institutions of Positive Progress.

Associations, not included above, for advancing the physical, intellectual, æsthetic, spiritual, and political welfare of the community.

Aggressive movements of local government, school authorities, churches, clubs, societies, for such advanced purposes.

See *Catechism for Social Observation*, by C. R. Henderson, for further details.

TOPICS FOR PAPERS AND DISCUSSIONS

CHAPTER I

Write out a definition of "society"; after studying the book, write another, and compare them.

Give an account of some local association, club, or lodge, — its purposes, officers, and their duties; and estimate the usefulness of the society to its members and to the community.

CHAPTER II

Make a chart of our solar system, and note the orbit of the earth.

Distinguish the fields and subjects of chemistry, physics, and geography. Illustrate the influence of climate, soil, and temperature on human beings. Make a map, and write an account of the mineral, vegetable, and animal products of your county or township. Examples of waste of material resources. Ask old settlers about effects of drainage of land on drought, floods, etc.

Illustrate the law of Diminishing Returns by some field or garden. State the Law of Variation. Local illustrations of conflict and struggle. State the meaning of "natural selection."

Define "race." On a map of county or township locate families of different races. Describe personal differences by physical marks and characteristics.

Write out examples of hard aspects of nature, and also illustrations of its beauty, sublimity, and service to man. Criticise the quotations from Walker and Mill, and show where they are defective. Find passages in Shelley, Wordsworth, Shakespeare, and other poets revealing the spiritual meaning of nature. Discuss the value of knowledge of nature to the farmer.

Discuss the value of nature-study in relation to social life, and add your own reflections.

CHAPTER III

Describe for yourself the parts, organs, and members of the human body and their functions. Define "function." What is anatomy? Physiology?

Define "organism" and "organization." Compare a physical body with a social community and state resemblances and differences.

What are the chief topics of psychology ? What are the chief kinds of motives which impel men to action ? Describe the characters of various persons known to you. Can you throw light on the causes of the differences among them ? Give examples of the union of persons induced by their differences.

Can you define the objects and give some of the results of "Child-study" ?

Write an account of cases of inheritance of nature and traits. Is there any other cause of these traits aside from heredity ?

State what you owe to several books or teachers. Trace the origin of various ideas and impulses in your own life and among your neighbors.

Describe illustrations of the many-sided experiences and connections of some prominent citizen.

Is it ever proper to use a human being as a means to some social end ? What gives worth ? What is worthiness ?

CHAPTER IV

The House. — Draw a map of a small district, and locate all the houses. Point out defects in two or three dwellings, and give reasons for criticism.

Housekeeping. — Describe changes in your neighborhood during a half-century, and give causes. Are these changes improvements ? Why ? What industries have been transferred from home to factory ? Illustrate and give reasons. Ask old citizens.

What is the personal organization of the home ? What are the relative duties of each member of the family ?

What are the social functions of the family ? Give reasons.

Family Government. — Give examples of failure. How may the home life prepare for citizenship ?

Why does society interfere with family life and make laws for it ? Give examples and reasons.

In what respects does the family differ from other social institutions ?

How may the family contribute to social order? And to progress?

What are some of the perils to which the family is exposed? Give reasons for divorce laws. Need of local reprobation of quarrels and divorce.

Suggest ways of bettering the intellectual, moral, æsthetic, and spiritual life of homes.

Discuss the educational opportunities of intelligent home life.

CHAPTER V

Protection. — Add local illustrations of social means of protecting health, morals. Is there need of rural police? Why? What is the need of a national navy, army, and state militia? State Board of Health?

Collect other examples of means of comfort and convenience provided by the community. Discover local defects. Make a drainage map of a district.

Space. — Give reasons for the location of certain farmhouses, villages, towns. Describe the means of transportation and communication of your neighborhood. Point out defects, and find out who is to blame. Note the contents of the nearest general store, and reflect on the origin of the commodities. How many nations helped to prepare your breakfast? How many to provide your clothing? Suggest improvements in the postal system. What would be the value of telephones to farmers if the price could be made low?

Time-keeping. — Illustrate the social value of clocks and watches. Illustrate the necessity for standards of weights and measures.

CHAPTER VI

Useful Arts. — Discuss the use of tools, implements, utensils, and machines. Give the history of some machine known to you through several decades, and show the value of the improvements: for example, a sewing-machine, or a reaper. Give an account of the training for six trades, time of learning, modes of instruction, terms of apprenticeship. Why are agricultural and other trade schools more necessary than they were forty years ago? Classify the useful arts. How can school children be interested in observing and understanding the useful arts?

What is the social function of language? What are the various modes of expression: as voice, writing, etc.?

Publicity. — Write an account of the means of publicity in your community. Analyze the contents of a local newspaper. How much of this could be profitably read in school? Can you mention any evils connected with the advertising columns? Why are vicious notices inserted? What hinders newspapers from giving all news correctly and impartially? What magazines circulate in your locality? If you have a public library, how is it supported, and what can be done to improve its working? How much is it used? What books are most popular? Why?

Fine Arts. — Discuss the special means and limitations of each art. What is the social function of art? Illustrate. What are the social means of æsthetic culture in your community? What more can be done? Has your schoolhouse one good photograph of a great picture?

CHAPTER VII

Wants. — State the desires which are satisfied by five industries known to you: as gardening, coal mining, etc. Do you know any family whose members would be better people if they had more wants? Is discontent ever a good? When?

Work. — Is work necessary to life? Is work always a sacrifice and painful? Give examples of "predatory" people and social "parasites." Is the manual laborer the only productive worker? What is the relation of

2 D

school teaching to the production of coal and woollen goods? Is a skilful physician a parasite? When can a "leisure class" be of advantage to society? What is the "labor cost" of an article?

Do we ever have to economize in sunshine and air? Why is economy necessary in gaining and using grain? Is war a source of wealth? Can workingmen increase the amount of work by idling? Who pays for losses when the fire insurance company indemnifies a loser? Is extravagance at a great ball or party a benefit to mechanics?

What are the permanent forms of capital? Describe the division of labor in a shop or factory. Why do not all do the same acts?

What service is rendered by a foreman on a railroad or in a shop? What is the difference between slavery and serfdom? Describe the factory system.

Describe local examples of barter, exchange, price, money, banking, management of a business. Give arguments for and against " free silver " bills in Congress.

Combinations of capital. What is a " trust "? How do large combinations arise? Have they any use ? State evils and dangers. How can society regulate them and make them subservient to the public good?

Define various forms of income, — wages, rent, profits, interest. Is it right for a man to receive rent or interest from workers when he does not work?

Why must governments have income? How do they raise funds? Who pays taxes? Is there any worker who does not pay taxes?

Discuss the limits of political economy. Are economic interests the only interests?

Chapter VIII

Definition of " social progress " in industry.

Evidence of economic progress. Growth of wealth and productive power. Sum up and criticise the points made under this head in the text. Compare the conclusions with old account books of wages and expenses of households. Ask old persons to help you from memory.

Causes of economic progress. State the points in the text and add others.

Has any social class been excluded from the advantages of economic progress? State objections to the factory system. Is it altogether an evil that " the rich are growing richer "? Does the wealth of a capitalist make others poor? In a trade must one party lose, or may both gain? Give examples of the injury done by speculation.

Chapter IX

Ask several labor agitators and leaders what they mean by the " labor movement," and what they are seeking to gain, and by what ways.

Is there need of a trade union among agricultural laborers, — " hired hands "? Reasons. Ask some of them as to their grievances and hopes.

Have school teachers trade unions or any organization which serves the purpose? Have "domestics" or "hired help" any unions? How do your neighbors regard trade unions? What arguments are used on both sides? What are the statistics of unions in your county or state? State the objects of unions. What is the "minimum wage"? Does the union seek to prevent men of superior skill from receiving higher wages?

Explain methods of industrial peace: conciliation, arbitration, etc. What are the duties of a State Board of Arbitration?

Explain profit sharing, and state the arguments. How may consumers unite to protect themselves and to favor wage-earners?

What is the aim of Socialists? How do they differ from Anarchists? What truths have they urged?

Offer further illustrations of "practicable socialism." Think of practicable improvements needed in your state.

CHAPTER X

Discuss, with local illustrations, the condition of the "social residuum."

Give a classification of the people of your county on the basis of their wealth and employments. Give examples of the separation of these classes and the causes of their feelings.

Inquire into the conditions of several families who depend on the public for aid, and study the causes of their dependence. In how many cases is drunkenness the reason? In how many cases is some form of physical or mental weakness the cause? And how did they come to be weak?

What social organization have you for distributing relief to the needy? What defects? Why are there any unemployed? Narrate the biography of some young man who has been sent to the penitentiary from your county, and discover the causes which led to his ruin. Visit county jail and poorhouse, and report defects. Inquire what is the effect on employment and wages of supporting able-bodied poor by taxation. Do "politics" affect the modes of distributing public relief? Do the poor demand aid as a right? Are they grateful for such help? Does it help them?

CHAPTER XI

Describe the organization of your state school system.

Discuss the opinions of local leaders about the value and needs of the public schools.

Criticise and improve the definitions of the end or purpose of education.

Discuss the question, "What knowledge is of most worth?"

Is there a natural order of studies? What is it?

Give examples of experiments in training children to care for social problems and interests.

Add suggestions about the improvement of rural schools.

Enlarge the argument as to the duty of society to its schools.

CHAPTER XII

Discuss the topics of the text, and select others for discussion. Suggest ways in which the churches may, without compromise of principles and beliefs, join in some common work for the benefit of the community, and so increase a sense of social unity.

CHAPTER XIII

Give local illustrations of the influence of family feeling, neighborhood sentiment and interests, class prejudices, race and denominational bonds, on social conduct under your observation.

Define the word "people" as used in the text. Criticise the discussion. Describe the influence, for good or evil, of some of these social bonds.

CHAPTER XIV

Distinguish "People" and "State." What are the functions of government? Describe the organization of government in your county. Note defects and the causes of these. Describe a political club. Explain the nature of a political party.

Explain the principles and history of civil service reform.

Explain the "Referendum." Give the history of the nominations of county and town officials. Describe a primary election, and give the law governing such elections in your state.

CHAPTER XV

What are some of the problems which social psychology seeks to study? Illustrate the influence of nearness in space upon community of thoughts. Explain the causes of human association. What is the social mind?

Give examples of the influence of suggestion and imitation on a crowd or on a school.

Give illustrations of the testing of an idea in a school or in a political campaign. Explain the method by which ideas and inventions are conserved and improved.

CHAPTER XVI

Define "social order." Illustrate the fact that a community has a belief in a right order of society. Give examples of customs and sentiments which regulate conduct, and show their use. Give examples of acts which are forbidden by morality but not by law, and give the causes of the difference.

What are the chief social virtues? Describe from observation the way in which influential persons have gained leadership.

CHAPTER XVII

Define "social progress." Explain the function of invention. What do you think of the importance of "great men" in relation to social progress? How do you explain the existence of great men?

Give illustrations of retrogression. Discuss methods of improving the physical well-being of a people. Methods of gaining greater command of natural forces. How can people be induced to enlarge and refine their enjoyments and entertainments?

The relation of the public school to race progress.

MAPS

Numbers I–IV are from Kalamazoo, Michigan, and Numbers V–IX are from Franklin, Indiana. Materials were kindly furnished by Rev. Caroline Bartlett Crane and Professor Paul Monroe, Ph.D., former students in the Department of Sociology at the University of Chicago.

I. KALAMAZOO, MICHIGAN. Physical features of the county; lakelets, streams, and watersheds. Early Indian trails; camps and homes of first white settlers. Township divisions.

II. Physical features of the city site.

III. The central part of the city, illustrating a complex system of artificial community arrangements.

IV. The systems of the water and fire departments.

V. FRANKLIN, INDIANA. The settlement in 1825.

VI. The town in 1840–41.

VII. The additions to the town by decades.

VIII. A population map for one race.

IX. Public buildings, and location of subscribers to a local newspaper.

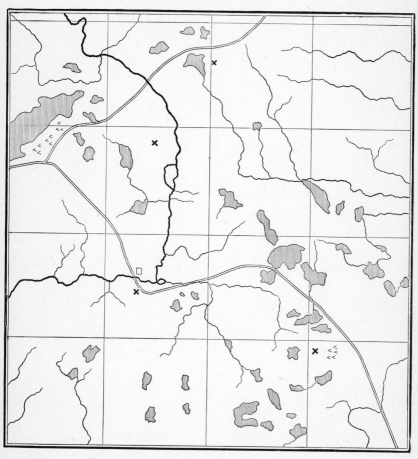

Kalamazoo: Physical features of the county; lakelets, streams, and water-sheds.
Early Indian trails, camps and homes of first white settlers.
Township Divisions.

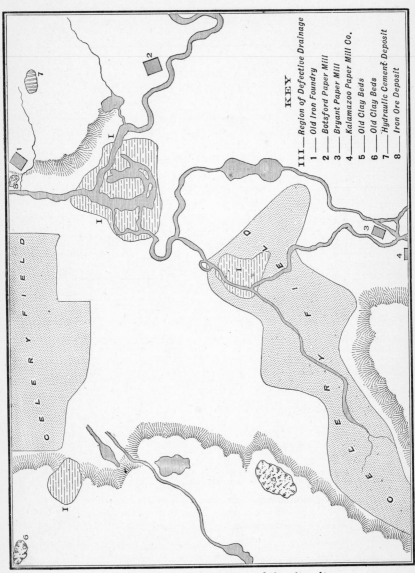

Kalamazoo: Physical features of the city site.

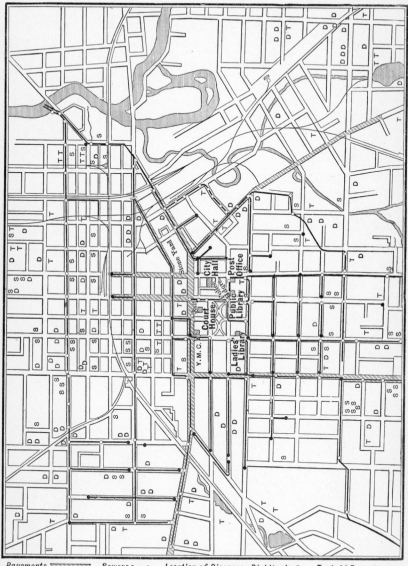

Pavements 〰〰〰〰〰 Sewers ●─○─ *Location of Diseases: Diphtheria* D *Typhoid Fever* T,
Scarlet Fever S,

**The central part of the city, illustrating a complex system of
artificial community arrangements.**

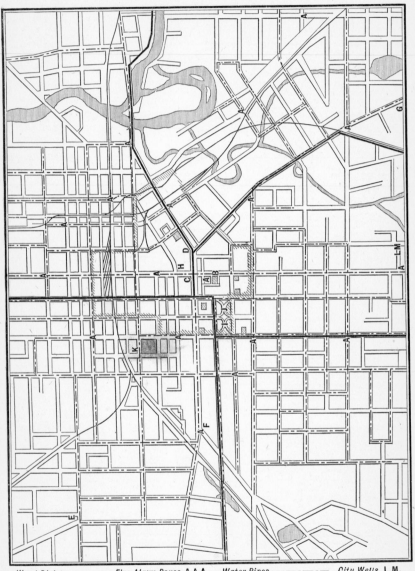

Ward Divisions ——— Fire Alarm Boxes **A,A,A,** Water Pipes —·—·—·— City Wells **L,M,**
Drinking Fountains, B,C,D,E,F,G,H,I,J,K, City Fire Limits

The systems of the water and fire departments.

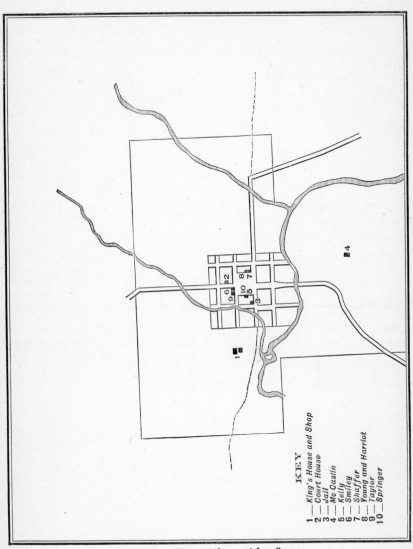

KEY

1 — King's House and Shop
2 — Court House
3 — Jail
4 — Mc Caslin
5 — Kelly
6 — Smiley
7 — Shaffer
8 — Young and Harriot
9 — Taylor
10 — Springer

Franklin, The settlement in 1825.

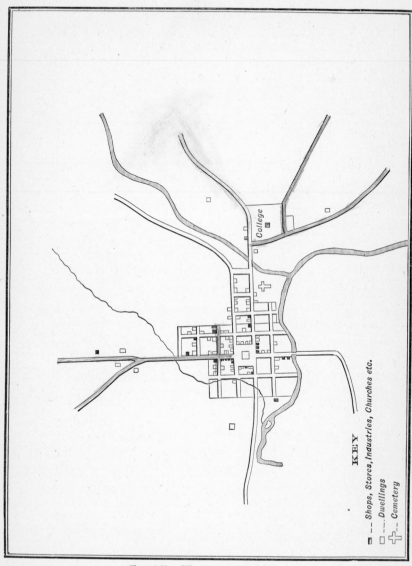

KEY

■ – – Shops, Stores, Industries, Churches etc.
□ – – Dwellings
✚ – – Cemetery

College

Franklin, The town in 1840-1.

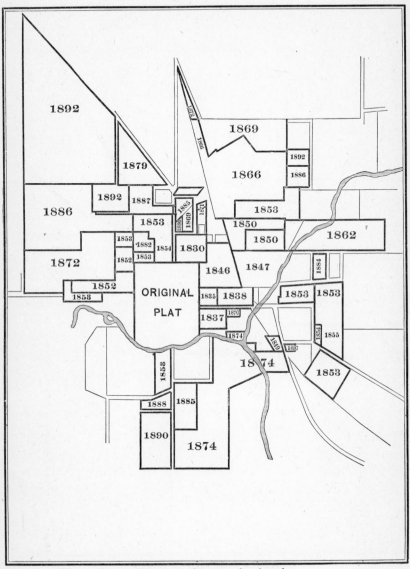

The additions to the town by decades.

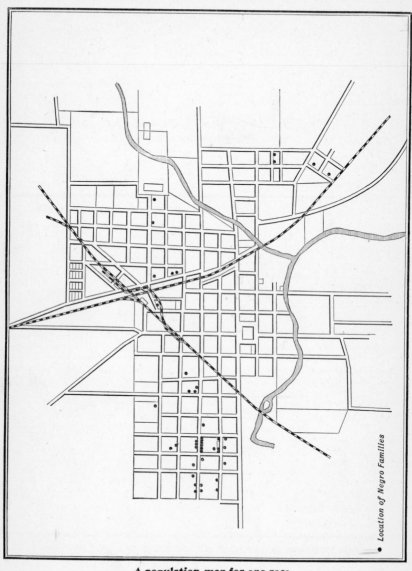

• Location of Negro Families

A population map for one race.

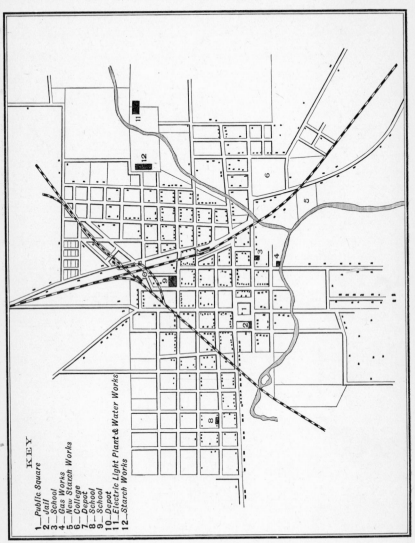

KEY

1—Public Square
2—Jail
3—School
4—Gas Works
5—New Starch Works
6—College
7—Depot
8—School
9—School
10—Depot
11—Electric Light Plant & Water Works
12—Starch Works

Public Buildings and location of subscribers to a local newspaper.